Balkans into Southeastern Europe

Related titles from Palgrave Macmillan

Leslie Benson, *Yugoslavia: A Concise History*, 2nd edition

Dennis P. Hupchick, *The Balkans: From Constantinople to Communism*

Ann Lane, *Yugoslavia: When Ideals Collide*

Carl-Ulrik Schierup (ed.), *Scramble for the Balkans: Nationalism, Globalism and the Political Economy*

Geoffrey Swain and Nigel Swain, *Eastern Europe since 1945*, 3rd edition

Balkans into Southeastern Europe

A Century of War and Transition

John R. Lampe

palgrave
macmillan

First published 2006 by
PALGRAVE MACMILLAN
Houndmills, Basingstoke, Hampshire RG21 6XS and
175 Fifth Avenue, New York, N.Y. 10010
Companies and representatives throughout the world

PALGRAVE MACMILLAN is the global academic imprint of the Palgrave Macmillan division of St. Martin's Press, LLC and of Palgrave Macmillan Ltd. Macmillan® is a registered trademark in the United States, United Kingdom and other countries. Palgrave is a registered trademark in the European Union and other countries.

ISBN-13: 978–0–333–79346–6 hardback
ISBN-10: 0–333–79346–3   hardback
ISBN-13: 978–0–333–79347–3 paperback
ISBN-10: 0–333–79347–1   paperback

This book is printed on paper suitable for recycling and made from fully managed and sustained forest sources.

Logging, pulping and manufacturing processes are expected to conform to the environmental regulations of the country of origin.

A catalogue record for this book is available from the British Library.

A catalog record for this book is available from the Library of Congress

10   9   8   7   6   5   4   3   2   1
15 14 13 12 11 10 09 08 07 06

Transferred to Digital Printing in 2009

Contents

List of Maps and Tables

Maps

Tables

Preface

As early as 1960, leading American scholars had gathered to discuss the European transformations under way in what had been the Ottoman Balkans. Their papers became *The Balkans in Transition*, as edited by Charles and Barbara Jelavich for the University of California Press in 1963. Their purview reached from the eighteenth century only to the immediate transition to Communist regimes after 1945. In his contribution, John C. Campbell contrasted the "generally liberal and democratic form" of nationalism that had inspired the struggle for national independence from the Ottoman Empire with the "fires of hatred and massacre" that ethnic conflicts had unleashed during the Second World War (p. 298). Surely their destructive potential and the Communist regimes that at least served to suppress it were moving the region further away from the European promise of the nineteenth century.

My vantage point, 40 years later, sees the region's European credentials and aspirations as having grown to maturity across the twentieth century, if hardly always in the service of political pluralism and a liberal market economy. Following from where Mark Mazower left off in his Epilogue to *The Balkans* (New York: Modern Library, 2001), I emphasize the problems as well as the promise of these European directions and institutions themselves. The idea of the nation-state and the dynamics of its central government have posed particular problems. The region's recurring decades of prolonged warfare and ethnic conflict, forced migration and foreign intervention, only made postwar reconstruction and further transition more difficult.

My own interest in any sort of post-Communist transition in a Western direction started when it seemed an unlikely prospect. When I became Director of East European Studies at the Woodrow Wilson International Center for Scholars in Washington in 1987, Yugoslavia seemed to have the best chance. By the time I returned full time to the University of Maryland in 1997, Yugoslavia had broken apart in just the sort of warfare that John Campbell had feared. Its successor states and the rest of the region, with no help from non-Communist Greece, were not managing their transitions to democratic institutions and liberal economies as well as their northern neighbors.

But by the turn of the new century, when this volume was first conceived in 2001, prospects were brighter across Southeastern Europe. Even in two of the most problematic locations, minority returns of refugees had finally started in Bosnia-Herzegovina and popular protest had overthrown the Milosevic regime in Serbia. Both Greece and the wider European Union also were beginning to play a constructive role. I therefore welcomed the invitation from Palgrave to survey the region's twentieth century. The full turn away from the warfare and troubled transitions of the 1990s that I had hoped might be complete by the time that I finished this volume has not materialized.

The importance of that turn has not however diminished. The warfare, ethnic conflict, and foreign intervention of the twentieth century are not a promising prospect for the new century, either for the region or for the rest of Europe. This third postwar reconstruction in less than a century needs to succeed. With this volume, I seek to make a modest contribution by offering a broad spectrum of readers, from students and scholars to the general public and policy makers, both here and in the region, a widely informed yet accessibly brief account of the past century's most relevant background to present challenges. In the forefront of that background, I see war and transition.

My sources are more varied and more direct than my footnotes indicate. I use them primarily to point readers to the most recent or authoritative publication that elaborates on the most relevant issues, where possible in English. Their limited number also reflects my effort, much encouraged by Palgrave, to avoid the lengthy, less readable volume that this could so easily have become. I should take this occasion, however, to record the insights on the century's first half obtained from American diplomatic reports. Collected on microfilm in the Hoyer Room of the US National Archives in College Park, they include reports from European diplomatic representatives and the local press, as well as more informed analysis than that with which they are sometimes credited. On the century's second half, Research Reports from Radio Free Europe and the collections of articles from the domestic presses of the Communist regimes, available at the Open Society Archives in Budapest, and the Romanian materials assembled by the Wilson Center's Cold War History Project were most helpful.

I also benefited from ongoing visits to the region. Consultations with Roumen Avramov of the Center for Liberal Strategies in Sofia, Ivo Bicanic of Zagreb University, Mark Wheeler of the International Crisis Group in Sarajevo, and Jean Tesche, a US Treasury representative in all three locations, were particularly valuable. So were meetings with younger scholars from the region at the several Young Scholars' Conferences organized by the Center for Democracy and Reconciliation in Southeastern Europe, based in Thessaloniki, and a number of classes and lectures for history and nationalism students at the Central European University in Budapest. Meetings with policymakers, official and nongovernmental, at the several conferences organized on regional cooperation and reconciliation by the Stanley Foundation in 2002–3 should also be mentioned.

These visits also allowed me to follow the range of new scholarship being published in the region. Especially valuable in this regard was a 2003 review of university curricula in the region with Christina Koulouri from Athens, Andrei Pippidi from Bucharest, Nikola Jordanovski from Skopje, and Sonja Dumjović from Sarajevo. My knowledge of recent Bulgarian scholarship greatly benefited from a comprehensive survey and summaries of selected works prepared by Ivanka Nedeva Atanasova of George Mason University.

The centerpiece for preparing and drafting the resulting manuscript was appropriately the Wilson Center. During my fellowship there in 2003–4, discussions with Martin Sletzinger, my successor as Director of East European Studies, Sampel F, Wells, Jr., the Center's Associate Director, and current Fellows helped to focus the project's policy relevance. The Center's library staff, Dagne Gizaw in particular, provided unfailing assistance. A succession of interns, Mathew Larsen, Jens Frederick Olsson, and Sofia Plagaskis, searched out the most recent data on the post-1989 period. Sofia deserves special thanks for careful preparation of the volume's statistical tables.

Beyond the Wilson Center, I was once again fortunate, as in my previous publications, to have the services of Larry Bowring and Bowring Cartographic in the preparation of a set of instructively detailed maps. Final revisions of the manuscript took advantage of a complete reading by Duncan Perry, Dean of the Graduate School at Scranton University, a partial reading by Gary Gerstle, Chair of History at the University of Maryland, and some detailed and well-informed suggestions by a reader for Palgrave. And further, I owe a great debt in the final preparation of the manuscript not only to my wife, Anita Baker-Lampe, but also to Palgrave's Juanita Bullough and Songa Barker for editorial and technical assistance respectively.

Finally, I dedicate this volume to Theofanis Stavrou, who introduced me to the study of Balkan history, and to the late Dennison Rusinow, who introduced me to the value of an historian's perspective on contemporary Southeastern Europe.

Introduction – Transitions at the Turn of Two Centuries

Once again there was trouble in the Balkans, once again conflict over ethnic rights had provoked bloodshed in Macedonia. Just as several nearby sources of turmoil seemed to subside, another local dispute was threatening to destabilize the entire region. Before this latest spark could set off the notorious Balkan powder keg, the major international powers felt obliged to intervene. The year was 1903. Yet the scenario reads at first glance like the confrontation of 2001 between the new state's ethnic Macedonian majority and Albanian minority. This recent dispute threatened to spill over into the Kosovo protectorate and the neighboring states until the European Union and the United States brokered an agreement between the two sides at Lake Ohrid in August of 2001. NATO thereupon deployed a small force and the European Union its much larger financial leverage. Both were needed to persuade the ethnic Macedonian government to step back from demanding full integration and Albanian representatives from insisting on full autonomy.

The Ohrid Agreement preserved the fragile successor state within its republic borders from the former Yugoslavia. It also preserved the wider set of borders whose maintenance Western capitals were calling crucial to regional stability at the turn of the twenty-first century. The set included Kosovo, autonomous as a UN protectorate while still formally part of Serbia since the NATO intervention of 1999 expelled Serbian authority. They extended to Bosnia-Herzegovina, still a NATO and UN protectorate. The Dayton Agreement in 1995 had ended three years of war but left the former Yugoslav republic territorially divided into a Bosnian Muslim–Croat federation and a Serb entity. Their failure to cohere into a viable state and Kosovar Albanian demands for independence, including a feared readiness to add the heavily Albanian territory of northwest Macedonia, fed the urgency of the Western initiative at Ohrid. The instability persisting from the wars of Yugoslavia's dissolution feeds a wider temptation: that is, to judge the entire region as the European powers judged it in 1903 – the back-

1

ward and eternally conflicted Balkans. Premodern limitations can then be presumed to explain ethnic disputes and to set their peoples apart from Europe as well as from each other.

Southeastern Europe's standing today is however better judged by its current governments' representations for full membership in the European Union and the members belated but finally forthcoming response. The European Union's meeting at Thessaloniki in June 2003, led by a Greek presidency, approved an agreement to open membership to all states of the region, not just to Slovenia in 2004 and Bulgaria and Romania in 2007 but subsequently to all of the successor states to the former Yugoslavia and to Albania. In order to understand how the region's standing evolved from the genuinely distinct and disadvantaged Balkan position of the pre-1914 period, we must read the history of the wider region, even its still troubled parts, forward through the twentieth century. That course is a repeatedly troubled but recognizably European one. The century had admittedly begun with trouble that prompted unilateral European intervention.

Unlike the recent meeting at Ohrid, the intervention of 1903 was not negotiated in Macedonia. Nor were any local or Ottoman representatives present at Emperor Franz Joseph's hunting lodge in Muerszteg, where the Austro-Hungarian and Russian rulers and their Foreign Ministers simply agreed among themselves to a detailed program. Its articles promised a Europan peacekeeping force and a Financial Commission to restore order in Ottoman Macedonia, an area much larger than the present republic and wracked by revolt and repression in August 1903.[1]

The Muerzsteg Agreement thus presaged the 1995 Dayton Agreement for Bosnia. It was to provide some 200 European police officers to train a new force from local ethnic majorities. Officers and men from Britain, France, and Italy as well as Austria–Hungary and Russia were to be recruited for three-year tours and assigned to districts divided between them like the recent NATO demarcations in Kosovo as well as Bosnia. The larger responsibilities went to Russia in the Salonika district and to Austria–Hungary in Kosovo. A German delegate was to join representatives of the other five on a Financial Commission. Its charge was to coordinate with Ottoman authorities the increase in Macedonian tax revenues needed to pay for the police reforms. Sultan Abdul Hamid II's regime reluctantly agreed, in the absence of any international Donors Conference on the recent Bosnian pattern.

In the event, the Financial Commission raised little new revenue, and the police-training mission never put more than 50 officers in place. They could not prevent an escalation in political violence that left 8000 locals dead and forced another 10,000 to emigrate. Paramilitary bands mixed local bandits and peasants with respective support from Bulgaria, Greece and Serbia. They clashed with each other as well as the supposedly reformed Ottoman authorities. By 1908 the mission was judged a failure and the European gendarmes withdrawn. The Austro-Hungarian contingent led the way, transferred to support the Habsburg annexation of Bosnia-Herzegovina in October of that year.

The Balkan Wars of 1912–13 and the First World War were left to expel first Ottoman and then Habsburg authority. The final settlement of 1919 ratified or drew new borders between Greece, Bulgaria, and enlarged Romania, now joined by Albania and Yugoslavia. To what became a decade of conflict and forced migration from 1912 to 1922, we must add the civil warfare that would again set the region largely apart from the rest of Europe during the Second World War and a half century later when the wars of Yugoslavia's dissolution followed the end of the Cold War. Altogether, some 4 million people would die, the majority of them civilians. Another 6 million would be forced to flee or migrate, the great majority of them at neighbors' hands, near or far. This recurring violence and attendant European (and finally American) intervention to reorder the region may too easily be taken for the singularly Balkan thread that ties together its history across the past century.[2] The lagging performance of the region's post-Communist economies when compared to those of their northern counterparts during the 1990s seemed to confirm the damning distinction of backwardness and a presumed democratic deficit. Greece's experience drops out in such a scenario.

The chapters that follow will however suggest that Greece deserves its place in the region's recent history, a recent history best understood as a set of European processes, ideas, and institutions, at work as they were elsewhere on the Continent. Here they moved at a faster, simultaneous pace, complicated by new borders after 1918 and burdened with longer, more internecine warfare. Of course, the continuing appeal of Balkan singularity cannot be denied. It attracts those outside the region seeking to stereotype it away from the rest of Europe as endemically unstable and politically as well as economically backward. Cultural historians have at least deployed the tools of literary criticism to trace the persistence of denigrating Balkan stereotypes in the language of Anglo-American politicians, journalists, and even scholars into the most recent decade.[3] And singularity also serves those within the region ready to blame foreign intervention, near neighbors included, for violence and their other misfortunes. Neither the indictment of Western stereotyping nor the continuing concentration on a victimized national history read backward, most noticeably in Yugoslavia's successor states, relates the region's peoples to each other or to the larger narrative of twentieth-century European history.

Such a comparative history, read representatively forward through the century rather than selectively back into it, is one purpose of this volume. Some separate treatment of individual states or regions cannot be avoided, but their comparison will be the rule. A second purpose is to concentrate on war and transition. Recent Western and regional scholarship allows us to assemble a more informed, better-balanced understanding of the region's experience and the major powers' role during the two world wars and the Cold War. These wartime upheavals had fateful postwar consequences. The resulting political and socioeconomic reconstructions involved enough systemic change to be called transitions. This concentration will not provide the comprehensive history that would also require a much longer volume. But it does address the historical background that seems most relevant to the region's capacity to enter the twenty-first century on the even terms with the rest of Europe that its peoples desire.

Southeastern Europe and the Post-1989 Transitions

The region's first designation as Southeastern Europe dates not from 1989 but from 1919. By the last pre-1914 decade, moreover, modern European aspirations and institutions were already at work in the imperial borderlands as well as the independent Balkan states. There followed across the twentieth century three separate decades of prolonged warfare. Each of them demanded a postwar transition that combined reconstruction with changing borders. Each time new domestic regimes faced a newly constituted international order. Social scientists, crowding around the post-1989 transition from Communist regimes, have neglected the century's two earlier sequences of war and transition. These experiences, their memories still fresh across the region, formed an essential background to the failings of the initial post-Communist transition, the wars of Yugoslavia's dissolution, and the wider regional discord to which Greece also contributed. Such an historical perspective helps us as well to make sense of the transition's virtual second wind since the late 1990s. It has begun to provide constructive political connections within Southeastern Europe and to pursue the region's wider economic ties to Europe. And here Greece has played a positive role.

The initial Western model for all of Eastern Europe after 1989 posited multiparty democracy and a free market economy as mutually reinforcing. Their easy combination, dubbed neoliberalism, would facilitate a uniform and relatively rapid transition to parliamentary democracy and a market economy from the discredited *nomenklatura* regimes and hemorrhaging command economies of the last Communist years. International organizations, primarily the International Monetary Fund, the World Bank and the European Bank for Recovery and Development, would join with Western governments in providing the necessary financial stability for the transition under an informal agreement known as "the Washington consensus."

Then the pace of economic change slowed and its handy correlation with political pluralism became less clear, even for Poland and Hungary. Close coordination among international organizations and with Western governments did not come automatically. Area specialists had already doubted that the recently negotiated democratization of authoritarian regimes in southern Europe or Latin America could be transplanted and have the same success. Sociologists and political scientists then focused on Communist legacies, assets as well as liabilities, informal as well as formal, to explain why the neoliberal transition was not proceeding smoothly.[4] This "path-dependent" approach introduced some historically valid distinctions within Communist Eastern Europe but neglected the largely European path along which all of these states have proceeded for most of the twentieth century. It is along this broader path that an open political process and the market mechanism have repeatedly contended with centralized state authority. In our region, the very weakness that had in fact characterized its states earlier in the century returned to provide the same authoritarian stimulus even after the Communist regimes had collapsed in 1989. Still, as the century ended, opposition parties revived the prospects for political pluralism and the promise of a market economy reemerged. Lessons from the initial transition combined with the magnetic attraction of the European Union to make economic prospects brighter. Comprehensive political stability remained elusive.

The wars of Yugoslavia's dissolution had indeed left a trying political legacy at the center of the region. How tempting to see the future of all Southeastern Europe as mortgaged to the continuing instability of what was now called the Western Balkans, reaching from Macedonia at least to Croatia. Such scenarios rested on a presumably uniform Communist legacy of collectivism, ignoring the case of Greece. They also emphasized paramilitary and patriarchal traditions of the pre-Communist period. They neglected any illiberal European legacies before the Second World War. We join Geoffrey Pridham in acknowledging this broader range of illiberal legacies and then only as "a powerful but not a predictive force."[5]

Confronting them were liberal ambitions, some centered on national identity, and periodic practice in multiparty politics and market economics. The rural peasantry shared some in that practice and brought its own populist egalitarian legacy along. Together these liberal, illiberal, and populist legacies faced a surfeit of warfare, international rivalry, and forced migration. In the process, wartime memories and postwar reconstruction challenged Southeastern Europe three times during the twentieth century. We follow these regimes and societies from war to peace and back again to the Kosovo conflict of 1999, the last violent chapter in the breakup of Yugoslavia. Each time, native political leaders confronted a changing international context and new international organizations as well as this broader contest of ideas, identities, and institutions. Albania, Bulgaria, Greece, Romania, Yugoslavia, and now its successors as nation-states found themselves within borders that were disputed after the First World War, reestablished after their violent reordering during the Second World War, and then called into question immediately after the Communist collapse of 1989. Virtually across the entire century, the region has thereby faced what Claus Offe and others have aptly called a triple transition – the simultaneous formation of nation-state identity along with the pursuit of political legitimacy and modern economic development.[6]

The recurring decades of war and postwar peace settlements, mass migration, and social upheaval, would compromise the sort of continuity that Western Europe enjoyed across most of the nineteenth century and after the Second World War. The three wartime decades indeed witnessed the direct foreign intervention that some mistake, as noted above, for the only significant European connection to the region's modern history. But the longer postwar transitions that followed the two world wars depended on domestic efforts to build modern European states and institutions, based on a single representative government (the Communist definition included), an educated population, and an integrated economy. So too has the post-1989 transition, especially since its second phase has taken hold after the end of warfare in the former Yugoslavia. But national politics still struggle with the consequences of the century's past wars and national identities with their memories more than in Western and even Central Europe.

A volume entitled *Balkans into Southeastern Europe* obviously suggests some parallel to Eugen Weber's seminal study of pre-1914 France, *Peasants into Frenchmen*.[7] Weber argued that public schooling, rail and other communication links, and the military draft contributed significantly to creating a common French identity in the four decades before the

First World War. This structural process worked to advance two other transitions already underway in France – a government elected from a growing franchise and an integrated national economy. Together they served the Radical Party's vision of a single national consciousness built on the citizens' rights of the French Revolution – *Fraternité* combining with *Liberté* and *Egalité*. Nineteenth-century Central European politics would call this combination of civic and ethnic representation National Liberalism.

Our region's twentieth century started down the same path. Its further experience, ideology and ethnicity aside for the moment, fits well with Charles Maier's structural narrative for all of modern European history.[8] He identifies four features common to continental European state-building from the 1860s to the present. Please note how these features include no reference to political pluralism or a market economy, thus applying to the authoritarian regimes of the last interwar years and the post-1945 Communist regimes as well as those that came before and now after:

1. centrally controlled government institutions, mainly ministries with growing administrative authority and larger staffs, at the expense of local authority and on the basis of a common language;
2. continually mobilized internal military and police forces as a "resource for governance" and maintenance of order;
3. cooption into the ruling political elite of leaders in finance, industry and the professions, education in particular;
4. a growing industrial infrastructure based on coal and iron technology and a railway network, all on the assumptions that efficiency is proportional to size and to central control, preferably from the capital city.

Maier sees the identification of this "bordered political space" with the native or assimilated ethnic majority as the legitimizing ideology that has moved state-building ahead, for good and for ill. The fit with modern France and its centrally propagated national identity, as described by Weber, is too tight to support any sharp separation of civic, West European nationalism from the ethnic German and East European nationalism. And yet, as Eric Hobsbawm reminds us, this liberal nationalism of nineteenth-century Europe did not privilege all local ethnic majorities with the right to state-building. Only those occupying a larger territory, which therefore promised advantages of economic integration and military security, were assumed to have that right, and then only if combined with some historical or cultural continuity. And that right included the assimilation, as in France, of smaller, therefore presumably lesser, ethnic groups.[9]

In the wake of the First World War, the new, still presumably liberal principle of "self-determination," as posited by American President Woodrow Wilson, seemed to promise a much broader right. Its appearance left the earlier, assimilationist model, closer to Wilson's own thinking as we shall see in Chapter 3, to contend with a longer list of national claimants, most obviously in Yugoslavia. From this time forward, ethnic self-determination justified at least demands for minority rights in liberal democracies advancing majority assimilation, and at most justified minority demands for secession and independence. Joining the two conflicting liberal rationales were other ideological frameworks – what Maier would call "moral narratives" – populist or religious as well as fascist, socialist and Communist, anti-fascist and anti-Communist. All of them have moved critical masses of people across twentieth-century Europe, sometimes weakening but more often strengthening the structural process we might call "modernization by centralization." A recent volume of essays from the region's younger scholars explores the relation of this range of European ideologies to the mass politics and popular culture that emerged across the region after the First World War. These ideologies, Communism included, confronted or combined pre-1914 political parties and elites that were already recognizably European.[10]

Domestic political leaders deserve our attention as individuals, rather than simply as representatives of an ideology or an elite group. These key figures would count, and not just for the parties or monarchies that they led. They all had to come to terms with or confront government establishments more powerful than any private interests or social class, hence making access to political power dangerously attractive. This attraction unsurprisingly produced what Bulgarians called *partizanstvo*. Clientelist networks of personal favors and public employment for supporters first displaced and then coexisted with ideological party programs across the region's twentieth century, even into and past the Communist regimes. Individual leaders, whether patriarchal, charismatic, or neither, were also essential to the mass politics that spread across most of Southeastern Europe by the interwar period. Countrywide organizations, large public meetings, and press coverage that inspired public confidence or resolve were needed to mobilize support beyond access to favors and jobs. Patriarchal figures, from the Serbian Radicals' Nikola Pašić to the young interwar monarchs and aging Communist leaders like Bulgaria's Todor Zhivkov, struggled with the problems of mass politics. Parties dependent on a modern charismatic leader struggled simply to continue after he was killed, like the Bulgarian

Agrarian's Stamboliiski, or stayed past his prime, like Greece's Liberal Venizelos or Yugoslavia's Communist Tito. They and the uncharismatic majority of the region's national leaders all sought domestic legitimacy for their regimes. They are better understood in the light of shifting European patterns of multiparty, one-party, or nonparty rule rather than simply advancing or opposing "democratization" as post-1989 approaches are tempted to assume.

Finally, we must not leave the region's socioeconomic development across the twentieth century, the Communist period included, simply to the centralizing dynamic of state institutions. Before 1945, as David Good has pointed out, the "institutional arrangements" of the region's state structures had proved "highly vulnerable to the shocks of war and depression"; in the post-1945 Communist regimes, as Valerie Bunce has argued, their uniformly centralized institutions received enough internal autonomy to struggle with each other and thereby subvert their presumably superior coordination of economic growth.[11] Heavy industry and capital cities did grow considerably under such initiatives. The same may not be said for agriculture and light industry, especially under the Communist regimes. In those sectors, private or cooperative enterprise responding to market signals rather than state direction would do better. Nor was the state's preeminent position in education matched by its control of the press and the new mixture of mass and high culture. University students took the lead in making the mixture volatile by the first decade of the twentieth century. By the interwar decades, a several-sided civil society was growing up in the capital cities to challenge the primacy of state interests and employment. This milieu combined with cafes, streetlights, and trams to make the centers of Athens, Belgrade, Bucharest, and Sofia look and feel remarkably like their European counterparts.

The unstable juxtaposition of nation-states and empire with lagging economic development and overwhelmingly rural societies still set the region apart as the Balkans during this last pre-1914 decade. They did indeed reflect a more contested geographic location and historical legacy than the northwest of Europe in particular. At the same time, the region's increasingly educated elite sought to emulate Europe's contemporary political and socio-economic models for national development. This was an effort visible, as Chapter 1 will demonstrate, in the surrounding Habsburg and Ottoman borderlands as well as the independent Balkan states. Memories of that initial effort and of the larger role of Great-Power intervention before 1914 would be called back to life during the three subsequent periods of warfare and postwar transition. Just where and how Western and Central Europe, and then Russia/the Soviet Union and the United States actually did intervene will be a special concern in subsequent chapters. But throughout we focus on the domestic intersection of European ideologies and institutions with the states and societies of Southeastern Europe. Their further intersection, three times during the twentieth century, with war and postwar reconstruction has made recurring transitions unavoidable.

1 Balkan States and Borderlands before the Balkan Wars

We begin with the Balkans generally regarded both as a single region and as one distinct from Europe. The five independent states of Bulgaria, Greece, Romania, Serbia, and Montenegro could all make ethnic claims to the surrounding Habsburg or Ottoman borderlands. With the constituent peoples of those borderlands, they shared what the European powers regarded as a common danger-zone. Local unrest and Great-Power intervention in the borderlands left the independent states to be courted or confronted primarily to control their irredentist ambitions. But the wider region, and not just its capital cities, had more in common by the last pre-1914 decade than this reputation for instability. Other common elements, some traditional and local, some modern and European, were struggling with hastier juxtaposition than elsewhere across Europe early in the twentieth century. In the process, disjunctures between state or provincial majorities and minorities also emerged, often to endure across the rest of the century. These too became part of the process changing the Balkans into Southeastern Europe.

Legacies of Geographic and Imperial Division

Two distinctions set the region most clearly aside from the rest of Europe during the pre-modern period. Both an isolating upland geography and the prolonged experience of fragmented imperial domination divided the Balkan peoples from each other. Yet these also facilitated their separate survival by preventing the emergence of a single dominant state. Both the English and French monarchies would achieve such domination by the early modern period. And both would enjoy advantages in location and physical geography conspicuously absent from the Balkan Peninsula.

The region does not in fact enjoy the access to the sea implied by its designation as a Peninsula. Only Greece is surrounded on three sides by water, and even there, as along the narrow Dalmatian coast on the Adriatic, the predominately mountainous or upland terrain comes too close to allow large hinterlands to develop around accessible ports or navigable rivers. Indeed, the only river fully navigable across the region is the Danube. And it flows away from Central Europe, with offloading required at the Iron Gates until the end of the nineteenth century, with its access to the Black Sea divided into a difficult delta.

The largely upland territory reflected in Map 1.1 also suggests the far smaller share of arable land available across the region than in the northern half of the continent. For Greece the arable fraction within present borders is barely 20 percent, and for Albania 10 percent. Their northern neighbors do better, up to 40 percent, thanks mainly to a belt of good soil running from Slavonia and the present Vojvodina across northern Bulgaria and into southern Romania. Its grain crops would however face the problem of limited rainfall that further declines from west to east. Punctuated by periodic droughts, the annual average of 20 inches a year is half that for Northwestern Europe.

The three mountain ranges (Dinaric, Balkan, and Carpathian) also provided unfortunate if common distinctions. No foothills contained sufficient deposits of iron ore or high-quality coal to provide the potential focal point for industrialization that the two found close together had afforded the English Midlands, the German Ruhr, or the Czech lands. Yet none of the mountains were high or continuous enough, on the Swiss pattern, to keep invading armies from finding their way through. The uplands, on the other hand, provided a refuge for the native population, one offering little economic advantage but allowing them to keep their small arms.

That population would not surprisingly remain small into the modern period. Rough estimates suggest densities averaging 20 per square kilometer by the early nineteenth century, in contrast to figures from Western and Central Europe that approached 100. Rapid growth would be required to bring those densities up by 1910 to the averages of 40–60 noted in Table 1.1.[1] Exaggerating the fragmented physical geography of the region were two empires that divided virtually all of the region between them across the early modern centuries.

No native state of the medieval centuries save the Romanian principalities would survive the advance of first the Ottoman and then the Habsburg empires. By the eighteenth century, a long military border on the Habsburg side stretched along the present Croatian–Bosnian border past Serbia and into Transylvania. Towns were scarce and small, dominated by imperial authority and the official religion (Muslim and Catholic respectively). Relatively little migration from the imperial centers, significant only for the Bulgarian and Macedonian lands, kept the overall population low. The

Map 1.1 Balkan physical geography and state borders, 1910

——·—— 1910 international boundaries
—————— 1910 provincial boundaries within Austria-Hungary and the Ottoman Empire
• selected cities

native nobility survived only in the Romanian principalities and Croatia–Slavonia, retaining at least local authority.

Their peasantries faced feudal obligations, as did the Romanians in Hungarian Transylvania, which encouraged some native movement to obtain land for service in the military border. But the larger share of this

Table 1.1   Balkan state and borderland populations and densities, *c.* 1910

	Population (in millions)	Urban % (over 2000)	Density (per sq. km.)
Independent States			
Bulgaria	4.34	19	45.6
Greece	2.68	24	41.8
Montenegro	–	9	24.6
Romania*	7.03	16	54.0
Serbia	2.92	11	60.5
Habsburg Borderlands			
Bosnia-Herzegovina	1.90	13	37.1
Croatia–Slovenia	2.62	18	61.7
Dalmatia	0.64	–	49.6
Slovene Carniola	1.32	27	51.3
Transylvania	4.23	13	37.1
Vojvodina	1.55	–	68.7
*Ottoman Districts***			
Kosovo	0.95	–	–
Monastir	0.89	24***	–
Salonika	1.00	28***	–

Notes: *1912; **1906; ***1895.

Sources: Michael R. Palairet, *The Balkan Economies ca. 1800–1914, Evolution without Development* (Cambridge: Cambridge University Press, 1997), Tables 1.4, 1.9, 1.10, pp. 13, 24–7; John R. Lampe and Marvin R. Jackson, *Balkan Economic History, 1550–1950, From Imperial Borderlands to Developing Nations* (Bloomington, IN: Indiana University Press, 1982), Tables 6.4, 9.1, 10.3, 10.11, pp. 166, 281, 334–5, 363.

native movement to the border settlement came from Serbs moving west from or across the Ottoman's own Bosnian border districts. We must resist the temptation to trace this movement either to an ethnically self-conscious mobilization or to an exploited lowland peasantry.[2] In general, the huge peasant majority in the Ottoman Balkans could maintain their ethnically centered Orthodox Christianity, sustain themselves by raising livestock in the uplands or extensive, uncleared forests, and keep the same small arms as their Ottoman overlords. From there they could venture forth to trade with the Adriatic or Greek coasts to the south or across the Danube to the Habsburg lands. Some did, but more remained isolated except for those resorting to banditry. Local memories of resistance to the Ottoman conquest legitimized such banditry if conducted against local authorities or warlords, typically Turkish. In any case, communal and egalitarian values were favored over the commercial or individual.

The fragmented nature of the two sets of imperial borderlands themselves, as I have argued elsewhere, contributed to this premodern history of isolation across the region, separating one area from another as well as from the wider continent.[3] Paramilitary autonomy in the face of foreign domination was also easier to sustain. The final legacy of the two empires also followed from the disparate set of regimes under which they maintained their ethnically mixed borderlands. Their two cultural spheres often overlapped the formal borders, borders also unable to keep wider Mediterranean and Central European influences from penetrating at least to some towns. Scholarly efforts across the years to draw a single cultural border across the region between these latter two influences have produced too many lines from southern Greece to north of the Danube to accept any of them as definitive.[4] The indeterminacy of that earlier division suggests that the region would be open, despite its limitations, to a wider European connection as the modern era began with the nineteenth century.

Nation-States versus Imperial Borderlands

During the course of that nineteenth century, a group of native Balkan states emerged. Overcoming much of their initial dependence on the two surrounding empires by the last pre-1914 decade, they provided the principal political distinction between the region and its northern neighbors in what would more recently be called Eastern Europe. No separate Polish, Czech. Slovak, or for that matter Hungarian state existed before the First World War. One of the war's major consequences was to break up the imperial German, Russian, and Austro-Hungarian regimes that divided those territories between them. To the south, the states established successively in Serbia, Greece, Romania, Montenegro, and Bulgaria had until then remained divided from imperial borderlands that still covered the other half of the region. The Habsburg lands reached from present-day Slovenia and Croatia into Bosnia-Herzegovina and across the Vojvodina through Transylvania. Ottoman rule still held from Albania and Kosovo through Macedonia broadly defined and Thrace. As may be seen in Map 1.2, the overlapping of ethnic settlement was most pronounced in the borderlands of Bosnia, Kosovo and Macedonia.

Map 1.2 Ethnic composition of the Western Balkans, 1900

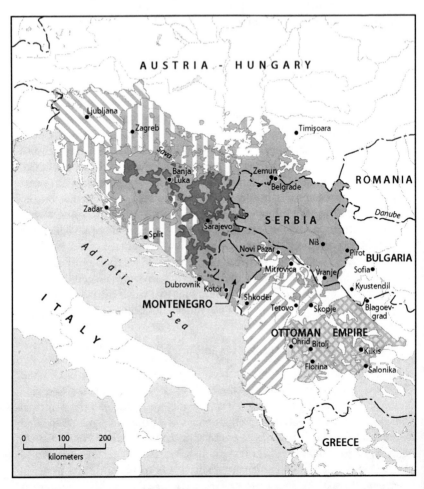

Source: Adapted from Paul Robert Magocsi, *Historical Atlas of Central Europe* (Seattle, WA: University of Washington Press, 2002)

Major concentrations of ethnic populations, *c.* 1900

The increasingly independent Balkan states themselves nonetheless fit perfectly into the European pattern that came to identify proper political borders with the predominant ethnic group. By the end of the nineteenth century, their populations were being counted with overwhelming majorities of Serbs, Greeks, Romanians, Montenegrins, and Bulgarians. Included in proportions that averaged 90 percent were a small number assimilated from minorities; a larger number of minorities had left or been forced to leave during the course of the century. The stage was well set for the formation of nation-states on the pattern best exemplified, as already noted, by nineteenth-century France. We might recall France's pre-1914 claim to Alsace-Lorraine after its loss to what became Germany in the Franco-Prussian War of 1871 before judging the claims of the Balkan states to their imperial borderlands as un-European behavior. French provinces only since the seventeenth century, their mixed population proved no barrier to the perception in Paris that their territory's transfer separated them from an established national identity. There were enough presumed ethnic kin of Balkan state majorities in the adjoining imperial lands to kindle similar demands. Some drew on claims for restoring lost medieval borders. All were driven by the idea that, like the Italians after the Risorgimento of the 1850s, all of their people belonged in the same state.

The Berlin Congress of European powers in 1878 had redrawn regional borders in order to limit these claims. The meeting's primary purpose was to rebuff Russian efforts to replace the Ottoman regime as the region's other imperial power. British support and German mediation helped Austria–Hungary to force a reluctant Tsarist Russia to abandon the Treaty of San Stefano. Forced on the Ottoman Empire in March 1878, after its third defeat of the century by Russian arms, the Tsarist terms had created a large Bulgarian state through Vardar and Aegean Macedonia almost to Salonika and through Thrace to the Aegean Sea. A Russian Prince was to be the likely ruler. The new treaty signed in Berlin that July trimmed the borders of the new Bulgaria back to remove even Pirin Macedonia and all of Thrace. The core area south of the Balkan Mountains reverted to Ottoman suzerainty as Eastern Rumelia. The truncated Bulgarian state to the north was only given autonomy from Constantinople, and then under a German rather than a Russian Prince.

The treaty did however provide formal independence to Serbia, Montenegro, and Romania. Their principalities now or soon became independent monarchies. Each received some territory from the Ottoman Empire, but not as much as they desired. Serbia, autonomous since 1830 after two earlier revolts (1804–13, 1815), was given the triangle bounded by Niš, Pirot, and Vranje. The small area at least bordered Kosovo, already sought after as the center of the medieval Serbian state and the site of its Orthodox monasteries. Montenegro lost only a little of San Stefano's huge inland addition to its coastal nexus but remained separated from Serbia by the Sandžak of Novi Pazar, now garrisoned by Habsburg rather than Ottoman troops. Greece had originally received nothing, but by 1881 pressure from the new Gladstone government in London had secured at least Thessaly from the Sultan's regime. Moving beyond the small southern core carved out in 1829, Greece acquired better land for grain crops, and a border with Epirus and Aegean Macedonia, both with sizeable Greek populations. The Romanian principalities of Wallachia and Moldova had been separated from Ottoman oversight by the Russian regime of Organic Statutes (1829–34) and united in 1859 by their election of a common Prince. Romania received only the Danube delta, as it had under San Stefano. Its representations for southern Bessarabia had no effect, nor did the those from Greece for Aegean Macedonia. Serbia was not even allowed to state its case for Kosovo or Bosnia. More immediately, its independence was mortgaged to Habsburg oversight.

Perhaps the most important legacy of the Berlin settlement to the region was the presumption through the twentieth century that the Great Powers would set its borders and decide its fate. For European strategic thinking, Russia excepted, the obvious legacy was that no one power should be allowed to dominate this crossroads to the rest of the continent. The less obvious legacy was that joint European intervention there could preserve stability at relatively little cost and with no reference to regional states. After all, the frontiers fixed at Berlin would continue unchanged until 1912. Since then, however, even joint intervention has proved to be much more costly.[5]

Austria–Hungary was at least rewarded in 1878 for its leadership against any Russian advance with the right to occupy and administer Bosnia-Herzegovina. Ottoman forces duly relinquished control, although Bosnian Muslims, led by their landholding elite, engaged Habsburg troops, largely Serbs and Croats from the military border, before order was restored. After a brief revolt in 1882 by returning Serbs balking at higher taxes, the province enjoyed 20 years of relative calm under an able Habsburg administrator, Benjamin Kállay. He allowed religious representation but forbad political organization to what was now a plurality of Serbs, a large minority of Bosnian Muslims and a growing Croat minority. The Ottoman system of land tenure was left in place, under Bosnian Muslim begs and agas whose sharecroppers were largely Serbs. His successor would allow political organizations to form, quickly coalescing under their ethnic leaderships. But before land reform could be launched, the Habsburg leadership had seized the chance to win Russian approval and formally annexed Bosnia-Herzegovina in 1908.[6] This Austro-Hungarian breach of the Berlin Treaty opened the way for the Balkan states themselves to challenge the remaining Ottoman borderlands. By then an explosive mixture of reform, resistance, and irredentism was also at work across the region.

Independence and Autonomy, Turmoil and Transition in the Last Prewar Decade

Less attention has of course been paid to transition than to turmoil on the eve of the First World War. Unrest had been building both in the national states and the imperial borderlands since the late nineteenth century. Disquiet boiled over after 1900. Accompanying the unrest, however, were assertions of independence in the national states and autonomy in the borderlands, sometimes including demands for national unification. The examples of nineteenth-century Italy or Germany were increasingly cited. Irredentist violence and unrest did indeed make the region a powder keg by the last prewar decade. It exploded in 1914 with the Bosnian Serb assassination of the Habsburg heir Franz Ferdinand in Sarajevo. The consequent Austro-Hungarian attack on Serbia triggered the First World War. In examining that turmoil, however, we find its roots embedded in a series of centralizing and legitimizing reforms that were typical of European political culture and economic development at the time. They were directed to or at least served the purpose of advancing national independence or autonomy.

Both the Balkan states and the borderlands were still small in population, if not in size, when compared not only to the European Great Powers but also to the two surrounding or containing empires. Table 1.1 spells out this contrast to the 21 million in the Ottoman Empire and the 51 million in the Habsburg lands by 1910. Between them the independent states totaled 16.8 million and the borderlands 15.1 million. Their overall densities, from 40–60 per square kilometer, and low urban proportions, from 20 percent for the states and up to 30 percent for the Ottoman and Slovene lands, fit the Ottoman rather than the European pattern of the period.

Political Ferment in the Independent States

All of the national states, save Montenegro, made significant advances in legitimizing their political frameworks. In the process, a series of political leaders emerged whose parties, policies, or personalities would carry over into the interwar period. The final executive authority in all of them rested in monarchs, three of them from Central European families. Serbia and Montenegro had native dynasties, but of the five, only Serbia could be called a constitutional monarchy, at least after 1903. Its advent was inauspicious. A band of military officers (later the notorious Black Hand) assassinated the young King Aleksandar Obrenović, bringing Petar Karadjordjević, the claimant from the other native dynasty, to the throne. But he returned from decades of Swiss exile to endorse parliamentary government as prescribed in a new constitution. Modeled on the Belgian constitution of 1830 and the Serbian precursor of 1888, it provided at least some separation of powers between a legislature elected by near-universal male suffrage and the Belgrade ministries staffed by the ruling party. It also enjoyed substantial leverage in the electoral process.

For the first five years, a new Independent Radical Party was indeed able to compete with the one nationally organized party, the Radicals, led by Nikola Pašić. Trained as an engineer in Zurich, Pašić had returned to Serbia to found this first modern political party in the Balkans by 1881. Its local network helped Pašić and the party to survive as the major opponent of the restrictive, Austrian-backed Obrenović regime. The Radicals' party platform was dedicated to popular sovereignty and universal male suffrage. Yet Pašić in power after 1903 proved indifferent to mass politics and domestic reform. A master of secretive maneuver, he preferred to rule through the Belgrade ministries. The wily Prime Minister used the ongoing tariff war with Austria–Hungary (1906–11) and indignation over the Habsburg annexation of Bosnia-Herzegovina in 1908 to reestablish Radical dominance over the Independents. Considerable freedom of the press remained. Increasing freedom from Austria–Hungary came with victory in the tariff war, Russian diplomatic backing, and two large French loans, one for armaments. Pašić used this leeway and the Serbian cultural activities still permitted in Bosnia after annexation to strengthen further his domestic position. In the small Montenegrin state, Prince Nikola continued his far more arbitrary regime but took advantage of the same chance now available to Serbia and the other Balkan states. That was to maneuver between the European powers, encouraging them to compete for support with loans and other favors.[7]

In Bulgaria and Romania, the originally German monarchs Ferdinand and Carol also used their power in foreign affairs, greater than that of Serbia's King Petar, to the same national advantage. The presumption that they would favor their native Central Powers over the emerging Entente between Russia, France, and Great Britain would however not be justified before the First World War. If still supreme in foreign policy, their domestic powers were increasingly constrained.[8] In Bulgaria, Ferdinand seized on the Bosnian annexation's violation of the Berlin Treaty to declare the state fully independent of the Ottoman Empire and to proclaim himself Tsar in 1908. But the domestic parties among which he had maneuvered to divide and rule now became more assertive. The pro-Russian Democrats' regime of 1908–11 forced Ferdinand to relax press laws, recognize professional unions and reappoint the dissenting professors he had dismissed from Sofia University. Its Prime Minister, the Macedonian Aleksandar Malinov, favored a Balkan federation of small states with limited central powers. When hopes faded that this project would attract Russian support to force Ottoman concessions on Macedonia, Ferdinand dismissed Malinov. His successor, the English-educated Ivan Estatiev Geshov was the last Bulgarian Minister President to pursue a policy of Ottoman appeasement, even restraining border raids into Macedonia by irredentist bands. Unlike Malinov, he pushed ahead with the accumulating regulatory powers, protective tariffs included, that were the hallmark of the developed European states during this decade. His greatest achievement was however the new constitution approved by a more widely elected Grand National Assembly in 1911. Its delegates included representatives of the two new mass parties that would fight for control of Bulgaria after both world wars, the Agrarian Union of Aleksandar Stamboliiski and the Narrow Socialist, later Communist, Party. His ruling coalition of the three strongest, and far less ideological, parties would include none of their members. And despite their opposition, the new constitution reaffirmed the government's right, if no longer Ferdinand's alone, to conclude secret treaties.

Romania's King Carol I celebrated 40 years on the throne in 1906. His governments had alternated between the two major parties: National Liberals based in Wallachia and Conservatives based in Moldova. The King allowed them in turn to conduct and therefore win parliamentary elections based on an extremely narrow, propertied franchise. Both parties were dominated by the landed boyar elite and faced no constitutional crisis in the last prewar decade. Carol preferred the Russophobe Conservatives but continued to accept the Liberal governments, despite their anti-Habsburg interest in Transylvania. Neither of them challenged royal prerogatives in the electoral process or foreign policy. It was instead the two parties who faced challenges from a rising urban elite, professional as well as commercial, and thereby found themselves pushed toward modernizing reforms. Established in 1908, the new Democratic-Conservative Party split the Conservatives. It demanded agricultural reforms in response to the peasant revolt of 1907 that the Liberal Party had brutally suppressed. The new party also proposed to codify for the first time the regulations under which any ruling party's Interior Ministry and its powerful, French-style prefects administered each local district, or *judeţ*. It soon shared power in a coalition government with the Conservatives. Before then, the brief Liberal government of 1908 had witnessed the ascendancy of a younger leadership.

Forward came the Brătianu family's most charismatic member, Ionel, to a position that he would consolidate during and after the First World War. Modern Greek politics began in 1910 with a Liberal Party more broadly constituted than that of Romania. It took shape and came to power under the leadership of the most charismatic of the prewar Prime Ministers, Eleftherios Venizelos. "Tall, articulate, graceful in appearance . . . a metallic voice full of life, power, feeling, decision," as a journalist described him in his native Crete, Venizelos moved large crowds with his speeches, first in Athens and later in Salonika. His rhetoric spoke of national regeneration and sounded like a call to arms.[9] In fact, he took office after a military coup but, like Serbia's King Petar Karadjordjević, quickly established a more legitimate political regime than his predecessor. The Danish King George, on the throne since 1863, did not oppose the new government. The Liberals amended the 1864 constitution but stopped short of seeking a new one. The amendments nonetheless gave civil servants the chance for tenure denied them under the existing practice of clientelism. It gave the party winning a parliamentary majority the right to appoint members to every level of state employment. The quorum in the often deadlocked parliament was reduced from one half to one third, primary education was made compulsory, and some initial social legislation passed. Helping to push through these reforms were Venizelos's credentials as a Greek nationalist from Crete, still under Ottoman rule. His zeal for claiming the northern borderlands as well could not be questioned. The very army officers whose Military League had overthrown the government in 1909, primarily to expel a number of royal Princes from the high command and then pursue irredentism more effectively, had brought Venizelos to Athens as their political advisor. He kept the ministries of the army and the navy for himself to advance their wider reform. They should be ready with regular forces, rather than relying on the irregulars easily defeated by Ottoman troops in 1897, when another chance to move north or to claim Crete appeared.[10]

Economic Unrest and Limited Advances

The pressures for change common to the two sets of imperial borderlands and the independent Balkan states came from their huge peasant majorities. Military and tax reform had already combined to incite comparable peasant revolts in Habsburg Croatia–Slavonia and independent Serbia in 1883. The end of the military border with its support structure for regimental families was primarily responsible for unrest in Croatia. In Serbia, peasant militia members revolted against handing in their weapons so that a modern, disciplined army might take their place. Ottoman forces had easily turned back the Serbian irregulars who entered Bosnia to support the peasant uprising there in 1876.

These two revolts pale by comparison with the one widespread peasant uprising of the prewar decades and the massive internal use of regular army troops to put it down. In February 1907 the Romanian peasantry of northern Moldova rose up when confronted with new annual contracts. The terms cut the retained share of their crops to barely 30 percent on the leased lands of the typically large noble (boyar) estates. The beating of largely Jewish estate agents and riotous destruction spread rapidly across Moldovan villages and headed into Wallachia toward Bucharest. A Conservative government hesitated, despite its Moldovan base. A new Liberal regime intervened with army troops. They suppressed the spontaneous uprising at the cost of some 10,000 lives. Also responsible for the revolt were reform efforts by the previous National Liberal government to set up communal banks, village cooperatives, and primary schools. They raised expectations but failed to take control of more than a small fraction of leased land.[11] Similarly severe sharecropping arrangements predominated across the Ottoman Balkans, contributing to the aforementioned Illinden Uprising and Kovoso Albanian rioting of 1903. Sharecropping also survived in Bosnia, creating rural Serb resentment of Bosnian Muslim landowners whom they called Turks.

Agriculture across the region was plainly backward by European standards. Extensive methods faced the pressure of a growing rural population. Only some estate farming in Slavonia and smallholding in the Vojvodina could keep pace with the productivity of the Hungarian agricultural revolution underway to the north. In the independent Balkan states, the real per capita grain production and acreage cultivated per capita that had risen so promisingly in the last decades of the nineteenth century began to drop after 1900. Their rural shares of a rising total population stayed at 80–90 percent as national and borderland averages per square kilometer doubled from mid-nineteenth century levels to reach 40, tripling to 60 in Romania and Serbia. A growing network of credit cooperatives and even some producers' cooperatives in Bulgaria and the Slovene lands pursued improved techniques of intensive agriculture but with few financial resources.[12] The two networks were in any case more significant as vehicles for political organization and protest, in particular the Bulgarian Agrarian National Union (BZNS) of Aleksandar Stamboliiski.

The principal recourse of this prewar Balkan peasantry, especially in the borderlands, was in any case to emigrate abroad or to migrate for seasonal work on the Hungarian or Romanian estates. Remaining in the disadvantaged upland areas, such as much of Herzegovina, still left them with their

Table 1.2   Economic indicators for Balkan states and borderlands, 1910–11

	Exports per cap. (mil. franc equiv.)	Bank assets per cap. (mil. franc equiv.)	Rail lines (km per 100 pop.)
Balkan States			
Bulgaria	42	167	43
Greece	46	263	56
Romania	98	290	49
Serbia	40	355	31
Habsburg Borderlands			
Bosnia-Herzegovina	67	37	74
Croatia–Slovenia	56	223	82
Slovene Carniota	121	–	82
Transylvania	–	331	96
Ottoman Macedonia	31	42	18

Source: John R. Lampe and Marvin R. Jackson, *Balkan Economic History, 1550–1950, From Imperial Borderlands to Developing Nations* (Bloomington, IN: Indiana University Press, 1982), Tables 9.2, 9.7, 9.8, pp. 282, 302, 304.

small arms and rising resentment at premodern poverty. The opportunity for education but not subsequent employment in a town like Sarajevo (or like Priština for Kosovar Albanians in the 1980s) only added to the resentment. These were the origins of Gavrilo Princip, the young Bosnian Serb who fired the fatal shots at Franz Ferdinand.

Let us now turn from the turmoil associated primarily with this disadvantaged upland peasantry, a restive student generation, and newly assertive Balkan governments to a potential economic transition. Based on foreign trade and European finance, it had at first promised to advance lowland agriculture. Table 1.2 indicates the progress toward European levels in these areas by the last prewar years, progress that had however failed to provide the broad, export-led growth associated with, say, Denmark and Canada during the same period.

Led by grain sales to Western and Central Europe, real per capita exports from the borderlands and national states had indeed risen steadily during the late nineteenth century. Then, after 1900, they turned down. Export surpluses for Bulgaria and Serbia shrank away, without having generated the imports of European capital for industry or railway construction that were in fact flowing into Tsarist Russia. Only Romania kept its large surplus from grain shipped out through the Mediterranean and attracted direct investment, mainly to the region's one oil industry. And only Romania's per capita exports and railway trackage could match those of the Habsburg borderlands, where even Bosnia's 1910 figures exceeded Serbia's by more than one half.[13]

European capital was of course coming into the national states, and in far greater amounts than to the borderlands, but it was coming to the state administrations. Their governments had pushed revenues up as fast as taxing the export boom would carry them. Their appetite for even greater expenditures had kept those budgetary totals the fastest-rising economic indicator in the region after 1900. They had all doubled by 1911, tripling for Romania. Sustaining these increases were a series of large loans, most often from the Paris capital market but subscribed more widely. Their total of almost 2 billion francs was also double that for either of the two preceding decades. Typically for political purposes, the most successful were the two French loans to Serbia in 1906–7. Their funding allowed the state budget to endure the tariff war with Austria–Hungary and to supply modern rifles and artillery to its newly reformed army, more of which shortly. For all the Balkan state budgets, however, government accounting reforms, in Serbia with French consultants, had reduced the irregular expenses that had allowed European lenders to attach revenues from specific domestic taxes in return. Ottoman state revenues had been so attached in 1881, Greece's in 1897 and Bulgaria's in 1902.

More impressively, all the Balkan states including Montenegro by 1906, had established national banks with exclusive powers of note issue. By the last prewar decade, they were discounting bills of exchange and extending other credit to a network of domestic commercial banks. All save the Bulgarian National Bank had established sufficient independence from state demand for credit to be called central banks on the European pattern. And for Bulgaria, the region's one large agricultural bank in place before the First World War, the Zemedelska Banka, made up for the otherwise limited number of commercial banks. All of them aspired to the Gold Standard under which most European central banks managed their currencies. While never accumulating sufficient gold reserves, they nonetheless kept their silver-backed currencies stable at par with the French franc after 1900. This achievement made their governments more attractive to foreign lenders, while probably making exports more expensive and imports cheaper than if exchange rates had been allowed to float freely. Total bank assets across the Balkan states approached 80 percent of domestic national product as roughly estimated for 1910, a proportion reached by the developed European economies as recently as 1880.[14]

For any transition to modern economic development, however, these domestic financial institutions and foreign loans made little contribution. The earlier emphasis on railway construction now gave way to paying interest on past debt and covering military or administrative expenses. Their combined totals took over 70 percent of the effective lending received. By 1910 state employees minus the military exceeded 5 percent of every labor force, double the small fractions of industrial workers and more than the French percentage, the largest in pre-1914 Europe. State jobs, especially in the capital cities, were better paid and more prestigious than those in manufacturing, thus making them more attractive.

National Aspirations and European Capitals

State employees were not only the largest occupational group in all of the state capitals save Bucharest. Debate over the state's national mission predominated in what was the broader cultural milieu familiar to the other major European capitals. Joining this enterprise in just the fashion suggested by Charles Maier's model (see Introduction) were university and artistic communities, a growing set of journalists and publicists, and bank officials if not industrialists. Their stages were cities that had by 1910 grown to nearly 100,000, save Montenegro's capital of Cetinje, and to over 300,000 for Bucharest. Street lights and trams were in place to make their central locations and gathering places accessible even after dark. Their municipal administrations had used some of the foreign loans to build up this infrastructure, extending to water and even telephone systems. British consular reporting noted Sofia's connection by phone with Bulgaria's main towns by 1906. Municipal governments collected taxes and challenged Interior Ministries for control over their own affairs in all areas except police and education. In Belgrade, the municipal elections of 1906 resulted in a narrow victory for the otherwise small Social Democratic Party, a victory that was allowed to stand.[15]

Urban literacy exceeded 60 percent, led by Belgrade. Levels in the countryside were still short of 20 percent. The rough overall figures for Bulgaria, Greece, Romania, and also Croatia–Slavonia and Transylvania were slightly higher than Serbia's 40 percent, while only the Slovene lands matched the Austrian or Hungarian levels of 60–70 percent.[16] At least an urban readership was also in place for the flood of newspapers and pamphlets, typically tied to one of the half dozen political parties on the continental rather than the Anglo-American pattern. With the founding of a university in Sofia in

1904 and in Belgrade in 1905, the four Balkan capitals all had functioning universities (Athens since 1837). So did Zagreb, Ljubljana, and Cluj, at that time known by their Austro-Hungarian names of Agram, Laibach, and Kolozsvar. Sofia was also the site of the Bulgarian Economic Society, founded in 1896 to hold public meetings and publish a near-monthly journal. Its membership grew to 300, and increasingly included government officials such as Ivan Estatiev Geshov. Its journal articles reflected serious debate from conflicting points of view, drawn basically along Central European lines over tariff protection, savings banks, and industrial encouragement. Graduates of the American high school founded near Sofia by Protestant missionaries often went on to the American Robert College in Constantinople. They also came back to contribute to Sofia's intellectual life, as did those returning from German schools as often as from the radicalizing Russian universities.[17] Together they built on what Bulgarians were already calling their *chitalishte* tradition of an educated civil society, named after the reading rooms so important to the cultural revival of the late Ottoman period.

In Belgrade, the new French-inspired literary journal, *Srpski književni glasnik*, promoted a modernizing reform of the Serbian language that also attracted some of Zagreb's young writers restless with archaic forms in written Croatian. The Serbian capital's most renowned young intellectual, Jovan Skerlić, used his *Istorija nove srpske književnosti* (History of New Serbian Literature) to emphasize the urban, European origins of this literature in the Habsburg Neusatz (Novi Sad) of the eighteenth century. He dubbed it "the Athens of Serbia" and made the Enlightenment cleric and scholar Dositej Obradović its central figure. It was Obradović, neglected during the Communist period as an Orthodox priest, who had first called for a reformed alphabet and standardized vernacular.[18]

Such modernizing ferment in the national states, often directly inspired from the wider European spectrum, cannot however be confined to the politically benign examples cited above. Young intellectuals such as Skerlić in Belgrade, Ion Dragoumis in Athens, and Nicolae Iorga in Bucharest used their literary talents to advance strident ideas of the national interest. They might disagree about socialism, the former in favor because it was Western and modern and the latter two opposed for the same reason. Skerlić had admittedly begun by speaking of some sort of South Slav, that is, Yugoslav, state. He promoted the South Slav congress that brought Serbs and Croats together in Belgrade in 1904. After the Austro-Hungarian annexation of Bosnia-Herzegovina in 1908, however, Skerlić turned away from even the Serbia-centered Yugoslav federation advocated by the small socialist party. Explicitly celebrating Serbia's "national consciousness," he spoke of a modern but separate state to which Bosnia, with its Serb plurality, should belong. He did continue to swim against the ethnically exclusionary tide flowing through Serbian and for that matter Habsburg-Croatian textbooks. Skerlić continued to criticize romantic concentration on the lost Kosovo battle of 1389 and kept advocating a place for Croatian literature in elementary school readers.[19]

Dragoumis and Iorga turned against Western cultural influence. Dragoumis criticized English philhellenic attentions for confining Greeks to their ancient history and lands. He also sought to shift the modern Greek focus from the past century's *Megali Idea* (Great Idea), recreating the huge Byzantine Empire centered on Constantinople, to incorporating the adjacent and more ethnically Greek lands to the north.[20]

French rather than British penetration troubled Nicolae Iorga. While university students staged demonstrations in Belgrade in 1903 demanding press freedom, and in Sofia in 1907 to whistle down Prince Ferdinand for his manipulation of the ministerial regimes in order to assure their own elections, Iorga led the student demonstration in Bucharest against the performance in French of a play whose very title, *Madame Flirt*, suggested modern decadence. Already the preeminent Romanian historian, Iorga, was reacting in part against the long-standing influence of students returning to Budapest from Paris. They had made French the Romanian capital's second language. Born in a Moldovan town with an increasing Jewish population, Iorga had overcome his initial anti-Semitism but not his conviction that Romanian national identity must be isolated from foreign influence, liberal and socialist ideas included. His opposition to corrupting modern influence extended to the so-called popular schools that the modernizing Minister of Education, Spiru Haret, was organizing in rural villages. Iorga saw them as "uprooting the peasants" from the setting that made most ethnically Romanian.[21]

Nor were the borderlands any quieter. Croat students had also joined in an anti-Serb demonstration in Zagreb in 1902. Prompted by an inflammatory article in the aforementioned *Srpski kniževni glasnik* that anticipated a cultural "war to extermination" between Serbs and Croats, the rioters sacked Serb houses and businesses. The Habsburg Ban had to declare martial law. Still, a Croat–Serb coalition emerged following the demonstration to dominate the 1906 elections, the first allowed to the Sabor of supposedly autonomous Croatia–Slavonia since the 1870s. Two Dalmatian Croats, Frano Supilo and Ante Trumbić, who would be the leading advocates of new loosely federal Yugoslavia during the First World War, founded the coalition. Yet its major figure forcing confrontation with Habsburg authorities in the last prewar years was the Serb Svetozar Pribićević. He championed the coalition's idea of national unity (*narodno jedinstvo*) between Serbs and Croats, rejecting the ethnically exclusive program of Serbia's ruling Radical Party that sought to regain corporate rights for the Serbian Orthodox Church. His Independents appealed instead for support to the Independent Radical Party that had split with Pašić's Radicals. After the First World War, as we shall see in Chapter 3, Pribićević would lead the cause of central control from Belgrade in order to advance the rights of the Serbs outside of Serbia in the new Kingdom of Serbs, Croats, and Slovenes.

Equally portentous for interwar Yugoslavia's politics was the appearance of the Croatian Peasant Party (HSS). Denied more than the smallest representation in the Croatian Sabor by the notoriously restrictive Hungarian franchise, the party attracted a growing membership under the leadership of the young Radić brothers, Stjepan and Pavel.[22] Their resentment of the Croatian Catholic hierarchy cut into the Church's political influence. Only in Bosnia-Herzegovina did that hierarchy, under the proselytizing Jesuit Archbishop Josip Stadler play a part in mobilizing the separate Croatian party that emerged after 1903. Separate Serb and Muslim National Organizations took their place along with the Croat representatives in the advisory assembly that Austro-Hungarian authorities allowed to convene by 1910. Fatefully, there would be no Croat–Serb coalition in Bosnia, other than the forerunner by 1911 of the terrorist youth organization whose members assassinated the heir to the Habsburg throne three years later in Sarajevo.

In Habsburg Transylvania, even more under Hungarian control since 1867 *Ausgleich* had given Budapest considerable autonomy in its half of the monarchy, its Romanian majority found younger voices seeking at least political rights. Aurel Popovici was just 28 when he authored the *Replica* of 1891 to challenge the Budapest university students who had upheld the restrictive Hungarian Law on Nationalities of 1868. By 1902, a Romanian newspaper in the small Transylvanian town of Orăştie was calling for an end to the passive pursuit of autonomy. In 1906, Popvici published in Sibiu, then Hermannstadt, a provincial rights treatise entitled *Die Vereinigten Staaten von Gross-Oesterreich* (The United States of Greater Austria).[23]

Young intellectuals' demands for language reform had also been part of the Young Turk Revolution of 1908. Its Salonika-based Committee for Union and Progress (CUP) replaced the reactionary regime of Sultan Abdul Hamid II. A mixed Albanian gathering of the two ethnic subdivisions, southern coastal Tosks and northern inland Gegs, met at Priština that same year and again at Monastir in 1909. They agreed on a single literary language of their own. The Young Turks backed the Ottoman alphabet favored by the Gegs, including the Kosovar Albanians. More importantly, some 20 Albanian deputies entered the new Ottoman parliament. None of this could overcome Albanian resentment at higher taxes after the new regime had made promises of local autonomy within the Ottoman Balkans but left them unfulfilled. Open resistance flared in Kosovo in 1909 and grew stronger in 1910–11, ironically attracting some official Serbian support to undermine Ottoman authority. The same resentment spread across Macedonia. Membership in Bulgarian, Greek, and Serbian bands and attendance in the respective school networks had increased after the initial Mürzsteg restrictions in 1903 closed down local initiatives. Some 1200 Bulgarian schools, the largest of the networks funded by the neighboring Balkan state, had enrolled 70,000 students by 1912. Greek schools were not far behind in Aegean Macedonia and ahead in what would become Albania. Only the Jewish plurality in Salonika joined Macedonia's Turks and recently arrived Bosnian Muslims in standing by the anational Ottomanism initially advanced by the CUP.[24]

The Young Turks were proceeding with greater success in reforming the Ottoman army under the guidance of German advisors than in countering these bands and networks. The Balkan states were also going ahead with military modernization on the European pattern. Budget appropriations financed the import of new magazine rifles and rapid-firing cannons. French sales of Schneider-Creuzot's field artillery and Maxim guns went to Bulgaria and Greece as well as to Serbia. The paramilitary local units that had led to crushing defeats for Serbian forces in Bosnia in 1876, for the Greek penetration of Macedonia in 1897, and for the Bulgarian-sponsored Supremists there in 1903 were now pushed away from the regular armies. More officers and career soldiers were recruited. Military drafts created the potential to mobilize huge national armies in case of war, from 150,000 in Greece to 550,000 for Bulgaria. Standing armies doubled during the last prewar decade, rising past 50,000 for all but Greece, which had the one naval force in addition, and Montenegro. For all of them, state military expenditure per capita was three-quarters of the German figure for 1911.[25]

Such modern armies were after all the European institution most likely to secure Italian-style unification with their ethnic fellows in the remaining Ottoman and also Habsburg borderlands. By the last prewar decade, the image of the uniformed soldier as the defender of the national interest was spreading military romanticism across the entire continent. Then the Ottoman defeat and loss of Libya to Italy in 1911 whetted the appetites of the respective Balkan governments. Their political leaders and their army generals were by this time awaiting their chance. It would come in 1912, when a short, victorious war would subsequently plunge them all into the first of their century's three decades of warfare and upheaval.

2 Balkan Wars, First World War, Postwar Settlements, 1912–1922

The region's first wartime decade of the twentieth century started spectacularly well for the five independent Balkan states. By the summer of 1912 only Romania abstained from an alliance that would send off their apparently united armies against the Ottomans' Balkan forces. The allied governments quickly mobilized massive reserves from an established system of conscripted service to supplement their standing armies, just as the European powers would do in 1914. Within a few weeks that October they overran all of Macedonia broadly defined and drove the Ottoman defenders back to within 20 miles of Istanbul. European observers compared the bravery and determination of Bulgarian and Serbian soldiers to Japanese troops, newly renowned for their defeat of Tsarist Russia in 1905. The prime Aegean port of Salonika, also the largest city in Ottoman Macedonia, surrendered to Greek forces on October 27. Montenegrin units were besieging the Ottoman's Albanian stronghold of Shkoder. By December the Sultan's government was obliged to sue for peace. Just months before this First Balkan War, a massive Albanian uprising concentrated in Kosovo was actually encouraged from Belgrade. This inadvertently raised the prospect of a new Albanian state that the remaining imperial power, Austria–Hungary, soon championed to check Serbia.

Among the many Serbs in the dual monarchy's own South Slav lands, Serbia's victorious advance to the south raised visions of expanding to the west. Bosnia-Herzegovina at the least might be broken away from Habsburg rule. For many Slovenes and some Croats, from Austrian-administered Dalmatia in particular, the Yugoslav idea of some federal or confederal union with Serbia acquired its first popular support. And, in Romania, the hasty visit to Bucharest that November of the Habsburg Chief of Staff, General Conrad von Hotzendorf, revealed the monarchy's anxiety that its one alliance to the southeast would slip away, as indeed it did within the year.

But within the space of that year, the Second Balkan War left the alliance of independent states in a shambles. Within two years, the First World War started the region down a far longer and more costly road. Allegiance to either the Anglo-French and Russian Entente or the two Central Powers added to the cost. Before it was over, the toll of military and civilian dead approached 2 million. Still more survivors were forced to flee or migrate. Bulgaria and Serbia respectively suffered the largest proportion of military and civilian losses to their prewar populations across Europe. Not only Serbia and Montenegro but also much of Romania and a newly created Albania faced occupation by the Central Powers of Germany or Austria–Hungary. The Habsburg's South Slav lands bore a heavy burden for defending the monarchy on the Italian front and supplying it on the home front, as would Bulgaria on the Salonika Front. Its troops plus a small German contingent faced an Entente expeditionary force from France, Britain, and briefly Russia, supplemented by large Serbian and eventually Greek contingents. Bulgaria also paid an unexpectedly high economic price at home for its German alliance.

Romania's belated decision to join the Entente in 1916 would make a difficult Russian alliance its only defense against the Central Powers. That defense collapsed with heavy losses even before the Russian Revolution. Defeated and then largely occupied, Romania at least rallied a surviving military force in 1917 that allowed it to rejoin the winning side just as the war ended. New political divisions emerged even as Austria–Hungary's collapse opened the way to incorporate Transylvania and Bukovina. The transfer of Bessarabia from an embattled Bolshevik Russia also beckoned.

Greece's government joined the Entente only in 1917, and then against the wishes of its pro-German King. The decision deepened the domestic political division between his southern supporters and northern opponents. Attracted to the victorious Anglo-French partition of the Ottoman Empire after 1918, the northern side plunged into the ultimately disastrous Anatolian campaign. The returning royal regime of 1920 felt obliged to continue the advance. With its complete defeat in 1922 and the resulting Greek expulsion from Asia Minor, the region's full decade of warfare and forced migration would finally end.

A complete set of new borders now covered the region. Their mixtures of population and memories of wartime losses would make the nation-building to which they all aspired in the 1920s difficult indeed. So would the expectation that the European powers would continue the great interest in the region that had in fact characterized only the first years of the First World War.

From the Balkan Wars to Sarajevo, 1914

The diplomatic prelude to the First Balkan War already revealed dangerous internal divisions between the Balkan states. Its aftermath, on the other hand, would initially re-create the Balkan Concert of European Powers, last convened to help settle the Greek–Ottoman war in 1897. From 1912, Germany and Italy, Britain and France now entered prominently into the region's affairs, if only to check the presumed revival of Russian influence. Yet they pursued increasingly separate policies as the First World War wore on and finally brought down the surrounding empires: Austro-Hungarian, Tsarist Russian, and Ottoman. The Second Balkan War pitted Bulgaria against Serbia and its other erstwhile Balkan allies, a division that helped to undo the Concert led by Germany and Britain. What opened up in its place were efforts by the rival European alliances – the Central Powers of Germany, Austria–Hungary, and Italy versus the Entente of France, Britain, and Russia – to win over one side or the other. This was of course the rivalry that would trigger the First World War, following Serbia's presumed role in the assassination of the heir to the Habsburg throne in Sarajevo in 1914.

The Two Balkan Wars, 1912–13

The Bulgarian government of Ivan Estatiev Geshov took note of its predecessor's failure to win Russian support against the increasingly restrictive Young Turk regime in Ottoman Macedonia. It turned reluctantly in the spring of 1912 to Serbia, its irredentist rival for Vardar Macedonia. Tsar Ferdinand, obliged to share the responsibility for foreign policy under the 1911 constitution, favored the initiative because of his long-standing aversion to Russian ties. He also shared Geshov's desire to undercut the *komitadji* guerrilla bands operating into Ottoman Macedonia from bases in Bulgaria. Discussions of alliance with the Serbian government of Nikola Pašić quickly stumbled over a secret annex specifying the territorial division of a liberated Macedonia. The northern Vardar area, including Skopje, had to be left as a "disputed area." The Russian Tsar's authority was to determine its postwar disposition. Bulgaria's interest in assistance from Greece's navy prompted negotiations with the Venizelos government, quickly concluded in May. Discounting the capacity of the Greek army to seize Salonika, Bulgarian negotiators did not even raise the issue of territorial division for Aegean Macedonia. Greek exchanges with Serbia and Montenegro over the summer reached oral agreements that also omitted any mention of territorial division. Only then did King Nikola's Montenegro sign agreements of alliance with Bulgaria and finally, in September, with Serbia. Their Balkan League, the region's one internal military alliance of the twentieth century, was thereby complete. Behind it stood an encouraging Russian government, eager to reassert the influence lost in agreeing to illusory access through the Dardanelles in return for the Austro-Hungarian annexation of Bosnia-Herzegovina in 1908.

The campaigns and conflicts that followed nonetheless support the hard verdict of the most recent Western scholarship on the two Balkan Wars. The four-member Balkan League "was a flawed and flimsy diplomatic instrument, accomplished in haste and based on self-interest."¹ Nor would Russian influence in holding it together go beyond passive mediation. Seeds of conflict were already planted with the triumphant Serbian campaign that swept through Kosovo and Vardar Macedonia, most of the "disputed zone" included. Facing Ottoman forces of barely half their 320,000 men, the Serbian advance began at Kumanovo on October 19. General Putnik's First Army won a stunning victory, to be celebrated as the greatest in Serbian military history. Its superior use of modern artillery counted for more than the audacious infantry assaults that press reports credited with carrying the day. Ottoman forces thereupon fell back, leaving Skopje undefended. They lost a last stand at Monastir (Bitola) on October 28, the day after Salonika's surrender to the Greek army. Greece's navy had meanwhile rendered the larger service to the Serbian campaign by preventing any Ottoman reinforcements or supplies from reaching the Macedonian front.

The Serbian side had not expected to have that crucial front to itself. But Bulgaria's commanding General Fichev had ironically declined Belgrade's request for 100,000 men. He wanted the full force of his 350,000 men, with another 250,000 mobilized, to be marched south to Thrace. He had not expected to proceed east toward Istanbul, but the same superior use of modern weaponry and tactics as that of the Serbian army opened the way. Tsar Ferdinand urged him on, dreaming of a Christian reconsecration of the great Haga Sophia mosque.² Facing a smaller Ottoman contingent of barely 100,000 and wisely bypassing the fortified city of Edirne (Adrianople), two Bulgarian armies converged on the fortified redoubt of Chataldzha, almost within sight of Istanbul, by early November. And there they stayed. The tighter Turkish command that would continue through and beyond Gallipoli, where British Commonwealth forces were repulsed in 1915, held the now-depleted Bulgarian armies at bay. The armistice of December 3 left Edirne in Ottoman hands and, worse, all of Vardar Macedonia in Serbian hands. A reconstituted Bulgarian force ended the siege of Edirne by March 1913. The belated conquest encouraged the Geshov government to refuse Serbia any renegotiation of their prewar agreement on Vardar Macedonia's division.

Peace negotiations began in London that May, with Bulgaria's Minister President Geshov unwisely not in attendance. The persuasive Venizelos won British support for the Greek claim to Salonika. The Russian support Bulgaria had expected for Macedonia went instead to Serbia. Geshov resigned the day after the Treaty of London was signed on May 13. His successor Stoyan Danev could not resist the arguments of Ferdinand and the General Staff that war against Serbia and Greece was the only answer. Ferdinand spoke of certain German support and feared assassination by Bulgarian–Macedonian bands if he did not act. Army leaders wished to act before the deterioration of its huge mobilized force after six months of fighting went any further. Attacking in July, they pushed into Serbia rather than the presumably more friendly Vardar region. The depleted Bulgarian divisions could sustain neither that advance nor a drive toward Salonika against Greek forces. The Romanian government, neutral until now under the pro-Habsburg leadership of the Conservatives and King Carol, despaired of Vienna's assistance in pressing their one Balkan claim, the Black Sea border with Bulgaria. Fully 330,000 Romanian troops thereupon moved south across the Danube, one army into northern Bulgaria and a second to take over the ethnically mixed southern Dobrudja that had been pursued since 1909. This decisive blow allowed Ottoman forces to recapture Edirne and what would become European Turkey.

The Treaty of Bucharest in August effectively ended the Second Balkan War. As may be seen in Map 2.1, Bulgaria still held only Pirin Macedonia and Eastern Thrace from its original gains.[3] Bulgarian and Greek treaties with the Ottoman Empire remained to be signed in the next few months, but their relations with each other and the European powers now became more important. In the Bucharest negotiations, Austro-Hungarian and Russian pressure on Serbia to be generous with Bulgaria's western border failed to move the Pašić government beyond a minor concession. France and Germany successfully pressured Bulgaria to accept Greece's incorporation of Kavalla, Thrace's major Aegean port. This was to be the last occasion, however, for the revived European Concert to work across the lines of the rival alliances.

The Enlarged Balkan States and the Great Powers

The powers' individual competition for influence had of course begun well before the Balkan Wars, as we saw in Chapter 1. But the French and German advantage had come to the recent fore on the strength of state loans and

Map 2.1 State borders after the Balkan Wars, 1913

Source: Adapted from Richard and Ben Crampton, *Atlas of Eastern Europe in the Twentieth Century* (London and New York: Routledge, 1996)

Acquired by Montenegro from Ottoman Empire	Acquired by Romania from Bulgaria
Acquired by Bulgaria from Ottoman Empire during First Balkan War, but lost again in Second Balkan War.	Acquired by Bulgaria from Ottoman Empire
	Acquired by Greece from Ottoman Empire
Southern Dodecanese Islands, occupied by Italy	Acquired by Serbia from Ottoman Empire
	— - — 1911 international boundaries

arms sales. The classic case was French success in tying its large 1906 loan to Serbia to the purchase of artillery and small arms from Schneider–Creuzot, thus overcoming the rival Austrian offer to buy from its Czech Škoda works. German arms also found their way into the equipment of all the Balkan armies save Montenegro's, where only some old Russian rifles had been obtained. French trainers were busy working with both the Greek and Romanian armies. The greater German effort had been devoted to reforming and equipping the Ottoman army, an effort that only increased after the Balkan Wars.[4] Yet as leader of the Central Powers, Germany could not pass up the chance to win the favor of defeated Bulgaria in the last months before the First World War. Serbia's ties to the Entente seemed too strong to shake, and Greece's new King Constantine, although the Kaiser's brother-in-law, could not overcome the preference of the Venizelos government for British and French support. A new French loan of 500 million francs confirmed Greece's connection. Hence the comparable German loan worth 500 million francs from the Deutsche Bank in April 1914 to a Bulgarian government seeking to repair its strong prewar position. The new Minister President, Vasil Radoslavov, saw this connection to the Central Powers as replacing failed reliance on Russia.

Behind Bulgaria's apparently restored strength and the expanded territories of the regional victors lay more weakness and difficulty than most of their leaders realized at the time. The two wars had cost them all dear, and the consolidation of new, mixed populations was off to an ugly, unpromising start. The remaining regional empire, Austria–Hungary, was also primed to bring down Serbia, the major winner. The several estimates of the economic cost of the wars, including lost trade, center on 2.5 billion francs (half a billion dollars). Bulgaria suffered at least half of that loss, nearly three times the value of the new 1914 loan. Serbia lost slightly more military dead, in battle or from disease, than Bulgaria: 36,000 versus 32,000. Montenegro's loss of 3000 was proportionally more than the larger Greek figure of 8000. All of the armies had found it difficult to maintain unified command and provide the supplies needed to sustain these mass mobilizations for more than a few weeks. Their portentously heavy losses in the celebrated "Japanese-style" assaults on positions defended by machine guns and artillery went unnoticed by the few European observers the combatants allowed.[5]

International attention did fall on the initial treatment of populations in the newly acquired territories. It also marked the start of American interest in the region as a whole. Pioneering the path taken by several nongovernmental organizations and the Organization for Security and Cooperation in Europe (OSCE) in the recent wars of Yugoslav dissolution, the Washington-based Carnegie Endowment for International Peace assembled a balanced International Commission. Their detailed 1913 report addressed the conduct of all the contending armies toward civilian populations. Protestant American missionaries in Bulgaria had pressed for such an inquiry to counter Greek charges that Bulgarian troops alone had committed widespread abuses. The commission collected testimony from all sides save the Albanian. Its report faulted all of the Balkan armies and especially the small irregular forces accompanying or joining them. Details or testimonies are missing only for the Serbian advance into Kosovo. The charges are familiar – summary executions of men, the rape of women, and looting and burning of the village's houses.[6]

Invariably perpetrated against people seen as ethnic rivals with a rival claim to the territory, these war crimes would be called "ethnic cleansing" in the recent post-Yugoslav tragedy. Then as now, the past Balkan experience and memory of paramilitary violence created a climate that mixed fatally with the pre-1914 European imperatives for a modern nation-state. These ethnic abuses, and the fear that more would follow, prompted the first set of the forced migrations that would burden the region across the century. Some 135,000 Turks and other Muslims fled through Salonika to Ottoman safety. Following the Second Balkan War, 112,000 Slavs (whether ethnically Macedonian or Bulgarian is disputed) were forced to leave Aegean and Vardar Macedonia for Bulgaria. 150,000 Greeks were also pushed out of wider Macedonian locations and Smyrna on the Anatolian coast. Bulgarian and Ottoman authorities even signed a formal agreement that confirmed the recent wartime transfer of 50,000 Turks from Bulgaria and 50,000 Bulgarians from Ottoman Thrace. A similar convention between Greece and the Ottoman Empire in 1914 could not be implemented before war broke out. It spoke of voluntary transfers but set a precedent, as we shall see, for the compulsory exchanges of population concluded after the First World War between the successor regimes.[7]

Slav Macedonians remaining in Serbia and Greece, greatly enlarged by one half in size and by two-thirds in population to 4.4 million each, found that only ethnic assimilation could win them legal and individual rights. We know more about the Serbian case. Protests arose from within the opposition parties to the policies of Pašić's Radical government in Vardar Macedonia, if not in Kosovo. The initial regime of military occupation in the Vardar area was not discontinued after the end of the Second Balkan War and the peace settlement. The army's own postwar disarray there helped to encourage its leadership to resist any relaxation. Meanwhile, all local school teachers, Orthodox priests and officials who had not declared or proved themselves to be Serbs were dismissed. No rights to vote in Serbian elections were granted to any of the new population. The economy fell into the hands of officials from Serbia. Their corrupt private dealings, according to the liberal nationalist Jovan Skerlić, were infecting the "political hygiene" of the entire state. Matters were worse in Kosovo for the majority Albanian population, although the historical record is regrettably sparse. Between perhaps fifteen and twenty thousand had been killed in the initial months, and several times that figure had been forced to flee. Scattered resistance to the new Serb authorities was used to justify martial law and the confiscation of property. The Greek administration in the new lands north of Salonika was also forcing the assimilation of Slav Macedonians, along with forcing the departure of Turks and Albanians.[8] Despite the Carnegie Report, abused minorities and their migrations did not concern the European powers during this last prewar year.

Italy and Austria–Hungary were indeed concerned with the Albanian question but because of the Adriatic coast rather than internal conditions in Kosovo. Italian interest in supporting Albanian independence, first proclaimed by local leaders in the port of Vlore in November 1912, foresaw a southern coastal presence building on existing commercial ties and secular schools. Long-standing rights from the Ottomans for Catholic representation and then Catholic schools had given the Austrians a northern foothold. Habsburg diplomacy was more concerned with preventing the long-feared Serbian foothold on the Adriatic coast, now threatened as its troops advanced during the First Balkan War. Austro-Hungarian Foreign Minister Count Berchtold promptly pursued the creation of a separate Albanian state. Italy joined the dual monarchy in nominating the young Prussian Prince Wilhelm of Wied to head the new entity. He would not set foot there until 1914, and then for barely half a year. But by September 1913 all the other Concert powers had accepted him and recognized Albania's sovereignty.

Two international commissions fixed Albania's borders, virtually the present ones, compromising between a narrower Russian set of lines and a wider Austrian one. The continued presence of Serbian troops on some of this new if uncontrolled territory prompted an Austro-Hungarian ultimatum to Serbia that October. It demanded their withdrawal and threatened war in almost the same terms as the fatal message that would be the last spark to set off the First World War the following July.[9] The Serbian government accepted this first ultimatum, already worried about the over-stretched and unrepaired state of their large, still fully mobilized army as the last year of peace drew to a close.

The Austrian ultimatum of July 1914 was intended to be unacceptable. Behind it lay not simply the assassination in Sarajevo as the culmination of rising if still scattered resistance to Habsburg rule in Croatia and Bosnia-Herzegovina. It also reflected the Dual Monarchy's growing concern over a

Russian diplomatic offensive in the region. All this gave the Austro-Hungarian Chief of Staff, still General Conrad von Hotzendorf, the arguments he needed. Conrad had been advocating a "preventative war" against Serbia since 1908. By early 1914 the end of the alliance that Conrad had personally pursued with Romania was at hand. Plans for the Russian Tsar's visit to Bucharest in June were already under way. The Russian Ambassador in Belgrade, Hartwig, continued to speak to the Pašić government of support under any circumstances.

Meanwhile, in Bosnia-Herzegovina, Habsburg authorities had reacted to signs of Serbian sympathies after the First Balkan War by declaring martial law. This only encouraged the small, largely student band noted in Chapter 1 and now calling themselves *Mlada Bosna* (Young Bosnia). They were already inspired by the nineteenth-century Italian example (Mazzini's Young Italy) and already attracted to the terrorist assassinations that anarchists had introduced to European politics before the turn of the century. They included Croats and even a few Bosnian Muslims, but a majority were Serbs. A handful of Serbs banded together at the March news of the forthcoming visit to Sarajevo of the Archduke Franz Ferdinand. The heir to the Habsburg throne had inadvertently chosen June 28, the very anniversary of the Serbian defeat at Kosovo in 1389 that spelled the end of their medieval state. Gavrilo Princip and his associates did receive pistols and a day of training from a major in the Black Hand camarilla in Serbian military intelligence, but probably no other support or direction. The idea of the assassination was theirs.

It succeeded by sheerest chance. Princip could fire the fatal shots only because he was standing just where the Archduke's car inadvertently stopped. His chauffeur had started making a wrong turn to leave the crowded center of Sarajevo after the other conspirators had managed a few hours before to throw one bomb at a trailing car. Two days after the murder of the Archduke and his wife, Foreign Minister Berchtold admitted that "a final and fundamental reckoning with Serbia" was now the only answer.

Serbia and Bulgaria: Two Roads to the Salonika Front

This ill-fated reckoning began with the Austro-Hungarian ultimatum to Serbia on July 23, 1914 and its declaration of war five days later, exactly one month after the assassination. Assuring rejection was the demand that Habsburg authorities be allowed to enter Serbia in order to "take part in the judicial inquiry" to be instituted against the Serbian officials and officers presumed to be involved in the plot. Reinforced by the German Kaiser's famous "blank check," the Austro-Hungarian decision triggered Russia's mobilization and the consequent German decision to mobilize for defeating France first. The decisions that set the two Central Powers at war with the rival Entente by August may be the most widely studied sequence in modern diplomatic history.

The most widely remembered and revered sequence of events in Serbian military history are, however, the three initial Austro-Hungarian attacks of 1914. It took the combined German–Austrian–Bulgarian invasion of 1915 to force the Serbian government and surviving army to retreat across Albanian territory to the Adriatic coast. The Entente transferred them from there to Corfu and finally in 1916 to its Salonika Front.[10] Bulgaria's road to defend itself and the Central Powers on the other side of that front would burden the country's historical memory as the first of its two ill-fated German alliances.

We start with Serbia's experience, not just because of its role in remembrance but also because it prompted the Pašić government to take its first official interest in a wider Yugoslav state. That interest would however not be expressed until the last of the three Austro-Hungarian invasions had pushed the Serbian army deep into the interior and the government to the southern town of Niš. The first assault in August had been repulsed in less than two weeks; the second came across the Drina River from Bosnia in September but did no better, despite massing 460,000 troops. The third in November took Belgrade and enough of pre-1912 Serbia to prompt the Austrian military command to name their notoriously harsh governor in Bosnia, General Stefan Sarkotić, as "governor of Serbia."[11]

It was in these desperate circumstances that the Pašić government issued the Niš Declaration on December 7. It did not mention a Greater Serbia or even the Serb-led South Slav state that Pašić had advocated that fall. Belgrade scholars led by the geographer Jovan Cvijić contributed to the new declaration. It spoke only of a future union of three presumably equal tribes – Serbs, Croats, and Slovenes. Intended as an anti-Habsburg appeal to the Entente for supplies and to the monarchy's South Slavs for support, the declaration soon became a dead letter. The counterattack launched by Serbia's last reserves that same week succeeded in liberating Belgrade and again driving out the monarchy's forces by the end of December. The following February, Frano Supilo, a Dalmatian Croat leader of the émigré Yugoslav Committee founded in Florence the previous fall, met with Serbian authorities in Niš but could come to no agreement on the shape of a common state.[12]

Such joint discussions did not resume before the new German command of the Serbian front, under General Mackensen, had launched a several-sided attack in October 1915. Supporting his ten divisions were four Austrian divisions. Another six from Bulgaria attacked from the east. Already weakened by a typhus epidemic that had killed some 150,000 soldiers and civilians, Serbian forces were now outnumbered and driven out. The army with King Petar in tow retreated in December weather across largely mountainous territory, harassed by repeated attacks from local Albanian bands. At most 135,000 of the original army of 320,000 survived to reach the Adriatic coast. French transport took them first to Corfu and then to Salonika. Their transfer had its origins in the Entente's establishing a base at the northern Aegean port earlier in 1915, ironically in order to supply Serbian forces against that fall's irresistible, German-led offensive.

Bulgaria's government had not rushed down the road that brought it to the side of the Central Powers, to their joint attack on Serbia, and from there to the Salonika Front. True, both Tsar Ferdinand and his Minister President Radoslavov favored the Austro-German side. The Anglophile Geshov and his pro-Russian Democrats argued for joining the Entente. But the Tsar's government had had the advantage since 1914 of a prorogued *Subranie* (parliament) and a censored press. Whether worried that public opinion continued to favor Russia or bargaining for the largest promise of territory, the Bulgarian leadership entertained offers from both alliances during the first year of the war. The Entente had won Italy away from the Central Powers in May 1915 with the Treaty of London and its postwar promise of the Dalmatian coast. The Entente's ties to Serbia confined their offer for Bulgaria to Ottoman territory and possibly an eastern slice of Vardar Macedonia. The Central Powers could offer instead all of the Vardar and much of Thrace. Here were Bulgaria's major war aims even for the Russophile opposition. Yet Russian reverses in its Polish borderlands that summer were still needed to push Ferdinand into final negotiations with Berlin and Vienna by September.[13]

By the end of the year, Bulgarian troops and officials had moved in to occupy Vardar and northeastern Aegean Macedonia following the Serbian expulsion. The attendant euphoria confirmed Bulgaria's allegiance to the Central Powers. Radoslavov led the so-called maximalists in calling for postwar annexation of Serbia's fertile Morava valley, all of Thrace and some Aegean islands as well to make up a Greater Bulgaria. After all, the 800,000 men that Bulgaria had mobilized by 1915 were in place, while the Serbia's initial force of 700,000 had long since been reduced and expelled. Surely Bulgarian troops and their German allies would be able to hold the high ground north of Salonika against the Anglo-French expeditionary force of 150,000 and the battered, poorly equipped Serbian survivors. Largely inactive or ineffective from their arrival in October 1915 through 1917, they were dismissively dubbed "the Gardeners of Salonika" by general staffs in Britain and France who saw the Western Front as the only key to victory.[14] Their French commander, General Franchet d'Esperey, was however a committed "easterner," determined to see his Army of the Orient ready to play a decisive role sooner or later.

But to understand the reversal of Bulgarian fortunes by 1918 and d'Esperey's October breakthrough on the Salonika Front, we must do more than follow the Serbian revival. The Entente was able to recruit more manpower from the wider region, while the Central Powers experienced growing difficulties in mobilizing supplies as well as soldiers. Their Balkan home front now stretched from Bulgaria and largely occupied Romania across all of the future Yugoslavia to the Italian Front. Competing Anglo-French and Austro-German mobilizations would have more to do with the postwar shape of the region than any of the promises made by the rival alliances early in the war.

Romania and Greece: Two Roads to the Western Alliance

The French connection would be a crucial advantage for Romania from 1917 into the postwar settlement. Already in 1916 Paris clearly encouraged the Liberal government's declaration of war on Austria–Hungary that September. But the Romanian government's decision only then to forsake the neutrality declared in August 1914 was taken, like Bulgaria's, primarily to pursue the ethnic unification of an enlarged nation-state. Unlike his Bulgarian counterpart, however, the Prime Minister Ionel Brătianu enjoyed more independence from the throne. King Carol, drawn by his descent to German sympathies, had died in October 1914. The succession of his nephew Ferdinand reinforced what Keith Hitchins has called the Liberals' "expectant neutrality."[15] The Conservatives, deposed from power at the start of the year, suffered for their discredited reliance on the Central Powers in the Balkan Wars. The Liberals expected the Entente to win the war and offer Romania support that made ending its neutrality worthwhile. Neither happened in 1915. Russian defeats in Poland and the failed British and Commonwealth expedition to force the Dardanelles open at Gallipoli made the Eastern Front look even less promising than the stalemate in the West. The Entente refused to entertain Brătianu's proposal to send Romanian troops to the Salonika Front in return for half a million Russian troops to forestall a likely Bulgarian attack on Dobrudja.

The Russians' Brusilov offensive of the next summer convinced the Brătianu government that the Entente would win after all.[16] Its earlier postwar promise of Transylvania, with Romanians in the clear ethnic majority, and the Bukovina, might now be kept. Public opinion was reportedly indifferent, but pressure from the Romanian general staff, eager to lead their mobilized force of 660,000 men, added to the impetus for war. Unfortunately, their massive numbers were poorly trained and woefully under-supplied. Some units had a bullet a day per man. Their plan of attacking only Habsburg forces in Transylvania failed to anticipate either Austro-Hungarian reinforcements being rushed up by rail or any German, Bulgarian, and Ottoman contribution to a counterattack. Both quickly materialized. The resulting debacle pushed the Romanians back from the eastern third of Transylvania and into Wallachia. By December a combined German-Austrian force had occupied Bucharest. Some 250,000 Romanian troops had been killed, wounded, or taken prisoner. Only 90,000 remained in the retreating columns that finally consolidated a defensive position in northern Moldova under the wing of 40 Russian divisions.

This humiliation had two consequences. First, Brătianu was obliged to renew postwar promises of universal male suffrage and land reform, first made in 1913, on behalf of his new unity government. Secondly, French support now became crucial to the revival of Romanian fortunes. General Foch was strong enough as Chief of Staff in 1917 to resist the British disposition, to be repeated in the Second World War, to discontinue any support for what the Foch called a "*mole de résistance.*" Already in October 1916, a French military mission, 1500 strong, had arrived to start the substantial rebuilding of the Romanian army. Its politically adroit leader, General Henri Barthelot, opposed Russian efforts to move the bulk of its manpower back from the crowded Moldovan Front and instead established a close relationship with Brătianu. Badly needed French shipments of machine guns, artillery, and telegraph equipment followed, allowing a retrained, adequately armed force of 460,000 to take the field in July 1917.[17] They now held their own in two major engagements against Austro-German forces, albeit without breaking through. Romanian military dead alone rose to 235,000.

By December the Bolshevik Revolution had removed all prospect of Russian support or diversion. The Brătianu government thereupon agreed to a cease-fire. He himself shrewdly stepped down as Prime Minister in February 1918. This left a new, largely Conservative Romanian government to sign the Treaty of Bucharest in May as dictated by Germany and Austria–Hungary. With limited powers and reduced territory, it had only months to live before the Central Powers were finally defeated in November. Its collaboration with the defeated enemy spelled the immediate demise of the Conservative Party. Brătianu, his Liberals, and their French connection received a free reign in the peace settlements that lay ahead. Against the objections of d'Esperey in Salonika, General Barthelot hastily detached three French and one British division from the Army of the Orient in order to form a new Army of the Danube. On November 10, Barthelot led it from defeated Bulgaria to link up in Bucharest with the large Romanian force advancing from Moldova.

No such mandate and Western military support awaited the winning side in Greece's political rivalry following the First World War. Instead, the "national schism" that had divided Eleftherios Venizelos and his Liberals from the monarchy in 1915 spread into the army, where it would remain until the last decades of the twentieth century. The assassination of King George in 1913 replaced the ruler who had picked Venizelos to be Prime Minister in 1910 with his son Constantine. The new King was closer to the older army officers and the southern Greek interests who opposed the Liberals. Support from the northern lands acquired in the Balkan Wars buoyed the Liberals. Venizelos saw the European war as a chance to join with Britain and France in order to enlarge the Greek nation-state still further at Ottoman expense. King Constantine, a brother-in-law to the German Kaiser, both favored and expected the Central Powers to win. Only supporting them could win any concessions from their Ottoman ally.

Venizelos, on the other hand, jumped at the British proposal to force open the Dardanelles in early 1915. The chance to send Greek troops to join the British and Commonwealth expedition to Gallipoli might well secure Smyrna and its western Anatolian coast, home to 800,000 Greeks as well as part of the Great Idea's Byzantine homeland. Both the King and the royalist staff officer assigned to the Prime Minister, Colonel Ioannis Metaxas, opposed the enterprise. They favored Germany and feared a Bulgarian attack. Venizelos resigned in March. Metaxas, the future dictatorial ruler of 1936–41, was left to prevent any preparations for the dispatch of troops. The Colonel's military arguments against sending a detachment to the Dardanelles deepened the King's distrust of Venizelos. So did the political arguments of Ion Dragoumis, as noted in Chapter 1, against the Greater Greece of the Great Idea.

Constantine could not prevent the June victory of the Venizelos Liberals in parliamentary elections but delayed the formation of their new government until August. Venizelos's final break with the King came in October. Constantine rebuffed his proposal to send Greek troops or invite an Entente force to oppose the imminent German, Austrian-Bulgarian attack on Serbia. The first British and French divisions landed in Salonika anyway. Metaxas retired rather than accept their presence. The King now obliged Venizelos to resign. The Liberals boycotted the December elections, leaving the King's supporters in the south and, fatefully, the non-Greek minorities in the north to win a commanding majority.

Younger army officers, especially those trained by France's prewar military mission, joined the deposed Liberals in resisting royal authority in the new northern territories. By August 1916, pro-Venezelist officers led the coup that established a separate "State of Thessaloniki." Venizelos soon returned in triumph and formally established a new army as well. Yet the new regime was powerless even to move the surviving Serbian army from Corfu to Salonika until the Entente stepped in. Quite prepared to override the sovereignty of the royal regime, the new British government of Lloyd George first pressed Constantine to dissolve the parliament and replace his army command. After his refusal, a small contingent of British and French troops tried in vain to force their way into Athens in December 1916. The subsequent British and French naval blockade of the southern port of Piraeus that supplied Athens created public privation and added to royal resentment. In the south, Constantine authorized a heavy-handed purge of Venezelist officers and officials. But, by June 1917, relentless Entente pressures forced Constantine to leave the throne to his son Alexander, although he did not formally abdicate.

The counterpurge of the King's supporters cost some 1500 military officers their positions, completing the first set of these "schismatic cleansings" that would revisit the Greek armed forces repeatedly in the decades ahead.[18] It was this Venezelist cadre that led the nine divisions that Greece contributed to the Salonika Front for the breakthrough in September 1918. They would proceed ahead without the formal Entente promises of new territory that had been tendered to Romania in 1916. All the more reason for the Venizelos government and its officer corps to start the postwar Anatolian campaign, again at British urging. Its disastrous conclusion would ironically be left to Constantine and his officers, back in power, as we shall see, following a sweeping Liberal defeat in the elections of November 1920.

Mobilizing for War: Home Fronts and Occupation Regimes

The Liberals were turned out by a war-weary population, especially the townspeople. The huge Entente presence in Salonika dated from the 150,000 troops evacuated there from Gallipoli by early 1916. They had continued to strain the city even after the Anglo-French fuel blockade of Athens and Piraeus had been lifted in 1917. A massive fire in Salonika in August 1917 left 70,000 of its 170,000 people homeless, primarily from the still-large Jewish population that had been a plurality before the war. Unemployment still surpassed 40 percent in Athens by 1918, and prices continued to rise, up 400 percent since 1914. Entente controls accompanied some limited financial assistance, but food shortages persisted even in Salonika. Soup kitchens and medical facilities provided by the American Red Cross were swamped. The resulting resentment would break fertile ground for the new Greek Communist Party. Yet it hardly affected the Entente's war effort, buoyed by the swelling American troops arriving at the Western Front as well as the addition of Serbian and Greek divisions to their forces north of Salonika.

The breakthrough on the Salonika Front and the advance on the Italian Front would not have been possible had the Central Powers been able to mobilize needed resources behind their own long lines with less local resentment. This mobilization was crucial to a German economy cut off from the Atlantic by British naval blockage and an Austrian economy whose largely Hungarian food supply became less accessible as the war wore on. German officials secured the Romanian oil fields at Ploeşti by December 1916, placing them under what was to be 50 years of further German control by the Treaty of Bucharest. All of Wallachia's industrial enterprises except for food-processing also came under direct German control. This included the right to ship useful machinery or equipment back to Germany. German authorities mobilized forced labor for agricultural production but favored industrial crops to the neglect of the grain needed for the domestic food supply.

The rest of the region proved more difficult for the Central Powers and their allies. Their efforts relied on the centralization that Charles Maier, as noted in the Introduction, has called the structural thread running through the national histories of twentieth-century Europe.

Bulgarian centralization was at least domestically controlled. The Ministry of National Enlightenment overcame its prewar hesitation to work with the army's Cultural Department. They centralized primary schooling, its curriculum, and its teachers, under a system of six districts, with special emphasis on "national knowledge" in the new territories. Although Bulgaria was the one Balkan state allied with the Central Powers during the First World War, we find no cultural connections beyond the adoption of Julian over the Orthodox Gregorian calendar in 1916. Yet the country's sizeable prewar production of grain, meat, and tobacco now became supplies as valuable to Germany as petroleum. The Bulgarian government's efforts to conserve its resources for its war effort were arguably more extensive than those of either of its allies. It created several institutions that the authoritarian regime of the 1930s and then the Communist command economy could use as precedents. But the parallel role of German demands would frustrate these institutions.

Already in March 1915, half a year before Bulgaria abandoned its neutrality, the Radoslavov government had pushed through legislation that created a Central Committee for Public Welfare. Its purview was to broaden the price controls that had already been proclaimed in July 1914 and to restrict the export of foodstuffs to those reserved for Germany. The National and Agricultural Banks as well as local governments were empowered to buy grain, flour, and milk under these arrangements. Once at war, the army's own General Commission for Requisitions entered the competition for foodstuffs. The mobilization of manpower and draft animals cut the supply of agricultural labor horses to perhaps one-quarter of prewar levels. By 1916 the Committee's powers had been expanded to cover military supplies as well, but the army continued to collect its own supplies where it could. By 1917 the general staff had won control of a now reorganized directorate. Army agronomists were assigned to enforce specified acreage for grain cultivation. Troops sometimes helped with the harvest. More was thereby produced than the much reduced force of peasant labor would otherwise have done, but the directorate's decision to keep delivery prices low encouraged other crops and a growing black market. By 1918, troops were being used to collect forced requisitions against peasant resistance. Townspeople received ration coupons but found few goods for sale. Troops at the front could expect no new boots or medical supplies and only meager food rations.[19]

The German demand for Bulgarian supplies added to domestic shortages. Surging tobacco exports posed no problem, replacing grain exports to Western Europe and generating overall trade surpluses until 1918. But German control of the former Oriental Railway Line plus the copper and coal mines in Macedonia and Serbia denied this income to Bulgaria. The Deutsche Bank's management of the Pernik coal mine in Bulgaria paid only minimal prices for production. Food exports were modest according to official figures, but they did not include the five kilograms that German troops in the Bulgarian rear of the Salonika Front were allowed to send home each month. Their drain probably doubled the value of foodstuffs sent to Germany.

Resentment grew, despite a concerted German effort to convince Bulgaria's political elite of the benefits that final victory would bring them. Friedrich Naumann, wartime author of the economic vision of a German-dominated *Mitteleuropa*, raised the prospect of a postwar Bulgaria as the leading power of the Balkans, stretching from the Dobrudja to Monastir and Salonika. Yet even Aleksandar Tsankov, the economist and postwar Minister President and then a Director of the Central Committee for Economic and Social Welfare, did not allow his pro-German sympathies to overcome suspicions of political subjugation under Naumann's vision. As for Bulgarian public opinion, their commitment to a Greater Bulgaria went no further than Vardar Macedonia. And when the limited Entente offensive of July 1917 recaptured Monastir, even that prospect seemed threatened.[20] Occupied Serbia faced harsher conditions under a largely Austrian regime. The number of Habsburg troops in Serbia, initially 30,000 in 1916, shrank over time but not as much as their own food rations. Efforts to supplement them strained a food supply that was lower than Bulgaria's from the start. The Serbian manpower lost or departed in the defeat had combined with the typhus epidemic of 1915 to leave the force of peasant labor severely reduced. The deportation of some 40,000 Serbs and the detention of another 10,000 in concentration camps added to the absences as well as to bitter memories. The so-called Great Requisition of December 1915 sought out all cloth, leather, and metal goods, locks and church bells included. Another soon demanded housewares. Austrian *centrale* requisitioned crops and livestock with virtually no compensation other than modest rations to the surviving population. Austro-Hungarian forces imposed the same regime on Montenegro when they obliged Prince Nikola's government to flee in January 1916. There was no possibility here, as there was in Bulgaria, for public approval of a centralized war effort if only it were properly organized under domestic leadership.

Nor was there such a possibility in the Habsburg's South Slav lands to the west. To begin with, there was no Austrian or Hungarian effort, beyond one isolated inquiry from the Zagreb military command about a rail link with Belgrade, to connect occupied Serbia, Croatia–Slavonia and Bosnia-Herzegovina with each other in some constructive fashion. Their wartime experience was not much better than Serbia's.[21] Serbs in Bosnia in particular were also subject to detention or deportation. Under the harsh regime of the province's Bosnian-Croat military governor, General Stefan Sarkotić, some 5000 Serbs were interned and another 100,000 forced from their homes. And, for the population as a whole, the same *centrale* operated to requisition foodstuffs with increasingly arbitrary powers and meager rations in return as the war wore on. By 1916 hunger had become a problem in the food-deficit areas of Istria, Dalmatia, and Herzegovina, while peasant hoarding was reported in the grain-growing Croatian north and Slavonia. The Habsburg military command in Zagreb tried in vain to keep town and troop rations from dropping as well.

Despite these hardships, the South Slav contribution to the monarchy's military numbers had risen to 17 percent by 1917. Croat, Slovene, and Bosnian-Muslim troops, with virtually no Serbs by this time, furnished 17 percent of Habsburg forces. They were naturally concentrated on the nearby Italian Front. It was there that most of the 300,000 Croats died in the First

World War, with smaller numerical and larger proportional losses for Slovenes and Bosnian Muslims. Habsburg Serb troops had increasingly deserted on the Serbian and then the Russian Fronts. But by 1917, Croat and Slovene desertions were also mounting. During the last year of the war they were joined by their fellows who had been Russian prisoners of war. These so-called Green Cadres totaled as many as 200,000 men. Their armed resistance to any central control became one of the disparate elements that would trouble the creation of the first Yugoslav state as the First World War drew to a close.

Establishing Albania, Enlarging Romania, Creating Yugoslavia

The breakthrough on the Salonika Front in September 1918 and the Serbian army's contribution had more to do with shaping the new Yugoslav state than did unrest inside the monarchy's lines. That unrest and the breakthrough nonetheless combined in October to end the Austro-Hungarian capacity to continue the war or even continue as a single state. The Entente's initial advance from Salonika had broken the long-strained morale of Bulgaria's conscript army. Then internal unrest would, as we shall see in the next section, rapidly take Bulgaria out of the war and turn radical mass politics loose. Still worse for the Habsburg monarchy, the French-led force of 28 divisions, spearheaded by the six reformed Serbian divisions, was now heading straight for Belgrade. By the end of October, the young Emperor Karl in Vienna was promising federal autonomy to the Austrian lands in a desperate attempt to fasten on the American President Wilson's Fourteen Points as a basis for ending the war equitably. Point Nine promised to maintain a democratic Austria-Hungary. Meanwhile, the Hungarian half had simply broken away, and the monarchy's army ceased to be a fighting force. By November the former Romanian Prime Minister Brătianu was back in power, leading a Romanian government that was dispatching its army, now unopposed, into Transylvania as well as back to Bucharest.

On December 1, 1918 the National Party of Romanians in Transylvania assembled a huge crowd of 100,000 at Alba Iulia in order to proclaim union with Romania. On the same day, Serbia's Regent Aleksandar received a delegation including Zagreb's newly broadened National Council and proclaimed the Kingdom of Serbs, Croats, and Slovenes in Belgrade. The last Habsburg military forces in the field now abandoned northern Albania. They left the proclamation of a reunited state to a local leader who was acting under the Italian aegis that would challenge Albania's independence throughout the interwar period. At least the prospects for independence looked brighter for the Romanian and Yugoslav states that between them absorbed all the former Habsburg territory of Southeastern Europe. Yet there were devils in the details of how the war's end and the international peace settlements that followed affected all three of them. None would result in a happy ending.

Albania Resurrected

The 100,000 Italian troops occupying Albania in 1918 at least kept Greek and Serbian or Montenegrin forces from pressing in from south and north. The Italian claim to Vlore and the southern coast had been frustrated by the European Concert's creation of Albania in 1912. It now revived with the Treaty of London that brought Italy into the war with the Entente. The Serbian army had launched a treaty-endorsed incursion into the north earlier in 1915. By December its entire surviving force was retreating in the face of an irresistible Austro-German offensive to the Albanian coast and then to Corfu. The Serbian interlude had also compromised the war's initial Albanian leader, Essad Pasha. He had collaborated with their command in return for local autonomy in the central highlands.

The subsequent interwar ruler Ahmed Zogolli (later Zogu and from 1928 King Zog) ironically did better by the Austro-Hungarian occupation. It followed the Serbian retreat of December 1915 and the Montenegrin surrender a few months later. A leader of the largest single Albanian tribe, the Mati, and already a rival to his uncle Essad, Zogolli was able to begin formal organization of Albanian army units under Habsburg auspices. Austria commanders soon doubted that he would keep the new units subordinate, and Zogolli was summoned to Vienna. There he stayed, barred from returning but learning lessons about how European ministries operated and royalty was respected. Meanwhile, the Greek units that had moved from Epirus into the south had by 1917 been pushed back. Italian and French contingents intervened, each of them allowing and then undermining some proclamation of Albanian independence. Disputing this manipulation for military advantage against the Central Powers was Fan Noli, the American-based Christian Orthodox Bishop who was the main leader abroad and briefly Prime Minister in 1924. He argued for independence and against the Treaty of London. He appealed to the American government in particular as a representative of the 60,000 Albanian immigrants recently arrived in the United States.[22]

The complex of external interventions during the war turned out to be an appropriate prelude to the immediate postwar period. By the time that Zogolli returned in 1919, British and French troops joined the Italians in the north, French and Greek troops were mixing in from the south, and Serbian units were pressing in from Kosovo. There was some limited British, American, and even Serbian support for independence within the 1912 borders. It was, however, the Albanians' own national congress that convened at Lushnje in January 1920, and its committee of national defense that generated the June ultimatum obliging the 20,000 Italian troops to withdraw. By August the Italian government had signed a treaty at Tirana, soon to be the new capital, recognizing the territorial integrity of Albania, Vlore included. Italian support had already helped at the Paris peace conference in rejecting Greece's claims to the south. The emigré Kosova Committee could win no support against the favored Serbian claim to the controversial province.

Within the imposed borders, Zogolli had already received the powerful position of the Interior Minister in a provisional government of four regents, one Sunni and one local Bektashi Muslim, one Catholic and one Orthodox. He secured Belgrade's support in return for an agreement conceding Albania's claim to Kosovo. The assassination of his old rival Essad Pasha, in Paris attempting to represent Albania at the peace conference, also helped. By the end of the year Albania had been admitted to the new League of Nations, although Italian pressures delayed general diplomatic recognition until 1921. Internally, however, the new state was divided, but more between tribes than between Gegs and Tosks or between the Muslim, Catholic, and Orthodox religions. Supplies of basic foodstuffs were scarce, especially for refugees from the wartime upheavals. Perhaps 10,000 of them alone had died of starvation or exposure by 1920, a figure that would have been higher but for the emergency aid supplied by the American Red Cross.[23] Otherwise, the United States sought no official role in the postwar settlement for Albania. There were, however, a couple of emigré inquiries asking that Albania become an American protectorate, but the US State Department paid them no recorded attention.

Romania Expanded

If Albania's road out of the First World War was the most complex for any state in the region, Romania's was the simplest. It was also the most frustrating one for the major peacemaking powers gathered at Paris – Britain, France, and Italy now joined by the United States. The collapse of Austria–Hungary had put the ardently pro-Entente Ionel Brătianu and his Liberals back in power and in Bucharest by November 1918. By January 1919 Brătianu had arrived in Paris expecting to sit as an equal participant with the Big Four. He also planned to place Romanian representatives on the two relevant territorial commissions. Both expectations were denied. Romania's capitulation to the Central Powers in 1918 was the reason, or the excuse.

Brătianu reacted against this unexpectedly subordinate position. He became the conference's most ardent and inflexible advocate of territorial demands. These included not only Transylvania (from Habsburg Hungary) and the Bukovina (from Austrian Habsburg Galicia) as promised by the Entente in 1916 but also Bessarabia (from Tsarist Russia). In all three, he could point to a Romanian ethnic majority of two-thirds. From the start, Brătianu refused to entertain an American request, originating with the academic experts on Eastern Europe accompanying President Wilson, for drawing borders that reflected ethnic lines of demarcation in Transylvania in particular.

Although the Big Four's irritation with Brătianu's demands spread even to the pro-Romanian French delegation, radical regimes threatening the region from Russia and now Hungary cleared the way for his Greater Romania. In March 1919, pro-Bolshevik insurgents led by Bela Kun seized power in defeated Hungary. Their Soviet Republic was soon promising to spread revolutionary Hungarian rule across all of the prewar territories as soon as Trotsky's Red Army arrived to link up. The Russian relief never arrived of course, but neither were there British or French troops available to deal with the Kun regime threatening Transylvania. The powers in Paris refused the request of General Franchet d'Esperey to move his French and Serbian forces north to Budapest. All of them were thus obliged to stand by as the Romanian army advanced westward. It reached the Tisza River by May and forced Kun's regime to collapse by August 1. Three days later, Romanian troops occupied Budapest itself. And there they stayed, defying repeated demands to leave from the peacemakers and confiscating considerable equipment as reparations for what the German occupation had taken in Wallachia. Simply withdrawing in November helped to win agreement on a generous western border for Transylvania in Paris, overcoming American objections to including the key cities of Satu Mare, Oradea, and Arad plus the rail lines linking them with each other.

This apparent triumph was not enough to save Brătianu's Liberals from defeat in the election of November 1919. The Transylvanian National Party joined the opposition Peasant Party to mobilize rural votes in a franchise greatly expanded by universal male suffrage. The resulting Parliamentary Bloc, in fact a loose coalition government, promised agrarian reform. Its radical terms allowed Brătianu to win King Ferdinand over quickly to replacing it with one headed by the war hero General Alexandru Averescu. He used the threat from Russian and some Romanian Bolshevik agitation in Bessarabia to overcome a last American request for a plebiscite. By late 1920 the eastern province was simply included within interwar Romania's borders. These borders also included half of the western Banat, divided with the new Yugoslav state, along with Transylvania and the Bukovina.[44]

Brătianu and his Liberals would return to power in 1922, ready to centralize control of this enlarged, if ethnically more diverse Romania.

The Yugoslav Kingdom Assembled

The new Kingdom of Serbs, Croats, and Slovenes combined a still more diverse population than that of Romania. European diplomacy and two camps of domestic actors had struggled with each other over any prospect for this equally large state until 1918. Then the military tide turned in Serbia's favor at the Salonika Front. Its advancing army and the defense it offered against Italian claims brought representatives from the new National Council of Slovenes, Croats, and Serbs, convened that fall in Zagreb, to Belgrade. Serbia's Regent Aleksandar proclaimed the new kingdom with French approval on December 1. The Council's belated connection with Belgrade would hold at Paris, if not easily, through a peace conference that settled all borders except the one with Italy.

Italy's contradictory wartime role began in May 1915 with the aforementioned Treaty of London. Its promise of Istria and the central Dalmatian coast to postwar Italy in return for joining the Entente gave new life to the Yugoslav Committee ironically formed in Italy six months earlier by the two Dalmatian Croats, Frano Supilo and Ante Trumbić. Now based in London, they concentrated their efforts on winning British support for a postwar Yugoslav state that would deny Italy those Adriatic territories. They enlisted support from the two Western specialists most influential among the various friends of the respective Balkan peoples at this time, the scholar R. W. Seton-Watson and the journalist Henry Wickham-Steed. It was Seton-Watson who founded the weekly *The New Europe* in 1916, in order to advocate that a South Slav state be carved from Austria-Hungary and joined to a liberated Serbia and Montenegro. Then in 1917, as the Italian army struggled with its own war effort against the Habsburg monarchy, its government passed the word to Trumbić that the London terms might be open to revision. It even set up a commission at Padua, perhaps disingenuously, to explore ties with the Yugoslav Committee.[25]

Little would come of these Italian contacts, but they brightened the prospects for a postwar state after the committee's inconclusive meeting with Serbia's government on Corfu that July. Prime Minister Pašić had asked the Committee to abandon its demand that at least some of the 30,000 volunteers deserting from Habsburg units or returning from emigration be allowed to form an Adriatic Legion separate from the Serbian army. Instead, they were all incorporated into it. But after discussing a common postwar state, the two sides could agree only on the ambiguous Corfu Declaration. *Its* 14 points implied autonomy for each of the three peoples – Serbs, Croats, and Slovenes – who would unite under the Serbian dynasty, but left any specific autonomous rights to a future constituent assembly. Both sides, as I have argued elsewhere, were in fact too weak at this time to insist on more.[26]

By the fall of 1918 the breakthrough on the Salonika Front greatly strengthened the Serbian hand. Its army units had in August already joined French troops in entering Montenegro. There they not only replaced the evacuating Austro-Hungarian occupiers but also prevented King Nikola from restoring the independent state. Their presence bolstered the northern Whites that desired union with Serbia and conciliated the southern Greens. Their attacks, some atrocities included, against Albanians intermixed on the contested border also helped.

The Yugoslav Committee's hand was weaker, despite its closer contact with Western diplomacy. Taking the committee's place in the Habsburg's Slovene lands in particular was a domestic movement that had already been pressing the monarchy for federal, really confederal, autonomy from the start of the war.[27] The Slovene urban elite, mainly schoolteachers and clergy, formed the vanguard. They all feared Austrian-German domination in a victorious Austria–Hungary as much as the loss of territory to Italy if the monarchy went down. Unlike the other territories of the future Yugoslavia, the Austrian urban presence was large enough during the war years to make ethnically German theater and cultural life, German language instruction in the schools, even the use of German in public and religious life more prominent than it had been before the war. The clergy took the lead. By 1917 Bishop Jeglić and the interwar Slovene leader Msgr Korošec readily joined the reconvened Reichsrat's "South Slav Club" and endorsed its May Declaration for internal autonomy. But by October the Slovenes were rejecting any internal reorganization of the monarchy. The following fall they formed a separate National Council in Ljubljana as Croats were forming theirs in Zagreb. On October 6 they joined forces in Zagreb and, by the end of the month, declared for secession.

The new council had no military force at its command to stop the Italian units that were advancing into Istria. Nor could it suppress the so-called "green cadres" of primarily Croat troops from disintegrating Austro-Hungarian units who were seizing land as a law unto themselves. Only the Serbian army could stop the Italian advance and restore order. And it came as soon as called by the National Council. Stjepan Radić of the Croatian Peasant Party and the hard-right Party of the Pure Right objected but were outvoted. Its arrival doomed the Yugoslav Committee's last stand for a confederal state, an agreement signed at Geneva on November 9 by Trumbić and Korošec with Pašić as Serbia's foreign representative. His own Radical government repudiated it a few days later. The National Council was obliged to join Serb-dominated delegations from Bosnia, the Vojvodina and Montenegro in traveling to Belgrade. On December 1 they accepted Regent Aleksandar's declaration of a unitary state. French diplomacy readily backed such a state in order to deny Italy wartime claims to the vanished Habsburg lands. This further strengthened the Serbian position.

Continuing Italian pressure to claim some of Dalmatia as well as the Istrian Peninsula helped to justify Belgrade's rejection of joint or coequal ministries when the unelected Interim National Parliament convened in March 1919. Opposition to unitary Serbian terms was nonetheless strong enough to delay elections to a constituent assembly until November 1920. Radic's Peasant Party was again the main opponent of the constitution drafted for the new kingdom by Pašić's Radicals. The Croatian party's abstention was needed to secure the assembly's approval six months later in 1921. The election also included a large protest vote in Macedonia and Montenegro for the new Communist Party and a division into competing parties among only one major ethnic group, the Serbs. This division plus total Serb numbers that were barely 38 percent of the population (40 percent with Montenegrins) did not bode well for the successful consolidation of power and legitimacy from Belgrade.

Although the election stoked the domestic conflicts of the 1920s (see Chapter 3), the new kingdom's borders were nonetheless secured. The afore-mentioned division of the Banat with Romania at the Paris peace confer-ence and the southern border with Greece were uncontested. Not so the transfer from defeated Bulgaria of several strategic frontier enclaves and, more importantly, Vardar Macedonia. The new kingdom's Serbian leader-ship would press against the border fixed between Kosovo and the Albanian state well into the 1920s. The fledgling League of Nations inter-vened only in Carinthia. A plebiscite in 1920 awarded the disputed territory with its Slovene minority to Austria.

The kingdom's delegation to Paris, led by Pašić, Trumbić, and Korošec, advanced their argument for self-determination in Istria, and Italy's Sidney Sonnino refused any concession. The Italian army and navy had pressured British and French contingents to retreat from the Dalmatian coastal zones that a Rome agreement had assigned them. Throughout 1919 the Italians had however been confronted by the US naval and marine units. They had been dispatched to the central zone around Split in order to deliver food relief directly inland to the defeated Habsburg territories as well as liberated Serbia. Their deployment and American readiness to intervene in general ended with the President Wilson's term of office in 1920. The Interim National Parliament was obliged to accept Italy's terms, the loss of Istria and tenuous international status for the major port of Rijeka (Fiume). The Treaty of Rapallo left half a million Croats and Slovenes inside Italy.[28] Here then was a set of contested borders, even when Istria was incorporated after the Second World War, whose defense would remain one justification for strong central government in both Yugoslavias.

Bulgaria and Greece: Refugees and Radical Divisions

The collapse of the Salonika Front in September 1918 was as portentous for Bulgaria as was the breakthrough there for Greece. Bulgaria's defeat started a massive influx of refugees and brought one of the two now-prominent radical parties to power. Greece's apparent victory would lead first its pro-Entente Liberals and then their royalist opponents into Anatolia and the catastrophic retreat, basically back to the present border with Turkey, by 1922. As a result, the largest forced migration anywhere in post-1918 Europe brought 1.4 million refugees to Greece. The majority came fatefully to the post-1912 northern area of Aegean Macedonia and Thrace. Their influx sharpened the wartime political division that would by 1924 make Greece the one regional state to replace its monarchy with a republic. Sensitive to any threat to Greece's sovereignty over their new home from the northern neighbors, they would help to keep the Macedonian question alive through the twentieth century.

Bulgaria Defeated

By September 26, 1918 the Bulgarian divisions falling back dispirited and in disarray from the Salonika Front reached Radomir, only a few miles from Sofia. They threatened to seize the capital and declare Bulgaria a republic. Desperate to stop their advance, Tsar Ferdinand released the Agrarian party leader, Aleksandar Stamboliiski, imprisoned for opposing the war, and sent him off to dissuade the rebels. Stamboliiski's legendary decision to support them instead probably reflected no prior plan. Nor did it prevent German and Macedonian units from quickly putting down what became known as the Radomir Rebellion. The other Agrarian leaders did not support his decision. Neither did the Narrow Socialists, flush with the success of the Bolshevik Revolution in Russia and from 1919 the Bulgarian Communist Party (BKP).

Rather than the rebellion, it was the French General Franchet D'Esperey, at the head of the advancing Army of the Orient, who obliged Ferdinand to abdicate a few days later. The dispatch of an armistice delegation to Salonika was left to Andrei Liapchev and other Democratic Party opponents of the alliance with the Central Powers. Ferdinand's son, the 24-year-old Boris, succeeded to the throne, thus preserving the monarchy. The coalition government's delegation to the Paris peace conference stood little chance of preserving the wartime borders. A belated proposal from Bulgarian academics for a Balkan federation after all sank without a trace. Stamboliiski was in Paris with this unhappy delegation when the elections of August 1919 gave his Bulgarian Agrarian National Union (BZNS) a plurality in the new National Assembly. To supplement the 85 BZNS deputies elected, he reluctantly reached out to the next largest party. But the BKP with its 47 seats rejected cooperation out of hand. The rivalry between the region's two largest radical parties would leave its mark on Bulgarian political life after both of the world wars. This time it was the Agrarians' turn.[29]

By November of 1919 the victorious powers in Paris had agreed on peace terms for Bulgaria that would make Stamboliiski's turn difficult indeed. In addition to levying reparations over the next 37 years that would have amounted to more than ten times the state budget's revenues in 1911, the Treaty of Neuilly demanded Bulgarian military forces be reduced to 20,000 men. To ensure demobilization, British and French Military Missions remained at strategic locations, excluding Sofia, through 1920. The territorial terms took away Aegean and Vardar Macedonia, all of Thrace, even the southern Dobrudja. This last revision in Romania's favor deprived the economy of 20–25 percent of its annual wheat exports. A bad harvest in 1918 on the remaining grain land created a desperate domestic shortage. Only an emergency American delivery of wheat through Herbert Hoover's Food Administration, sold in return for gold from Bulgaria's reserves, prevented starvation. Then came the refugees, over 220,000 by 1920. Barely 50,000 of them came under the Convention Respecting Reciprocal Emigration signed with Venizelos's government in November 1919. It provided for the departure of 30,000 Greeks from Bulgaria and avoided any language which suggested that the migration was not voluntary. But for much of this fraction and all of the rest who had started coming during the war and continued afterwards, their transfer amounted to forced migration under a variety of informal pressures. They streamed into southwest Bulgaria and Sofia from all the lost lands. They accounted for half the increase in population from 4.4 to 4.8 million on postwar territory between 1910 and 1920. Their minimal accommodation and irredentist agitation, particularly from groups in the Internal Macedonian Revolutionary Organization (VMRO), would pose continuing problems to Bulgarian governments across most of the interwar period, as we shall see in Chapters 3 and 4.

Stamboliiski's government met this assortment of challenges with mass politics and political repression. He also resisted European pressures whenever he could. American diplomatic reports follow his consolidation of power with grudging admiration.[30] In November 1919, on the eve of the Neuilly treaty, he protested that "an unjust peace cannot last" but also called himself "the last optimist left in Bulgaria." Among the 25 points of his initial October speech to the National Assembly, he had promised to reestablish lawful authority but also to "punish the authors of the national catastrophe." There would be further talk of trials, and members of the wartime Radoslavov cabinet were indeed arrested. But unlike the Venizelos regime that returned to power in Greece in 1922 (see below) the Agrarian regime stopped short of convictions or executions. It turned aside the British Military Mission's request for 600 indictments.

Stamboliiski concentrated on winning a clear majority in the next parliamentary elections. His mass party had the cadre to organize village support, if not the trained personnel needed for subsequent administration. They and their paramilitary organization, the Orange Guards, had already put down two strikes organized primarily by the BKP in the fall of 1919. Now they disrupted Communist meetings and otherwise made political opposition difficult, albeit without any decision from Stamboliiski to ban the rival party. The monarchy, the 1879 constitution, and the old parties were also left in place. Among those parties, only the Democrats won as much as 10 percent of the vote in the elections of March 1920. The Broad Socialists faded to 6 percent. Some 915,000 male voters cast their ballots, twice as many as in 1908 and half again as many as in 1919. The Agrarians, with 38 percent, gained seats but so did the Communists with 20 percent, winning some urban and Greek minority support just because the BKP had been harassed. The BZNS disqualified 13 seats of 233 in order to make their 110 into a ruling majority.

Stamboliiski promptly named himself Foreign and War Minister as well as Prime Minister, perhaps reflecting the inexperience of his young colleagues. He himself was only 40, in sharpest contrast to the Yugoslav Kingdom's Pašić, who was 74. Romania's Brătianu and Greece's Venizelos were both 56. Stamboliiski and his Agrarians were at least in a stronger position in 1920 to carry out their version of a postwar transition than any of the other three.

Greece Overextended

Venizelos was clearly in the weakest position. Like Brătianu, he would be forced from power in 1920. But before he returned in 1922 Greece would have lost as much as Romania gained in the final postwar settlement. As in the aftermath of the Second World War, Greece's divided political leadership would keep the country involved in armed conflict for another four years. Rather than the civil war that lasted from 1946 until 1949, it was the territorial expansion that one side had started in 1918 and the other took over which kept the country at war until 1922.

This modern Greek tragedy began at the Salonika Front, with the closest postwar relation that any of the region's leaders would have with his counterpart among the European powers. This was the growing wartime connection between Venizelos and the British Prime Minister, Lloyd George. Once the Greek army had been mobilized to a surprising strength of 300,000 men for the breakthrough at Salonika, its further deployment around the Black Sea attracted both men. Lloyd George sought support for the Anglo-French intervention against the Bolsheviks in the Ukraine. Venizelos wished to protect the Greek minority, over half a million from Odessa eastward. But that minority and the dispatch of a couple of Greek divisions to the Black Sea coast made the landing of more troops to protect the larger Greek settlement on the western coast of Anatolia, some 600,000 people in and around Smyrna alone, irresistible. Lloyd George's religious roots in the Welsh Chapel attracted him to the idea of liberating all Christians, Orthodox included, from Muslim rule. So did representations made to him on behalf of the Armenians massacred during their forced deportation by Ottoman forces in 1915.

Venizelos started with more credit as a supporter of the Entente than any other small state's representative. He took further advantage from Italy's temporary absence, because of the aforementioned dispute over Rijeka, at the Paris peace conference. Greece was thereby able to take over the postwar Italian claim to occupy a coastal zone in western Anatolia. The conference's Big Three, Britain, France and the US, obliged Italy as well to agree to the landing of Greek troops at Smyrna in May 1919. The landing fired Venizelos's interest in a larger Anatolian enclave, if not the incorporation of Istanbul as foreseen in the Great Idea. It also kindled the Turkish resistance under Mustafa Kemal (later Attaturk) which would prove overpowering three years later.

The major players for the denouement were already in place by the end of 1920.[31] In January, Kemal and other Turkish leaders had proclaimed their National Pact, abandoning the authority of the Ottoman Sultan and rejecting any imposed peace or foreign presence in Anatolia. The Paris conference proceeded blithely ahead to draft a peace treaty with the fading Ottoman authority. The terms presented in May provoked first Turkish resistance and then a further mandate from Paris for Greek forces to restore order. By June, those forces had rapidly taken control of eastern Thrace, as far as the same Chataldzha line that had been the furthest point of

Bulgarian advance in 1912. Greek units also advanced significantly inland from Smyrna. The Treaty of Sèvres duly imposed on the Sultan's representatives in August made these advances seem permanent. After this latest of his lengthy absences at the conference, Venizelos now expected to return to Greece in final triumph. But the young King Alexander died suddenly, after a bite from his pet monkey. This left his father, the deposed Constantine, as the only logical successor.

The National Schism that Venizelos and the Entente had pushed aside in 1917 by installing Alexander was instantly recalled to life. Royalist supporters in the south and among the older army officers mobilized the discontent that had been building against Venizelos's Liberal lieutenants at home, fueled by the long, hard years of military mobilization. The new Greek Socialist Party, already a Communist party, stressed the unremitting urban hardships already noted above to win 100,000 votes in the parliamentary elections of November 1920. It was, however, Constantine's People's Party which won a majority of the million votes cast and two-thirds of the seats. Venizelos left the country as a hasty plebiscite approved the recall of Constantine to the throne. His cadre of 1500 army officers turned out the Venizelists who had replaced them in 1917. But neither they, with the exception of Metaxas who returned from exile only to retire, nor the King could resist the temptation of proceeding to advance still further into Anatolia and toward Istanbul as well. They would have to do it without international support. British backing for the enterprise wavered with the restoration of the Greek monarch who had favored the Central Powers during the war. France withdrew all support. Italy now switched openly to the Turkish side.

Over 200,000 Greek troops were able to sustain the ill-fated military campaign until September 1922. The seminal role of its defeat in the founding of the modern Turkish state under the victorious Attaturk is well known. We are more concerned with the consequences of the forced migration to Greece that followed. Perhaps 30,000 civilians, Greeks and Armenians, were killed in the Turkish sacking and burning of Smyrna. The losses to the Greek army were larger still.

By the end of the year, some 1.4 million of almost 2 million Greeks in Anatolia and eastern Thrace had fled. Almost all of them, 1.2 million, came to Greece. Their transfer under harsh conditions to Aegean Macedonia, western Thrace, and the environs of Athens created a problem of subsequent settlement that would leave its mark on Greek political and economic life for the rest of the century. By November 1922, the peace conference with Turkey that would ratify this forced migration had already convened at Lausanne under the auspices of Britain, France, and Italy on behalf of the League of Nations. The League's initial report cited the Greek exchange agreements with Bulgaria and the Ottoman Empire in 1913–14, noted above, as precedents. The subsequent convention forbade refugee return, Istanbul excepted, and also provided for the further transfer of the 200,000 Greeks remaining in Anatolia outside of Istanbul and most of the 350,000 Turks and other Muslims still in Greece, with those in western Thrace excepted.[32] The Greek, Turkish, and European representatives had negotiated only in terms of compulsory exchanges, although each of them paid lip-service to voluntary departures. The convention's signing completed the disgrace of the royal regime.

Venezelist officers and some royalists as well had already forced Constantine to abdicate. Venizelos himself and the Liberals returned to power. He used the obligation to represent Greece at Lausanne to blame the settlement's onerous terms on the King's military failure. This time, over 2500 royalist officers were cashiered. Within months, Constantine's Prime Minister and five other cabinet members were tried and executed for their part in the catastrophe. Yet, along with this divisive transfer of political power, 1922 also marked the year in which Greece settled into her modern, Southeastern European borders, a year that Greek historians call "the true divide between the old and the new century in Greece."[33]

The decade of war that finally ended in 1922 had brought few advantages beyond the new borders to this region now composed entirely of independent states. Forced migration, primarily of Greeks and Bulgarians, nearly matched the number of war dead from the prewar states, some 2 million soldiers and civilians from a population of 22 million. Now the 38 million surviving in the expanded post-1918 states would at least have the advantage of independence to establish themselves according to prevailing European standards. How their political leaders, their ethnic majorities, their economies and societies pursued those standards concerns the next chapter. But first we must consider how the European powers so involved with the region at the start and the end of the First World War would proceed.

3 Struggling with Liberal and National Transitions in the 1920s

Under the standards of democracy and self-determination unfurled by the American President, Woodrow Wilson, liberal ideals were to serve national independence. The former imperial borderlands and the prewar Balkan states should combine and cohere into a single set of independent, representative governments. It was the lack of "complete independence" before 1914, Wilson told his European colleagues at the deliberations in Paris in 1919, that had invited wider international rivalry and led to the First World War. "One of the great results of this conference," he concluded, "is to liberate the Balkan Peninsula from the intervention of the Great Powers."[1] It would, however, prove to be the powers' political disinterest and their economic differences rather than the peace treaties that diminished intervention as the postwar decade progressed.

Nor did the Paris conference or Wilson himself privilege self-determination to the exclusion of the less generous standards for statehood left, as noted in the Introduction, from the liberal nationalism of the nineteenth century. The common framework for conflict resolution under which the new governments of Southeastern Europe would now conduct their international relations, the Covenant for Wilson's beloved League of Nations, did not mention self-determination, let alone any far-reaching right to independent statehood. As the conference subsequently came down to decisions made by the so-called Big Four – the US, Britain, France, and sometimes Italy – none of them endorsed the prospect of an unlimited number of smaller states. Wilson himself did take a special interest in supporting the three new states of Czechoslovakia, Poland, and what became Yugoslavia, but all were large enough to promise economic viability and military security. Their considerable minorities would be served by a set of Minorities Treaties intended to afford them the same individual rights as the majorities, not the regional rights to "autonomous development" promised in Wilson's 14 Points (see Chapter 2) when Austria–Hungary still survived and still might reach a separate peace with the Allies.

Democratic governments were to guarantee those rights. Multiparty elections and universal male suffrage would provide parliamentary representation, and an autonomous judiciary would uphold individual rights. Private enterprise was to combine with limited government regulation to facilitate the national integration of market economies. Access to free trade, long a core principle for Wilson's Democratic Party and its southern base, would advance their international integration.[2]

By October 1918 Austria–Hungary had refused his 14 Points and begun to disintegrate. It was then that Wilson took up "self-determination," a term already coined by Lenin in 1916 to appeal to non-Russians in the Tsarist empire. For the American President, this newly "imperative principle" justified the independent, elected governments that would stand as a barrier against Bolshevik claims to Poland or serve to replace the imperial regimes of the Habsburg and Hohenzollern monarchies. Never defined by Wilson to mean the right to independence for ethnic minorities, its application during the subsequent peace conference was confined to the limited number of typically larger states that would now become Eastern Europe. His priority at Paris in any case was keeping the support he had initially won for a League of Nations. He and his advisors advocated ethnically drawn borders for the Southeastern European states in particular, but they typically retreated when necessary to maintain British, French, and Italian endorsement for the new international organization.[3]

By 1920 Wilson had failed to win even American support for the League. His international influence fell with his physical decline and ceased with the end of his term in office. Succeeding Republican administrations went on to steer clear of asserting the liberal economic leadership that would have been consistent with League membership as well as being the principal postwar creditor. Tariffs rose instead of falling, and financial support for reconstruction was left to the private sector, as in the Dawes Plan for a stabilization loan to Germany.[4]

Nor was Wilson's liberal political framework for Eastern Europe falling easily into place. Regionally representative government was particularly daunting for the insecure regimes of these newly created or expanded states. Their territories were also ethnically diverse or divided by a refugee influx and challenged by the Bolshevik rejection of multiparty elections. The Southeastern European states did indeed join the rest of the continent in rejecting the Communist alternative after the First World War. Like all of the newly defined or redefined states of Eastern Europe, they struggled with national integration and economic recovery. Their more heavily rural populations faced the further challenge of socioeconomic modernization.

The region's royal regimes and Greece's republic followed the pre-1914 Western model for structuring legitimate states and creating a conscious loyalty. New constitutions limited royal or executive prerogatives and proclaimed a common commitment to the rule of law and the rights of representation. As applied, however, their provisions seemed more national than liberal. They resisted international authority, celebrated a majority-based national identity, and defended the national economy against free trade. The League of Nations, without German membership until 1926 and Soviet membership until 1934, and missing the US throughout, lacked the leverage to overcome the national interests as pursued by its major European members – Britain, France, and Italy. Their regular Conferences of Ambassadors carried more weight than the League's deliberations in Geneva.

British interests quickly turned further east following Greece's Anatolian debacle. Lloyd George's Conservative successors devoted their reduced postwar resources to defending the non-European Empire and the new mandates in Palestine and Iraq. An army of 1 million men in the Middle East alone quickly shrank to less than 400,000 overall. By 1921 the Anglo-French intervention against Bolshevik Russia had been abandoned. These two remaining Great Powers also turned away from each other. Britain eschewed a military alliance with France and reluctantly opted for closer ties with the United States. In its relations with Southeastern Europe, London naturally liked the idea of constitutional monarchies but confined its diplomacy to supporting the territorial settlements, stable central governments, and, as we shall see, independent central banks. Minority claims even to political autonomy were discouraged. On the Macedonian question, for instance, the assimilationist policies of Athens and Belgrade were preferred to endorsing local rights that sounded like Irish demands and might encourage Bulgarian claims.

French diplomacy did support the so-called Little Entente by 1924, formed under Czech initiative in 1921. But the alliance of Romania, its regional favorite, the Yugoslav Kingdom and Czechoslovakia focused primarily on the threat of Hungarian revanchism, secondarily on restraining Bulgaria, and not at all on the containment of Germany which was the understandable French obsession. France continued to maintain its million-man army, but steadily reduced its budget, training, and equipment. Its government's original post-1918 interest in the region had been for collective defense against Bolshevik Russia, a resurgent Germany, or a reconstituted Austria–Hungary. This military interest vanished behind the Maginot Line even as its construction began in 1928.

Mussolini's Fascist regime built on Italian dissatisfaction with the postwar settlement. Italian foreign policy cut away Albania's economic independence and readily confronted Greek and Yugoslav territorial integrity. In 1923 the League stood back when an Italian occupation of Corfu followed the assassination of an Italian General adjudicating the Greek–Albanian border. The Conference of Ambassadors secured withdrawal only through Greek concessions. In 1927 and again in 1929 the Duce provided arms and financial assistance to VMRO's pro-Bulgarian organization. Its terrorist raids served to unsettle Vardar Macedonia and prevent any Yugoslav rapprochement with Bulgaria.[5]

The principal transition facing post-1918 Europe as a whole was not systemic change but economic recovery, preferably recovery for the victors on prewar terms at the losers' expense. The wartime losses of men, matériel, and markets were heavy. Reparations were supposed to compensate for property damage, however difficult to calculate the cost. Prospective collection from the defeated states threatened their overall recovery, even when actual payments were reduced. In what now became Eastern Europe, any Western loans or investments were inhibited not only by the reparations imposed on Austria, Hungary, and Bulgaria but also by Greek, Romanian, and Serbian war debts to the United States, primarily for food relief in 1919. Washington would resist any request for postponement, and New York now became the center of the postwar capital market. European agricultural markets suffered from demand reduced by war deaths and supply permanently increased by American and Canadian imports. Prewar levels of grain exports would never be regained in real per capita terms. Where mineral exports were available, governments continued to manage the mines as before the war. Romania's ruling Liberal Party stepped in to restrict foreign management of oil investments. Protective tariffs rose again across Europe, dragging in even the last bastion of free trade, Great Britain, by the end of the 1920s.

Before then, Britain had provided the one major initiative from liberal orthodoxy that was intended to transform and then coordinate the European economies. Montagu Norman, the Governor of the Bank of England, proposed to reduce both reparations and debt repayments from governments and then to make central banks independent of state budget demands in general, all to allow them to stand behind currencies fixed to exchange rates dependent only on their gold and Western currency reserves. The result would hopefully prevent inflation and revive capital markets at least for reconstruction loans, while removing the state from the making of monetary policy. Norman's final goal was to bring the victors and the vanquished together in an international consortium of central banks, independent of national interference and foreign (read French) political influence. This early version of the International Monetary Fund (IMF) had no resources of its own and would not materialize. Still, the League's Financial Committee encouraged or pressured the central banks of Bulgaria, Greece, Romania, and the Yugoslav Kingdom to establish their independence.

Belated efforts by the Bank of France to insert itself separately into the process succeeded by 1928–9 in organizing a consortium and credit for the formal stabilization of Romania's currency. Its advisors there joined others dispatched elsewhere by the League's Committee to push for reduced state expenses and employees as well as central bank independence, an early version of the IMF "conditionality" of the 1990s. The exchange rates that they helped to stabilize were generally overvalued like the British pound, if not bound as it was to prewar parity. Had their rates of exchange not been set above open market values, stable currencies would have helped in resuming the prewar growth of exports and discouraging higher tariffs.[6] For our region, the flow of new foreign lending which high, stable rates of exchange should have encouraged did not appear before the Depression closed off any such prospect.

The universal franchise promised by the new constitutions, and provided for males, created a common practice of mass politics but precious little sense of a common European identity. As in Western Europe, appeals to a common national identity or against a common adversary promised more votes. Wartime propaganda against the enemy as a people and not just a government had paved the way. Witness the first British and French postwar elections. Both endorsed the imposition of heavy reparations on Germany. The Soviet Comintern soon split off separate Communist parties from the various socialist parties, but only briefly in the interest of some unified European movement. By the late 1920s the Comintern was using its early proposal for a Communist Balkan Federation to support minority claims for self-determination in order to divide or weaken the successor states Communist disdain for multiparty elections also helped to strengthen the Western faith in such elections, regardless of how they were held, as the principle indicator of democratic governance. West European Liberal parties per se faded into the background, most noticeably in Britain.

What did not fade was the centralization of governance, with the exception of municipal politics, in the national ministries. The wartime mobilizations had advanced the collection of information and organization of the home front from these ministries, old or new, even in Britain. Dismantled there, they remained in place for France most noticeably. Smaller military forces did not diminish their powers in other areas. These extended to public education, the judicial system, and the conduct of the parliamentary elections, all presumably independent of the executive branch by liberal standards. Public employment grew in the new states of Eastern Europe, as it had in Western Europe before the war. Where the ethnic majority, as in Poland or Romania, or the ethnic plurality as in Czechoslovakia or the Kingdom of Serbs, Croats, and Slovenes, could dominate the ministries, that domination provoked minority resentment or resistance. The monarchs surviving as titular chief executives everywhere in our region but Greece also used the ministerial framework to authoritarian advantage.

All the same, competitive elections allowed opposition parties sizeable representation in the Yugoslav Kingdom from 1923 to 1927. One election ousted the ruling party in Romania and another validated the largest party in Greece in 1928. And, in 1931, Bulgarian multiparty elections brought at least a faction of the Agrarian Union, violently overthrown and its leader assassinated in 1923, back within a coalition government.

A wider Western popular culture now spread across Europe during the 1920s. Here was one point of common connection across national borders that otherwise resisted political or economic integration. Hollywood films and jazz music made an American presence felt for the first time. Mass press and sporting events built on their British origins. As the sensation and celebrity of this popular culture grew, so did the connection with a common European high culture. Russian emigrés provided particular encouragement to the arts and universities in Belgrade and Sofia. For all of Southeastern Europe, this cultural ferment was concentrated in the few major cities. These included the capitals of the prewar Balkan states but also rivals from the new territories. Zagreb, Ljubljana, Cluj, and Thessaloniki (respectively Agram, Laibach, Kolozsvar, and Salonika before the war) challenged the predominance of Belgrade, Bucharest, and Athens as cultural centers. Widely publicized ceremonies to commemorate war dead and preserve memories of victorious national sacrifice also divided Belgrade and Zagreb, and Bucharest from Cluj as well as from defeated Bulgaria.

Still setting our region apart were Europe's smallest shares of urban population, typically 20 percent, and far less in larger towns. Greece passed 30 percent only because of the refugees that had flooded into Athens and Thessaloniki as well as Macedonia and Thrace. The broad political incorporation of this huge peasant majority remained a transition too far for the national liberal regimes of this first postwar decade. But the presumption that their ethnic majority and peasant culture stood for national identity would nonetheless advance, to the further disadvantage of regional or European connections.

The Postwar Starting Points: New Borders and Divided Populations

Both the new state borders and the ethnic, religious, or regional entities within those borders divided populations that the postwar governments were determined to integrate. We cannot proceed without a mental mapping of these borders and divisions. Agreement demarcating the Yugoslav Kingdom from Albania in 1926 completed a set of international borders (see Map 3.1) that would stand for the rest of the interwar period. But the ethnic and religious diversity seen in Table 3.1 failed to cohere within any of those borders and pressed across some of them. Romania and the Yugoslav Kingdom faced the greatest ethnic diversity, Greece and Bulgaria the major influx of refugees. The conflicting interests of Bulgarians and ethnic Macedonians, Serbs and Greeks spilled across the borders between Bulgaria, the Yugoslav Kingdom, and Greece. Other demographic divisions – between urban and rural populations, between regions, or, as in Albania, between tribal clans – also challenged national unification. Together, these starting points posed a greater challenge than those faced by any other region of Europe after the First World War.

Greece and Albania appear from Table 3.1 to be ethnically homogenous on the prewar Balkan pattern, each recording ethnic majorities of 92 percent. These official numbers are deceptive. The Greek percentage must be reduced below 90 percent by the undercounted Slav Macedonian minority that remained after the 1913 and 1920 exchanges of population with Bulgaria. To their 150,000 or more in the northwest must be added 200,000 Turks remaining in eastern Thrace. But the 1.4 million newly arrived Greek refugees from Anatolia and Bulgaria were over 20 percent of a total population that climbed to 6.2 million. The refugees were largely responsible for swelling the urban population from 27 to 33 percent by 1930. Albania's religious divisions were relatively straightforward – Catholics in the north, the Muslim majority in the center, and the Orthodox minority occupying the southern Adriatic coast and bordering Greece. More relevant to interwar Albanian politics were the larger number of tribal divisions, compounded by the distinction between the southern coastal Tosks and the northern upland Gegs who extended into Kosovo. The final Albanian borders with the Yugoslav Kingdom's Kosovo and similarly with Greece's northern Epirus still divided ethnic Albanians from traditional market towns on the other side of both borders.

Interwar Bulgaria contained a smaller but still predominant ethnic majority of 83 percent of its 4.8 million. The large Turkish minority of 11 percent posed no political problem across the interwar period. Included in

Map 3.1 Southeastern Europe, 1922–1939

Source: Adapted from Richard and Ben Crampton, *Atlas of Eastern Europe in the Twentieth Century* (London and New York: Routledge, 1996)

Territory lost by Russia

Territory lost by Austria-Hungary

Territory lost by Bulgaria

Territory regained by Turkey from Greece in 1923

– – – – – Previous borders

——·— New international boundaries

Table 3.1   Post-1920 ethnic and religious composition (%)

Country, year, and population	Ethnic composition		Religious composition	
Albania (1930)	Albanians	92.4	Muslims	70.0
1 million	Greeks	4.7	Orthodox	20.0
	Vlachs	0.9	Catholics	10.0
	Others	2.4		
Bulgaria (1920)	Bulgarian	83.4	Orthodox	83.3
4.85 million	Turkish	11.2	Muslim	14.3
	Greek	1.0	Jewish	0.9
	Jewish	0.8	Other	1.0
	Other	3.6		
Greece (1928)	Greeks	92.0	Orthodox	94.0
6.2 million	Turks	3.0	Muslim	4.0
	Macedonian Slavs	2.0	Jewish	1.0
	Jews	1.0	Other	1.0
	Other	2.0		
Romania (1920)	Romanian	72.0	Orthodox	72.6
15.6 million	Magyar	7.9	Uniate	7.9
	German	4.1	Catholic	6.8
	Jewish	4.0	Jewish	4.2
	Ukrainian	3.2	Calvinist	3.9
	Other	9.0	Other	4.6
Yugoslav Kingdom	Serbs	38.8	Orthodox	46.7
(1921) 12 million	Croats	23.8	Catholic	39.3
	Slovenes	8.5	Muslim	11.2
	Bosnian Muslims	6.1	Protestant	1.9
	Macedonian Slavs	4.9	Jewish	0.5
	Germans	4.2	Other	0.4
	Hungarians	3.9		
	Albanians	3.7		
	Other	5.0		

Sources: Richard and Ben Crampton, *An Atlas of Eastern Europe in the 20th Century* (London: Routledge, 1996) pp. 52, 117, 124; and Paul Robert Magocsi, *Historical Atlas of Central Europe* (Seattle, WA: University of Washington Press, 2002), pp. 166, 173.

the Bulgarian majority, however, was the large refugee influx that amounted to perhaps 5 percent of the total. Its designation as Bulgarian rather than ethnic Macedonian was less controversial inside the country, but its cross-border links with ethnic fellows in Vardar and Aegean Macedonia widened the political divisions between Bulgaria and its two neighbors throughout the decade. An ugly incident on the Aegean side in 1924 raised the brief prospect of a permanent international presence in such areas of mixed population, namely resident agents appointed by the League of Nations to enforce the Minorities Treaties discussed below. British support for Yugoslav and Greek objections quickly killed its addition to the existing agreement on population exchange. Internally, the refugees' autonomous control of southwestern Bulgaria challenged the national integration of the state. Their rural concentration kept the urban share of total population at 20 percent through the 1920s.

The two larger states were Romania, with 15.6 million, and the Kingdom of Serbs, Croats, and Slovenes, with 12 million. Here the new borders and ethnic minorities reflected in Map 3.1 and Table 3.1 raised problems that would persist until the Second World War made them worse. The peace settlements left such problems to the Treaties for Minority Protection demanded from all the East European states. All were duly signed, and a Minorities Committee set up by the League of Nations convened to address grievances. Yet little protection was in fact accorded. None of the bare 13 petitions that the Committee deemed worthy of legal action during the 1920s concerned Romania or the Yugoslav Kingdom, despite the fact that they were the objects of some 50 of the 300 grievances submitted during the 1920s.

For Romania, the ethnic majority had fallen from a prewar 90 percent to 72 percent. There would be little difficulty from the smaller minorities of Roma, Ukrainians, Serbs and Turks who combined in that order to account for 12 percent. The greatest objections came from a large Hungarian minority now separated from the small surviving Hungary, some just across the new border and more in eastern Transylvania. The League Committee received over thirty grievances filled on their behalf, ranging from loss of property and religious and educational rights to censorship and restricted movement. Joining the Hungarian 8 percent of the population was another 8 percent, equally divided between Saxon Germans and the Ashkenazim Jews who joined a slightly smaller number within the prewar borders. Both groups had formed Habsburg or Hungarian identities in Transylvania or the Bukovina to complement their own during the prewar period. Adding a Romanian identity would be difficult. The Jewish contingent from Bessarabia was less attached to a Russian identity but also more newly arrived from the Russian lands. Almost all of the Jews lived in towns, as they did in prewar Romania, Moldova in particular. Their concentration encouraged anti-Semitism in an overall urban population that the new territories increased from a prewar Romanian fraction of 15 percent to 22 percent.

For the Kingdom of Serbs, Croats, and Slovenes, there simply was no ethnic majority unless Serbs and Croats were counted together. Even then, the 74 percent of the 12 million recorded by the Belgrade government's census of 1921 as Serbs and Croats added Bosnian Muslims, Macedonians, and Montenegrins to reach that predominant percentage. When their likely numbers are subtracted, as in Table 3.1, the potential majority of the two largest ethnic groups falls to 62 percent. Their own division between 38 percent for the Serbs versus 24 percent for the Croats would persist at roughly that ratio through the history of both Yugoslavias. Further complicating their relations were the sizeable Serb populations that constituted a minority in historic Croatia–Slavonia and, until the 1970s, a plurality in Bosnia-Herzegovina. Neither Serbs nor Croats would come to terms with a coalition that subsumed their differences. Instead, their leaders would seek support from the Slovenes and Bosnian Muslims, each with 8 percent in 1921. The Serbs were successful in the interwar period, and the Croats in the last years of Communist Yugoslavia. The German and Hungarian minorities in the Vojvodina, each with 4 percent, posed no political problems during the 1920s. The Kosovar Albanian and ethnic Macedonian or Bulgarian minorities, also about 4 percent each of total population, found themselves politically powerless in what the new Yugoslav Kingdom called South Serbia. The Pašić interim government had successfully excluded them from the Kingdom's Minorities Treaty signed in 1919. British diplomats tacitly supported the assimilationist policies of successor regimes in Belgrade. Violent resistance from Kosovars seeking union with Albania or VMRO activists seeking Macedonian independence of union with Bulgaria only encouraged further repression from Serbian gendarmes or army troops.

Both Romania and the Yugoslav Kingdom faced the immediate issues of reconstructing industry, and establishing communications and a common currency across their large territories. Both Serbia and Romania had seen at least half of their prewar industrial facilities destroyed. Rail links from Transylvania and the Bukovina favored Hungary. Those from Bessarabia ran primarily to Russia and on broad-gauge track which had to be replaced. There were at least some tracks in place to Bucharest from east and west, in contrast to the virtual absence of rail links between Serbia, Croatia, and the Dalmatian coast. Important rail and also road connections remained to be built in both countries, some not until after the Second World War.[7]

The two regimes chose opposite strategies for replacing the Austro-Hungarian crowns of the defunct monarchy with their own existing currencies. In order to aid the advance of the large Bucharest banks into Transylvania and the Bukovina, crowns were exchanged for Romanian lei at the attractive rate of two for one. Croat and Slovene requests to the provisional Belgrade government for a similar rate for dinars were rebuffed. The Serbian side at least thought better of an initial offer of 10-1 but settled on 5-1, arguing that by 1919 this was the market rate for the remaining crowns in Vienna.[8] The large Croatian banks in Zagreb suffered accordingly, and the economic integration of the new kingdom was thereby off to a difficult start.

Land Reform, Trade Restriction, and Financial Transition

European trade relations and capital flows would never recapture their prewar levels before the Great Depression descended in 1929. Our region's largely agricultural economies struggled more than the industrialized majority of Europe to recover in the face of new international competition and markets reduced by war losses or new borders. The large Ottoman and Austro-Hungarian markets were now subdivided and reduced, to the disadvantage of all save Romania. But Romania even more than Bulgaria faced new competition from the United States and Canada. Their grain had entered the West European market during the war and did not leave when it ended. Depleted rolling stock and disrupted shipping lines made it difficult even to attempt reentry into the West European market during the early 1920s. Interregional trade remained small, about 9 percent of total turnover in 1929. In the absence of significant industrial production, the largely agricultural exports were too much the same from country to country to have expected a larger percentage.

The decade's urban and industrial growth did not reduce the 70–80 percent of the population dependent on agriculture anywhere by more than 2 percent. This high dependency on agricultural employment correlates almost exactly with the low levels of Gross Domestic Product (GDP) per capita, 20–30 percent of the British figure, that, by both measures, put Bulgaria, Romania, and the Yugoslav Kingdom at the bottom of 24 European countries ranked for 1929. With only 54 percent dependent on agriculture, Greece's GDP was 45 percent of the United Kingdom's level.[9] Table 3.2 records postwar indices for GDP, foreign trade, state budgets, and currency-note issue that were generally if not uniformly lower than prewar levels. These distinctions do not alter the overall picture of national economies whose reconfigured borders and reduced circumstances put any prospect of catching up with the more developed European economies out of the ques-

Table 3.2 Main economic indicators, 1911–30 (indices of real per capita values)

	Bulgaria	Greece	Romania	Yugoslav Kingdom
GDP (crop value) 1911 = 100				
1922	74 (66)	97 (73)	71 (72)	(71)*
1929	122 (91)	119 (80)	100 (88)	133 (106)
Exports/imports 1906–10 = 100				
1921–25	139/123	127/209	52/64	129/176*
1926–30	147/127	145/224	74/87	161/204
State budget expenditure (millions in constant for exchange)				
1911	46.5	67.2	65.6	40.7*
1920	35.7	194.6	48.6	88.4
1926–30	56.6	120.9	58.0	79.0
Currency notes issue (millions in constant foreign exchange)				
1911	25.4	59.4	62.5	40.7*
1920	59.2	174.3	68.6	88.4
1926–30	24.5	55.7	58.0	79.0
State debts (including war debts and reparations) 1911 = 100				
1920	548	307	179	140*
1930	129	126	135	103

Note: *Serbia only.

Sources: John R. Lampe and Marvin R. Jackson, *Balkan Economic History, 1550–1950: From Imperial Borderlands to Developing Nations* (Bloomington, IN: Indiana University Press, 1982), Table 10.5, pp. 338–40; Table 10.6, p. 343; Table 11.2, p. 384; Table 11.3, pp. 386–87.

tion. Little new foreign lending arrived during the 1920s. As for direct foreign investment, Romania had attracted barely $100 million by 1930, primarily to its oil fields, and the rest of the region combined only half that amount. At least the state debt that had risen sharply from prewar levels by 1920 because of war loans or, for Bulgaria, reparations then declined just as sharply during the rest of the decade.

The land reforms that redistributed large estates as smallholdings to individual peasant families were initially blamed for setting the recovery back even further. Yet the reforms varied too widely in their impact, especially beyond grain cultivation, for the old interwar notion of agricultural overpopulation on inefficiently small and primitive farms to apply as another Balkan pejorative. Only Albania, with surely the region's most backward agricultural practice, remained unreformed. Romania and the Yugoslav Kingdom reapportioned the largest amount of land, 6.5 and 2.5 million hectares respectively. These totals covered 20 and 17 percent of their agricultural land, as compared with only 6 percent for Bulgaria.[10] Most of the Bulgarian total came from state land, as only 5 percent of prewar holdings had exceeded even 50 hectares. Estates over 250 hectares were the target in Moldova and Transylvania, as were the "large estates," size undefined, in Croatia–Slavonia and the sharecropping properties of Muslim owners in Bosnia, Kosovo, and Vardar Macedonia.

The prewar distribution of Serbian land contained no more large holdings than did Bulgaria. The initial postwar plan of the Radical government to make Serb war veterans from the new territories the primary beneficiaries went ahead in Kosovo and Macedonia, but these controversial allocations accounted for less than 10 percent of the land distributed. The Greek government, with Western assistance as we shall see, carried out the largest proportional distribution. It was also the most consciously targeted, favoring the refugees from Asia Minor in the allocation of fully 40 percent of Greece's limited agricultural land. It came principally, and with little political difficulty, from the former Muslim sharecropping estates in Aegean Macedonia and Thrace. The smaller share taken from Slav Macedonians or Bulgarians did however add to political unrest.

The failure of the region's grain exports per capita to approach prewar levels has with justification been laid at the feet of the land reforms. But this single standard neglects the revival of domestic grain production and consumption across the region during the decade. Exports could also advance if other crops were substituted, especially for wheat where the American and Canadian advantage was greatest. Tobacco cultivation stepped into the breach for Bulgaria and Greece, jumping from single digits before the war to 38 and 55 percent of their respective export values for 1926–30. When tobacco prices slumped from 1926, Bulgarian smallholders switched to sugar beet and other industrial crops. As a result, real Bulgarian exports per capita were 47 percent higher in 1926–30 than in 1906–10. Greece's increase was 45 percent and the figure for the newly assembled territories of the Yugoslav Kingdom comparably high but hard to calculate. Grain- and oil-dependent Romania, with its 26 percent decline, was therefore an exceptional case.[11]

The region as a whole redirected its postwar trade from Western Europe and the former Ottoman Empire to Germany, Italy, and the Habsburg successor states. By 1926–30, this shift accounted for 80 percent of Yugoslav exports, and 60 percent of exports from Albania, Bulgaria, and Romania. For Greece, the one economy trading primarily with Britain and the wider world, the figure was still 40 percent. The new concentration on Central Europe, whose problems of postwar recovery were comparable, helped to advance the imposition of protective tariffs all around.[12]

The first wave of increased duties on agricultural as well as manufactured imports between 1924 and 1927 jumped Greek, Romanian, and Yugoslav rates past 40 percent ad valorem and made the Bulgarian rates even higher. They were triple the prewar rates for agricultural goods and quadruple those for manufactures. Then the drop in world agricultural prices in the late 1920s prompted another round of increases across the region, for foodstuffs in particular. Only the Greek economy may be judged to have benefited from agricultural protection. The sheltering of grain production and the heavy involvement of the refugees therein prompted a one-third increase in domestic cultivation and a corresponding drop in food imports. The food-deficit areas inland from the Yugoslav and Albanian coasts were not noticeably relieved, and the corn-dependent deprivation of the Wallachian and Moldovan peasant diet did not improve.

The aim of manufacturing tariffs across Central and Eastern Europe was, of course, to encourage the domestic industry that would attract low-cost agricultural labor and mobilize new investment. Greece's prewar industrial production did indeed triple in real terms, and that of Bulgaria quadrupled by 1929. This growth was however concentrated in too many small, unincorporated firms for Greece and from too small a base for Bulgaria for us to speak of an industrial transition. Manufacturing's share of net output reached only 8 percent for Bulgaria by 1929, as compared with 18 percent for Greece. Croatian and Slovene manufacturing accounted for the larger part of the Yugoslav Kingdom's 19 percent share, consolidating a politically unsettling advantage over Serbian enterprises more than half of whose plant and equipment had been destroyed during the war. Albanian industry made negligible progress from a minuscule prewar base. More damaging, given its precedence in state policy, was the failure of Romanian industry to build on what had been the region's largest prewar sector. By 1929 its manufacturing and oil extraction as well had barely been able to reach their prewar levels. Romania's industrial share in net output now fell just short of 18 percent, trailing both Greece and the Yugoslav Kingdom. Given a West and Central European advance in industrial production for 1920–9 that exceeded 40 percent everywhere but Britain and Germany, its far greater weight in those developed economies meant that our region's GDP probably lost ground by comparison.[13]

The Western liberal formula for gaining such ground in the course of postwar reconstruction probably did more harm than good. This was first a transition not to free trade but simply back to the convertible currencies of the prewar period, now backed by hard currency as well as gold reserves and fixed at stable rates of exchange. Although having depreciated to less than 10 percent of prewar parity, these rates were nonetheless "overvalued" (above likely free-market levels) in order to facilitate the repayment of war debts and reparations but also to attract direct Western investment. In the shorter run, Montagu Norman's aforementioned push for independent central banks sought to reduce state obligations for debt repayment and reparations, the same realistic process applied to Weimar Germany. For Bulgaria, Greece, and Romania, state debt per capita dropped sharply between 1920 and 1930, as noted in Table 3.2, to a real level only 29–35 percent more than before the war. But these reductions also established the same commitment to balanced state budgets that would cause all European governments such difficulty at the start of the Depression.

The League of Nations Financial Commission had started this campaign for independent central banks in 1921 by dispatching advisors to the Romanian National Bank. They could build on its established reputation for independence. Not until 1927, however, did the bank set a fixed rate for the leu free of inflationary pressures from the Brătianu government. The final stabilization, as noted earlier, did not take place for more than another year and then under the politically encouraged auspices of the Bank of France. An attendant state loan of $101 million arrived in 1929, just as the Depression descended. In the Yugoslav Kingdom, the former National Bank of Serbia became the new country's central bank. The Finance Minister from 1922 to 1925, Milan Stojadinović, supported its independence and welcomed British advisors. Trained in London himself, he backed the liberal priority of fixing a stable international rate of exchange for the dinar. Committed to financial orthodoxy, he imposed the rate to prevent the currency's inflationary depreciation even without the budgetary support of a League loan.

The tougher tests were in Bulgaria and Greece, where League loans were needed in both cases.[14] The Bulgarian National Bank's stabilization of the lev in 1924 still left it with large state debts unpaid and under pressure to provide more for an unbalanced state budget. Only a League Stabilization Loan of $22 million in 1928 made it possible to wipe out those debts and repair reserves which had become dangerously undercapitalized. To assure continued independence, an advisor was posted from the Financial Commission to the bank. For Greece, the long-predominant position of the National Bank of Greece, as a commercial and investment bank as well as the bank of issue, posed the problem. Its close ties to the Liberal Party helped to fend off the Financial Commission's demands for a separate central bank until 1928. Then the desperate need for a new refugee loan in 1928 combined with the Western offer of further support to launch a separate Bank of Greece as the bank of issue and lender of last resort only.

There were, however, minimal gains during the late 1920s from the state's much-reduced budget deficits and from note issue that was half the per capita levels of 1920, as recorded in Table 3.2. New state loans on the prewar pattern were not forthcoming from London and less so from New York, the new center of the Western capital market. Direct foreign investment also remained minimal.

Western banks combining commercial lending and stock investment on the German pattern arrived as a major new presence only in Sofia. Some five banks, variously French, Italian, and Belgian, did in fact provide the largest part of the credit and investment that allowed Bulgarian industry to record significant growth during the decade. In response to this competition, the Bulgarian National Bank used its new independence in 1929 to underwrite a rash of commercial loans that soon became bad private debts. Central European capital also found its way into the same sort of universal banks in Zagreb, allowing them to do business without recourse to the kingdom's central bank in Belgrade throughout the decade. Their initiatives in industrial investment were matched in Bucharest not by the French and Italian banks but by the domestic Jewish-owned Bancă Marmarosch-Blanc and the Liberal regime's Bancă Românească. Their rivalry eventually forced the latter's dangerously low liquidity on the former.[15] Only the small Albanian central bank established in Rome in 1925 could proceed ahead with inflationary note issue for a state budget severely in deficit, and only in return for almost complete Italian control.

Central Governments versus Political Pluralism

The postwar political transition received less attention from the presumed Western guardians of the League's liberal principles than had the economic standards. The region's reconfigured states faced domestic divisions with only sporadic international support for political pluralism. The chances for a democratic electoral process to emerge, for royal and military influence to recede, or for the civilian political elite to abjure the abuse of executive power seemed slim indeed. Only hostile neighbors raised the prospect of some higher national consciousness. Foreign threats also heightened the appeal of charismatic political leaders who could appeal for special powers to defend the nation. Such charisma, as argued by George Mavrogordatos for Greece, could perpetuate the right of the ruling party to appoint a clientelist network to official positions and to emphasize cleavage from the opposition.[16] Clientelism and cleavage, based on ethnic or regional rather than class distinctions, surely characterized the post-1918 ruling parties. But charisma of the sort that helped bring Mussolini and Hitler to power in Italy and Germany would be harder to create or sustain in these states. In addition, competing party organizations and newspapers spread the practice of mass politics sufficiently to open the recurring elections to some genuinely democratic outcomes by the end of the decade.

The only surviving leader with charismatic appeal before a mass crowd was Greece's Eleftherios Venizelos. Assassinations had claimed the two magnetic agrarian populists, Bulgaria's Aleksandar Stamboliiski in 1923 and the Croatian Stjepan Radić in 1928. Radić's Serbian rival, the venerated if uncharismatic Nikola Pašić, had died a natural death in 1926. So did the artful Romanian Prime Minister Ionel Brătianu and the respected King Ferdinand in 1927. The relatively young monarchs, King Boris of Bulgaria and Aleksandar of the Yugoslav Kingdom, respectively 37 and 33 in 1921, were building up public personas but lacked effective powers beyond foreign affairs.

Albania as a Balkan Exception

Perhaps the most unconstrained and yet the most insecure monarch on a regional throne by the end of the decade was also the newest. Ahmed Zogolli, now shortened his name to Zogu on becoming President of Albania in 1925. He then forced through his coronation as King Zog by 1928. His decade of advance and survival began with Zogolli's return from Habsburg house arrest in 1919. He arrived to assume the position of Interior Minister by 1920 (see Chapter 2). Under the constitution's French framework, he appointed the chief administrative authorities, or prefects, in each of the ten prefectures into which the state was divided. More important at the start, he pulled together a force of 4000 Albanian irregulars who pressed the disaffected Italian troops that remained, perhaps 15,000, into evacuating entirely. Zogu also formed an alliance with the Belgrade government that secured its assistance to keep the Italians from returning. In return, he forced the Kosova Committee and its leaders, Hasan Prishtina and Bajram Curri, out of the loose People's Party and out of Tirana. Curri would return in January 1924 and lend his support to replacing Zogu with the brief unhappy regime of Bishop Fan S. Noli.

The emigré Orthodox Bishop Noli had represented Albania as its Foreign Minister at the initial League of Nations meeting in 1921. Soon concluding that he could not work with Zogu, he resigned and moved to Rome. By June 1924 he led a disparate opposition to power. Its Kosovar militants obliged Zogu to leave for Belgrade. Noli promised to provide the loan for food relief and infrastructure from the League of Nations that had been refused Zogu. He also promised land reform to a peasant majority still bound to share-cropping obligations owed to native beys who survived from the Ottoman regime. Had Noli been able to obtain the League loan, instead of some vague Soviet promises, or to launch the land reform, his regime might have survived longer than the last six months of 1924.[17] Zogu seized on those failures. He mobilized the assistance of his Mati tribe and northern Catholic support. Paramilitary intervention from General Wrangel's White Russian emigrés, again courtesy of Belgrade, also helped to force Noli to flee. Curri was hunted down and killed.

Zogu quickly recalled his supporters from the Constituent Assembly of 1923. They pushed through his election as President of what now became a republic, with executive powers concentrated in his hands. These unseparated powers allowed him to appoint not only cabinet members but also the judiciary and a majority of the bicameral senate. Sole rights to initiate budgetary measures or constitutional changes, plus veto power over any measure passed by the continuing constituent assembly, completed the list. Impressed by the respect he saw for Habsburg royal authority in wartime Vienna, Zogu declared himself King Zog in 1928. The assembly dutifully amended the constitution for one last time. It abolished the Senate and left the new King with full powers to introduce or veto legislation. He now monitored membership in the sham parliament.[18]

By 1925–6, however, Zogu was nonetheless obliged to come to terms with Italian predominance. For economic survival, this was surely unavoidable. The Albanian national bank empowered to issue paper currency was, after all, established in Rome in 1925. Direct Italian payment to Zogu for army salaries trumped a British offer to found the bank and secured Rome's controlling interest. Its directors, three of five of whom were Italian, were given the commanding authority to issue all contracts for public works. Italian funding for the construction of desperately needed infrastructure soon arrived in the form of a loan that Albania had otherwise been unable to obtain. In 1926 Mussolini's government created a new Agency for the Support of the Economy of Albania (SVEA) to administer the 50 million gold francs now provided, albeit at a high rate of interest. The resulting construction of roads, bridges, and harbors, plus a rail line from Tirana to the coast, all served to advance Italian commercial penetration. Land reclamation to relieve the grain deficit was promised but then neglected.[19] Imports twice the value of exports, half of both with Italy, sustained the population.

Despite the secret military pact and then the formal treaty that Zogu was obliged to sign with Italy, also in 1926, his regime nonetheless preserved considerable internal autonomy. Some Italian restraint must of course be acknowledged. But, more important, as President and then King Zog he drew on independent British assistance to establish his own trained and disciplined gendarmerie. This force rather than the less reliable army prevented the establishment of paramilitary bands that could challenge his authority. Colonel W. R. Stirling, late of Lawrence of Arabia's wartime contingent, became the Inspector General for Zogu's fledgling gendarmerie in 1923. In 1926 another former British officer took over and remained in the position until 1938. His small staff succeeded in training a force of several thousand who made commercial travel safe and were sufficiently disciplined to earn respect across tribal lines. The army also continued to grow, reaching 8000 men. Together with the gendarmerie, it took nearly half of the state budget by 1929–30. The arrival of 50 Italian officers and much equipment from 1927 did not, however, create the political leverage over Zogu that was anticipated. He continued to trust the gendarmerie and to suspect a regular, Italian-style army of the sort that he and his irregulars had expelled, albeit with little prolonged combat, in 1919.[20]

What remained in the isolated capital of Tirana, so designated by Zogu in 1925 for inland security close to his tribal base, was a central government that survived despite as well as because of its economic and diplomatic dependence on Italy. Roughly 90 percent of the population remained rural and illiterate. In the upland majority of the country, the state's presence was weak overall, but police powers were sufficient to prevent any semblance of separate political organization. In the towns, the ruler's staying power seemed to represent the national interest, and Zog was able to cultivate a certain charisma as King. After 1930, as we shall see in Chapter 4, Zog's royal dictatorship attempted to close some of the gaps that still set his country apart from the rest of the region. Even then, the political contests waged elsewhere in Southeastern Europe over economic policy and over national identity did not arise in interwar Albania.

Bulgaria, Greece, and the Refugee Challenge

Southeastern Europe witnessed two radical attempts at broader political representation during the decade. One was Bulgaria's Agrarian Party regime and the other was Greece's rejection of the monarchy in favor of a republic. Declared a year after a coup had assassinated Stamboliisksi and driven the Agrarian regime from power in 1923, the Republic of Greece would endure until the monarchy's return in 1936. The republic lasted in large measure because of support from the huge refugee influx with which both countries had to deal. The smaller number of Bulgarian refugees were on the other hand instrumental in overthrowing the Stamboliiski regime. Thereafter they formed the main resistance to the centralization of executive power that the Agrarian initiatives had advanced and their successors only continued. The refugees, dispossessed and insecure by definition, also played central roles in the evolution of small Communist parties in both states, and in Greek pressures on the remaining ethnic minorities. Such domestic intimidation defied the Minorities Treaties that the peace treaties and the League of Nations had obliged their governments to sign.

Stamboliiski's electoral mandate was never overwhelming, and his populist rhetoric sounded threatening to urban ears. He faced opposition from the Communists on one side and a combination of the old parties, the army high command, and the Macedonian VMRO refugees on the other. His Agrarian Union (BZNS) had, as we saw in Chapter 2, won the barest of majorities in the 1920 elections to the National Assembly. They now fell short of one in the local elections of 1922. The old parties pointed to the inexperience of many Agrarian appointees, and the corrupt gains of some, in a state bureaucracy that still continued to grow. Pet proposals such as obliging urban professionals to help with the harvest and barring lawyers from marrying peasant girls further soured his standing. Generals chaffed under Stamboliiski's appointment of a civilian War Minister. Some 6500 officers resigned their commissions and formed a separate Military League. This left the army's strength under even the maximum of 20,000 prescribed by the peace treaty. By 1921 the regime's new Compulsory Labor Force had drafted almost twice that number for a year's service in building public works. Stamboliiski's defiance of the treaty's demands for reparations won some wider support. Yet the equally defiant new Grain Consortium, formed under the existing state banks to raise and fix export prices, also distressed private Bulgarian traders. By 1921 the Inter-Allied Reparations Commission had forced both some initial payment of reparations and the disbanding of the Consortium.

Other, more positive Agrarian initiatives went forward. They expanded the party's network of agricultural cooperatives by one half. Educational reforms created new faculties of Agriculture, Veterinary Science, and Medicine at Sofia University and established primary schools in many cooperatives. Finally, there was land reform. The regime intended it to provide refugees as well as some 100,000 landless or dwarf holders with the "labor property" by which Stamboliiski wished to level the already egalitarian distribution of arable land. Yet the state's land fund confiscated only one-third of the acreage projected from larger holdings by 1923. And, like other agencies of the Agrarian regime, the fund operated outside the control of the National Assembly and officials from the established ministerial bureaucracy.

The old parties railed against the explicit demand for "the unity of state power." Here was an unfortunate populist precedent for Communist rule following the Second World War. In September 1922 the parties' new Constitutional Bloc attempted to hold a convention in Turnovo, but the Agrarians' Orange Guards either stopped the delegates' trains from arriving or roughed up and humiliated those who got through. The ruling party then secured a bare absolute majority (53 percent) in the April 1923 elections to the *Subranie*. But by abolishing proportional representation, the Agrarians took 212 of 245 seats. For Stamboliiski's populist ideology of a ruling peasant estate, this huge majority appropriately reflected the rural share of Bulgaria's population.[21] Confident of that peasant majority's support, he rejected the advice of moderates who now left his government.

The Agrarian regime faced violent overthrow less than two months later. Centralizing state authority in their party and allowing the abuses of the Orange Guards mobilized members of the prewar parties. The dismissal in May of that year of several generals from the high command, together with the regime's order making several Macedonian organizations illegal, brought the army and the irredentist refugees into the opposition. Both carried firearms rather than the wooden clubs of the Orange Guards. The VMRO leadership was already incensed over the treaty that Stamboliiski had sought out and signed with the Yugoslav Kingdom at Niš in March. It recognized the new border with Vardar Macedonia and committed Bulgaria to end its repeated crossings by irredentist bands of refugees. As it came into effect in May, Stamboliiski had threatened the town and other areas that had supposedly supported the Central Powers during the war with paying all of the country's reparations if they objected.

Little wonder that his Macedonian assassins reportedly cut off the hand that had signed the hated treaty before killing him in June. The Bulgarian Communists stood by but were soon obliged by an indignant Comintern to show that they would now be able to take power after the overthrow of the "reactionary smallholders" they so disdained. An arbitrary new regime from the old guard headed by Sofia University Rector Aleksandar Tsankov had already taken power. It used the army and gendarmerie brutally to suppress the BKP's hasty September uprising in just a few days.

The Communist effort to play the Macedonian card against the new regime also failed. The irredentist leadership of the VMRO rejected separate status from Bulgaria for Vardar and some of Aegean Macedonia in the Balkan Communist Federation that the region's parties endorsed at Comintern urging in March 1924. In a failed attempt to assassinate Tsar Boris, BKP militants carried out the deadly terrorist bombing of the Sveta Nedelya Cathedral in April 1925. The blast killed 160 people, mostly leading officials attending the funeral of an assassinated general from the Military League. The aftermath brought a new wave of repression down on the party as a whole. This White Terror was the last step in pushing the leaders and middle membership of the largest Balkan Communist party into Soviet emigration.[22] More were killed than in September 1923, pushing the total toward 5000. VMRO assassinations accounted for some of these numbers.

The subsequent regime nonetheless retreated from these dictatorial origins and allowed multiparty politics to reemerge. It ruled from 1926 to 1931 and then accepted election results that returned its opposition to power in a coalition which even included an Agrarian faction. Bulgarian Communist historiography went little farther than soul-searching over the fiasco of the September uprising and charges of monarcho-Fascism against all successors from the 1923–6 regime of Aleksandar Tsankov forward. True, the young Tsar Boris had stood by while the army played its part in overthrowing Stamboliiski and took the lead in suppressing the Communist uprising of 1923. But he soon joined a number of generals in objecting that Tsankov's Democratic Alliance of old parties, initially legitimized by elections held under restrictive provisions for national defense in December 1923, was making the international image of defeated Bulgaria even worse. The uncharismatic Tsankov himself mobilized no personal political support, either for the semi-fascist ideas that he would openly advocate in the 1930s nor for the economic ideology of centralized state control he favored during the First World War. British backing in 1926 for a badly needed League of Nations loan for refugee resettlement was conditional on his departure from office. The ruling coalition promptly replaced him with Andrei Liapchev, a former Macedonian Supremist but now a moderating influence.

Now, as well, the Agrarians' economic program that Tsankov had grudgingly allowed to continue could go ahead with genuine support. Liapchev, as noted in Chapter 2, was a lifelong advocate of the cooperative movement and the cooperative bank. The land reform presumably cut short in 1923 actually redistributed more land in the late 1920s than under Stamboliiski. A tobacco consortium had stayed in place after the Reparations Commission had disallowed the grain consortium. It took on greater importance when international tobacco prices tumbled in 1926. The Compulsory Labor Service still assembled its annual force of 20,000 or more. Only the financial transition, as noted in the previous section, went well beyond what the Agrarians had proposed.

Political pluralism advanced under the Liapchev regime but not to the advantage of representative government. The advance followed the parliamentary pattern of interwar France. Disputes within the ruling coalition resisted resolution and instead encouraged new divisions. The Democratic Alliance counted some 19 groups by the 1927 elections, barely coming together to win just 39 percent of the votes. In the continued absence of proportional representation, they received 167 of 273 seats. Despite village intimidation by officials bound to the Alliance, the largely Agrarian Iron Bloc won 22 percent of the vote for 56 seats, the next largest grouping. Even the Bulgarian Communist Party, formally illegal since 1924, was able to put forward a shadow Bulgarian Workers Party and capture 2 percent of the vote. The Agrarians were, however, divided among themselves. And VMRO irredentists in the southwest simply appointed their own parliamentary representatives. In the Balkan tradition of the late Ottoman period, they used paramilitary authority to administer their own region.

All of this ironically strengthened the Sofia ministries. They were able to proceed with their central administration of the country's other provinces and districts against an increasingly fractured political spectrum. The high salaries and other benefits attached to these positions remained the most attractive available to the growing number of university graduates. Unsurprisingly, the 87,000 state employees in Bulgaria by the end of the decade represented one of the highest ratios, 17 per 1000, to total population in Europe. The aforementioned mandate to reduce those numbers from the League of Nations financial advisor to the Bulgarian National Bank from 1928 had little effect.[23]

The Liapchev regime's control of this large state apparatus is rightly faulted for sympathies that left the VMRO's paramilitary enclave outside central control. But there were positive features as well. The regime's representatives negotiated the abovementioned League loan of 1926 that allowed the construction of refugee housing elsewhere in Bulgaria. The resulting transfer reduced the refugee population of the southwestern enclave by one-third. By the late 1920s the regime had already allowed a free press to reappear and reigned in arbitrary police procedures. In 1931 it accepted first a new system of proportional representation and then electoral defeat at the hands of a newly formed National Bloc. The old Democrats joined with the accomodationist wing of the Agrarians and a new Liberal group to win for the Bloc what amounted to a two-coalition contest. Its 590,000 votes translated into 152 seats, versus 417,00 votes and 78 seats for Liapchev's Democratic Alliance. The coalition's high hopes and ultimate displacement by a military coup in 1934 awaits the next chapter. Yet with the Depression already under way, Bulgaria's genuinely democratic election displaced a ruling government after a decade whose early confrontations had promised little pluralism.

The Greek elections of 1923, 1926 and 1928 frame an equally uncertain start toward an eventually promising political process. Unlike Bulgaria's experience with a charismatic leader of a radical party, cut short by a coup d'état in 1923, Greece's post-Anatolian decade would revolve around the charismatic leader of a so-called Liberal Party. His party's election victory in 1928 and the full four-year term he then served as Prime Minister marked the high point of the still-flawed practice of open politics in interwar Greece.

Eleftherios Venizelos was nearly 60 in 1923 when King Constantine's abdication after the defeat in Anatolia opened the way for his Liberals, the largest party since the last prewar years, to return to power. The King's supporters and other anti-Venizelists had abstained from the parliamentary elections of December 1923. The Liberals and the more radical Republican Union swept up all but 27 of 397 seats. Venizelos returned from his latest exile to become Prime Minister in January 1924. Less than three weeks later he left again, distressed to find that his unchallenged Liberals were divided into factions who could agree on little more than the plebiscite that made Greece a republic. Over the next year and a half, those factions struggled with each other and against increasing interference from the Venezelist army generals to form six short-lived governments.

Then, in June 1925, the architect of the trial and execution of the six ministers from the Asia Minor catastrophe, General Theodoros Pangalos, took power in a military coup. He obliged the parliament to elect him President of the Republic. His domestic puritanism and foreign overreach neatly presaged the Colonels' regime of 1967–74 (see Chapter 7). Regulating the length of women's skirts proved less difficult than challenging the borders set down by the final peace settlement. In October 1925 an exchange of shots across the frontier with Bulgaria killed a couple of Greek border guards. Pangalos rushed enough troops forward to press several miles into Bulgarian territory on a broad front. Britain took the lead in bringing the full weight of the League to bear on the one international dispute that it would success-fully resolve during its lifetime.[24] Greece was obliged to withdraw its troops and pay Bulgaria compensation. Pangalos's nationalist pretensions suffered accordingly. His own military guard joined in forcing him out after barely one year in power.

The road for Venizelos to return opened yet again with the parliamen-tary elections of November 1926. They were the first of several interwar elec-tions to be based on proportional representation for voting strictly by party lists. Here, as often in interwar France, the results produced a stalemate. The anti-Venezelist People's Party and Metaxas's new Free Opinion Party won virtually the same share of seats – 38 percent – as the Liberals. Only the last-minute payment of overdue agricultural compensation to refugee interests saved this crucial segment of Liberal support from going over to the Metaxas party. The small Greek Communist Party made its first inroads with the urban refugees. It won 10 seats despite the suspicion, always hanging over the Greek party, that it would support a separate Macedonian state in the Balkan Federation proposed by the regional Communist congresses from 1924 forward. Moderates in the two major parties, the Liberals of Venizelos and his opponents' People's Party, now tried to overcome the long-standing National Schism and agreed to form an Ecumenical Cabinet. They managed to craft agreement on a constitution for the republic and accepted the return of at least some anti-Venezelist army officers to duty. But the new cabinet could go no further. It bore the burden of economic austerity imposed to stabilize the drachma and open the way to a Western loan badly needed for refugee resettlement.

Venizelos came back again from exile in April 1928. Already appointed Prime Minister by the current parliament, he led his now-reunited Liberal Party to a sweeping victory in the August elections. Adding to the advan-tage that control of the Interior Ministry and local police afforded such an incumbent was the return from proportional representation to individual seats decided by winner-take-all majorities. Districts were purposely made wider in the north, thereby increasing the rural refugees' weight. The Liberals alone took 47 percent of the vote and 178 of the 250 seats in the Chamber, while their allies added another 48 seats. Their progress as an organized mass party deserves some credit for this victory, along with the continuing appeal of Venizelos to the refugees in particular. He still had the ability to stir a large crowd with his speeches and to use press coverage to spread his inspirational exhortations still further. We should also acknowl-edge the continuing absence of any coherent ideology, liberal, populist, or otherwise. Venizelos himself had tried and failed from 1928 forward to prompt the rest of the leadership to draft a written constitution for the party. None of the three drafts was ever approved, evidence for the seminal study of Greece's interwar politics that the party had relied too much on the charismatic but also quixotic leadership of Venizelos.[25]

Much was accomplished all the same during the full four-year term which ended, as in Bulgaria, with an election sufficiently open for the government to lose it. As noted in the previous section, Greek industry had grown rapidly and the financial system was restructured to include a separate and independent central bank. The Liberal regime also constructed twice as many primary schools during these four years as in the previous hundred. Instruction in the demotic language familiar to the refugees helped to spread its ascendancy over the Byzantine *katharevousa* that the southern elite had imposed on secondary and university education from the nineteenth century forward. The many new schools in Aegean Macedonia and Thrace nonetheless struggled to find trained teachers.

Quicker results for the refugees came from the creation of an agricultural bank in 1929 and the continued spread of agricultural cooperatives. These initiatives allowed the Refugee Settlement Commission, the major Western program for continuing assistance across the region, to conclude its operations in 1930 and pass them on to a domestic framework that would have continued to evolve constructively had the Great Depression not intervened. The League loan of 1924 had allowed the Commission, created the year before under American, British, and Greek management, to construct housing for fully half of the refugees by 1926. The subsequent League loan of 1927, joined by Greek budgetary resources and an internal loan, provided the resources to finish the job, at least in the rural north. The commission expended a total of $230 million and employed some 1500, largely refugees, to dwarf the other Western loans and programs in the region during the decade.[26]

The refugees' political loyalty to Venizelos fell significantly following his 1930 negotiation for a final settlement of wartime claims with the Turkish government. The Ankara Agreement provided only limited compensation, even for the families who had fled for their lives from Smyrna. Venizelos's monarchist opponents in the south and the small Greek Communist Party based in the north benefited accordingly. Beyond the domestic political price, however, the agreement marked a general improvement in inter-Balkan relations to which Greece's rapprochement with Bulgaria also contributed.

Romania, the Kingdom of Serbs, Croats, and Slovenes, and the Ethnic Challenge

The national governments in Bucharest and Belgrade faced a different challenge to broader political representation during the century's first postwar decade. Both responded with confidence that came from wartime membership in the winners' circle. They were nonetheless reluctant to undertake any radical change from the prewar patterns of the smaller and far more ethnically compact Romanian and Serbian Kingdoms. Both constitutions, ratified in 1923 and 1921 respectively, maintained the pattern of winner-take-all elections conducted by the party in power. Even a plurality of the vote thereby provided a large parliamentary majority. Central control over local government continued through the French system of prefects appointed from the Interior Ministry for a large set of small districts. How the ethnic minorities and new territories could be represented, accommodated, or suppressed within new borders proved problems even more difficult to address than the accommodation of refugees facing Bulgaria and Greece. The same multiparty coalitions or mergers familiar to West European politics would struggle to provide wider representation.

Romania's National Liberal Party made the clearest effort on behalf of an explicitly integrationist and assimilationist ideology in the region. Its hold on power from 1923 to 1927 did not, however, prevent a coalition led by representatives of the new territories, although not including the ethnic minorities, from winning a parliamentary election in 1928. The Liberals had initially ignored the peasant and regional parties, despite the fact that their membership had risen with the universal male suffrage that replaced the restricted prewar franchise. This neglect had already cost them the election of 1919. The winning Parliamentary Bloc then quickly foundered. The Bloc's coalition was too loose to carry through the decentralizing reforms it proposed against the combined opposition of King Ferdinand, the army and the Liberal elite of Bucharest.

The return of Ionel Brătianu from the Paris peace conference quickly reestablished his longtime party leadership. Citing the Bloc's radical agenda as noted above, he persuaded King Ferdinand to appoint the wartime hero General Averescu as Prime Minister. Averescu struggled to introduce new taxes for financing reconstruction and also to implement the much-anticipated land reform. These difficulties soon undercut the general's personal popularity. He also offended the largely Romanian representatives of Transylvania, Bessarabia, and the Bukovina by abolishing the separate Directing Councils. Each of them had voted to enter the enlarged state with the promise that their regional councils would continue. The prewar network of counties (*judeţ*), were simply expanded to 76. Locally elected general councils were to provide assistance to the government-appointed prefects. Yet these bodies had little independent influence, their own election included, during the National Liberal regime that followed. Its local government law of 1925 allowed the Interior Ministry to dismiss the local councils or local mayors and even to dissolve the county itself.[27]

By January 1923 King Ferdinand had used his continuing power to appoint a new government and again made Brătianu the Prime Minister. Brătianu used that authority generously. His prefects and their local police ensured a sweeping victory in the parliamentary elections two months later. The Liberals won 222 of 369 seats in what now became a constituent assembly. The constitution that it duly drafted and ratified by March 1923 confirmed the King's continuing authority and the Prime Minister's executive powers. Both restricted the mass politics promised by universal male suffrage and the initiatives promised to the bicameral legislature, a Chamber of Deputies and a Senate. Article 1 proclaimed Romania to be a "unified and indivisible national state." At least it spoke of the population as individual citizens rather than ethnic Romanians.

This last stipulation presumably ended the long struggle over citizenship for a Jewish population that more than doubled within the new borders. Brătianu himself had resisted Western pressures at the Paris peace conference and in the League's subsequent Minorities Treaty for Romania to provide blanket citizenship to its Jews. There were over 700,000 in all, one-quarter of them in newly acquired Bessarabia. Some 80,000 would remain unnaturalized even after legislation was finally passed to afford individual citizenship. The treaty did frustrate the demands of student nationalists and the Moldovan League for National Christian Defense (LANC) for a *numerus clausus* like Hungary's. It would have limited Jewish university enrollment to the share of population, or about one-third of the 14 percent then attending. (The fascist Legion of the Archangel Michael was formed by radical students who broke with the LANC in 1927, but became important for Romanian politics in the l930s. It will be addressed in Chapter 4, as will the evolution of the small Romanian Communist Party, illegal from 1924 and finally freed from its support for returning Bessarabia to the Soviet Union in 1935). Legal recourse against the local denial of citizens' rights was available to minorities only through claims for individual rights, and then before judges whose advancement would depend on approval by the thoroughly Romanian ruling party. And, as we have seen, the League of Nations had failed to act on any of the numerous grievances from Romania's Hungarian minority laid before its Minorities Committee. More broadly, a fledgling constitutional court could set no precedents for future legislation but rule only on individual laws. It overruled just nine such laws as unconstitutional during the decade.[28]

This framework left the National Liberals free to press ahead with a variety of state-centered initiatives to promote industrial development "through ourselves alone" (*prin noi înşine*). Little came of the effort to repair and expand state railways or to transform state monopoly enterprises such as tobacco processing into commercially viable activities. More important was the 1924 Law of Mines. It made mandatory Romanian majority ownership of stock and two-thirds representation on Boards of Directors, measures aimed directly at the Western oil companies that continued to extract the bulk of petroleum from state lands. Their position had already been weakened by nationalization of the largest prewar enterprise, the former Austro-Hungarian and German Steaua Română. Only the American Standard Oil concession pressed for an exemption and failed. The US State Department turned down its request for the desired American government concession on Romania's debt owed primarily from the food relief of 1919. The others, except for Anglo-Dutch Shell, complied but then restricted further investment.[29] In the meantime, however, the state's Steaua Română found that it could not proceed without new Western funding of its own.

The centralization of primary and secondary education went ahead but with other limitations. Transylvania was the scene of the principal transition, from the heavily Hungarian prewar system to one that taught Romanian language and history in order to create, according to the Liberals' Education Minister, "a cultural cordon." The number of new schools built there surpassed the prewar total for all of Romania. Lycée libraries were emptied of predominantly Hungarian books and replaced with Romanian volumes. Of greatest interest to the Ministry in Bucharest were the Romanian rural peasantry, still largely illiterate, and the Szekler Hungarians. The latter had migrated to their eastern concentrations, far from the new borders with Hungary, in the fourteenth century. Surely these were "hidden Romanians," just as the ethnic Macedonians were "hidden Serbs." By late 1922 the Liberal Ministry had dissolved the separate Directorate of Education in Cluj. Thereafter the construction of new schools in the Szekler region proceeded apace. But few Romanian teachers could be found to replace the old ones. They continued to teach in Hungarian. The non-Szekler Hungarians in the western border areas attended the primary and secondary schools in Hungarian as guaranteed by the Minorities Treaty. The previously Hungarian university at Cluj was however nationalized. Hungary's refusal to recognize its degrees, typical of Budapest's uniform rejection of the Trianon settlement, allowed the Romanian side to reciprocate.[30] None of this was advancing the ethnic or regional reconciliation that would have been needed to create an integrated society or economy.

The postwar decade all the same concluded with elections that Keith Hitchins has called "the most democratic in Romanian history."[31] They were won by the Liberals' major opponents, the National Peasant Party, which thereupon launched a promising set of political and economic reforms. The winning side in the parliamentary elections of December 1928 took shape two years earlier. It was then that the Transylvanian National Party and the Wallachian–Moldavian Peasant Party reached long-discussed agreement on merging into a single National Peasant Party. Recall that the demise of the Conservatives for their support of the Central Powers in the war had left the Liberals with no comparably large rival. The Nationals' leader, Iuliu Maniu, had been an early advocate of moving beyond regional representation. The Peasant Party had been founded in 1918 under the leadership of a rural schoolteacher, Ion Mihalache. It promoted the cooperative movement in terms similar to Stamboliiski's Agrarians but soon sought to reach out beyond a peasant constituency. Shocked by Ferdinand's decision to ignore them as separate parties, the two finally combined to form a second-party alternative to the Liberals in 1926. That year the King had turned back to General Averescu and his small People's Party in order to replace a Liberal regime that had grown unpopular in the absence of a mass base. By 1927 Ferdinand was asking Brătianu to return as Prime Minister, but within a few months both died of natural causes. A regency succeeded Ferdinand, a decree of 1925 having barred his playboy son Carol from the throne for having left the country and his wife, a Greek royal princess. It appointed Brătianu's brother, Vintilă, as Prime Minister, but he lacked Ion's political skills.

The Regency finally approached Maniu. He used their mandate to appoint new prefects prior to the 1928 election but otherwise restricted press censorship and police interference. The new joint party won 78 percent of the popular vote and 348 of 387 Chamber seats. In 1929 its regime made promising political and economic starts. The 76 *judeţ* were overlaid with seven regions, one each for Transylvania, the Banat, Bessarabia, the Bukovina and Moldova, with two for Wallachia. All seven now enjoyed their own elected administrative councils and separate budgets. Maniu hoped that greater minority as well as regional representation would follow. He lifted the press censorship that the Hungarian border towns of Transylvania had faced throughout the decade. The Law of Mines was revised in 1930 and other measures restricting foreign investment were removed. Protective tariffs for domestic industry remained in place. Then the Great Depression and the return of Carol to claim his throne in 1930 cut short prospects for these genuinely liberal reforms.

The prospects for political pluralism did not finish the decade with such promise in the Kingdom of Serbs, Croats, and Slovenes. Its dramatic conclusion is well known. First, a Montenegrin deputy shot the effusive, populist leader of the Croatian Peasant Party (HSS), Stjepan Radić, in the

Belgrade parliament in July 1928. He died of his wounds a few weeks later in Zagreb. Neither the HSS deputies nor the party representing Croatian and Bosnian Serbs could be persuaded that the largest single party, Serbia's Radicals, had not been somehow responsible. They refused to return to Belgrade. As the rump remainder struggled among themselves, King Aleksandar and his army advisors intervened. In the first week of the new year, the King dissolved not only the parliament but all "ethnically based" political parties. In the absence of any parties that did not fit that description, the new Kingdom of Yugoslavia entered the world in 1929 as a royal dictatorship.

Why had multiparty politics failed to find the balance that had produced constructive results, albeit short-lived, in Greece and Romania in 1928 and in Bulgaria by 1931? Indicting Serbian hegemony is a necessary but not a sufficient answer.[32] A Serb plurality became the majority needed to ratify the 1921 Constitution. That was because the Croatian delegates from Radić's Peasant Party, as noted in Chapter 2, and the smaller Communist contingent had abstained. Its provisions centralized power in the national ministries and 33 administrative districts under prefects appointed from Belgrade. The requirement that they have 15 years of previous government service favored experience in the prewar Serbian state. Serbs made up some 60 percent of the huge Ministry of Internal Affairs, itself over half a state bureaucracy of 172,000 that was proportionally even larger than that of Bulgaria. The army's 6000 officers were overwhelmingly Serbs by the late 1920s, as most of the 2500 initially taken from the former Austro-Hungarian military resigned or retired.

Yet Serbian political leverage to sustain this structure was limited. In addition to the absence of an overall numerical majority, the Serbian political spectrum was divided among several parties. Such divisions would not burden the Croat, Slovene, and Bosnian Muslim representatives who won sizeable if still minority shares of seats in the parliamentary elections. Their territories would also be insulated by the Habsburg legal codes that would remain in force through the 1920s. None of this representation or insulation was available to Kosovo and Macedonia, where districts were drawn to justify the appointment of Serb prefects.

The now aged Serbian Radical leader, Nikola Pašić, formed ten cabinets between 1921 and 1926. Their number testifies to his party's status as a parliamentary minority, dependent on temporary coalitions in order to stay in power. Radical efforts to become a national party went no further west than Bosnia. Their first principal rivals, the prewar Independent Radicals, now renamed the Democrats, had won as many seats as the Radicals in the Constituent Assembly of 1920. But they lost support in the three subsequent elections (1923, 1925, 1927) by emphasizing the country-wide approach of their originally Serbian party. By 1925 they were reduced to 37 of 315 seats when the disputatious Svetozar Pribićević , briefly the Radicals' Interior and then Education Minister in 1918–21, led his Croatian Serbs into a separate party of Independent Democrats. They won 22 seats. Already in 1923 the only other party with country-wide aspirations, the peasant-based Agrarian Union, had seen its 1920 representation of 39 drop to 11. Into this breach stepped steady support for the clerical, cooperative-based Slovene People's Party (SLS) and Bosnia's secular Yugoslav Muslim Organization (JMO). A Kosovar Albanian party, the *Xemijet*, found itself suppressed by 1925.

The largest Radical rival was the Croatian Republican Peasant Party (HRSS), led by the decade's one charismatic political figure, Stjepan Radić.[33] He grounded the party's agrarian populism in his own lifelong suspicion of central authority, religious or secular. The HRSS mounted its strongest challenge in 1923, winning 22 percent of the vote and 70 seats of 313, second only to the Radicals 26 percent and 108 seats. Only the aforementioned series of coalitions kept Pašić in his position as Prime Minister for all but four months until 1926. His last coalition must have been the most difficult, bringing Radić himself to Belgrade as Education Minister. In return, Radić removed the word "Republican" from the party's name and endorsed the monarchy. He had even met agreeably with the King. Pašić died at age 82 in 1926, in a fit of anger after Aleksandar refused to appoint him yet again. An awkward coalition formed by Pribićević and Radić then struggled through 1927. Yet Radical influence fell still further. The impasse of 1928 began with Aleksandar actually asking Radić to form a government. Failing this, the Croat leader still returned to Belgrade in July 1928, but not to contest Serbian hegemony. He came instead to oppose the ratification of the Nettuno Convention with Italy. It acknowledged Italian sovereignty over Istria, Zadar, and several Adriatic islands.

Radić's subsequent assassination notwithstanding, Serbian dominance was hardly the burden in the former Habsburg lands that it was in Kosovo and Macedonia, now simply designated as South Serbia. There, armed resistance persisted from bands of Kosovar Albanians or VMRO irredentists, respectively moving back and forth across the Albanian and Bulgarian borders. This helped to justify the regime of semimartial law unregulated by the 1921 Constitution and enforced by the regime's largely Serbian gendarmerie. Also justifying the stationing there of fully two-thirds of its 20,000 men was the regional strength of the Communist Party of Yugoslavia (KPJ). Illegal since 1921, it survived in "South Serbia" by its promotion of a separate Macedonian republic in the aforementioned Balkan Communist Federation – a protest vote against absorption as South Serbia had already won the Communists their highest share of the balloting for the Constituent Assembly in 1920, 38 percent of the Macedonian vote with 15 of their 58 seats.

The Serbian gendarmerie struggled to suppress attacks from Kosovar Albanian *kaçak* and the pro-Macedonian or pro-Bulgarian VMRO bands. Violence from all sides made South Serbia a lawless region and its border areas genuinely dangerous until at least the mid-1920s. Some 80,000 Kosovars had fled to Albania or Turkey and 30,000 Macedonians/Bulgarians to Bulgaria at the start. The *kaçak* raids took a far smaller toll than the VMRO assaults and assassinations. They alone accounted for the deaths of nearly 200 Serbian officials and 600 gendarmes by 1924. Deaths on the two other sides surpassed that number. The gendarmerie burned out 14 villages by their own account, over 100 by others. Recent Serbian scholarship deserves credit for detailing these and other widespread abuses. They ranged from police brutality and corrupt collection of taxes and seizure of property to annual impositions of forced labor.[34]

Serbian pressures had forced the fledgling *Xemijet* party of urban Kosovar Albanians out of existence in 1925. Like Macedonia, Kosovo now provided no legal political representation outside the parties. The judicial system functioned only in the Serbian language, and almost all primary schooling was conducted with Serbian textbooks and by largely unqualified teachers. Some 40 percent of school-age children simply did not attend, and the figure was much lower for the Albanians. The government's Special Commission for agricultural reform in Macedonia and Kosovo meanwhile moved Serb families of war veterans mainly from land-poor Herzegovina and Montenegro into deserted or confiscated properties there as "colonists," but with little state support even for housing. This effort would add perhaps 100,000 to the existing Serb minorities, large only in Kosovo but still short of the majority desired there. The largest part of arable land remained uncultivated.

The transition in the formerly Habsburg northwest was hardly so unpromising or unambiguous. The agricultural reform of 1921 had favored Serb peasants previously sharecropping Bosnian Muslim lands, but included many Croats and Slovenes elsewhere. True, the typically Serb prefects in Bosnia, Dalmatia, and much of Croatia could overrule decisions from municipal governments and deploy police or paramilitary pressures against the rural supporters of Radić's party in particular. Prior to the 1925 elections, for instance, over two thousand homes were searched and still more Croatian Peasant activists detained. Radić himself had been arrested after his controversial trip to the Soviet Union. And yet his million-strong party increased its share of the popular vote slightly in 1925, to move past 22 percent. The party's rural organization, if not yet well coordinated, reached into every village. Half of its elected representatives were peasants themselves. The failure of parliamentary sessions in Belgrade to agree on a single new civil or criminal code left the prewar Habsburg variants in place, helping to keep Croat and Slovene judges in place as well. This allowed the prewar owners to continue contesting peasant titles to land distributed under the 1921 reform through the 1920s.

As would again be the case after the Second World War, the initial effort to establish a single curriculum and set of textbooks for primary and secondary schools failed to win approval. In 1921 the heavy-handed Svetozar Pribićević, then Education Minister, and the parliament's predominately Serb education committee proposed new laws that would have made a unitary approach mandatory. But their definition of Yugoslav unity rested on prewar Serbian assumptions about language and history that subsumed Croats and left Slovenes subordinate. Parliamentary opposition kept any such law from passing before 1929. The Serbian side could at least spread its prewar textbooks, which made virtually no mention of Croats, to the Vojvodina, Kosovo, and Macedonia. Elsewhere, prewar Habsburg textbooks remained in use. They made little mention of South Slav ethnic connections and none of Serbian leadership.[35] This was the Kingdom that Aleksandar proposed to unite as Yugoslavia in 1929. Against its disparate and repressive features, we must fairly balance a set of European aspirations common to its neighbors in the region and concentrated in their capital cities.

National Capitals and the Contest over National Ideas

All of the national capitals grew significantly during this first postwar decade, roughly doubling in population. All of them save the new Albanian capital spread out from public centers that already afforded a familiar European appearance before the war and now included main shopping streets as well. Inland Tirana's population by 1930 was less than 30,000, and only a few, Italian-funded public buildings stood out in a center which was otherwise the marketplace of a prewar Ottoman town. A small technical high school started by the American Red Cross survived. The several European embassies became social centers. The other capitals contained a full set of European cultural institutions and amenities. University enrollments rose by half or more. The number of daily or weekly newspapers multiplied. Movie houses now joined theaters and concert halls. Shops, if not yet department stores, sold a full range of European fashions and furnishings. Tram networks linked the expanding residential area with the center. All of this connected an overwhelmingly literate population with European high culture or at least with a popular culture that now included American films and European football.

These rising cultural centers did more than promote European connections. They contributed to and also challenged the national integration to which each of these interwar states aspired. In every case they advanced the liberal, modernist, and urban version of that integration familiar from the short, unhappy but still promising life of Weimar Germany. But for Athens and Belgrade there were cultural and economic challenges from rival city centers, from Thessaloniki (no longer Salonika) in the northern new lands and from Zagreb and Ljubljana (no longer Agram and Laibach) in the former Habsburg lands. And from advocates for the Croatian, Bulgarian, and Romanian peasant majorities came populist challenges that favored the rural village and its traditions over any capital city as the proper center for national identity. The most explicit ideological struggle took place in Romania, but contestation emerged everywhere. In Bulgaria, as we have seen, it cost Aleksandar Stamboliiski his life.

For Greece, the contest between Athens and Thessaloniki would become an ideological one only during the Second World War and the two Greek civil wars that followed. In the 1920s there was nonetheless a rivalry between the capital city and the northern port. As Salonika it had been the larger and more cosmopolitan town, with more Sephardic Jews and mainly Turkish Muslims than Greeks until the Balkan Wars of 1912–13. The royal family in Athens, with its links to the old merchant families of the south, jousted with Venizelos and his northern support. The Liberal leader was credited, as we have seen, with acquiring the new lands in 1912 and then for backing the refugees who fled Anatolia in 1922. Yet even with the King's abdication that same year and the republic proclaimed in 1924, Athens maintained a postwar advantage. Thessaloniki, and the Jewish community in particular, struggled to recover from the great fire of 1917. Promising plans for renewal soon ran out of funding. Most northern refugees were placed in rural settlements, although there were enough in Thessaloniki to bring the Greek share of the population up to three-quarters. Athens meanwhile surged ahead, at least in population and public employment.[36] Its refugees and rural migration had already boosted the population from 110,000 to 200,000 by 1920. It climbed to 350,000 by 1930. The ancient Acropolis, unconnected to the city center below until after the Second World War, towered above the set of neoclassical public buildings begun not far away in the nineteenth century and the Plaka's unplanned sprawl of small shops and houses immediately below. Some "neovernacular" construction in the 1920s supplemented the university, parliament, and other neoclassical buildings already in place. Multistory buildings close to the Acropolis were banned.

State jobs still attracted the majority of university graduates, seeking positions if possible in the favored Ministries of Foreign Affairs and Justice. From 1925 forward, some were prepared in the Athens College established on the model of an English public school by wealthy Greek-American benefactors. Still, the university's restrictive commitment to ancient history and to the Byzantine Greek language of *katharevousa,* reinforced by the conservative influence of the Orthodox clergy, offered fewer links to European modernist trends than in the other capitals. Nor was their much in this elitist or religious identity for the rural refugee masses of the north and the newcomers that had crowded into Athens. The ruling Liberals, as we have seen, offered no discernible ideology, liberal, populist, or otherwise. They left the door open for both the integral nationalism of Metaxas in the late 1930s or the socialism of the Greek Communist Party afterwards.

Belgrade seemed more open to European ideas and to cultural influences from elsewhere in the new Yugoslav state, from Dalmatia in particular. Yet by the end of the 1920s, as again by the end of the 1980s, the prospect of a multiethnic capital leading the way to a new sense of Yugoslav identity had largely played itself out. The city's population had climbed from 95,000 in 1910, to 110,000 in 1920, and to 225,000 by 1930. Joining immigrants from Serbia, Macedonia, Bosnia, Dalmatia, and the Vojvodina were some 40,000 White Russian refugees from the Bolshevik Revolution. Officially welcomed by King Aleksandar, they made a major contribution to the city's cultural and intellectual life. As university professors, architects, and artists, they mixed fruitfully with the young Serbian officers and refugees, who took up the offer as the war was ending to attend universities in France. Belgrade University's new Carnegie Library provided an Anglo-American presence. Mass spectator sports arrived with European football. Modern multistory buildings and shops with plate-glass windows spread along the French-style boulevard leading to the central Terazije. Café life and bohemian circles flourished, while the city formed its special attachment to Hollywood films, "a new form of religion" as one newspaper put it.[37]

Efforts to create a common Yugoslav consciousness centered on Belgrade met with limited success, probably less than the growing sense of membership in a common European culture and, for Serbs, membership in the winners' circle from the war. The initial surge in Yugoslav consciousness drew on major Serbian writers and intellectuals who were simply not attracted, as Andrew Wachtel concludes, to any "strong preference for a unitary culture, much less one based . . . on Serbian terms."[38] Ethnically mixed contingents from Dalmatia and the Vojvodina were conspicuous contributors. Let the Croatian poet Tin Ujević's arrival and then disillusioned departure from bohemian Belgrade late in the decade stand for the final failure of some multicultural synthesis to emerge. Stjepan Radić would not have opposed such a synthesis, only its centering in a city and in the Serbian capital at that.

War memories, as well, worked against a single Yugoslav identity. Keeping them alive were memorials that were also multiplying in Britain, France, and Belgium during the decade. In the new Kingdom of Serbs, Croats, and Slovenes these were almost entirely ceremonies and cemeteries for Serbia's military dead. King Aleksandar and the new army's largely Serb leadership made the most of their dedication ceremonies. Croat and Slovene losses on the defeated Habsburg side were left unrecognized.[39] The heroic Serbian memory of its army's role in the First World War encouraged their civilian elite to assume the right to lead the post-1918 state. But unlike Romania, where a less heroic war effort was also celebrated as a validation of national identity, the Serbian standard bearers did not represent an ethnic majority.

Another challenge to Belgrade as a single center for national integration came from the cultural and economic growth of Zagreb and Ljubljana. Zagreb's population also kept pace, rising to 185,000 by 1929. Buoyed by greater industrial growth, the municipal governments of both cities supported plans from local architects that transformed their centers in impressive modern fashion. Interference from the central government's ministries made Belgrade's General Plan of 1923 a dead letter. The new building for the National Assembly, or *Skupština*, was left unfinished until 1935. The political opposition to Belgrade's leadership came from Zagreb as well as Radić's Croatian Peasant Party with its rural base. The Croatian Union, drawn from the urban elite in the prewar Croat–Serb Coalition and wartime supporters of a Yugoslav state, began the 1920s with liberal hopes for a single market economy and a federal government. Within a few years, however, their program had attracted little attention. Former Union members joined Radic's confederal camp without accepting his rural populism. The alternative of a Croatian Catholic Party gathered no support, while the Church's mobilization of young people in gymnastic societies, to be considered in Chapter 4, was successful mainly in rural areas or small towns.

In Sofia, ideology played a more important and more contentious role. The city had grown from 95,000 before the war to 200,000 by 1929. Some 30,000 of that increase came from the refugees driven in from Vardar and Aegean Macedonia by the peace settlement. Their cramped and ramshackle quarters on the city's western edge were the scene for factional violence throughout the decade. "Another Macedonian murder" became a common newspaper headline. Perhaps a thousand people died in the violence, more than were killed advancing the irredentist cause in Vardar Macedonia. The main lines of battle were drawn between the "autonomists," favoring the reincorporation of as much of Macedonia as possible into Bulgaria, and the "federalists," favoring a largely independent Greater Macedonia in a Balkan federation.

For Sofia and Bulgaria as a whole, the costly defeats of the Second Balkan War and then finally of the First World War turned national consciousness away from the ethnic self-assertion so central to its neighbors. Recent Bulgarian scholarship has rightly called the shock of these two "national catastrophes" sufficient to end the period of "national revival" that had begun in the nineteenth century.[40] A massive crowd still turned out in Sofia for the funeral in 1921 of Ivan Vazov, the novelist most revered during the prewar decades for championing the revival. Yet his influence had already faded because of the unwavering support he had given the war effort. Defeat transferred cultural, if hardly official, authority in postwar Sofia from the so-called "apologists," such as Vazov, to the "humanists," who had opposed the war at least in its later stages. The Bulgarian Orthodox Church also found its influence constrained by the decision of its ruling Synod to preserve the Exarchate it had received under Ottoman aegis to represent believers in Thrace and all the Macedonian lands. Now, although the Greek and Serbian Orthodox Churches had quickly displaced their clergy in this wider territory, the Bulgarian Church refused to retreat to Bulgaria alone and kept its exarchal headquarters in Istanbul. By leaving its jurisdiction unresolved in hopes of regaining the lost lands, the Church limited its legal authority and state support for domestic activity.

The two major political opponents of the lost war from the start had of course been Aleksandar Stamboliiski's Agrarians and the Narrow Socialists, the Bulgarian Communist Party from 1918. But by 1923 both had been put down, as we have seen. The coup assassinating Stamboliiski and the suppression of the Communist uprising formally removed their two radical ideologies from the city's public life. Even informally, Stamboliiski's peasant populism was not attractive to the educated urban elite he had wished to see sent off to the countryside every summer to help with the harvest. It was instead postwar European modernism that struck the responsive ideological chord in Sofia. The intellectual elite turned to this mixture of symbolism and expressionism. It found its political place in a civil society that disdained even the successors to the governments that had overseen the catastrophes. Its links with the cultural ferment in defeated Germany and in the early Soviet Union combined with Stamboliiski's egalitarianism to provide the region's one interwar cultural legacy on which a post-1945 Communist regime could plausibly draw. There was also a more pragmatic connection to vocational training, through the agricultural, veterinary, and medical faculties added to Sofia University by Stamboliiski's Minister of

Education. The same emphasis came from the American College that succeeded the high school in outlying Samakov started by Protestant missionaries in the 1860s.

Sofia was still the capital of a defeated and reduced state, its irredentist ambitions for recovering the lost lands further compromised by the warring Macedonian factions. A sense of national failure or frustration hung over the city. In the discourse of the day, café conversations spoke bitterly of *bulgarska rabota*, any initially promising "piece of work" gone bad because Bulgarians had laid their hands to it.

The Romanian capital of Bucharest was not only the largest but also ideologically the most open. Already numbering 382,000 in 1920, its population climbed to 631,000 by 1930. Houses and villas in the several exclusive central neighborhoods reminded visitors of Berlin or Chicago. The rough huts of the *mahale* quarters on the periphery were poorer than any regional counterpart. Broad boulevards connected this largest urban space in the region. By 1922 a wooden replica of the Arc de Triomphe in Paris had gone up across the main avenue to the center from the north (redone in stone by 1936). It was erected to celebrate the promise of Greater Romania. The city itself offered a variety of promises. The cafés, restaurants, and shops for the commercial and official elite made some streets in the center look like the "Paris of the East." So the city aspired to be for a smart set that typically spoke French as well as Romanian. The large if not overwhelming Jewish presence in private commerce and finance helped to stoke resentment. Particularly resentful were the rural migrants recently arrived to swell the *mahale*. The fascist Legion of the Archangel Michael would exploit their alienation in the 1930s (see Chapter 4). Ten such villages were absorbed by the city in 1920 and another ten by 1930.

More important for the 1920s were the growing number of industrial workers and university students closer to the city center. Some 20 percent of the enlarged country's industrial employment was in Bucharest. Joining the huge rail yards, the Malaxa metallurgical works, and related enterprises were many small textile manufacturers in the Lipscanj district, home to the one concentration of Jewish factory labor in any of the capitals. The future Communist activist Ana Pauker came from there and was already active in socialist agitation before the First World War. It was, however, the faculty and students of Bucharest University that provided the ideological constituency for the overwhelmingly anti-Communist ferment of this first postwar decade. Student enrollment tripled in the 1920s to reach 23,000, and the faculty fivefold to approach 1000, both the largest in the region. Faculties, institutes, and other institutions of higher learning elsewhere in the city multiplied as well. Newspapers, journals, and book publishers flourished.

Political pluralism found some chance to challenge the Interior Ministry's past leverage in administering the Romanian capital. Municipal elections selected over half of the city's governing council or *Primarie*, and more from 1929.[41]

This was the setting for what Keith Hitchins has aptly called "the great debate."[42] There were two sides for the 1920s, to be joined by a defensive third in the 1930s that would include the fascist Legion. One side embraced Western liberal values and industrial development explicitly, more than any other advocates in the region. Eugen Lovinescu, holding a Sorbonne doctorate in literature and philosophy, stressed Romania's connection to European high culture. His three-volume history of modern Romanian civilization found a common Latin cord connecting Romania and Western Europe from the nineteenth century forward. A complete connection only awaited the continuing growth of an educated urban middle class. They would "synchronize" business and intellectual perspectives for a national identity on what he assumed to be the French model. The Romanian Orthodox Church remained as much of a barrier to this transition for him as Byzantine and Ottoman hegemony had been. Stefan Zeletin, with a doctoral degree in economics from a German university, represented another sort of liberal determinism. Drawing him was the magnetic attraction of modern economic development, not European culture. Rapid, even forced industrialization on the pattern advocated by the Liberal government would create the urban society that would make Romania the modern European country that its enlargement after the war promised it should be.

Opposing these "Europeanists" were a still more disparate group that may be characterized as peasant populists. The prolific historian Nicolae Iorga, another holder of a German doctorate, had already founded his Sowers (*Sămănăturist*) organization before the First World War, as we saw in Chapter 1. He and his followers idealized village life and peasant culture per se as the unalloyed essence of Romanian national identity. Its protection from the corruption of urban ways and Western influences would be the only way to realize the promise of Greater Romania. Cooperative organization and vocational education would help to promote gradual evolution into a modern but still primarily agricultural economy. But, for Iorga, religious or ethnic discrimination against the newly increased minorities would not help. He deserves credit for opposing anti-Semitic or anti-Hungarian restrictions on access to education.[43]

The separate and more philosophical circle, called *Gîndirea* after their literary review, had two branches. Let the eclectic poet Lucien Blaga stand for the moderates who accepted broader European and regional influences in Romanian history but harked back to pre-Roman, and thus pre-Latin, origins of a national character already identified in ancient Thracian times. The review's editor from 1926 to 1944, Nichifor Crainic, represented what became the more influential branch. The ways of rural folk did not interest him other than as a reflection of Orthodox Christianity. Its spirituality, entirely divorced from the secular corruptions of modern Europe, had left peasant villages as the repository of Romanian national identity. Russian religious thinkers in the Slavophile tradition were his only foreign inspiration.

The potential for religious and ethnic intolerance in his "autotochtonist" thinking would find an echo in Romanian political life, as we shall see, in the 1930s and again in the 1970s. For the 1920s its primary connection was with a Romanian Orthodox Church newly concerned with a much less predominant position in the new territories of greater Romania than within the prewar borders. Transylvania, with its Romanian majority in the rival "Greek Catholic" (or Uniate Orthodox) Church plus the large Protestant minorities of Germans and Hungarians, was particularly troubling. Only the Church's success in acquiring control of the Hero's Cult organization to spread war memorials across to the new borders gave it the increased leverage that the hierarchy desired.[44] Their massive numbers, some 3500 memorials by the 1930s, would not however consolidate a single Romanian identity to the satisfaction of the contending groups noted above.

Nowhere had the promise of the 1920s been brighter than in Romania, its prewar borders enlarged and its postwar population not burdened with the influx of refugees experienced by Bulgaria and Greece. Nor were there the Albanian and Yugoslav burdens of creating new states. Yet Romania had struggled even more than they did with economic recovery in the face of rural–urban as well as ethnic divisions. Its return to international trade was also the most difficult. Politically, Romania had joined the other royal regimes, Albania excepted, and the Greek republic in pursuing European standards of constitutional government under elected parliaments and a wider franchise. It was after all in Romania that an opposition party had won a national election by 1928. At the same time, the equally European pattern of pursuing national integration around the state's identification with the ethnic majority had not helped this liberal transition anywhere in the region. Its Western sponsors had done little beyond the reform of the central banks and the settlement of refugees. Worse lay ahead in the 1930s when much of Europe called the liberal model itself, first economically and then politically, into question.

4 Illiberal Directions During the Depression Decade

Neither political pluralism nor economic liberalism would survive the 1930s in Southeastern Europe. Little ideological underpinning remained beyond national self-assertion, with its emphasis on the ethnic majority. The political examples of Mussolini's Italy and then Hitler's Germany stood between all of the states we would know as Eastern Europe after the Second World War and the multiparty electoral processes of Western Europe. Poland had already forsaken parliamentary government by 1926; the Southeastern European states would follow suit after 1930. The Depression also hit their economies hard. Although less vulnerable to industrial unemployment than Weimar Germany, they were heavily dependent on agricultural exports whose prices suffered the sharpest declines and whose markets contracted still further from their pre-1914 range.

Western historians have emphasized Nazi penetration of the region's troubled economies. Their counterparts in Communist Eastern Europe presumed growing political influence and ideological inspiration as well. Marxist–Leninist orthodoxy demanded that the domestic regimes be branded "monarcho-Fascist," rather than simply "royal dictatorships" as in standard Western accounts.[1] The best East European scholarship of the Communist era concentrated on economic history. It paid particular attention to the Depression difficulties of the market mechanism and the state's growing economic role. Both experiences made the post-1945 transition to state planning and ownership seem like a logical progression.

The most recent research finds the assumption of effective Nazi penetration premature. It did indeed spread from March 1939, when the bloodless German destruction of Czechoslovakia put European diplomatic relations on a war footing. Before then, the bilateral barter agreements through which the region had come to conduct the majority of its foreign trade did indeed constitute an important transition from the market mechanism to state control. Yet such agreements appeared before the Nazi economic offensive of 1935. The pacts that followed did not bring decisive investment from the Reich in their wake. The various state initiatives across the economies of the region also appear less connected to the decade's relatively strong industrial growth than were a growing number of joint-stock enterprises, domestic as well as West European or American.

The more unambiguously illiberal transition during the 1930s was the subordination of parliamentary government in all five states. Monarchic authority sought to keep some constitutional sanction but reserved to itself the independence from legislative oversight of the Kaiser's Germany. The royal regimes often relied on emergency decrees and expanded the intrusive authority of their Interior Ministries in particular. This was surely some precedent for the establishment of more comprehensive Communist power after 1945. None of these prewar governments could sustain dictatorial powers for more than a few years. Still suffering in the process were autonomy for local government and ministerial responsibility to elected parliaments.

The royal regimes also undercut the established political parties and left them seriously weakened as the decade drew to a close. Yet they failed to create successful new "state parties" that represented the desired national consensus and hence might have sustained their dictatorial ambitions. This failure, plus the restrictions on legal position in general, helped radical dissenters. The Communist parties in particular gained legitimacy as well as experience through already established frameworks for clandestine survival. Right-wing radicals relied on assassinations and other confrontational violence. The Internal Macedonian Revolutionary Organization (VMRO), more populist than fascist, did not survive to future advantage. The Second World War would give the Croatian *Ustaša* and the Romanian Iron Guard, more fascist than populist, an early advantage that both used to destroy themselves (see Chapter 5).

Until 1940 the royal regimes and their Interior Ministries consistently prevailed over the established parties and radical alternatives. Their monarchs, a majority of them descended from European royalty rather than native stock, sought to spread a sense of national identification with the state. Confounding their efforts were continuing urban–rural disjunctures, especially between modern capital cities and the huge majority of peasant villages. These social disparities compounded the regional differences with which these newly created or reconfigured states were already contending. Together they undermined the very ethnonational unity by which the royal regimes sought to exclude any political alternative.

These regimes nonetheless concentrated enough executive authority to hasten the liberal retreat and statist advance that the Great Depression pressed on the respective national economies. The advance was striking for public over private finance but much less so for agriculture and industry. Limited agricultural growth relied more on local cooperatives, peasant initiatives, and their access to credit than on state agencies. Manufacturing grew despite the retreat of transnational bank credit and the advance of domestic cartels. Joint-stock incorporation joined direct Western investment and new access to central or state bank credit in promoting an industrial recovery, mining included, that exceeded the European average.

Finally, we must acknowledge the international constraints which did indeed press in on all of Southeastern Europe. Closer regional relations offered some initial promise, and some connection with the United States and the Soviet Union also emerged. But the main arena for foreign policy, in which all five countries maneuvered with varying success to preserve their independence, became a broadly regional contest between Britain and Germany. By the later 1930s it replaced the Franco-Italian rivalry that had previously continued the Great Powers' pre-1914 practice of seeking special relationships with individual states. Not until 1939, when Hitler was preparing to launch the European war denied him at the Munich conference, would Nazi Germany's economic advantage in bilateral trade arrangements finally produce comprehensive economic hegemony and decisive diplomatic leverage.

Royal Regimes, Regional Divisions, Radical Alternatives

Albania's royal regime aspired to be the strongest and yet remained the weakest of the decade's nonparty governments. Ahmed Zogu had proclaimed himself King Zog of Albania in 1928 (see Chapter 3) with no intention of allowing any legislative or judicial body to challenge his right to rule as he saw fit. And indeed none would challenge him. That December's new constitution reduced the previously bicameral legislature to a single, smaller body of 56 deputies. It rarely met and received no separate authority. No political parties were allowed; individual candidates ran for election unopposed after approval by Zog's local representatives. In order to tighten local control after 1930, Zog divided the country into ten prefectures on the French model, each under a set of prefects, subprefects, mayors, and communal leaders. All of them were responsible to the Ministry of the Interior. A version of the Italian penal code adopted in 1930 gave the ministry and the monarch broad powers to impose or overrule any sentence.

All the same, Zog lacked the wider administrative apparatus away from his small capital city to carry out the economic and educational reforms to which he also aspired. Tribal authority and local arms still held too much sway in the rural areas that included 90 percent of the population of 1 million. The land reform of 1930 succeeded only in redistributing 10 percent of state land and none of the larger private total still held for exploitative sharecropping by local beys. Budgetary revenues were small to start with, perhaps one-fifth of the neighboring states' levels per capita. By 1931 they had fallen further and forced a nearly 50 percent reduction in state expenses. Even the army and gendarmerie, which took nearly half of the budget, were affected. Only another Italian loan that year allowed any economic initiatives to proceed. They came at the price of accepting the services of Italian experts in the four relevant ministries as well as Italian officers in the small army of 6000. In 1933–4, Zog made little progress with his efforts to establish more state schools and to close the Italian and Greek religious institutions that provided the bulk of primary education. He appointed a presumably reformist Prime Minister in 1935 to press ahead with education and land reclamation but dismissed him in less than a year. Zog apparently feared that the police powers he struggled to maintain against local tribal leaders and their armed followers were being called into question.[2]

The other four royal regimes mobilized more resources, made far greater progress in their efforts to centralize authority, but also faced more organized opposition. Their record tells us more about the decade's contested transition to centralized royal power than does that of King Zog. Their lineage also connected them to major European royal families and to each other. Carol II was the son of Queen Victoria's granddaughter, Queen Marie of Romania until King Ferdinand's death in 1927. One of her daughters married Yugoslavia's King Aleksandar, and another Greece's George II. Bulgaria's King Boris III, like his father, married an Italian princess, the daughter of powerless King Victor Emmanuel III. This common background in prewar royal privilege must account for some of the powers these rulers assumed were theirs, despite the fact that monarchies had vanished or retreated across the rest of Europe by the 1930s.

Two comparisons seem instructive: Yugoslavia with Romania, and Bulgaria with Greece. The first royal regimes were established in Yugoslavia in 1929 and in Romania the next year. Although Aleksandar's personal regime was cut short by assassination in 1934, his framework stayed in place. So did the opposition that prevented a Yugoslav state party from predominating. Carol's regime worked to subvert the political pluralism he detested. The Romanian monarch manipulated an increasingly subdivided set of parties until assuming dictatorial powers in 1938. In Bulgaria an elected government ruled until 1934, and in Greece the Republic endured until 1936. Then,

Bulgaria's Tsar Boris stood back from simply building on the military regime that seized power in 1934–5, as Greece's George II did not. He returned from exile to allow retired army general Ion Metaxas to impose the most dictatorial of any of the four regimes.

From Aleksandar's Yugoslavia to Carol's Romania

On January 6, 1929 King Aleksandar used the eve of the Orthodox Christmas holiday to dismiss the elected parliament and to disband all political parties, even confiscating their properties and records. This abrupt announcement and the flurry of emergency decrees that followed seemed to promise the most draconian of the royal regimes. It also started with more popular approval than any of the others. But by 1931 Aleksandar was obliged to retreat. He faced rising opposition even before his assassination in 1934 at the hands of his most radical adversaries.

The appointment of his closest military advisor, General Petar Živković, as both Prime Minister and Interior Minister set the course for these first two years. It aimed to exclude the smallest legislative oversight and also any significant representation for non-Serbs. Only five Croats and one Slovene were appointed to the new cabinet of 16 members. Still, the parliamentary disarray that had followed the assassination of Stjepan Radić in July 1928 prompted his successor, Vladko Maček, to welcome removing the "badly buttoned vest" of the 1921 constitution. Among the 163 measures subsequently decreed in 1929, a number addressed issues of national integration that should have been faced from the start. Perhaps most needed was the single legal code to replace the patchwork of six prewar systems. But the unified tax code and reduction in the number of ministries, officials, and even army generals left advantages for Serbia and Serbs in place.

Four decrees proclaimed during the first weeks of the new regime concentrated unlimited power in the hands of the King and his Interior Minister. They stipulated royal authority to appoint all ministers and decree legislation, to impose security measures against any opposition, and to create a court for state protection. Amendments to the 1925 press law stiffened it significantly. A new Central Press Bureau was charged with preventing any domestic publication expressing "hatred of the state" and monitoring the reports of foreign correspondents.

Aleksandar's often stated but never elaborated intention was to create a single Yugoslav nation from the state he proclaimed in Belgrade in 1918 as the Kingdom of Serbs, Croats, and Slovenes. As he saw it through soldier's eyes, victorious Serbia had then invited Croat, Slovene, and Bosnian Serb representatives to bring their formerly Habsburg lands into a Serbian state to which his army's advance had already added Macedonia, Kosovo, and the Vojvodina. On the same day in October 1929, he renamed the state as the Kingdom of Yugoslavia. Aleksandar also announced a revision of internal boundaries and administration that was intended to end the "tribal" and Ottoman- or Habsburg-imposed divisions that had impeded national integration. Set around river valleys and given ahistorical names, the nine *banovine* were nonetheless configured to provide Serb majorities or pluralities in six of them. At the special urging of the Bosnian Serb Milan Srškić, the Minister of Justice, Bosnia-Herzegovina was artfully divided between four of them and Kosovo between two.

It was however the Ministry of Interior under General Živković that made the central government's police powers greater rather than less than they had been under the 33 provinces of the Vidovdan Constitution.[3] Among the seven new departments set up in each *banovina*, the Administrative Departments worked closely with the Interior Ministry to coordinate their own Divisions for State Protection. These typically Serb-staffed divisions covered villages as well as towns in their efforts to recruit a network of informers on antistate activity or statements, to keep all suspects or any foreigners under surveillance, and to order arrests by the gendarmerie or local police. Education Departments worked with the Ministries of Education and the army and navy in Belgrade to oblige student participation in the new Yugoslav Sokol Union. It was to replace the several separate societies for youth gymnastics for Serbia, Croatian Serbs, Croats, and Slovenes. Security and education officials coordinated the monitoring or dismissal of "anti-state" teachers.

Whatever precedent this intrusive framework would set for the postwar Communist government, it was not sufficiently effective during the rest of the 1930s to stifle dissent. Nor did it create the sort of Yugoslav state identity that would submerge ethnic or regional interests.[4] By the mid-1930s the one Slovene Minister, the longtime leader of the powerful People's Party Msgr Anton Korošec, resigned over the abolition of the Slovenian Sokol and the further threat to separate Catholic schools. The project for a single set of primary and secondary school textbooks, boldly proclaimed in 1929, struggled to overcome regional objections, Serbia included. No agreed volumes would be distributed until late in the decade. Aleksandar proclaimed a new constitution in 1931 and promptly held nonparty elections. Low turnout, under two-thirds of eligible voters, and the high proportion of Serbs elected, over two-thirds, did not reassure non-Serbs. Bosnian Muslim religious leadership was objecting in any case to that year's decision from Belgrade to create a single Islamic council for the country. It threatened to undercut Sarajevo's long-standing local authority. The Croatian

Peasant Party's membership honored the anniversary of Radić's assassination rather than the King's birthday, while its new leader Maček languished in prison on false charges. By 1932 Maček had been acquitted, to the Interior Ministry's embarrassment. He and Korošec each issued public lists of grievances, the so-called *punktacije*, that challenged the royal regime. Before then, student protests in Belgrade had helped push the King to dismiss General Živković as Prime Minister. But Aleksandar's choice for his replacement, the zealous and corrupt Bosnian Serb Srškić, hardly improved the regime's standing. Its attempt to found a new political party, Yugoslav Radical-Peasant Democracy, made little headway in 1932, or in 1933 when renamed the Yugoslav National Party. King Aleksandar alone retained some popularity across the country.

In October 1934 two radical groups calling for the breakup of Yugoslavia joined forces to assassinate Aleksandar. They shot him down, along with France's Foreign Minister, as he arrived in Marseilles for a state visit. The Internal Macedonian Revolutionary Organization (VMRO) furnished the gunman, a chauffeur to the leader of its exiled pro-Bulgarian faction that had been, as we shall see, recently suppressed in Sofia. Croatian *Ustaša* exiles in Italy and Hungary were, however, the organizers. They had already tried to kill Aleksandar during his visit to Zagreb in 1933.

Ante Pavelić, a lawyer originally from Herzegovina, had founded the movement in immediate response to Aleksandar's proclamation of the royal dictatorship of 1929. The small, illegal band quickly found its way to Italy.[5] Organized with fascist-style uniforms and symbols as a military movement with Pavelić as *poglavnik*, or leader, it won the same sort of financial support from Mussolini's government that the VMRO had received since the 1920s. In the furor following the assassination, both groups lost their Italian sponsorship. Only the *Ustaša* survived to reemerge in Croatia as the Second World War was beginning.

The VMRO lost ground in Vardar Macedonia to the other illegal party advocating the regime's overthrow, the Yugoslav Communist Party. Its membership was still small, perhaps five or six thousand, but the Soviet decision in 1935 to support a single Yugoslavia as part of an anti-Nazi Popular Front began to attract student followers. By 1936 the Comintern approved a new leader, the Croat-Slovene Josip Broz who took Tito as his party name. He consolidated control but also granted separate if subordinate status to Macedonian and Croatian party organizations in 1937. Dividends would accrue only as war approached.

Meanwhile, the administrative framework that Aleksandar had established stayed in place until 1939. The past and present Finance Minister, Milan Stojadinović, quickly emerged as the new Prime Minister. Prince Paul,

Aleksandar's cousin, led a group of Regents who would wait until the young Petar, the King's son born in 1923, came of age. Following a disputed election victory for the government list in 1935, Prince Paul took the advice of the British Ambassador and appointed Stojadinović. He started well. Stojadinović relaxed censorship and appointed the Slovenian leader Korošec and the Bosnian Muslim leader Mehmet Spaho to his cabinet. He also promised a "political reversal" in Croat relations with Belgrade. But he could not come to terms with the Croatian leader Maček. When Stojadinović endorsed a Concordat with the Vatican for Catholic religious rights, he lost Serbian support. Stojadinović also took his turn at establishing a new national party, the Yugoslav Radical Union (JRZ). It never caught on. Proto-fascist trappings for Sokol youths and *banovine* police pressures could not save the JRZ from nearly losing the 1938 elections. The opposing coalition included Maček's much enlarged membership in the Croat Peasant Party's cooperative network. Stojadinović's resignation signalled the end of the forced integration that Aleksandar had begun with so much determination in 1929.

In the neighboring Kingdom of Romania, the feckless reputation of the direct successor to King Ferdinand, his only son Carol, kept him from returning until 1930. Even then, three years after his father's death, the Prime Minister, Iuliu Maniu, agreed only on the conditions that Carol reconcile with his now former wife, Princess Helen of Greece, and break off contact with his mistress and companion in exile, Elena Lupescu. Maniu's National Peasant Party had seen the Depression undercut its liberal initiatives of 1929, particularly the opening to foreign investment. Maniu reckoned that Carol's resentment of the National Liberals who had sanctioned his exile and his popularity among army officers would undercut this rival party but not his own. The beleaguered Prime Minister also gambled that Carol would otherwise observe the restrictive conditions of his return. He quickly lost both gambles and resigned.

So began a sorry decade in Romanian political history. Carol first played the parties of an increasingly subdivided political spectrum off against each other. None could escape the web of royal favors and repression. Nor could the major minorities, first the Hungarians in Transylvania and finally the Romanian Jews, maintain the press freedom and other representative rights that the National Peasant regime had granted them. It was, however, only in 1938 that Carol finally assumed dictatorial powers comparable to those of Aleksandar.

The rise of the region's one radical movement seriously to challenge royal authority provided the eventual justification for Carol's dictatorship. This was not the Communist challenge that would serve as a justification, however exaggerated, in Yugoslavia and Greece. By the early 1930s the small Romanian Communist Party (PCR), illegal since 1924, had shrunk to barely a thousand members. Its ethnic Hungarian and other non-Romanian leadership won scant support for endorsing the Comintern's approval of irredentist claims across Eastern Europe and the specific Soviet demand for the return of Bessarabia. In 1935 Soviet policy shifted to favor existing states and borders as part of the Popular Front against fascism. The PCR took advantage of this shift, building on its reputed leadership of the Grivița railway-yard strikers in Bucharest in 1933. The gifted, forceful, and Jewish Ana Pauker also emerged as a leading figure. Membership probably climbed past 5000 by 1936. By then, however, Pauker, as well as other leaders including the one ethnic Romanian, Grivița strike hero Gheorghe Gheorghiu-Dej, were arrested and in prison. The PCR's membership and fortunes slipped back down to the lowest level for any Communist party in the region.[6]

The real radical challenge to Carol's regime came instead from the distinctively Romanian fascist movement best known as the Iron Guard. Its strikingly handsome leader, Corneliu Zelea Codreanu, had already founded the Legion of the Archangel Michael in 1927 to bring together strident nationalists from provincial universities. This student core shared his hatred of the Jews already numerous in his native Iași and now joined by more Jews plus the new Hungarian and other minorities of Greater Romania. Codreanu as *Capitanul* acquired the military loyalty to a charismatic leader common to all fascist movements. His Legion mixed its commitment to radical violence with a peasant populism and a messianic religious ideology, unlike any other fascist movement. The movement sought to ground itself in the Romanian Orthodox Church. In 1930, as the Depression spread distress from student youth to the countryside and the lower clergy, he refocused the movement on the fascist-style Iron Guard, his new, green-uniformed "combat organization." Codreanu had first formed it for a march beyond Iași into Bessarabia. The Guard's fortunes would rise unevenly, and without the Nazi support sometimes presumed, until King Carol appeared to have swept it aside in 1938.[7]

Before then, Carol had relied on no ideology of his own. He took the tactical advice his "royal camarilla," a curious circle of advisors that included both major Jewish bankers and industrialists along with heads of police and security services. Later on, he listened to several leaders of minor new parties or factions. In the meantime, the King had encouraged divisions that the Depression had started within the two leading parties. They split first the National Peasants and then the Liberals.[8] From 1931 to 1933 a succession of unstable coalitions included one that made the historian Nicolae Iorga the

Prime Minister until he pressed too hard on reducing state employment and salaries. Iron Guard demonstrations and disorders mounted, some of them financed by the government of Iorga's successor. In November 1933 Carol's Foreign Minister, the internationally respected Gheorghe Titulescu, helped to persuade him that tacit assistance to the Guard was threatening Romania's relationship with France, its major Western supporter. The King reluctantly called on his long-standing Liberal opponent, Ion Duca, to form a new government. Duca used his own authority, when Carol balked at any royal approval, to ban the Guard and arrest over a thousand members. When the Guard assassinated Duca a few weeks later, Carol now made a more comfortable choice, the compliant, authoritarian leader of the "young Liberals," Gheorghe Tătărescu.

His four-year term began in 1934 with martial law and press censorship. The same year, Carol had established a royal youth organization, the Guard of the Nation (*Staja țarii*), militarily uniformed to counter the Iron Guard. To match its rural appeal, the Royal Cultural Foundation authorized the eminent sociologist Dimitrie Gusti to establish a series of village "cultural centers" in 1935. They were staffed with student volunteers to promote improved hygiene, better agricultural techniques and rural education.

Tătărescu stood by while Carol allowed the merger of the two smaller right-wing rivals of the Legion to form a National Christian Party (PNC). They did not mount the expected challenge to the Guard. Codreanu's local groups, called nests, mushroomed up from 4000 in 1935 to 34,000 by 1937. Its surrogate Fatherland party then capped the movement's rise by winning 16 percent of the vote in the parliamentary elections of December 1937. The Tătărescu coalition won only 36 percent, short of the 40 percent needed for a majority of seats since 1926. Carol turned briefly to the PNC, despite the fact that it had won only 9 percent of the vote, to form a new government under his prerogative from the 1923 constitution. This brief regime distinguished itself only by a flurry of anti-Semitic decrees, banning Jewish publications and firing Jewish employees of the state for instance.

But by February 1938 Carol had cast both the government and the 1923 constitution aside. A hastily staged "oral referendum" approved provisions that banned all party activity and military formations. A new Front for National Rebirth was to be the only political organization. More importantly, ministers in the new Government of National Union, all of whom were now to be ethnically Romanian and over 30, were appointed by and responsible solely to the King. The National Assembly lost all effective power.

Much of that power now went to Carol's uncompromising Interior Minister, Armand Calinescu. Determined to finish the Guard for good despite its apparent dissolution, he arrested Codreanu in March on a petty charge and convicted him on a more serious one by May. The *Capitanul* was simply murdered that November, garroted by gendarmes allegedly transferring him to another prison. The killing marked Calinescu as the survivors' primary target for assassination, even when he became Prime Minister in March 1939. In the meantime, his Interior Ministry and their political police, the *siguranţa*, could proceed to establish tighter local control under the same framework installed by Aleksandar's *banovine*. Carol reduced the 70 *judeţ* to ten districts that cut across historical boundaries and transferred army officers into the district leaderships. But by 1940, as we shall see in Chapter 5, first Soviet and then Nazi-supported Hungarian demands had cut away two major areas of post-1918 Romania and forced Carol to flee the country.

From Boris's Bulgaria to Metaxas's Greece

Bulgaria's government would begin and end the 1930s under a more promising, less illiberal framework than any other state in Southeastern Europe. Despite the country's greater economic dependence on Nazi Germany, its last prewar years witnessed at least a limited revival of the electoral legitimacy with which it had begun the decade. Tsar Boris played a more constructive role than the other monarchs, ideologically no more clearly defined but personally more disposed to conciliation than to confrontation or manipulation. Two further features distinguished Bulgaria from the rest of the region, the self-destructive defeat by 1934 of the major radical alternative to the royal regime, the VMRO, and the absence of any significant regional division. More relevant to the Bulgarian Communist Party's postwar seizure of power than its inglorious role during the Second World War (see Chapter 5) was the success of its surrogate Workers Party in surviving the 1930s as part of the political process.

The decade began with the last of the region's few genuinely open interwar elections. By 1931 the ruling Democratic Alliance of Andrei Liapchev had lost its majority in the National Assembly. In addition to the Depression's agricultural crisis, a growing number of strikes and VMRO violence in Sofia diminished public support. At least the Alliance did not abuse its continuing ministerial authority to prevent a rival coalition from winning the June elections to the Assembly. Fully 85 percent of eligible voters (male citizens of 25 and over) cast ballots for proportional representation, again led by the rural balloting that had been the region's highest since the 1920s. The opposition People's Bloc took 48 percent of the huge turnout, leaving the Alliance only 31 percent. The Bloc of Labor that the Communists' surrogate Workers' Party had assembled with the left Agrarians won 13 percent. Although the Democratic Party headed the winning coalition, the accomodationist Agrarians (BZNS-Vrabcha) won the larger number of seats, 73 to 43, with only three for their Radical and Liberal partners. It was still too soon, however, for Stamboliiski's old opponents to accept the return of an Agrarian regime. The Democrat's aging leader, Aleksandar Malinov, was initially named Minister President in the new government but quickly gave way to his colleague Nikola Mushanov, whose refined manners made him more acceptable to Tsar Boris in any case.

The generally comfortable relationship between the two and the breakup of the rival Alliance did not save the Bloc from a series of debilitating problems over the next three years. Falling budget revenues forced cuts in the state's still outsized employment (as noted in Chapter 3). Salaries stayed unpaid for months at a time. Worse still for the Bloc, the tight budgets prevented officers' promotions already overdue in the small army of 20,000 still in place from the peace settlement. Urban workers continued to strike. The Workers' Party actually won Sofia's municipal elections in 1932, pushing the Bloc to nullify the election. Sofia also saw an upsurge in street violence between the two refugee factions vying for control of the VMRO. This was violence that the Bloc had promised to suppress along with the autonomy of the VMRO's Petrich district in the southwest. But renewed Italian support for the predominant and previously pro-Bulgarian faction in 1932–3 confounded suppression. Reacting to the regime's restrictions, its leader Ivan Mihailov now called Sofia "as dangerous as Belgrade or Athens" to the movement. Within the Bloc's coalition, splinter groups appeared as in Romania. Each group in turn demanded their share of official positions, if not ministries. The Bloc's government thus faced the same charges of *partizanstvo*, or clientelism, that had been used against the pre-1914 parties.

Acting without the Tsar's approval, a small group of army officers seized on the emerging impasse to take power in a bloodless coup on April 19, 1934. Zveno took its name from a journal started in 1928 by a disillusioned Social Democrat. The group had first attracted a number of younger officers from the Military College. Indeed, its commandant until 1928, Colonel Damian Velchev, was the coup's leader. Another retired Colonel, Kimon Georgiev, became the political leader of the new nonparty regime. Significantly, Boris would not recognize it until the Bloc's Prime Minister Mushanov had formally resigned. The new regime imposed press censorship and moved quickly to end VMRO autonomy in the Petrich district and to disarm the movement generally. Otherwise, Zveno struggled to establish its authority.

Several groups in the informal Military League, on which it had counted for full support, held back. The Tsar did as well, disquieted by the republican inclinations of some of its younger members. Absent a positive program let alone an identifiable ideology, Zveno formed four successive cabinets in order to win wider approval. By November 1935 Boris and his army allies simply forced them out. Velchev attempted a countercoup and was easily arrested when it failed.[9]

Now began what Richard Crampton has rightly called Boris's search for a middle ground between the growing political polarization of left and right while at the same time not allowing the generals of the Military League simply to continue the Zveno regime under another name.[10] Boris named the aged and respected Georgi Kiosseivanov as Prime Minister. He promptly dissolved the Military League and two paramilitary organizations, doubtless with the Tsar's approval. Boris's personal regime, as it has been called, soon became a search for controlled representation from a reduced political spectrum that now excluded Zveno, the army and the protofascist National Legion of the 1924–6 Prime Minister, Tsankov.

Still included was a Workers' Party newly emboldened by the Comintern's Popular Front against fascism, as were all the Communist surrogates in Southeastern Europe. In the Soviet Union, the BKP's prior leadership was purged for advocating an autonomous Macedonia, now anathema if a unified Yugoslavia was to be supported. The new Comintern head, Georgi Dimitrov, thereby reemerged in Moscow as party leader and consolidated his control in Bulgaria under the Front's banner. The Workers' Party joined the Constitutional Bloc of old Democrats and the Pladne Agrarian rivals to the Vrabcha group in demanding a return to the 1879 Constitution and new elections. Their so-called Petorka of five parties was able to contest new municipal elections in 1937 and then national ones for a reduced National Assembly in March 1938. A new electoral law trimmed the number of seats from 272 to 160. It also reshaped districts and raised the voting age from 25 to 30 to subtract potential votes against the government's list of candidates. Majority balloting again replaced proportional representation. At the same time, married or widowed women were allowed to vote for the first time. Almost half of them did not cast ballots in the face of rural intimidation. This pulled the overall turnout down to 65 percent of eligible voters. Still, the government list barely won with 95 of the 160 seats, including two that were disputed, and then with candidates almost entirely from the established parties. An Interior Ministry Report complained that its best repressive efforts had been undone by rural cooperatives and reading rooms, the lack of cooperation from other ministries, and "liberty not appropriate for the time."

By the same year of 1938, Greece's government came closer to qualifying as a totalitarian dictatorship than any other state in interwar Southeastern Europe, instructively under a monarch less influential than any of the others in the region. George II had been exiled since 1923, obliged to leave following the Asia Minor disaster. Finally, in November 1935, after a last Venezelist coup had failed, the army's monarchist opposition forced the government to stage a plebiscite on restoring George to the throne. Near-unanimous if partly contrived approval brought him back from London by the end of the month. Thus ended the Greek Republic, just as the civil war that would destroy the Spanish Republic was beginning.

The death throes of Greece's Republic followed quickly on the heels of its "golden age," the reforming and fairly elected Liberal regime of Venizelos from 1928 to 1932. Its primary opponents, the southern-based People's Party, had barely lost the last parliamentary election based on proportional representation to the Liberals in 1932. In 1933 they won under winner-take-all balloting. Liberal support suffered in part for the economic losses from the Depression. The party also faced the northern refugee's disillusion with Venizelos over the 1930 agreement with Turkey to limit claims to lost property in Asia Minor. Venizelos could not accept the narrow defeat. He did not discourage, as he could have, the military coup attempted by the leading Liberal General Nicolaos Plastiras. It quickly failed. So did a comparable attempt in March 1935, this time explicitly endorsed by Venizelos. An organization for Republican Defense failed to mobilize the expected support from army officers in the former northern stronghold. The way was open for martial law and the very dismissal of republican military officers that the coup had hoped to prevent. Some 1500 were cashiered in this latest turn of the carousel.[11]

The King's return did little to resolve the political divisions exposed by the aforementioned elections of January 1936 to the National Assembly. The People's Party won 143 seats and the Liberals 141. Adding the 15 seats taken for the Greek Communist Party (KKE) became the only basis for a working majority. Neither party could countenance accepting Communist support. A series of prolonged strikes in Thessaloniki just then helped them both to dramatize the threat from the KKE, now grown past 10,000 and well represented in unions that counted nearly 200,000 members. The Comintern's shift to the Popular Front in 1935 had proved especially helpful to the KKE. It was freed for the time being from the commitment to support an autonomous Macedonia, the Aegean region included, in a Communist Balkan Federation. The Liberals now suffered a further loss of northern refugee support to the KKE.

Their longtime adversary, Metaxas, stepped in, to the disadvantage as well of the People's Party to which he had never belonged despite his royalist sympathies. The deaths of Venizelos, the rival party's leader, Panaghis Tsaldaris, and Metxasas's major military rival, General Kondylis, all during the first half of 1936, helped to clear his way. Once appointed Prime Minister in April, Metaxas waited only a few months, until August 4, to dismiss the recently elected National Assembly. Seizing on the threat of a general strike he suspended the 1911 Constitution and began to rule by emergency decree. He empowered his Interior Minister, Konstantinos Maniadakis, soon a feared figure in his own right, to breathe new life into the *Idionymon* law passed under Venizelos in 1929. It authorized all measures to suppress Communist activity against the state. Now it also served to suppress strikes, the Slav Macedonian or Bulgarian minority, anyone suspected of Communist sympathies, and all other dissenters. Unknown numbers of them were exiled. By 1937 the Akronaupia concentration camp had collected the first of some thousands of prisoners (the number is disputed). They were all charged as Communists and only released on signing forced Declarations of Repentance. Meanwhile, the two major parties atrophied, never to recover. A decree of 1937 ended the municipal self-government that had been their last stronghold.

On August 4, 1938 Metaxas took the further step, unprecedented in Southeastern Europe to that point, of declaring himself Prime Minister for life. He did not create a new political party, arguing that "the whole of the Greek people constituted such a party." He took the additional position of Education Minister and also concentrated on promoting his new National Youth Organization (EON). His efforts to spread the study of demotic Greek, rather than the Byzantine *katharevousa*, through the school system were constructive, as was his resistance to the anti-Semitism that suspected the national loyalty of Thessaloniki's still large Jewish population and had provoked the rioting that destroyed the city's Campbell district in 1931. Much less positive was the promotion of EON through its own new bureaucracy and its use to provide a new set of informers for the Interior Ministry. To expand its membership further, he abolished the Greek Boy Scouts in 1939. EON also became the primary vehicle for advancing a personality cult around Metaxas as Greece's "first farmer, first worker, first warrior." At his frequent public appearances for state occasions, the short, aging, and overweight Metaxas hardly presented a military image, the creator of another ancient Sparta and a third Hellenic civilization. But for anyone who objected, spoke a language other than Greek in public, or failed to display the flag on holidays, Manadiakis and his expanded force of secu-

rity police were watching closely. They tapped telephones to identify dissenters. Decrees stipulating minimum wages, maximum hours, paid vaca-
tions, and even health insurance made some concession to urban workers,
proportionally the largest in the region, and to their fractious unions. More
useful to the regime were increases in military salaries and training for the
core of 5000 officers. Beyond promoting loyalty, these last measures also
contributed to the army's success in repulsing the Italian invasion of 1940
(see Chapter 5). Before then, however, Metaxas must be judged by his dictatorial political regime, its unusually repressive restrictions and the allegiance to his narrow view of a collective Greek identity that it demanded.[12]

Troubled National Transitions and Urban-Rural Disjunctures

Neither in Greece nor elsewhere in the region did these officially promoted
identities spread as widely as the royal regimes intended. Let us admit that
the challenge of national integration during these brief interwar decades
was under any conditions formidable for states either newly created like
Yugoslavia and Albania, greatly enlarged like Romania, or unexpectedly burdened with a huge refugee influx like Bulgaria and Greece. Nowhere had the
mass military mobilization for the First World War created the victorious,
unifying experience that was Eugen Weber's final phase in making peasants
into Frenchmen. Only the Serbian army could claim a full set of heroic
wartime credentials, and, as we have seen in Chapter 3, its experience had
not made Serb let alone non-Serb peasants into Yugoslavs.

Only in defeated Bulgaria did public education, the other pillar of official integration, bring the national figure for largely rural illiteracy down to
31 percent by the 1930s. Elsewhere it still exceeded 40 percent, at least double
that in Albania. The persisting limits on peasant education even for the
ethnic majorities or pluralities contributed to the continuing gap between
these predominantly rural populations and the increasingly modern capital
cities and universities. This disjuncture undercut the central control to
which the royal regimes increasingly aspired. It did not prevent and sometimes encouraged responses, rural as well as urban, that drew heavily on
European ideologies or organizational practice.

Urban Promise and European Models

All of the capital cities save Tirana continued their rapid growth of the first
interwar decade, moving well ahead of the pace for other towns. Bucharest
nearly doubled in size and Athens tripled to reach 1 million people by 1939.
They accounted respectively for one half and one-third of the total urban

population. Sofia grew by some 100,000 to reach 387,000 by the end of the decade. Belgrade also grew but by barely 10 percent to pass 300,000. One reason was surely the growth of Zagreb, the one near-rival in size across the region, to 200,000. Its well-established university constituted another sort of rivalry.

All four large capitals shared a number of features in common not only with each other but also with other European cities. Literacy rates exceeded 80 percent for Belgrade and Bucharest. They reached 90 percent for Athens and Sofia. A flood of books and other publications helped to make up for the periodic censorship of the press. For newspapers, magazines, and journals, Yugoslavia's censorship decree of 1929 had to contend with nearly 200 publications in Belgrade alone. By the early 1930s the industrial workforce that still lagged behind public employees on a national basis now surpassed their numbers in all four capitals. By 1938, industrial totals all reached 50,000. Membership in trade unions separate from the royal regimes and tolerated at best rose accordingly. They doubled for Athens, Belgrade, and Sofia by 1938 to include half or more of factory or state utility workers. Periodic strikes, always encouraged by Communist union members even in Bucharest, reflected an independent challenge to the Ministries of Interior in particular. All four universities now employed about two hundred faculty members in a full range of disciplines. Student enrollments ranged from 6000 in Belgrade up to 21,000 in Bucharest. Only in Belgrade did a shift not occur into scientific or technical fields and away from the law faculty and related fields, so often used to stereotype the region's interwar universities as merely training grounds for state employment.[13]

Reform-minded municipal government was another liberal prospect in this generally illiberal decade of European as well as regional politics. Bucharest and Sofia hung on to considerable autonomy into the mid-1930s and made good use of it. Both benefited from determined mayors and university faculties of architecture who were fully engaged with the prevailing European currents of urban planning.[14] The mayor's office in Bucharest had already solicited the Paris plans for traffic circulation and park space before the First World War. The city's leading theorist of explicitly French urbanism, Cincitat Sfinţescu, prepared a comprehensive plan to include all of the surrounding *mahale* (villages) in the city limits and to replace their substandard shacks with subsidized housing. By 1930 a reforming *Primar*, or mayor, Dimitrie Dobrescu had been selected from the 60 percent of a city council now elected for the first time. While he served until 1934, Dobrescu did more than spread the paved streets and indoor plumbing that earned him the nickname of "the pick-axe *Primar*." He pushed up municipal tax revenues from 30 to 50 percent of the central government's levy on the city. Frustrated in his effort to build subsidized public housing, he at least established the distribution of hygienically safe milk and effective regulations for meat processing. The rough-cut Transylvanian reformer recruited staff from the university's architecture faculty and drew on the international standing of Sfințescu and other Romanian urbanists to keep King Carol's Interior Ministry from interfering. By 1938, however, the ministry was again choosing the mayor and the city council.

Sofia's *obshtina*, or district council, had established a department for architecture and planning by 1931. Even after the council's right to an elected membership was suspended after the Zveno coup in 1934, it continued to play a surprisingly independent role. By 1937 the planning department had grown to 119 members. Its 31 architects and engineers had been trained mainly in German universities. They and their *kmet*, or mayor, Ivan Ivanov, remained more committed to the ideals of Weimar urban planning than the anti-urban ideas of Nazi Germany. Stamboliiski's Agrarian regime had already started the construction of low-rent, cooperative apartment buildings on the German model of the 1920s. Then a Nazi architect won the Zveno's competition for a new urban plan. Adolf Muesmann favored the "garden city" approach of Ebenezer Howard over more low-cost apartments. Mussman wanted to separate industrial workers in an outlying zone and also to isolate a Jewish population he wrongly believed to occupy half of the city center. Meanwhile, two-thirds of the rising factory labor force lived in largely substandard rental quarters between the small Jewish quarter and the shacks of the Macedonian refugees just to the west of the center. Ivanov and his colleagues stalled off final approval of the Mussman Plan until 1938. It was then abandoned as too expensive.

Belgrade, like Athens, had made little progress in advancing a French-inspired General Plan of 1923 for the city center before all municipal autonomy vanished in the 1930s. Serbian political infighting and the lack of tax revenues were responsible in Belgrade. The city council convened a planning conference in 1937 but failed to generate a new initiative for the city's rapidly growing urban area. Half of its streets remained unpaved and without plumbing. In Athens the chaotic, largely extralegal settlement of the Asia Minor refugees prevented the revival of promising efforts that had peaked in 1896 with construction for the first Olympic Games.

The Peasant Problem, Competing Ideologies and National Identity

Competition to represent the huge peasant majorities could proceed in the general absence, as we have seen, of any consistent commitment to rural reforms among the royal regimes. The problems of struggling rural small-holders and tenant farmers sometimes allowed peasantist ideologies to contest or speak for the national identity as well. In Yugoslavia the peasant problem added to regional and religious contention; in Romania it advanced an exclusionary ethnic identity. Elsewhere, nationalist ideology itself could trump peasant populism. In Bulgaria the decision of Stamboliiski's Agrarian regime to reconcile with the Yugoslav Kingdom on the Macedonian question had encouraged its overthrow. In Greece the huge refugee influx pushed the problems of the smallholding peasantry in the south aside for the Venezelist Liberals. They championed instead the Greek identity of the new northern lands in order to keep its refugees in their republican camp against the threat of a royalist revival. The Slav Macedonians remaining in Greece and those fleeing or transferred into Bulgaria, each about two hundred thousand, both served to confine the concern with national integration to issues of ethnic identity. In Albania, persisting tribal identities, scant access to higher education, and Zog's determination to prevent any wider identification with Kosovar Albanians all undermined discussion of national identity.

In Yugoslavia, King Aleksandar was determined, as we have already seen, to establish a wider Yugoslav identity that merged Serbs, Croats, Slovenes, and assimilating minorities together. Yet this transition was to be encouraged and enforced on the essentially Serbian terms that came from a central government based in Belgrade and with Serbs much overrepresented in the key ministries. The city's largely liberal intelligentsia did not enthuse over this reliance on state power or the assertion of Serbian ethnic or religious rights in the process. Three-quarters of Belgrade University's faculty expressed their opposition to what they saw as simply continuing the pre-1914 policies of Pašić's Radical Party. There was little backing there or in the broader cultural elite for the 1937 proposal of Vasa Čubrilović, much cited by Serb adversaries in the 1990s, to expel the Albanian majority in Kosovo to Turkey or Albania. Yet there was also little interest in national politics and no section for sociology in the Serbian Academy of Sciences and Arts. Attention to the country's huge peasant majority was confined to Serbia and its historical ethnography.[15] And that Serbian peasantry's primary point of contact with the country's other constituent peoples was the experience or the exaggerated schoolbook account of Albanian attacks on the retreating Serbian army in 1915.

As for the Serbian Orthodox Church, expanded state borders afer 1918 confronted it, like its Romanian counterpart, with the loss of the overwhelming majority it had enjoyed in the prewar population. The six Orthodox jurisdictions within the new Yugoslav Kingdom only brought the

Church's combined total up to 48 percent of the population, and unifying just those jurisdictions took over a decade. Neither the royal dictatorship's Law on the Serbian Orthodox Church or the Orthodox Constitution that finally united the regional hierarchies in 1931 promoted a wider Yugoslav identity. The Law provided increased budgetary support for priests' salaries, and the Constitution spoke of still more church or school construction in Serb areas of Bosnia. While not proclaiming Orthodoxy as the state religion, these measures surely placed the other confessions in a secondary position. Nor did Bosnian Muslims welcome the countrywide Islamic framework that Aleksandar's regime had forced on them in 1929. By 1935 their complaints had reestablished the statute of Bosnian-Muslim religious autonomy won from Habsburg authorities in 1909.

The Croatian and Slovene-Catholic hierarchies had meanwhile mounted a campaign to win rights comparable to those in the Orthodox Constitution. But the ensuing struggle over such an agreement required a Concordat between the Yugoslav government and the Vatican. Its conclusion had been a pet project of Aleksandar's. The Serbian opposition to the succeeding Stojadinović government seized on the issue and was soon joined in demanding rejection by the Orthodox Patriarchate of Belgrade. The death of the Patriarch on the very day the Concordat was ratified in Belgrade served to scuttle any implementation and leave the respective religious leaderships divided for the rest of the decade.[16]

Below this higher level, two mass organizations in Croatia stepped in to speak for their rural populations and to contest any imposed Yugoslav identity. They were each far more important than either the largely emigré *Ustaša* or the Croatian section of the KPJ. The cooperatives of the Croatian Peasant Party (HSS) and the Catholic Church's Crusaders were also in competition with each other. HSS leader Vladko Maček described the surge forward after his release from prison and the resumption of legal political activity in 1935 as "the boom of the party." The boom owed something to his own organizational skills but more to the regional impact of the Depression on the grain-deficit area that stretched down the Adriatic coast and inland into Bosnia, Kosovo, and Macedonia. North from Dubrovnik, this was largely a Croat population. They had received small plots of inhospitable land received in the redistribution of the 1920s (see Chapter 3). Efforts to cultivate them had soon left most recipients in debt and pushed families back into sharecropping to survive. Then the Depression discouraged Italian investment in coastal industry and brought back a quarter of the 75,000 young men who had gone primarily to France to work. On the Dalmatian coast alone, the HSS boosted the number of local cooperatives from 35 in 1928 to 202 by 1937. Their activities went beyond agricultural credit to adult education and social events. Instruction that reduced illiteracy also increased political engagement. Recent Croatian scholarship goes so far as to call this expanding cooperative network "the generator of Croatian national consciousness on the coast."[17]

Its competitor there and into Bosnia-Herzegovina in particular was a Catholic youth organization that attracted far more Croat participation than did the mandatory membership in Aleksandar's new Yugoslav Sokol, a gymnastics society for youth on the Czech pattern. The royal regime had created this single organization in 1929 to replace not only the existing Serb, Croat, and Slovene Sokols but also the Croatian Eagles. They had begun as a youth organization under the 1922 papal imprimatur for Catholic Action, new lay initiatives beyond the clergy. The Eagles had prospered as a Sokol-like society for gymnastics and mass meetings. They survived competition from a Croatian Sokol closely tied to an HSS then led by the anti-clerical Stjepan Radić. Both organizations were disbanded by the royal dictatorship of 1929.

The Eagles reconstituted themselves within a few weeks as a registered religious organization. Now under Jesuit supervision and confined to activities within church premises, the previous leader, Ivo Protupilac, proclaimed the Great Crusader Brotherhood and Sorority.[18] Now their weekly meetings consisted of moral instruction to the exclusion of gymnastics. Sunday parades, church meetings open to the public, mass attendance at Eucharistic conferences, or celebrations from 1932 of the Pope's Day constantly pressed the legal limits. Summer courses and brochures went out from an efficient central headquarters in Zagreb to a largely rural constituency. Anti-Communism soon joined antiliberalism and antisecularism as major themes, along with social strictures and the appreciation of Croatian history. Their materials never mentioned Yugoslavia, only "the state" within which "the homeland," understood as Croatia and most of Herzegovina, was located. By the later 1930s the slogan "God, Church, and Homeland" symbolized a political program that included no recognition of a wider Yugoslav identity. Head of all Catholic Action for Croatia from 1936, Protupilac tried but failed to come to terms with the less anticlerical Maček and his growing HSS. His relationship with the Croatian Catholic hierarchy, under the assertive new Archbishop Alojzije Stepinac from 1937, was no more successful.

These considerable Croatian challenges to a single Yugoslav state and national identity thus remained divided among themselves. The Croatian Peasant Party, the Catholic hierarchy and the Crusaders could not reconcile their differences as war approached. First the fascist *Ustaša* and then the Yugoslav Communist Party would exploit those differences as the Second World War progressed.

The search for a single, overarching national identity was most open and intense in Romania. There, not incidentally, university students were most numerous and their faculties more concerned with sociology or philosophy. In part because of the urban location or perceived advantage of the new minority populations, Jews as well as Hungarians and Germans, the decade's discussion focused on the ethnically Romanian peasantry. If their conditions could be improved and their values preserved, surely this would confirm the wider "national essence" to which the minorities would simply have to assimilate. Had not the tendency of the Roma minority to adopt the Romanian language and otherwise abandon their traditional identity reduced their numbers to less than 2 percent of the population by the 1930 census? Peasant devotion to holding their own land would also be the best bulwark against a Communist threat that the Soviet claim to Bessarabia kept alive. The majority of these approaches moved sharply away from liberal values of French positivism that had predominated in Romanian academia. The historian Nicolae Iorga had already started the movement back to Romania's peasant heritage before the First World War. Yet his approach and several new ones, presented with the same scholarly elaboration, stayed largely within the Western mainstream of the 1930s. The exception was Nichifor Crainic. By the 1930s he and his *Gînderea* (Thought) circle had moved beyond their celebration of Orthodoxy as the foundation of peasant culture noted in Chapter 3. They now joined forces with irreligious young intellectuals led by Nae Ionescu and including Mircea Eliade. They shifted to the far right, enthusing first over Mussolini's fascist regime and then turning to Codreanu's Iron Guard. They cloaked the Guard's ill-defined ideology of peasant populism and minority exclusion with some intellectual legitimacy.[19] Anti-Communist Romanian nationalists in the 1970s would rediscover and appreciate Crainic's ideas (see Chapter 7).

More important at the time, however, was a school of specific sociological or economic prescriptions for rural reform. Its programs promoted the state-building that the populists suspected or disregarded. Four individuals stand out. The country's leading sociologist, Dimitrie Gusti, probably had the greatest effect on public policy. His teams of young researchers detailed peasant poverty and deficiencies in diet and education that cried out for reform. And as Minister of Education in 1933 and then, as noted above, director of King Carol's "village centers," Gusti had more direct contact with peasant problems than any of the other intellectuals we consider here. He was also attracted to the eugenic determinism of Iuliu Moldovan, a Transylvanian trained in medical pathology in Vienna and at the front during the First World War. In 1919 Moldovan founded the medical school and the Institute of Hygiene and Social Hygiene in Cluj. In 1930 he used his brief tenure as Minister of Health and Social Welfare in fellow Transylvanian Iuliu Maniu's National Peasant government to put forward the so-called Moldovan Law. Much trimmed down as passed, it still relied on biological determinism to promote a more capable Romanian peasantry and also to exclude the minorities from participation. Gusti endorsed instruction in this genetic "wager on the strong" in his programs for rural education. And the American Rockefeller Foundation endorsed a comparable emphasis in Romanian medical education. Moldovan used Transylvania's existing Astra organization to establish the Carpathian Falcons. Its mission was to teach peasant youth national loyalty as well as personal hygiene. His later service in King Carol's Supreme Council and then in Marshal Antonescu's wartime regime does not seem surprising.[20]

The leading economist of the National Peasant regime, the Leipzig-educated Virgil Madgearu, was the one major reformer to stay the liberal course during the 1930s. He had favored the opening of Romanian industry to foreign competition before the Depression as a way of helping small peasant proprietors. His "peasantism" wagered not on their traditions but on their capacity to adopt modern methods to their smallholdings and to produce as well or better than the large estates that critics of the Romanian land reform assumed to be superior. Madgearu also assumed that an increasing number of peasants would eventually move to industrial jobs. The more influential economist of this period was, however, Mihail Manoilescu, trained as an engineer and a neoliberal opponent of peasantism. By the 1930s he had turned to corporatism and industrial protectionism. The state should provide a corporatist framework for the rapid industrialization that would push peasants away from an agricultural sector that Manoilescu regarded as permanently less productive.[21]

Surviving the Depression: National Economies and State Initiatives

To be sure, the shock of plummeting agricultural exports compounded by the burden of exchange rates tied to the Gold Standard encouraged a turning inward to rely on domestic resources and new state initiatives. The region's national economies could no longer rely on commercial bank credit supported by wider European connections nor on central banks whose primary concern was to protect currency values from depreciation. The record of limited economic recovery across the Depression decade deserves our attention. The advance was, however, less connected to what has been called "the genesis of etatism" across Eastern Europe (the rise of enough state economic initiative to make the post-1945 transition to socialist planning seem a logical progression) than previous scholarship, my own included, has maintained.[22] One precedent set for the post-1945 Communist regimes does stand up. Starting before the Nazi economic offensive across the region but spreading further under its auspices, bilateral clearing accounts largely replaced multilateral trade under internationally agreed exchange rates and tariffs. These bilateral agreements encouraged the survival of state agencies for controlling at least agricultural exports, agencies whose performance otherwise fell short of expectations.

Agricultural Retrenchment and Limited Growth

The largely agricultural economies of Southeastern Europe hardly closed the gap between their low levels of national income and the developed European economies during the 1930s. Their roughly estimated net incomes in 1938 all ranged from $70 to $80 per capita, with Albania further back at less than $60. These figures were one-third of the reckonings for France and one-quarter of those for Germany, while barely one-third for both of them in agricultural output per capita.[23] There is, all the same, no indication that the region lost ground to the developed, largely industrial economies during the course of the Depression. By 1932 the real value of exports suffered the same general European decline to about 40 percent of the 1929 level, with the exception of Romania and its advantage in oil. When and how these agricultural sectors, whose productivity per capita and marketed share of output remained at one-third of the leading Danish levels, managed to surpass at least their own 1929 levels still deserves attention.

Bulgaria did better than the other two grain-exporters, Romania and Yugoslavia. By 1936–8, Bulgarian cereal production had risen by 23 percent from the 1926–30 level without the increase in cultivated land seen elsewhere in the region. Wheat yields per hectare for 1935–9 were fully 31 percent above the pre-1914 level. Meanwhile, acreage in industrial crops and the production of vegetables had doubled, well beyond increases in neighboring economies. Greater access to credit from the cooperative network and the long-established Bulgarian Agricultural Bank (BZB) provided the advantage that allowed two constructive tendencies that had already begun in the later 1920s, as noted in Chapter 3, to continue. These were the import of agricultural equipment for grain cultivation and the diversification into other crops for export. The contrast with Romania is instructive. There a state Agricultural Mortgage Bank had only been established in 1929. Its loans charged high rates. While Romania's lower-interest Popular Banks were retreating from further lending in the face of unpaid debts, Bulgaria's cooperative credit associations were able to increase their loans by one-quarter between 1932 and 1934. The state had admittedly trimmed peasant debts by 20–40 percent. Perhaps more important was the new credit made available from the merger of the BZB and the cooperatives' Central Bank. It supported the consolidation of scattered plots that further strengthened peasant smallholdings during the rest of the decade.

Neither such consolidation nor the overdue shift away from excessive dependence on wheat and corn crops occurred in Romanian agriculture. Since the completion of the land reform, its peasantry occupied almost half of arable land in smallholdings of less than five hectares. Holdings of 5–50 hectares covered another 35 percent. Smallholders with less than ten hectares owed 70 percent of Romania's personal debt, by far the largest share in the region. For the majority under five hectares, their net earnings were barely half the total accumulated in agricultural rent, interest or profit from larger holdings, versus earnings from Bulgaria's smallholdings that equaled its comparable total from properties over five hectares. The Romanian peasant diet also suffered. Its unhealthy dependence on corn continued. A State Cereal Commission was established in 1932 in order to expand the wheat production from which Romania should have been retreating. It subsidized wheat exports at 30 percent above a world price that had fallen by twice as much, helping only to double wheat acreage by 1937 and to keep the export value of cereals over 30 percent of the Romanian total.

Bulgaria's experience with a state agency for subsidizing grain exports was hardly more promising. Founded in 1930, *Hranoiznos* paid full support prices for wheat and rye exports over the next three years, only to run up sizeable deficits. This prompted the 1934 decision to make the agency into a buyers' monopoly, or monopsony, for all domestic production. It then charged flour mills prices high enough to cover export losses but not high enough to leave a surplus for investing in agricultural improvements. Fortunately, cereals had slipped from 25 percent of Bulgarian export value in 1932 to just 10 percent by 1938.

The counterpart created in Yugoslavia a few months earlier, the Privileged Joint-Stock Export Company (*Prizad*) began with monopoly privileges for wheat and corn export. It could not, however, sustain the following year's monopoly on domestic sales. Its domestic price proved too low to cover the export premiums paid for the bumper harvests of 1931. The unsold export surplus had to be stored at extra expense in Hungary or Romania as a result of the lack of domestic facilities. By 1932, amid charges of kickbacks paid to the new state agency, *Prizad's* domestic monopoly was withdrawn. Its continuing export monopoly made little use of its profits to improve grain cultivation and none to encourage a turn to other crops.

Aggregate statistics for Yugoslavia suggest a more promising picture than that in Romania. Both cereals and industrial crops led the way in pushing overall crop output per capita and per hectare to increases approaching 20 percent for 1936–8 over 1926–30. In any case, animal and timber exports both accounted for a larger share of export value than cereals, 20 versus 15 percent, throughout most of the decade. But regional disparities rivaled only by Greece reduced this promise considerably. The increases of 1936–8, boosted by favorable weather, were confined to the fertile northern lowlands. In the upland south, smaller holdings on poorer land kept grain prices at twice their northern levels. These southern smallholdings also explained a Yugoslav average of land cultivated per capita that was half of the average of one hectare in Bulgaria and Romania. The Dalmatian coast, as noted above, and Vardar Macedonia both suffered from the Depression's reduction of foreign workers in Western Europe. For Macedonia, the state's sharp reduction of authorized growers for its tobacco monopoly, down by three-quarters from 1926 to 1934, made matters worse.

Greece's grain cultivation faced no crisis from falling export prices. Dependent like Albania on imports simply to feed the population, its challenge across the interwar period and beyond was simply to produce a greater proportion of domestic needs. Already in 1928 a state agency, the Organization for the Concentration of Wheat, had been created in order to pay peasants twice the price of Western or Russian imports. An agricultural bank opened the following year and lent freely, particularly through a special section for cooperatives. Peasant repayments nonetheless lagged until the good harvests of 1932–3. Imports of harvesting equipment now increased, and the use of improved Austrian and Italian seeds spread. Drainage projects begun by the Refugee Settlement Commission in Macedonia and Thrace resumed under several American contractors. Domestically grown wheat climbed from 40 percent of consumption in 1928 to 64 percent by 1933–7. Exports continued to depend on tobacco and raisins for two-thirds of their sales. They did not recover in real terms from the drop in prices and British demand, despite the increase in German purchases after 1935.[24] Here we find scant state support, unlike Bulgaria where a tobacco consortium of cooperatives had survived the deposing of Stamboliiski's Agrarian regime (see Chapter 3). For Greece, the drop in tobacco prices and the declining area under cultivation in the north stoked the aforementioned outburst of urban protest among the tobacco processors of Thessaloniki, typically refugees increasingly attracted to Communist-led unions.

Industry Growing, Commercial Banks Retreating

Manufacturing surely grew at a respectable pace across the region in comparison to the continent as a whole. Greece and Bulgaria led the way, with increases for 1929–38 of 5.7 percent and 4.8 percent. Romania and Yugoslavia recorded advances of 3.4 and 2.4 percent, still better than the European average of 1.1 percent, and even better when the surges in mining are added. The manufactured share of Romania's export value fell to the Bulgarian and Yugoslav level of 16–17 percent, all of them well ahead of 3–4 percent for Greece and its virtual absence for Albania. None of this growth was of course transferring enough labor and capital from agriculture to industry to generate the sustained, self-supporting, national growth that economists call development. Nationally, employees in public service remained larger in every case than the industrial workforce, both still dwarfed by the aforementioned majorities of 70–80 percent in agriculture. Manufactured imports continued to be primarily consumer goods rather than industrial equipment or inputs.

The state's role in this growth was also limited. It controlled prices and furnished new sources of credit rather than expanding state ownership or even direct investment. Private commercial banks, domestic as well as foreign, had been one cornerstone of the liberal framework for national economic growth in the 1920s. They now slipped well into the background. Another cornerstone, the joint-stock company, surprisingly did not, despite the decline in direct foreign investment. The central banks, whose independence as we saw in Chapter 3 had been an explicit Anglo-French initiative, were now less independent. They still expanded their activities rather than see them transferred to new state agencies.

Indeed, the respective central banks dominated the transition from private to public finance. Their share of bank assets rose at the expense of commercial banks through the 1930s, most strikingly for Romania where the former doubled and the latter fell by one half to reverse their relative positions. While the number of Romanian banks was also halved, the greatest blow to commercial assets came from the collapse of the region's largest private commercial bank, the Bancă Marmarosch-Blanc, in 1931. The failure of its main creditor, Vienna's Credit-Anstalt, combined with Jewish ownership to deny Marmarosch-Blanc more than token domestic support. Its rival, the Liberal backed Bancă Romanescă, survived. It was, however, new lending from the National Bank, supported by a two-thirds increase in note issue from 1934 to 1938, that funded rearmament orders. They helped the metallurgical sector to double the overall industrial growth rate of 3.4 percent. Yugoslavia was the only other state with a metallurgical sector of its own large enough to make the state's rearmament a major stimulus. There the State Mortgage Bank (DHB) advanced the credits that allowed new military production, primarily in Serbia, to swell state budget expenditures by one-quarter from 1935 to 1939.

Meanwhile, Yugoslavia's major commercial banks had barely survived the earlier collapse of the Credit-Anstalt and several German banks as well. These were the Zagreb banks whose extensive industrial investments and independence from the National Bank in Belgrade were noted in Chapter 3. That independence now left them with little state support, adding to the Croatian regional grievance against a central government dominated like the National Bank by Belgrade. They drew on their so-called iron reserves to stay in business, but the capacity for new lending vanished.[25] The Belgrade government had also supported trade sanctions imposed by the League of Nations against Italy in 1935. Private Croatian, Slovene, and Dalmatian enterprises who were the main exporters to this nearby market suffered accordingly. Enterprises under direct state ownership, primarily sugar, flour, and tobacco plus the railways, depended on sales taxes, the *trošarina*, for revenues. Their rates were set at higher percentages in these Western lands, but, as total collections shrank with the Depression, there was little left for new investment.

State-owned industry in Bulgaria and Greece did no better, but their central banks and domestic joint-stock enterprises combined to generate the higher rates of growth in manufacturing noted above. And they did so without metallurgical sectors that were too small to respond to the comparable efforts at rearmament. Like Romania and Yugoslavia as well, they had all been freed from the Gold Standard's constraint against devaluation by 1932. Britain's departure from the standard in 1931, ironically just as Yugoslavia had finally joined, left only France and a few others standing on this last cornerstone of liberal orthodoxy from the 1920s. The Bulgarian National Bank received state authorization in 1934 to combine the dozen leading domestic commercial banks into a single *Banka Bulgarski Kredit*.

For the Bulgarian enterprises in cotton textiles, chemicals, and paper which led the way in growth rates, however, their new capital came primarily from joint-stock incorporation. Little came from the cartels whose spread was later exaggerated by the region's Communist-era economic historians. Prevailing only in Romania's metallurgical sector, Bulgaria's cartels never covered more than 10 percent of Bulgarian industrial production. Even there they were effective only for short periods. Nor did direct foreign investment predominate, dropping from three-quarters to less than one-quarter of industrial capital from 1930 to 1939. Yet for Greece and Bulgaria too, the number of joint-stock incorporations literally doubled during the decade, while scarcely changing in Romania and Yugoslavia.

Greek manufacturing benefited from the region's only significant growth in commercial banking during the Depression. Leading this advance from 1933 forward was the National Bank of Greece. Reluctantly freed from its central banking responsibilities by the creation of the Bank of Greece in 1928, the still semiofficial National Bank boosted its share of commercial bank liabilities from 47 to 69 percent by 1934. Overall, commercial bank deposits exceeded total currency in circulation. This access to credit helped to make up for the region's smallest state promotion of new or larger firms as a response to the Depression. Indeed, the Ministry of National Economy under the Tsaldaris government of 1933–5 had only three employees. His regime also ignored export promotion and discouraged machine imports for modernizing the textile industry, preferring instead to protect the small-scale producers typical of its southern political base. The Metaxas regime that took power in 1936 did not hesitate to damp unrest among the increasingly large and fractious force of industrial labor by mandating higher wages and shorter hours. Its new Supreme Economic Council talked of new tariffs and production controls, but state economic policy remained passive. Mark Mazower is surely right in dismissing alarms from the American Ambassador that Greece was becoming "a planned economy."[26]

From Regional Relations to the German Trade Offensive

The louder and longer alarm before and after the Second World War was that a Nazi trade offensive, well coordinated across the entire region from 1935 forward, soon established economic hegemony and with it decisive political influence. Unless we proceed into 1939 and beyond, we cannot find support for this earlier orthodoxy. The separate state adoptions of bilateral clearing accounts under encouraging rates of exchange had spread from an Austrian initiative in the early 1930s. Neither direct German investment nor rearmament deals followed, even after Germany consolidated its existing position as the region's leading trade partner under a series of bilateral clearing agreements. Even less did the royal regimes regard these growing trade relations as anything more than a way to secure the neutrality that now became the primary goal of their diplomacy. The perceived French retreat from the region, the British reluctance to take their place, and the difficulty of dealing with the Soviet Union made some accommodation with Nazi Germany seem essential. At the time, the German potential for restraining fascist Italy seemed more real than Hitler's determination, now so clear in scholarly retrospect, to go to war.

Earlier in the 1930s, the royal regimes had tried to confront the Depression and its attendant political uncertainties by combining regional resources. By 1935, however, the economic efforts had failed. A new political alliance did not include Bulgaria or Albania. One of the conferences of agrarian states promoted by the League of Nations in 1930 had generated a proposal for a customs union between Romania and Yugoslavia that might also include Czechoslovakia. Here was the third member of the Little Entente of the early 1920s and the only one with enough industry to be a complementary trade partner. The proposal quickly died with the French-led furor that scuttled the Austro-German customs union of 1931. Months before, a meeting in Athens of what became the first annual Balkan Conference took up a broader range of alternatives for common protective measures and institutions. Yugoslavia's representative startled the delegates by observing that Denmark's agricultural exports nearly equaled those of Southeastern Europe, with ten times the population. But proposals at subsequent meetings to increase the small amount of interregional trade, about 9 percent of export and import value, foundered. They found few complementary exports and faced the threat of British-led opposition to any evasion of Most-Favored-Nation access to all tariff concessions. For 1931–8, the interregional share of total trade had instead fallen everywhere but Greece.[27]

Diplomatic negotiations in 1934 to arrange a Balkan Entente of security guarantees started well. A series of royal visits to the various capitals created considerable goodwill. But Greece's fear of revisionist claims from Bulgaria, despite disclaimers from Tsar Boris, and Italian pressure on Albania and also Bulgaria kept those two governments from signing the final agreement.[28] Had King Aleksandar not been assassinated that October, only a month after Boris's warm reception for him in Sofia, his preference for reconciliation with Bulgaria might have prevailed.

Hermann Goering's attendance at Aleksandar's funeral in Belgrade in November 1934 is sometimes cited as the start of a concerted Nazi campaign. He did broach the advantages of closer relations with Germany to all regional leaders attending the funeral. In reality, it was simply the first of his own personal initiatives, all promising more than Hitler's government was ready to provide. As may be seen in Table 4.1, Germany and Austria

Table 4.1   Directions of foreign trade, 1929–38 (% in current prices)

Country and year	Northwestern Europe*		Germany and Austria		Italy		Southeastern Europe and Turkey	
	Exp.	Imp.	Exp.	Imp.	Exp.	Imp.	Exp.	Imp.
Albania								
1929–30	0.5	12.3	1.0	8.3	60.5	48.2	22.2	11.8
1937–38	2.4	12.7	0.2	7.0	73.5	30.2	12.6	27.9
Bulgaria								
1929–30	17.8	27.3	38.2	29.9	9.4	12.2	8.7	13.3
1937–38	19.4	33.4	53.0	55.1	5.9	6.3	1.7	4.9
Greece								
1929–30	29.7	28.6	25.9	11.1	16.2	6.0	2.65	16.7
1937–38	17.6	19.7	36.6	30.1	5.8	3.2	6.0	17.4
Romania								
1929–30	20.6	21.5	32.5	36.7	10.3	7.4	7.6	2.6
1937–38	24.9	24.7	26.3	37.1	6.4	4.7	9.5	2.3
Yugoslavia								
1929–30	9.8	13.9	26.8	33.7	26.6	11.1	15.9	4.0
1937–38	22.0	14.1	37.0	43.6	8.5	10.3	4.5	4.1

Note: *France, Holland, Belgium, Britain, and Switzerland.

Source: John R. Lampe and Marvin R. Jackson, *Balkan Economic History, 1550–1950: From Imperial Borderlands to Developing Nations* (Bloomington, IN: Indiana University Press, 1982), Table 12.7, pp. 458–60.

accounted for over 30 percent of Bulgarian, Romanian, and Yugoslav exports and imports by 1929–30, making them the region's largest trading partners. From 1931, central banks across East Central Europe followed an Austrian lead and became the vehicle for exports and imports to be denominated in the domestic currency. The overall balance was to be settled in foreign exchange and then infrequently. Strict licensing requirements for buying foreign goods were also put in place across the region. Premiums of 20–35 percent on buying foreign exchange effectively devalued domestic currencies even when formally still bound to the Gold Exchange Standard.

(Only Greece had formally departed, and even then its initial devaluation of the drachma proved insufficient to meet the region's heaviest debt burden, some 40 percent of the state budget.) Together, these mechanisms served to prevent the import surpluses that would threaten both limited exchange reserves and any prospect of paying debt service. Payments had peaked as a percentage of slumping state budget revenues in the early 1930s. Only official agreements between trading partners could manage the clearing accounts and import licenses. By 1934 such precedents for postwar Communist practice covered over 70 percent of trade turnover for Bulgaria and Yugoslavia, nearly 60 percent for Romania, and 40 percent for Greece. All of them, save Italian-dominated Albania, already had clearing agreements with Germany. This plus a head start from the 1920s had already placed the region's trade with Germany and Austria in a preeminent position by 1934.[29]

The further shift in regional trade by 1938–9 to the German Reich (now including Austria) and the Reichsmark, as reflected in Table 4.1, was nonetheless considerable. From half of Bulgaria's foreign trade in 1934, the Austro-German total now reached two-thirds. This matched the degree of Albanian dependence on Italian trade throughout the interwar period. For Romania and Yugoslavia, it was Austro-German imports that climbed by one half after 1934 to close the export surplus that the initial grain sales had created. For Greece, tobacco and raisin exports to Germany under the 1932 clearing agreement boosted the German share of total exports to 36 percent, recovering from some slippage once the Austrian share was added in 1938. Here the boost in exports continued to reduce the huge import surplus from two to one, like Albania's throughout, to three to two. By 1936–8, real per capita exports approached the level of 1926–30 for all the region's economies except Romania's, which surpassed it by 22 percent.[30]

As Chapter 5 will demonstrate, Nazi trade hegemony did translate into real if not immediately effective political leverage over the royal regimes by 1939. Before then, whether German foreign policy pursued such leverage ardently or indifferently, it did not hold the economic or diplomatic cards to enforce compliance. Each of the royal regimes strove with considerable success to maintain their freedom of diplomatic maneuver. They made agricultural trade bargains that were initially to their advantage and then received too little direct investment to bind their industries or their armies to the growing import of German manufactures.

In addition, no royal ruler admired Hitler, nor could those Nazi leaders, primarily Hermann Goering and Alfred Rosenberg, who sought to spread Nazi influence into domestic parties proceed without being restrained by German diplomacy. The region's one political leader whose domestic regime and national ideology bears some comparison to Hitler's Germany, Ion Metaxas of Greece, was also the only one resolutely committed to alliance with Great Britain throughout. Tsar Boris would be equally resolute in relying on diplomatic maneuver to keep Bulgaria's neutral standing intact despite the growing dependence on German trade. In 1937 he backed Prime Minister Kiosseivanov in resisting the efforts of his War Minister and Hermann Goering to more than double the size of a modest German loan for rearmament. It was intended to replace obsolete equipment in an army grown to 50,000 men since forsaking the 1919 limits in 1934. As late as 1938, Boris tried vainly at British urging to join the Balkan Entente. He also admonished Hitler before the Munich Conference that a German invasion of Czechoslovakia would provoke British intervention and probably start the "fatal disaster" of another war.[31]

The Nazi trade offensive nonetheless began in 1935 with better political prospects, at least in Romania and Yugoslavia. Both the League of Nations and French foreign policy had just suffered serious damage to their reputations for assuring regional security. The League sought member sanctions against trade with Italy following Mussolini's invasion of Ethiopia. The sanctions did not deter Mussolini. Observing them hurt both the Romanian and Yugoslav economies, and created political resentment in the two governments. At the same time, the French efforts to add the Soviet Union as a guarantor of regional security succeeded only in arranging an agreement with Czechoslovakia. The other two members of the Little Entente, Romania and Yugoslavia, objected. In Bucharest, King Carol led the objectors and obliged the Entente's principal advocate, his Francophile Foreign Minister Nicolae Titulescu, to resign. Fear of Soviet claims to Bessarabia were still widely felt, and, as it turned out, realistic. In Belgrade, where even diplomatic relations with the Soviet Union would not be established until 1941, Prime Minister Stojadinović regarded the initiative as the end of the Little Entente. And across the region, the limitations on French and for that matter British trade were too severe to permit economic blandishments. These included systems of imperial preference for both, protective agricultural tariffs, plus an overvalued currency for France, and an aversion to clearing accounts in Britain.

By March 1935 the artful German Finance Minister, Hjalmar Schacht, had negotiated a trade protocol with Yugoslavia. It put still more favorable rates of exchange in place for grain and tobacco exports, and opened the way for German firms to explore further arrangements. Schacht launched similar negotiations with Romania a couple of months later. He then toured Sofia and Athens as well as Belgrade in June 1936 to sign the economic agreements with enough public fanfare to make the political implications clear.

Yugoslavia was plainly the initial target.[32] Prime Minister Stojadinović admired the German economic recovery, freed of the liberal orthodoxy he himself had abandoned, and appreciated Hitler as a successful politician. He also misjudged the Nazi leader as "a man of peace who wanted only a colony or two" and whose Balkan interests were "nothing more than an open door for our German economy."[33]

For the pre-1939 period, that was in fact all that Germany received for Stojadinovic's gamble. German investment and technical assistance were indeed directed toward metallurgy and Yugoslav rearmament. The Krupp project to construct a new modern steelworks, *Jugočelik*, at Zenica in Bosnia, began the week after Schacht's visit. Its purpose was to provide all of Yugoslavia's military requirements. But potential objections from the largely Serbian officer corps to Goering's favorite proposal, accepting weapons and equipment from their First World War adversary, kept Stojadinovic from even proposing such assistance. Orders were placed instead with Škoda of Czechoslovakia and an Italian firm, despite German objections. Even after Zenica was in operation and an Austrian steelworks and coal mines in Slovenia had been added in 1938, the overall German share in Yugoslavia's foreign investment amounted to only 6 percent. British and French firms continued to control 90 percent of the country's mining operations, resisting German offers to buy them out. Seeking Yugoslav support over the manufactured Czech crisis of 1938, German diplomacy openly rejected the irredentist efforts of the Croatian *Ustaša* emigrés. A German Foreign Ministry not yet under the Nazi zealot Joachim von Ribbentrop also obliged Alfred Rosenberg to tell the *Volksdeutsche* organization of Vojvodina Germans to back the Stojadinović government. The German Embassy in Belgrade had already stalled some economic initiatives in struggling for control with Goering's representative.

The German economic relationship with Romania started more slowly and faced still more obstacles. Schacht had not included Bucharest on his tour of new partners in 1936. Romanian reluctance, in a bad harvest year, to ship promised grain to Germany had gotten the trade protocol of 1935 off on the wrong foot. Such shipments were central both to Schacht's original plan to barter exports for imports and to broader Nazi aims for *Grossraumwirtschaft*. For such a "great-area economy," where planned coordination would replace currency payments and market controls, Southeast European agriculture and raw materials offered the perfect complement to industrial Germany.[34] Hard currency demand for its oil exports allowed Romania to resist the start that Yugoslavia and Bulgaria had made down this road.

Later in 1936, even after King Carol had replaced Titulescu as Foreign Minister, his government accepted Czech credits to begin a program to arm at least ten of its army's 37 nominal divisions. Goering and his representatives pushed hard to tie further rearmament to the Reich. They promised an unequivocal German guarantee for the integrity of Romania's borders, with Hungary in particular. Yet this assurance contradicted German diplomatic overtures to revisionist Hungary. Carol's government was not reassured. Deliveries on credit to start construction on the huge Ferrostaal project for a new metallurgical complex did close the Romanian export surplus with Germany for 1937. But, like the comparable Krupp project for Zenica, not much more followed until war was imminent. The German share of direct foreign investment in Romania was still only 2 percent in 1938.

By then, however, Romania's oil industry had become the priority for German military planning that it would remain throughout the Second World War. Goering's Four-Year Plan to prepare the German economy for war had started in 1936 with a memorandum signed by Hitler himself. It promised the domestic development of synthetic fuels, most prominently oil. By 1938 it was clear that the promise could not be kept. Now the promotion of oil imports from Romania could be covered with new investment in the Romanian armaments industry, much desired by the Bucharest metallurgical magnate Malaxa and the corporatist economist Mihail Manoilescu. Still, what had now become Carol's royal dictatorship held back from a comprehensive agreement with Germany, let alone support for its domestic political supporters. The regime's closest Nazi ally was not the Iron Guard but rather the Christian National Party of Octavian Goga, financially supported by Alfred Rosenberg's organization since its founding in 1936. German representatives stood by when Carol quickly abandoned the two-month Goga government of early 1938, specifically because its aforementioned anti-Semitic decrees had provoked Anglo-French protest abroad and a threatened Jewish boycott in Romania. Nor did they lodge more than a perfunctory protest when the Iron Guard leader, Codreanu, was first arrested and then murdered in prison on the King's orders later in the year.[35]

But war was coming. By March 1939 the royal dictatorship would be obliged to sign a comprehensive economic agreement with Nazi Germany, political strings attached. The century's second wartime transition now began for Romania and the rest of the region. Before it was over, the Soviet Union replaced Germany as the regional hegemon. For the Western powers, only Britain, now joined by the United States for the first time, could respond. Once again, the region's political independence, maintained as argued above in surprising measure even through the interwar period, would be suspended. That independence had survived during the Depression decade did not however preserve the practice of political pluralism or the state's commitment to the market mechanism. Nor had their statist, nonparty efforts succeeded in fostering a higher national identity before the Second World War swept away the royal regimes.

5 World War, Civil War, and the Communist Advantage

At the outset of the Second World War and at its end, the strategic interests of the major combatants once again did much to determine the fate of Southeastern Europe. During the course of the war, however, both the Allied powers and Nazi Germany concentrated on tactical choices that discouraged any of them from a major commitment of ground forces to the region. By 1945, with the Nazis gone, the Anglo-American alliance and the Soviet Union saw Southeastern Europe as a strategic crossroads whose location would make its loss to the other side, in whole or in part, unacceptable. The initial German conquest and reliance on the region's resources, the subsequent British support for resistance or opposition, and the final approach of the Red Army in 1944 just as American engagement began, did, all the same, exert fateful influences.

We must balance those influences against new evidence from the period 1942–4. Civil warfare among resistance movements contributed to divisions in British policy and opened the way to a belated Nazi effort to coopt anti-Communist resistance. It began when Italy's capitulation left the Reich with a larger area to occupy and allowed its regional specialists to encourage collaboration. At the same time, the racist determination of the Nazi leadership to continue pressing for the transfer of the region's Jewish minority to the death camps helped to discredit German influence, most clearly in Bulgaria. Throughout this long period, Soviet diplomacy remained cautious, and the region out of military reach. This balance, finally joined by the advance of the Red Army and the appearance of American interest, would work to the advantage of all the region's Communist parties. So would the massive destruction, loss of life, and forced migration that made some transition from the fractured liberal institutions and unconstitutional monarchies of the 1930s now seem essential to postwar recovery. Less evenly distributed and eventually more problematic was the legitimacy that came from linking Communist resistance to the Balkan legacy of rural rebellion and paramilitary forces under local leadership.

Let us review the more familiar chain of military campaigns and diplomatic maneuvers from 1939 to 1941 before proceeding to the fateful course of internal resistance and collaboration. The chain's first two links were Italian initiatives, both undertaken by Mussolini to match Hitler's easy advances. The hasty but unhindered Italian occupation of Albania on April 4, 1939 kept pace with the Nazi occupation of the Bohemia and Moravia that destroyed Czechoslovakia on March 15. Mussolini launched his ill-prepared invasion of Greece from Albania on October 28, 1940. It followed from his frustration at Hitler's June triumph in France and September partition of Romania, all the while denying Italy permission to attack Yugoslavia and thereby annex the entire Dalmatian coast. In Greece, its small but well-trained army quickly forced the Italian dictator's war-weary, ill-supplied troops and poorly coordinated commanders back into Albania.

This failure contributed to the German decision to proceed with and to expand Operation Maritsa. The plan was first conceived in November 1940 as a "peripheral strategy." The conquest of Greece would deny Britain Mediterranean leverage. Threatening just such leverage was the Churchill government's immediate dispatch of five RAF fighter squadrons to help its only regional ally repulse Italy's October invasion. By January 1941 Hitler had concentrated German military preparations instead on Operation Barbarrosa, the invasion of the Soviet Union planned for May. But the British air bases in northern Greece and the successful bombing from elsewhere of Italian ports raised the threat of an attack on the Romanian oil fields or German supply routes to Russia. By February, further Italian misfortunes in North Africa had prompted the dispatch of General Irwin Rommel and the first units of the Afrika Corps. Securing their supply lines also justified the conquest of Greece. In March the sizeable German force of 680,000 troops assembling in Romania moved south through Bulgaria. Nazi diplomatic pressure had secured passage by obliging Bulgaria to join the Tripartite Pact of Germany, Italy, and Japan. Yugoslavia was duly pressured to join as well. But when the Cvetković-Maček government reluctantly signed the pact on March 25, it was overthrown two days later in a bloodless coup. Serbian military officers, with some British encouragement and wide public support in Belgrade, replaced the regency of Prince Paul with the young King Petar. The new regime promised to negotiate the transit of German troops after all. Hitler refused to listen. He immediately added Yugoslavia to Greece as a military objective.[1]

On April 6, 1941 the German bombing of Belgrade launched the campaign that would until 1944 make Yugoslavia, Greece, and Albania occupied territory and lock the governments of Romania and Bulgaria into the German camp. Operation Punishment added Italian and Hungarian forces plus more German divisions to attack Yugoslavia from the north. The Maritsa force plus several Bulgarian divisions swept into Vardar Macedonia before moving south into Greece. Neither defending army slowed the German conquest. It was already complete by April 30. Both were not only outnumbered but greatly overmatched in mobility, armor and air power. Yugoslavia's army faced the further problem of heavy dependence on Serbian officers and on a command center in Belgrade that was immediately destroyed. Even without the welcome accorded German units entering Zagreb, Yugoslavia's large but immobile and hastily assembled army of 700,000 stood no chance strung out on the northern borders. The much smaller Greek army was burdened with maintaining the Albanian front against Italy. Still more damaging, its northern forces and a British detachment of 50,000 Commonwealth troops failed to agree on a single front. Their "catastrophic misunderstanding" left the British contingent south of Thessaloniki to be outflanked as soon as the German advance had breached the Greek lines to the northwest. All that may be said for damage to the German side is that this campaign made some contribution, how much is controversial, to the fateful delay in the Nazi attack on the Soviet Union until late June.[2]

More important for this larger part of Southeastern Europe was the oppressive framework in which it would now find itself trapped for three years, a framework that seemed likely, after the irresistible German conquest, to last for a long time. As recalled from early 1942 by a then teenage Croatian Serb, soon to be a Yugoslav Partisan, "who could ever imagine that Germany would lose the war?" Borders were redrawn and central authority divided between occupiers and collaborators. Their harsh regimes and the divisions within them generated rural resistance movements that were the largest across Europe in the Second World War. Their conflicts with the new regimes and the exiled old ones, with each other and with the British military missions, revived the sort of uncertainties that lay behind the original definition of the Balkans as a region apart from Europe. Hence the special attention needed to mark the new lines of demarcation from 1941 and areas of subsequent wartime resistance on Map 5.1.

Bulgarian participation in the attack on Yugoslavia and Greece placed Vardar Macedonia under its administration, with annexation pending the war's end, and western Thrace under its occupation. The Italian occupation of Albania attached Kosovo and was extended to Montenegro. Elsewhere, the lines of German–Italian demarcation deserve special attention. They divided the annexation of Slovenia and the occupation of Greece. There, only the German administration of Athens relieved Italian responsibility for the mainland south of Macedonia and all of the islands except Crete and

Map 5.1 Borders, partitions, and partisan movements during World War II

Source: Adapted from Richard and Ben Crampton, *Atlas of Eastern Europe in the Twentieth Century* (London and New York: Routledge, 1996)

- - - - - 1941 partition boundaries   ×××× × ×   Partisan movements

— · — 1939 international boundaries

the three closest to Turkey. And in the new Independent State of Croatia, minus the Dalmatian coast annexed to Italy, lines of primary Italian and German military responsibility ran from northwest to southeast. Between them lay a fateful zone of ill-defined, secondary Italian responsibility. There the region's largest resistance movement and its Communist leadership would first find the multiethnic support that carried it to power by 1945.

Royal Regimes in the German Orbit, 1939–1940

Before its Balkan campaign of 1941 reconfigured much of the region's map, the Nazi leadership sought to translate its growing economic leverage into military alliance with three of the four surviving royal regimes. Greece's ties to Britain made it an unlikely candidate. The others had tried, as emphasized in Chapter 4, to avoid such dependence as long as they could. To their credit, all four of them sought Anglo-French support as a counterweight and struggled to affirm national unity. To their discredit, they increasingly relied on repression and intolerance to assure that unity. Ethnic exclusiveness joined with German pressure to enact anti-Jewish restrictions. Political opponents faced or resorted themselves to violence. Conspiratorial skills allowed the small Communist parties to survive, but the Hitler–Stalin pact of August 1939 left them at a disadvantage in opposing German pressures. However compromised and repressive the royal regimes were by 1940, it was hard to imagine that these Communists would be the ones to challenge them, and with the exception of Greece, to dismiss them a few years later.

Romania and Bulgaria were both drawn into the German military orbit, but not in the reverse order that the latter's closer trade relations suggested. From March 1939, King Carol's government abandoned the prior Romanian reliance on exporting oil to Western markets for hard currency. Hungary's seizure of Ruthenia, as part of the German dismantling of Czechoslovakia on March 15, fed fears of a German–Hungarian alliance against Romania. Reichsmarschall Goering's past reassurances against Hungarian claims to Transylvania no longer seemed sufficient. This concern, plus the favorable exchange rates for Romanian exports and deliveries of military equipment that France and Britain had promised but did not provide, encouraged the Romanian regime to sign the Wohltat Agreement of March 23.

Its provisions offered German military supplies and equipment plus machinery for the arms industry, all in return for Romanian oil and agricultural exports. It also established joint, semiofficial German–Romanian companies, on more favorable terms than the Sovroms imposed by the Soviets after the war, for oil exploration, drilling, and refining. The German share of foreign direct investment shot up from 2 percent in 1938 to 50 percent by 1940, aided of course by the takeover of French assets following the defeat of France. But industrial investment went no further than agricultural processing, in line with the *Grossraumwirtschaft* principle of complementarity with the developed German economy. When this emphasis reappeared from the Soviet side in the 1960s, it prompted Romanian objections (see Chapter 7). In 1940 there were no protests. The Franco-British guarantee of Romanian and Polish independence in April 1939 had vanished as a realistic option when Poland itself was overrun that September. With the fall of France in June 1940, Carol abandoned the remaining British guarantee.

Reliance on Germany to guarantee the post-1918 frontiers also proved ill-founded. It was of no assistance in resisting the Soviet demand to evacuate Bessarabia and the Bukovina at the end of June 1940. Carol hastily appointed a pro-German cabinet in July, but they did no better. By August, German support for the Bulgarian claim to the southern Dobrudja had started negotiations for its transfer. It was ironically the leading advocate of the industrialization frustrated by the Wolhtat Agreement, Mihail Manoilescu, who was obliged as the new Foreign Minister to receive Hitler's terms for the concession to Hungary on August 30. This Second Vienna Award transferred most of northern Transylvania to Hungary, in return for a belated German guarantee of Romania's territorial integrity. Carol's domestic adversaries, led by the Iron Guard, forced him to flee the country. The new government of General Antonescu signed on to the Tripartite Pact on November 23, ready to join a German campaign against the Soviet Union that would at least win back Bessarabia.[3]

Bulgaria held out longer even though it already conducted a majority of its foreign trade with Germany, even before the Czech lands were incorporated in 1939. Tsar Boris shared the Romanian fears of the Soviet Union and had rejected Foreign Minister Molotov's offer of an agreement on mutual assistance in October 1939. Yet earlier that summer, before Hitler had come to terms with the USSR, Boris had also expressed relief when his Prime Minister Kiosseivanov had avoided a similar agreement with Germany in return for a limited delivery of military equipment. A personal conflict rather than German pressure triggered the Tsar's decision to replace his Prime Minister with the pro-German academic Bogdan Filov in February 1940. Boris continued to insist on his desire to remain neutral and hope for some British–German reconciliation despite the Hitler–Stalin pact. After Germany, Italy, and Japan signed the Tripartite agreement in September 1940, he resisted pressures to join which began almost at once from German diplomacy and several of his own generals. As late as January 1941, Boris impressed William Donovan, the American representative sent to survey the region, with his determination to keep Bulgaria out of the war. Only by the end of February did German demands for their troops' entry from the buildup in Romania make membership in the Tripartite alliance unavoidable.[4]

Yugoslavia's ability to hold out until the end of March also deserves respect. Neither the Anglophile Regent Prince Paul nor his Prime Minister Cincar-Marković wished to continue the predecessor Stojadinovic's policy of accommodation with Germany as the best guarantee of neutrality. More German credits for the Zenica steel project in 1939 and the German takeover of French mining interests by July 1940 did not change their minds. When the Minister of War, General Milan Nedić, pressed for a German alliance in November 1940, he was dismissed. German assistance to the Italian invasion of Greece helped to discredit him. The Cvetković-Maček government quietly sent munitions and horses to aid the Greek army. Although concerned about the security of access to Thessaloniki, their regime rejected the several German offers to control the key port in return for an alliance. Belated British and American diplomatic support early in 1941 encouraged Prince Paul in particular. By late March, however, Nazi Foreign Minister Ribbentrop made it clear that a German invasion was the only alternative to signing the Tripartite Pact.[5]

National Unity, Repression, and Response

The domestic record of the four royal regimes surviving these first two years of the Second World War is less admirable and less well known. Its repressive features nonetheless deserve attention. They did not promote the common national identity they professed to serve. The regimes would look the less attractive for it when they sought to return after the war. At the same time, the Hitler–Stalin pact worked more to their advantage while generally confounding the small Communist parties.

The region's most repressive regime, the outright Greek dictatorship of Ioannis Metaxas, drew popular support from its leader's defiant "no" to the Italian demand to surrender significant territory in October 1940. The mass response to his call to arms and the Greek army's quick repulse of the invaders impressed foreign observers, Germans included. The army's advance into southern Albania, with its Greek and Orthodox Albanian minorities was also popular. A number of republican officers volunteered to rejoin the army and were accepted. Jews, Turks, and other minorities were not pressed, with the considerable exception of the Slav Macedonians. Some of them had fought with the army when mobilized, but a smaller number of defections still served to make the recent deportation of suspected agitators to Bulgaria seem justified. Meanwhile, the Communist KKE struggled with the Comintern policy of rejecting support for war against a German ally. Party leader Nikos Zakhariadis had seconded the repulse of the Italian attack on October 31 but was soon obliged to withdraw it. Metaxas's notorious Interior Minister, Maniadakis, cleverly suppressed news of the Communist reversal, meanwhile continuing to infiltrate their ranks. Yet the monarchy missed a chance to capitalize on military success when Metaxas died after a brief illness on January 29, 1941. Richard Clogg rightly speculates on the future advantage that might have followed had King George II taken the occasion to signal a turn away from dictatorship.[6] He did not.

In Bulgaria, the Hitler–Stalin pact not only burdened the BKP and its surrogate Workers' Party but aided Boris's nonparty regime. In the elections to the National Assembly of December 1939, the government's slate won 140 of 160 seats, partly because of new procedures keeping any party's explicit nominees from running. But it could also advertize the Slavic bond to Russia, now tied to Germany as well. The Comintern advised the Bulgarian Communists, although still numbering only about eight thousand, to avoid another United Front that included Agrarian and Zveno candidates in the election. Their surprising defiance of the ban won party members seven of the twenty opposition seats, four of them in Sofia.[7]

The new Filov government of February 1940 left the Assembly and its small opposition in place, but otherwise moved the domestic regime away from the moderate diplomatic course on which Boris insisted. A paramilitary youth organization called *Branik*, or defenders, along the lines of Metaxas's EON, was finally organized. Filov reached into the leadership of the small fascist *Ratnik* organization for the new Interior Minister. By October, Petar Gabrovski, the cabinet's one genuine anti-Semite, was pressing for a Law for the Defense of the Nation (ZZN) patterned explicitly on the Nazis' Nuremberg Laws. Signed reluctantly by the Tsar in January 1941, it closed the Masonic lodges and sought to confine Jewish movement and property ownership. But a number of cabinet members remained Masons, and open objections in the National Assembly had watered down the measures restricting the country's 50,000 Jews. The *numerus clausus* limiting university attendance, for instance, was fixed at the Jewish percentage of urban population, five times a national figure of less than 1 percent. Neither the ZZN nor *Branik* rallied new support from a public mood whose caution and anxiety Boris mirrored.

In Yugoslavia the search for national unity struggled with open demands for internal autonomy. Prince Paul's new Prime Minister, Aleksandar

Cincar-Marković, spent the first half of 1939 bargaining with Vladko Maček, head of the Croatian Peasant Party, in order to provide enough autonomy to keep Croatian demands for separation in check. Their *Sporazum,* or Agreement of August 1939, created a specifically Croatian *banovina,* enlarged into Herzegovina and Dalmatia. The others were left in place. Soon the Serbian side was clamoring for its own enlarged district, one that would include the bulk of Bosnia-Herzegovina. More important in the agitation than Dimitrije Ljotić's small fascist *Zbor* party were leaders from the large Democratic Party and influential intellectuals in the Serbian Cultural Club. Meanwhile, as German flirtations with the Croatian political spectrum continued, the new autonomy allowed members of the fascist *Ustaša,* if not yet its leadership, to return from Italy and stoke demands for full independence. Albeit in the interests of autonomy rather than tolerance, the new Croatian *Ban,* or Governor, rejected the *numerus clausus* and bans on Jewish staple trading that the Cvetković-Maček regime imposed early in 1940.[8]

By this time, the regime's efforts to suppress the Communist KPJ and the pro-Bulgarian VMRO included the sort of detention camps that Maniadakis had set up in Greece. This could not prevent the convening of a KPJ congress near Zagreb in October 1940, the first held inside the country since 1919. There, Josip Broz Tito's now commanding leadership was able to take advantage of a new Comintern directive quietly to create "a united front from below." Instructions were to defend national independence even against Nazi Germany, while publicly supporting the Hitler–Stalin pact. With no Soviet or Comintern representative present, Tito was able to champion the multiethnic defense of the existing borders that would serve the party so well after 1941.

Romania's Legion with its Iron Guard became the one fascist party to hold power in the region before the German offensive. Their fortunes seemed at first to have fallen fatally following the strong electoral showing in 1937 (see Chapter 4). To avenge the prison murder of Guard leader Codreanu in 1938, his followers assassinated Carol's ruthless if pro-Western Premier and Interior Minister, Armand Calinescu, in September 1939. The King turned his *Siguranța* political police loose on them. Some 250 leading members were executed. Others fled to Germany, where Hitler was belatedly distressed over Codreanu's murder. Bucharest café wits joked that the Legion was now "like a potato, the best parts are underground."

But by April 1940 Calinescu's replacement as Prime Minister, the maverick Liberal Tătărescu, had failed to bring the Liberal mainstream or Maniu's National Peasants into a new government. Carol agreed to a reconciliation with the Legion in return for its cooperation. The loss of Bessarabia to the

Soviet Union further strengthened its hand as over two hundred thousand Romanian refugees poured in, many with tales of "Jewish attacks" as they were leaving. By August, Codreanu's successor as Legion head, Horia Sima, was Minister of Culture in the King's hasty new Party of the Nation. Carol accepted further anti-Jewish restrictions based on the Nazi's Nuremberg Laws that now, unlike the Goga measures of 1938, came into full effect. But his government could not survive the loss of Transylvania to Hungary and southern Dobrudja to Bulgaria. Ion Antonescu, the army general he had imprisoned in July for criticizing the abandonment of Bessarabia, now refused his offer to form a new government without full powers. Antonescu forced the King to abdicate on September 5. Guard members pursued Carol out of the country, missing the chance to kill him only because his train refused to stop. Another 300,000 refugees began to arrive as the King and his hated mistress, Magda Lupescu, departed.

Carol's son Michael had succeeded to the throne and appointed General Antonescu as *Conducator*, or leader of the Romanian state. Antonescu took control of national defense but left political control of the country in the Legion's hands. Sima and five other colleagues dominated the Council of Ministers, still headed by Antonescu. Their National Legionary State quickly wore out its welcome with urban workers by banning strikes and disbanding unions. Corrupt cronies took over the management of large industrial enterprises, further straining an economy struggling with troop mobilization and half a million refugees. Legionary leaders put forward plans, unprecedented in Romania, to isolate the Roma as "racially inferior." The Iron Guard's separate "legionary police" unleashed lawless violence against Jews and all perceived opponents. Let the murders of Nicolae Iorga and Virgil Madgearu, respectively Romania's leading historian and economist, stand for the unsavory reputation that had already put them in Antonescu's authoritarian disfavor by the end of 1940. The Guard's paramilitary regiments spearheaded Sima's bid to seize full power in January. Regular army units loyal to Antonescu easily crushed their assault on several government buildings.[9]

None of this internecine struggle on the right, which had already destroyed the institutional framework of the interwar state, could avail the tiny Romanian Communist Party (PCR) as war approached. The wider support of the Popular Front period vanished when the PCR endorsed the Soviet seizure of Bessarabia. Its main activists had almost all been imprisoned by the *Siguranţa*, the future leader Gheorgiu-Dej since 1933. Ana Pauker became the one important exception when she was traded to the Soviet Union for a Romanian political prisoner in 1941.

Axis Allies and Occupation Regimes

Between April and June of 1941, Germany's Balkan and Russian campaigns swept all of Southeastern Europe into the Second World War. The resulting burdens were heavy across the region. They were hardly the same burdens for the German allies of Bulgaria and Romania, for Albania annexed by Italy and then occupied by Germany, and for the divided occupation of Greece and Yugoslavia. The latter included the Nazi-installed Independent State of Croatia. This occupied Western Balkans would again, as in the First World War, suffer more forced migration and civilian casualties. By the end of 1941 another half a million deportees or refugees, mainly Serbs from Croatia and Bosnia, Jews from Bessarabia, and Greeks from Macedonia and Thrace, had been added to the half-million Romanians forced to move, as noted above, in 1940. This time, however, only one successor to the prewar monarchies and none of the prewar leaders would survive by 1945 as they all did after the First World War. And this time, the economic mobilization for war set useful precedents for the regimes which took their place.

Romania's fortunes became hostage to the region's one military alliance with the Nazi war effort. General Antonescu had already used the suppression of the Guard and thereby the Legion in January 1941 to establish what Keith Hitchins aptly calls a military dictatorship.[10] By February, some 9000 Guard members had been arrested and the "national legionary state" abolished. Antonescu explicitly wished to set aside all political parties, and any electoral process or appeal to individual rights in favor of control by the army and the security services. These were ironically the same two institutions on which the Ceauşescu regime would rely in the 1980s (see Chapter 7). The leaders of the two main interwar parties, the Liberals' Constantin Brătianu and the National Peasants' Iuliu Maniu, refused invitations to join what became a military cabinet. Neither they nor the young King Michael could raise any effective protest to the austere Antonescu's decrees and decisions. Carol's regime, in its last desperate months, had already placed all publications and even printing shops under strict censorship.

More anti-Russian than pro-Nazi, if still anti-Jewish, Anonescu could not resist the chance to join Barbarossa. The campaign's advance into the Soviet Union would thereby restore Bessarabia and the Bukovina to Romania. Antonescu called it "a holy war." Photos from Bucharest on June 22, the day of the attack, show ordinary residents kneeling and crossing themselves in response. Brătianu and Maniu felt obliged to give their approval. Antonescu committed one armored and twelve infantry divisions, the bulk of the

Romanian army. Half of them under German command, they advanced quickly and with few casualties across Bessarabia. But army units as well as returning civilians searched out and killed Jews presumed to have harassed them in 1940. That was only the start of a dishonorable record behind the front lines. In Iaşi, on the border with the lost province, the Romanian Intelligence Service and the mass panic following the brief Soviet bombing of June 24 triggered a pogrom that killed 6000 Jews in the city and another 2600 on death trains. The army's further advance across the Dneister River proved much more difficult than in Bessarabia. The long siege of Odessa cost 70,000 dead and wounded. In the wake of those losses, the October sabotage of the Romanian headquarters in what had become the capital of Romanian-administered "Transnistria" prompted a huge, misdirected reprisal. Romanian troops and police killed all of the 50,000 Jews they could find in Odessa. Meanwhile, another 10,000 had been shot in the Bessarabian capital of Chişinau and at least 120,000 deported to labor camps in Transnistria. A majority of them and the 25,000 Roma dumped into the countryside there did not survive.[11]

Neither would a majority of the Romanian army moving through the Crimea and on to Stalingrad survive. Reinforcements by 1942 put 18 still poorly equipped divisions on the southern flank of the ill-fated German salient to the Volga. The Red Army's breakthrough to surround Stalingrad destroyed two-thirds of the Romanian divisions by the end of the year, at a cost of 155,000 casualties. From this point, Antonescu began to husband within the prewar borders half of the new troops drafted to rebuild the army. He also opened contacts with the Anglo-American Allies and suspended plans for more Jewish deportations.

The growing drain on labor and other resources inside Romania encouraged centralization but also helped to save the sizeable Jewish population of 315,000 from deportation to the Nazi death camps. The supposed dismissal of all Jews from commercial enterprises left some 20,000 still employed by 1943. Another 20,000 of the 100,000 Jews drafted into labor battalions were assigned white-collar positions. German equipment and other essential supplies for oil production and other key industries operated under a Five-Year Plan that pressed Romanian production for more than the labor force could provide. German purchases also took a large share of declining agricultural output. Here, as in industry, Antonescu's response was to tighten his regime's own central controls. Local governing councils were abolished. Peasants were pushed to join small cooperative associations. Prices were centrally fixed, urban labor drafted for the harvest, and tractors imported from Germany. This completed a pattern of precedents that

Henry Roberts called "a bridge to the agricultural policy of the post-1945 government."[12]

Despite its continuing exemption from the Russian front, Bulgaria's contribution to the German war effort established even stronger economic precedents for the postwar Communist transition. The same strains and shortfalls also appeared, helping to discredit the royal regime. Maintaining an army of 400,000 men to secure Vardar Macedonia and western Thrace, plus dispatching 18,000 workers to Germany, created labor shortages in agriculture and industry. Food supplies for the Wehrmacht made domestic shortages from the bad grain harvest of 1942, just 40 percent of the 1939 figure, all the greater. The state's grain export agency from the 1930s, *Hranoiznos*, now expanded to control prices and requisition deliveries for 23 crops. The Directorate for Civilian Mobilization, already established in 1940, joined the Ministry of Agriculture in setting down a Five-Year Plan for all sectors in 1942. By 1943, as in the First World War, the army took over control of all production and trade through a High Command for the War Economy. Yet the lack of promised German imports or loans and any alternative export markets fed an inflationary spiral. Industrial production declined after 1941, and the urban black market for daily food supplies grew apace.[13]

The royal regime's political standing suffered a fatal blow when Tsar Boris died in August 1943. He succumbed to a heart attack after mountain climbing a few weeks after returning from Germany. His renewed refusal, during a last meeting there with Hitler, to commit Bulgarian troops against fellow Slavs on the Russian front fed the unfounded suspicion, widely believed in Bulgaria even under the Communist regime, that the Nazis had somehow poisoned him on the return flight. More important at the time, the one genuinely popular monarch among the region's royal regimes was now gone, to be replaced by a regency for his young son Simeon. The colorless Prime Minister Filov had vainly expected that his new position as Regent would increase support for the regime. But the public dismay at the Tsar's funeral in Sofia, assembling the largest crowd ever seen in the city, reflected a loss of confidence as well as an outpouring of grief.

By that time, the administration of Vardar Macedonia and the occupation of western Thrace had also lost its initial appeal. Despite the 800 new schools built in Macedonia and the university opened in Skopje in 1943, the easy integration of a population presumed to be Bulgarian had not happened. As in the First World War, direct administration from Sofia and German control of mines caused resentment and, as we shall see in the next section, fed resistance. Far harsher were the army's evictions and persecutions of the Greek majority in Thrace. Perhaps 100,000 Greeks had fled the initial advance. It was also in these two territories that Gabrowski's Commissariat for Jewish Affairs (KEV), created in August 1942 at Nazi urging, operated without royal restriction. Its agents rounded up some 12,000 Jews, on the grounds that they did not qualify as Bulgarian citizens, and put them on trains to the death camps.

In Bulgaria proper, however, the KEV and the prodding of both the German Ambassador and an SS representative of Adolf Eichmann failed in their efforts to send first 8000 and then all of the Jewish population north to the camps during 1943. Tsar Boris's final refusal to sanction their deportation was essential both times. But the threat of public exposure and then opposition provided the crucial basis for his refusal. In March the Deputy Speaker of the National Assembly, Dimitur Peshev, had responded courageously to pleas from the Jewish community. He launched the open dissent to which Boris could then respond. That summer, it was Stefan, the Orthodox Metropolitan of Sofia, who stepped forward after the city's 25,000 Jews had been shipped to labor camps in the countryside. Boris had approved the measure as a compromise to quiet German demands. Stefan's protests at plans for "further shipment," which the KEV had again tried to keep entirely secret, empowered the Tsar's refusal. Eichmann's representative soon left in disgust. These events, grounded in the established role of representative decision-making as well as the absence of anti-Semitism, have afforded the Bulgarian historical memory of the Second World War one point of considerable honor. The several Communist-led demonstrations that supported resistance to the deportation plans deserve mention, if hardly the predominant role assigned to them by the postwar regime.[14]

Italy's Greater Albania

In sharp contrast to the experience of Germany's two regional allies, Italy's annexation of Albania did not drain the economy for its war effort or threaten the Jewish or other religious minorities. Indeed, direct investment from 1939 to 1943, intended primarily for road and port construction, tripled the interwar Italian total. The customs union of April 1939 transferred the remaining third of foreign trade to Italy, but the huge, two-to-one import surplus did not decline. Italian authorities quickly came to terms with the Muslim religious leadership and the Orthodox Albanian clergy. The northen Catholics were freed from King Zog's 1927 civil code for marriage and divorce. The small Jewish population grew to 1800 during the war, partly as a result of refugees fleeing to the same safe haven that Italian authorities provided on the Dalmatian coast. As for King Zog, the failed reforms and harsh controls of his regime plus his own immediate flight in the face of a poorly executed Italian invasion left little regret that his arbitrary regime was gone.

Within the prewar borders, however, the Italian regime was already wearing out its welcome by the time that Germany's Balkan campaign gave them control of Kosovo in May 1941. There, a small Italian force turned quickly to Kosovar Albanians for administrators and police. Schools and instruction in Albanian, restricted since 1921, spread widely. These local Albanians were allowed to drive out the Serbian colonists who had settled there in interwar Yugoslavia. Perhaps 10,000 Serbs were killed and at least 20,000 more expelled, another of the reversals of ethnic fortune that has troubled the territory across the entire century.[15]

Kosovo's addition, and the added grain supplies it also promised, briefly revived the regime's popularity but could not compensate inside Albania for a series of Italian missteps that had begun almost at once. They not only discredited the Italian regime; they also destroyed the fragile framework of modern institutions that Zog had tried to impose. The customs union brought in Italian manufactures that put most of the small industrial enterprises out of business. The currency revaluation in Italian lira started an inflation that tripled the price of most daily foodstuffs. Corrupt Italian contractors and a disorganized administration wasted the majority of the new investment flooding in. The legislature, elected however imperfectly under Zog, became an appointed corporate council. The army was merged into the Italian military. The attempt to create an Albanian Fascist Party attracted few recruits, and the new fascist school curriculum little enthusiasm. A number of secondary schools, including the American technical high school, were closed to discourage subversion. Educational efforts concentrated instead on forming fascist youth groups. The new flag, surrounding Albanian eagles with fascist sheaves and topping them with a cross, aroused open resentment.[16]

To make matters worse, the Greek army's repulse of the Italian invasion of October 1940 carried the counterattack into southern Albania and threatened the permanent loss of that territory. The Italian military reputation was already in question after the 1939 invasion force which, in the often-quoted words of an Italian official, "a well-armed fire brigade would have driven into the sea." Even after the German campaign of 1941 had restored and expanded Italian rule, the stage was set for the resistance that appeared elsewhere in the western Balkans by 1942.

Divided Occupations and the Independent State of Croatia

Setting the wider stage for resistance was an ill-fated division of authority for the Axis occupation of Greece and Yugoslavia. Just the familiar contrast between the harder German and less rigorous Italian regimes tells only part of the story. Disputed responsibilities between the two and conflicts with the local collaborators fractured an occupation intended to coordinate the delivery of war supplies with a minimum of troops on the ground. Actual armed conflict broke out between the forces of the Nazi-installed Independent State of Croatia and the Italian army.

In Greece, the division of occupying authority alone produced what Mark Mazower has called "the chaos of the New Order."[17] The conquering German commanders had reluctantly ceded responsibility to the Italian army, on Hitler's orders, for the mainland and islands surrounding Wehrmacht headquarters in Athens and Piraeus (see Map 5.1). This major presence by the army that Greek forces had so recently defeated helped to encourage the idea of armed resistance from the start. It also placed the main source of grain for Athens and Thessaloniki outside of the German zone. When the war's disruptions reduced the normal grain harvest by as much as 30 percent in 1941, the resulting food shortage, especially in Athens, could be blamed on Italian administration or the absence of food shipments promised from Italy. These had indeed arrived but were delivered, contrary to German expectations, almost entirely to the western islands. There were other causes as well – a British naval blockade, the Bulgarian refusal to send some of their equally reduced harvest, and, most obvious to the population, German requisitions for their own troops. No German assistance or compensation came in return. Hitler had issued explicit orders that the Bank of Greece must cover all costs of occupation. By one recent and well-supported estimate, these charges took two-thirds of budgetary revenues and 20 percent of the entire country's domestic product for 1941–3; they were also the major cause of the hyperinflation that raged until the second half of 1942.[18] Prices rose by 3000 percent over that period, generating an extensive black market that traded on the division of occupying authority between Athens and the rural mainland.

The larger consequence was the actual famine that descended on most urban populations from October 1941. By April 1942 at least 40,000 people had died of starvation in Athens alone. A Red Cross estimate put the total for deaths from famine across Greece during 1941–2 at 250,000. Before the winter of 1942–3 arrived, the new German economic plenipotentiary, a former Nazi mayor of Vienna and an IG Farben regional expert, Hermann Neubacher, intervened to stem the inflation at least temporarily and increase the flow of supplies. Some foodstuffs from Romania and some from Italy together with Red Cross deliveries allowed through the British blockade eased urban conditions considerably.

Neubacher's accommodations did nothing to protect the largely urban Jewish population of 70,000, unless they were fortunate enough to be in the Italian zone. By July 1942, SS representatives and the Wehrmacht command in Thessaloniki had forced the males among the city's 50,000 Jews into hard labor battalions. By March 1943 they and their families had been sent to Auschwitz, along with those from the German-controlled area of Athens.[19] A few managed to escape and join the younger men and some women who had already fled from Athens and Thessaloniki to the countryside in order to survive the famine. Together they made up the one large urban component in the resistance coming together across the western Balkans. At the same time, the Bank of Greece and a number of other administrative agencies continued to operate under German or Italian oversight.

None of Yugoslavia's administrative apparatus continued to operate across the former state after the German conquest of April 1941. Hitler had decreed that the state should "cease to exist," and that was indeed the case. The division detailed in Map 5.1 includes areas under Hungarian and Bulgarian administration as well as the German and Italian areas annexed, occupied, or jointly held with the Independent State of Croatia (NDH). Holding sway across this complex of jurisdictions at the start were the overriding German goals of exploiting its resources and eliminating its Jews, all with as little drain as possible on the Wehrmacht.[20]

Serbia and the Banat north of Belgrade were the only areas under direct German occupation. In the valuable grain land of the Banat, the Nazi regime drew on the German minority of 130,000. Their *Volksdeutsche* administration concentrated on delivering the harvest and drafting recruits for the SS Division Prinz Eugen. In Serbia proper, first German and then Austrian Nazi generals ruled over an occupation that was the region's harshest. Serbs from Serbia were the overwhelming majority of the 200,000 prisoners captured from the royal army and immediately sent to prison camps or forced labor in Germany. Those continuing to resist in Belgrade were quickly rounded up, a handful hung from lampposts as an example. The university was closed, and the press confined to one official newspaper. The arrest or outright murder of the 16,000 Jews in Serbia and the Banat began at once and became systematic by the summer of 1941. Only a few thousand would survive. By August the German authorities had created a puppet Serbian administration under the aforementioned sympathizer, General Milan Nedić. But there were few others outside the small quasi fascist Zbor party of Dimitrije Ljotić. His forces formed the core of the Serbian Volunteer

Corps. They expanded to 12,000 men under Nedić's formal authority but remained under German military command, as did his 20,000 State Guards. Other than providing shelter for at least 200,000 Serb refugees from the NDH, Nedić's own authority also remained minimal. So did constructive economic activity within occupied Serbia, outside the direct German exploitation of the Bor copper mines. Only the transfer of about 45,000 Serbs to Germany for factory labor, where they were joined by 90,000 of the Serb POWs, aided the German war effort.

The Independent State of Croatia (NDH) was far more independent, despite recent comparisons to the Nedić regime. Ante Pavalić and his *Ustaša* government had indeed been installed by German authorities once the Croatian Peasant Party leader Maček and the Hungarian government had refused. And the *Ustaša* leadership returned from Italy to head a regime whose party had the support, even after 1939, of at most 10 percent of the population. The regime nonetheless attempted to take full control of a territory which, with Bosnia's addition, included 1.5 million Serbs in a population of barely 6 million. Their newly appointed police and gendarmes began in May 1941 to expel as many Serbs as possible to Serbia, already killing many out of hand. Their first dispute with German authorities arose from a flood of expellees that approached 200,000 and became unmanageable. As the Germans progressively closed down the official crossing points into Serbia, the regime's Culture Minister, Mile Budak, spelled out the fate that would await the rest: they would either convert from Orthodox to Catholic in order to "become Croats" or be killed.

The Jewish population of some 39,000 faced the threat of death in any case. Over two-thirds would perish. By 1942 a set of concentration camps to collect Serbs, Jews, and Roma as well as Communists were in place to supplement what local killing squads of *Ustaša* Blackshirts had not been able to accomplish. Together the camps would murder over 150,000 people, and leave the Serb side with the historical memory of a far larger number. Postwar Communist historiography would endorse that larger number and exaggerate the persecutory role of the Croatian Catholic Church and its controversial Archbishop, Alojzije Stepinanc, in this persecution. Emigré Croatian nationalists would in turn be tempted to dismiss the Archbishop's recurring expressions of support and refusal to condemn the regime publicly, even in 1944.

Before recognizing the stimulus this renegade regime afforded to wartime resistance, we should note the difficult relations it came to have with both German and Italian authorities. The German side had expected the NDH to feed its own population and deliver to them the Reich's one supply of bauxite as well as iron ore and timber from Bosnia. Corruption and incompetence disrupted the expected deliveries even before growing resistance cut them back still further.[21] The leading German general in Zagreb, another Austrian, sharply criticized the Pavelić regime and discouraged the efforts of Nazi political representatives to continue support. Matters were even worse with Italian authorities. Their responsibility for the demilitarized zone bordering their Dalmatian coastal annexations also extended into a central zone bordering the German area. It was in those zones, even before resistance added to frictions, that a number of Italian units fought the *Ustaša* militias which were conducting the roundup of Serbs and Jews and therefore creating rural disorder.

From Resistance Movements to Civil War and Allied Intervention

By the time that Italy left the war in September 1943, rural resistance movements stretched from the divided Slovene lands through the NDH and Serbia south to Macedonia, Albania, and Greece. Only in Bulgaria, where the smallest numbers were involved, did the Communist movement have the resistance to themselves. Only in Romania was there no resistance and, for that matter, almost no Communist party. Elsewhere, the "national bands" opposing what became a single German occupation were themselves divided. The local Communists had begun fighting immediately after the Nazi invasion of the Soviet Union on June 22, 1941. But they were not the only rural resistance, and Allied assistance would come from British and not Soviet Military Missions.

Historical controversy still swirls around the civil warfare that erupted between the larger Communist forces and other movements. Debate also continues on the British role in starting or settling such conflict. A mass of memoirs and scholarship has accumulated in Britain, Greece, and the former Yugoslavia and its successor states. In the region, the initial exaggeration of damage to the German war effort has given way to accepting the generally restrained judgment of British and also American scholarship.[22] Beginning with preparations for the Anglo-American invasion of Sicily in May 1943, the diversion of German forces to the western Balkans was the one significant accomplishment. This diversion counted just the same whether it was to respond to the deception of a planned invasion in Greece or to put down the larger resistance in the disintegrating Independent State of Croatia. More recently, Greek scholarship has struggled instead over the question of whether British intervention unduly weakened the Communist resistance, while first Yugoslav and then Serbian scholarship has debated whether intervention unduly strengthened it.[23]

Of greater concern to the region's postwar fate were conflicts within the resistance itself and the overriding loss of central authority and lines of demarcation that ensued as the German occupation tried to preserve itself. Caught in the crossfire were the exiled governments of Yugoslavia and Greece, both recognized by the Allies but increasingly isolated as the war continued. More relevant were the Yugoslav, Greek, and also Albanian experiences on the ground. There, connection to the premodern Balkan tradition of rural uprisings locally led would count for more.

Yugoslavia's Communist and major anti-Communist resistance both started in Serbia, and both drew heavily on that tradition. An uncaptured army colonel, Draža Mihailović, had pulled together the Chetnik movement. Loyal to the London government of young King Petar, its detachments adopted this traditional name of rural Serb bands resisting Ottoman forces. They soon suffered from the local autonomy at the core of this tradition. They also paid a high price later in the war for the traditional practice of temporary accommodation with the occupying forces. Ironically encouraging this accommodation was Mihailović's conviction, typical of European military training, that he should preserve his forces at all cost so that they could link up with the invading Allied armies. This strategy would also save the Serbian population from the disproportionate losses suffered in 1914–15. The Chetnik leader waited in vain for the British to establish another Salonika Front, as in the First World War, and quixotically sent his surviving Serbian forces to join with the advancing Red Army in September 1944. By then, the Communist leader, Josip Broz Tito, had already arranged for the far larger numbers of his multiethnic National Liberation Front to make that crucial connection.

Tito's Partisan forces had numbered no more than Mihailović's 10,000 during their half year of coexistence in Serbia from July 1941. Communist preparation for the sort of rural resistance of which the Soviet leadership disapproved had begun even before the Nazi invasion of the USSR on June 22, perhaps because Tito, like many others, knew it was coming. Several meetings that fall between Tito and Mihailović failed to resolve their differences. Partisan attacks on German rail transport provoked the Nazi reprisal that put the two movements on permanently separate tracks. The massacre of over two thousand schoolboys in Kragujevac on October 20 persuaded Mihailović to abandon his headquarters and disperse his forces. This newly passive strategy won tolerance from German commanders that were otherwise instructed to disarm them. Too many Serbs would be killed, Mihailovic reckoned, and all in vain unless British forces were reentering from freshly abandoned Greece. The Partisans pressed ahead with their small attacks on the assumption that more reprisals would force more townspeople into the hill country that began in western Serbia, and thereby into their ranks.

By early 1942 the first of the seven German offensives against the Partisans had forced them to retreat into Bosnia and the Chetniks remaining in Serbia to agree to passive autonomy in a few parts of Serbia. Then the *Ustaša* persecution of Bosnian and Croatian Serbs widened the gap between the Partisans and the Chetniks still further. Tito's beleaguered force grew as it played down its Communist leadership (but not its central military command) and played up its commitment to multiethnic resistance. An abortive Partisan uprising against the Italian occupation of Montenegro in 1941 failed to survive initial defeat. In addition, Communist reprisals against uncooperative villages had only created Chetnik recruits. Tito tried not repeat this "left deviation," a mistake made again by the Greek Communists in 1944, as we shall see, in the face of continuing German pressure. Their second offensive pushed his main force, still only about twenty thousand men and women, across Bosnia and into Montenegro and Herzegovina by the fall of 1942.

Stymied in Serbia, Mihailovic authorized his own Chetniks and new Bosnian detachments to come to the defense of persecuted Serbs in the NDH. Operating outside of effective central command, these units first fell on several undefended towns in eastern Bosnia. In Foča, in particular, they massacred Bosnian Muslim males on the faulty assumption, much advertised by NDH leader Pavelić himself, that these *Bošnjaci* were the original "pearl of the Croatian nation." Chetnik detachments generally avoided contact with the Germans and accepted Italian assistance against Croatian or by this time Partisan forces. In June 1942 they joined an Italian offensive in Montenegro, starting down the slippery slope to collaboration with the two major German offensives of 1943 against the Partisans.[24]

Two other decisive events – the start of British support and the end of Italian participation – framed the German offensives. They helped the Partisans simply to survive the year. In February the British Military Mission that had first reached Mihailović's headquarters in July 1941 sent back a damning report on the Chetniks' failure to attack German units. It quoted their leader's bitter (if accurate) complaints about the failure of any British arms to reach him. Ultra codebreaking intercepts confirmed not only the lack of Chetnik activity but also the Partisan success in doubling to 13 the number of German divisions committed to eradicating them. First Operation Weiss in the late winter and then Operation Schwartz in May 1943 failed to do so. Local Chetnik units joined both of them, Bulgarian and Croatian divisions the second. An Ultra intercept allowed the leader of the British mission to reach Tito's headquarters in eastern Herzegovina just as Operation *Schwartz* was under way. These and the other British missions were admittedly dispatched by SOE, the Special Operations Executive in Cairo. Its staff sympathized with Partisans and included at least one member of the British Communist Party. But unlike Greece, as we shall see, the Foreign Office and its Special Intelligence Service (SIS) did not dispute switching support entirely to what amounted to the Communist side. The common British aim was to tie down German forces that might otherwise be used in Italy or France. Had anyone on the British side known that Tito had dispatched Milovan Djilas from his inner circle to Zagreb, ready to talk truce with the Germans in case the Western Allies actually invaded the Dalmatian coast, they might have decided otherwise. As it was, Prime Minister Churchill approved the British decision in December 1943 to begin supplying Tito's forces.[25]

Already in September, Mussolini's overthrow had taken Italy out of the war and started the withdrawal of all Italian forces. Despite the earlier Chetnik collaboration with Italian units, the Partisans were by this time able to secure the bulk of the arms and equipment left behind. A number of Italian soldiers also joined their ranks. By December the Allied advance in Italy had proceeded far enough to make British support much more important. Their missions could now ferry what were increasingly American supplies to Partisan-controlled parts of the Dalmatian coast, as logistically they never could have to the Chetniks.

The Partisans' reversal of fortune brought their numbers across virtually all of prewar Yugoslavia except Serbia proper to 100,000 by the end of 1943. Mihailović had returned with his headquarters and the bulk of his force to Serbia. The Italian collapse had obliged other disparate units in the NDH to retreat to Slovenian territory where they survived on German sufferance. The Partisans' early core had been heavily Serbian, Bosnian or Croatian Serb, but now that changed. Tito had already promised as much at the first, difficult convening of the Anti-Fascist Council for the National Liberation of Yugoslavia (AVNOJ) at Bihać in November 1942. At the second meeting, also in Bosnia at Jajce in November 1943, delegates from all major ethnic groups save the Albanians assembled to speak of plans for a postwar federation. The influx of Croats, now over a quarter of Partisan forces, and some Bosnian Muslims from the NDH provided a broader base. So did the survival of the separate Slovenian Communist resistance and the start of some Partisan activity in Vardar Macedonia. When the Serbian core balked at separate postwar status for Bosnia-Herzegovina as a constituent republic, Tito turned them down. A member of the British

Military Mission looked on; no Soviet mission would arrive until the following February.

In the face of the growing Partisan resistance and the declining authority of both the NDH and the Nedić regime in Serbia, the German occupation turned to any forces that could be used against the Communists. In Bosnia, this search for support led to the creation of the SS Handžar Division from Bosnian Muslim volunteers. The Pavelić government objected strongly but could do nothing to stop the project. As it was, the recruits spent most of their time training in France and mutinied there unsuccessfully. They returned in 1944, unfortunately in time to take vengeance on some of the Serb population of eastern Bosnia in return for the atrocities of 1942. The memory of these misdeeds returned to feed Serb suspicions in the 1990s (see Chapter 8). More immediately, German military authorities, despairing by 1944 of any effective anti-Partisan activity from Nedić's State Guards, made grudging accommodations in Serbia with Mihailović's commanders as well. These ties allowed the postwar Communist regime to complete its indictment against the Chetniks as German collaborators from start to finish.

Reversing the experience of Yugoslavia's Partisans, Greece's *andartes* (guerrillas) of the People's National Liberation Army (ELAS) started from a broader base and became openly narrower as the war progressed. Their Communist leaders were caught in a closer but conflicting web of British policies. They were further compelled to pay more attention to the royal government in exile in Cairo than Yugoslavia's London government ever forced on Tito. The ELAS resistance would find itself bound by agreements with a smaller, anti-Communist rival long after the Partisans and Chetniks had failed to reconcile. The belated German effort to turn loose autonomous anti-Communist locals also had greater success than in Serbia.

Weakened by the persecutions of the Metaxas regime, the Communist Party of Greece (KKE) revived with the German conquest of April 1941. In the attendant confusion, a couple of hundred leading members escaped from prison. Even before the Nazi's June attack on the Soviet Union, party activists in Athens had already set up an underground organization to distribute emergency food rations. It offered some relief to the shortages that would create famine conditions by the fall. The KKE convened a July Plenum hoping to attract some of the exiled republican leaders to a broader front that already included non-Communist unions. Failing in this, and also missing their Soviet-approved leader, Zachariadis, already imprisoned in Dachau by the Germans for the duration, the KKE struck out on its own. Under the leadership of Gregorios Siantos, a former tobacco worker from

Thessaloniki, the party proclaimed its own National Liberation Front (EAM) in September.

The Front faced two limitations at the start. First, also in Athens in September 1941, the royal army Colonel Napoleon Zervas had announced the formation of the rival National Republican Greek League (EDES) under the presumed leadership of the Venezelist General Nicholaos. Here was just the sort of established republican figure that the KKE had not been able to enlist. Secondly, Siantos began Communist resistance with plans only for urban sabotage, even without the Soviet direction that would have favored it, rather than a guerrilla campaign in the hills.

By April 1942 the famine in Athens and other towns in the Italian-occupied mainland had in fact driven many young men into the countryside. German reprisals against rural resistance attacks had done the same for towns in the north. Siantos now approved the formation of ELAS, the EAM's guerrilla army whose name was not accidentally a synonym for Greece. Yet it was not until early the following year that he agreed to proposals from the party's "mountain men," led by its classic upland chieftain, Aris Veloukhiotis, to concentrate on spreading control over as many villages as possible. By then, a small British military mission dispatched by SOE became permanent. It had stayed on after succeeding in November 1942 to carry out its only assigned task: to blow up the Gorgopotomos viaduct on the Athens–Thessaloniki rail line. EDES as well as ELAS had assisted the enterprise.

Thus began the series of British missions to assist both, including a program to give a gold sovereign (worth about $25) to every resistance member for each month of service. British assistance and better war news combined to help both movements increase their membership. Still, the superior organization and wider appeal beyond Zervas's home EDES base of northern Epirus pushed ELAS well ahead. Its *andartes* numbered 17,000 by May and 30,000 by July, including now over a thousand former republican officers. EDES could muster only 5000. That same month, a British military mission had brokered the National Bands agreement between the two disparate forces. The agreement did not recognize them as political movements but gave EAM/ELAS the proportional advantage in a new joint command. This despite Zervas's declaration of loyalty to the King and the exiled government two months before. The agreement was to cement them both into the attacks desired for summer 1943. Widespread resistance and invasion rumors were to divert German and Italian troops from the Allied campaigns in Sicily and then the Italian mainland. The deception campaign called Operation Animals did indeed bring five more first-rate German divisions to Greece, boosting their total to close to 100,000. Only a couple of thousand Italian troops arrived to supplement the poorly supplied 160,000 men strung out across the mainland and the islands.

Fateful consequences, if quite different from Yugoslavia's case, followed for Greece from Italy's surrender in August 1943. True, a comparably large cache of Italian arms and equipment fell primarily into the hands of ELAS. They supplied the larger and more disciplined brigades that ELAS was now organizing along Partisan lines. But Tito's forces had survived the two German offensives of 1943, thereby drawing in sizeable German reinforcements, and were poised to win the British over from Mihailović by the end of the year. The KKE leadership had instead returned from their failed Cairo meeting with British authorities and the government-in-exile convinced that an Allied invasion was still imminent and that it intended to restore the King's government. To deny the invading British any domestic allies, Siantos and Aris threw ELAS into an all-out attack on EDES in October. This "First Round" of the Greek civil war, as it has been called, not only failed to eliminate Zervas's stronghold in the northwest, but the attackers' diversion and losses also helped larger German forces to mount a brutal offensive against ELAS in November. German reinforcements had come because of Operation Animals and stayed to take over the mainland occupation from the Italians. On the British side, the attack on EDES tipped the balance of an ongoing internal dispute away from SOE, who favored ELAS because of its larger and more active forces in the hills, and toward the Foreign Office's greater concern for the shape of a postwar government. From this point on, Churchill also weighed in with his preference for the King's return without the plebiscite that EAM/ELAS demanded. British supplies to ELAS virtually stopped, while those to EDES doubled.[26]

The First Round was over. By February 1944 the KKE leadership felt obliged to come to some agreement with EDES and the government-in-exile, signing a cease-fire at the Communists' Plaka mountain base. The fate of their new Political Committee of National Liberation (PEEA), proclaimed in March and including several non-Communist republican sympathizers, would have to await British and Soviet decisions later in the year. The Soviet side had already communicated its request for reconciliation to the KKE leadership in the weeks before the Plaka agreement.

In the meantime, German reprisals against ELAS villages continued. SS units rounded up all urban opponents while shipping off Jews to the death camps. These harsh measures continued to build support for the Communist-led resistance. Its own rural regime was, however, generating domestic resentment. EAM/ELAS increasingly demanded political control in those same villages, ignoring family networks and local traditions in order to begin a socialist transition. That the resulting village committees were not under central control and had democratic aspirations, best seen in the representation accorded women and the illiterate, should not obscure their dictatorial powers. These included confiscations of food for the war effort and special units for Protection of the People's Struggle (OPLA) that executed deserters and opponents. Forcibly recruited ELAS draftees were often assigned to the OPLA so that they would be implicated in a local killing.

All this created an opening into which German attempts to mobilize local support after the Italian surrender could step. A new SS representative of Hermann Neubacher's choosing worked with the collaborationist government of Ioannis Rallis, over Wehrmacht objections, to create the Greek Security Battalions. Their job would ostensibly be to protect villages from ELAS impositions and hence any risk of German reprisal. By January 1944 perhaps 10,000 had been recruited, some by forced draft from the gendarmerie or from prison. Their presence across the central and southern mainland would complicate the EAM/ELAS claim to exclusive power once the Germans were forced to evacuate Greece later in 1944. And already in the north, the growing numbers of Slav Macedonians in ELAS ranks and the belated efforts of Tito's Partisans to organize a wider ethnic Macedonian resistance was spreading the unfounded suspicion that the KKE leadership was already committed to ceding Aegean Macedonia to some new postwar state or federation.

By early 1944 such uncertainties would not confront the small Albanian Communist Party. Founded with Yugoslav Communist assistance in 1941, the small party took greater advantage from belated German assistance to Albanian adversaries, thereby discrediting them. Nor would much British presence or influence stand in the party's way. Italian units had quickly captured a small military mission dispatched from collapsing Yugoslavia in April 1941. A second one did not arrive until April 1943. King Zog had already found his way to London in 1939 but received no standing to form a government-in-exile since Britain had recognized the Italian annexation of Albania.

The handful of active Albanian Communists did not come together to establish a party until November 1941 and then made little progress over the next year.[27] Two of Tito's close associates had come to press for the party's formal creation, but whether they directed or observed the process remains controversial. What is clear is that the leading position in the new Central Committee belonged from the start to Enver Hoxha. He was a Tosk schoolteacher from the south with prolonged education in France and a commitment to promoting the Communist cause from joining the French party in 1931 and returning to Albania in 1936. By early 1942 the party could still count only a couple of hundred members. The aforementioned addition of

Kosovo reduced the appeal of resistance. The party was finally able to form a Movement of National Liberation (LNC) in September 1942, after launching a few sabotage missions during the summer. By November, anti-Communist but also anti-Zog opponents had formed their own National Front (*Balli Kombetar*). Their disparate peasant bands probably outnumbered the 2000 LNC recruits available to the Army of National Liberation finally formed in March 1943 on the model and advice of Tito's Partisans. Small British military missions began arriving in April 1943, somehow to coordinate resistance. They struggled over the summer and might still have succeeded if Italy had not left the war in September. The subsequent German occupation of Albania changed everything.[28] A small force of 36,000 second-line troops arrived with their own supplies. The Germans sold off Italian supplies left behind to the population at low prices. This was a welcome change from the demands of a larger Italian contingent of 55,000 forced to supply themselves locally. Nazi Foreign Minister Ribbentrop authorized the ubiquitous Neubacher to pursue the creation of an autonomous Albanian regency to replace the Italian administration. This included making agreements with and payments in gold coins seized in Kosovo to all local groups ready to oppose the LNC. In addition to northern Geg bands distrusting the southern Tosk Communists' indifference to Kosovo, they included the *Balli Kombetar* and also the newly formed Zogist *Legaliteti*. To make matters worse, German reinforcements arrived in November to launch a devastating attack on the National Liberation Army. Ballist units joined them in reprisals against villages aiding the Communist resistance. LNC numbers grew in response, although the total is uncertain. British support switched exclusively to its side.

By 1944, in other words, the LNC and its Communist leadership stood as the one resistance movement that had not collaborated with the Germans or spoken in vain of a forthcoming British invasion. Neither was there a Soviet presence. Instead, Tito's representative Tempo (Svetozar Vukmanović) offered Hoxha the chance to include Liberation Army officers in a Balkan Communist general staff. In January, after the Greek and Bulgarian party leaderships had demurred at forming such staff, Tempo arranged a Yugoslav–Albanian meeting at Bujan. Yugoslav representatives promised Kosovo's inclusion in the postwar Albania of a Communist Balkan federation. Tito would, however, quickly withdraw the promise.

Communist Advantage and Soviet Caution, 1944–1945

Enter the Red Army, from its August 1944 invasion of Romania through the November advance north from Yugoslavia to Hungary. Surely the region's

Communist parties would now receive the strong and exclusive Soviet support for which they had been waiting since 1942. But until the last weeks of the Second World War, they received little. Among those expecting that they would were British Prime Minister Churchill. His desire to keep the Communist liberation movements out of power in Greece and confined at least to sharing it in Yugoslavia lay behind the much analyzed percentages deal offered to Stalin in October 1944. In return for 90/10 predominance in postwar influence in Greece and a 50/50 split in Yugoslavia and Hungary, Churchill suggested Soviet advantages of 90/10 in Romania and 75/25 in Bulgaria. The Soviet side quickly pressed Churchill's Foreign Minister, Anthony Eden, to revise the Bulgarian and Hungarian figures to 80/20 and 60/40 in their favor.[29] Churchill's American allies had not been consulted. Soviet presumption of these percentages and subsequent American indifference to them would indeed play a part in the postwar period. Yet they would have less to do with the Communist political advantage as the war was ending than much anti-Communist analysis first assumed.

More important in the winter of 1944–5 was the advance of Soviet forces and their attendant military needs. Earlier in the year, American supplies to resistance movements and efforts to aid their downed bomber crews signaled renewed United States interest. The 1942 agreement to leave occupied or hostile Southeastern Europe entirely to the British was now set aside. The American arrival ironically contributed, along with the Soviet military advance, to the advantages already working for the region's Communist parties and against their domestic opponents.

Romania and Bulgaria

Despite their disparate size and standing, the Romanian and Bulgarian Communist parties each took considerable advantage from the arrival and also the departure of the Red Army. For Romania, General Antonescu's wartime regime lasted only three days after the Soviet breakthrough on the Moldovan front. King Michael responded to Antonescu's desperate attempt for an armistice with all three Allies by dismissing and arresting him on August 23. Another General close to Antonescu replaced him as Prime Minister and representatives of the four major opposition parties, generously including the Communists with perhaps a thousand members in the country, entered the new government. The four had agreed to form a National Democratic Bloc opposed to continuing the war only in June. It was their Liberal and National Peasant representatives, Brătianu and Maniu, who had coordinated the coup with Michael. They took the lead in the armistice negotiations with the Soviets. The Communist representative,

Lucretiu Pătrăşcanu, received no instruction from Moscow on how to proceed, let alone any deference in the agreement reached on September 12. It promised the Red Army $300 million worth of military supplies at 1938 prices and 12 divisions of the Romanian army. Pro-German generals were removed, but otherwise almost all of the remaining 300,000 men in its army went ahead into Transylvania under Soviet command. The prospect of regaining this territory lost to Hungary in 1940 united Michael and all parties in the Bloc. First there and then in Hungary and Czechoslovakia, the Red Army pushed those poorly equipped units into frontal attacks that cost them 132,000 casualties. Officers surviving the campaign still found themselves out of the country and under Soviet command.

If this Communist advantage is well known, the background to Soviet insistence on the Communist-dominated government of March 6, 1945 is not. Earlier Western scholarship and post-1989 work from Romania has traced Soviet intervention from the banning of the critical National Peasant newspaper *Universal* in October 1944 and then the dismissal of the August 23 government by November. The Red Army representative heading the Allied Control Commission did not hesitate to do both after the Liberals and National Peasants had combined forces to organize protest demonstrations in Bucharest. Yet recent research in the Soviet archives reveals that Andrei Vyshinsky, the same Foreign Minister who slammed the door and cracked the surrounding plaster on King Michael to punctuate his furious insistence in February 1945 on a pro-Communist government, had welcomed its predecessor in November 1944. Vyshinsky's several visits through December asked only that General Radescu's regime maintain civil order within 100 miles of the front and deliver the promised supplies, coal and oil in particular, as quickly as possible. Romania's Black Sea fleet was to be available to the Red Army for transport. Alfred Rieber argues persuasively that it was repeated Romanian failure to provide these deliveries or transport that prompted Vyshinsky's outburst.[30] Until that time, Moscow had seen the PCR as too weak and the problems of replacing the historic parties too great to be worth the effort.

By late February 1945, that small party had at least attracted 16,000 members. Prewar eminence Ana Pauker returned from the Soviet Union the previous September, but the leadership was already in the hands of the domestic leaders just released from prison in 1944. The eventual leader, Gheorghiu-Dej, had ironically headed the Transport Ministry whose performance the Soviets had found so wanting. Now he pressed for party union members to confront National Peasant supporters in a bloody battle at the Malaxa works just as Vyshinsky was arriving in February. The new Prime Minister named on March 6 was the maverick founder of the Ploughman's

Front and long-time Communist sympathizer Petru Groza. Dej became his Interior Minister. Only now was the road open to the Communist takeover of 1946–7.

The Bulgarian Communist Party was larger than its Romanian counterpart and also the beneficiary of disarray and hesitation in a wartime government formally allied with the Axis. King Boris's refusal to send Bulgarian troops against the Red Army stood up during the disarray that followed his death in August 1943. The Filov regime survived only until June 1944, under growing pressure from the regency for negotiations with the Western Allies. Its successor then delayed negotiations with the USSR through the summer of 1944, when Stalin might have agreed to its survival. Churchill, encouraged by the Americans, had not yet decided to consign the country to predominant Soviet influence. The regime's delay allowed the BKP to survive the slow revival of its fortunes. It failed to mount a resistance movement large enough even to seize power as the Red Army entered the country.

Although membership had climbed back toward 10,000 by early 1944, the party's efforts to organize armed resistance on the Yugoslav model had not gotten very far. A People's Liberation Army (NOVA) set up in spring 1943 had mobilized fewer than a thousand members when it was largely destroyed that fall by government forces. Encouraged by the government's disruption and mass public flight from Sofia after the largest of several Anglo-American bombings in January, Partisan numbers climbed past 2000. By May they had attracted the one British military mission to Bulgaria during the war. But Bulgarian army and police units quickly intercepted the ensuing expedition. It was decimated before it could reach Plovdiv, and its British officers killed. In Moscow, where he would remain until November 1945, party secretary Georgi Dimitrov was not yet in direct radio contact with his Central Committee in Bulgaria. He nonetheless discouraged his colleagues from coming to terms with the new government. Ivan Bagrianov had replaced Filov and his pro-Germans on June 1.

Anglo-American interest in forcing or luring Bulgaria away from the Axis faded with the success of the Normandy invasion. The Soviet side remained open to negotiation despite Dimitrov's clear opposition. But Bagrianov's fears of another 1919 settlement, i.e., losing the new territories and the right to a large army, kept him from responding. With the Red Army approaching, the Agrarian Konstantin Muraviev and the old Democrat Mushanov agreed to head the government that replaced him on September 1. They now left several places open for Communist members. Before they could negotiate, and without Dimitrov's knowledge, the Soviet Union declared war on Bulgaria on September 5. Only now were Soviet arms sent to the Partisans. They did not arrive in time for them to overthrow the government on

September 9, as the BKP would soon proclaim and celebrate annually. The actual seizure of power was left to army units loyal to Zveno, another partner along with some Agrarians and Social Democrats in the Fatherland Front that the Communists had cobbled together in 1942.

From September 9 forward, however, the BKP leadership made up for lost time.[31] They received only four ministries of fifteen in the new government of the Fatherland Front, but two of them were Interior and Justice. These key ministries allowed them to purge fully 30,000 state officials, including most police officers. A Communist-controlled People's Militia quickly took their place, while Communist mayors were appointed in three-quarters of the country's cities and villages. By early October the beleaguered regents, now minus Filov, had been obliged to sanction the convening of People's Courts. They worked quickly and arbitrarily as Communist political instruments but provided at least some semblance of justice. They convicted 6000 defendants of collaboration or related crimes, sentencing 2000 to death. In addition, the new Militia and Partisan groups killed another 3000 out of hand, including 800 in Sofia. Party leader Dimitrov, now in direct radio contact with the leadership although still in Moscow for another full year, urged restraint. This was doubtless Stalin's desire. The Front's wartime alliance was to be preserved at all costs because the war against Germany took precedence.

In November, over three-quarters of the large Bulgarian army of 400,000 men joined the Red Army and proceeded into Yugoslavia. They would suffer 32,000 killed and more wounded. By December, Communist appointees replaced a third of the remaining officer corps, after 800 had been initially dismissed. Here we see the first direct domestic result of the Red Army's continuing presence in Bulgaria. The Soviet head of the Allied Control Commission, General Biriuzov, had demanded the change. His rapid appointment came as a concession from the Western allies. In return, Stalin had agreed in October to a British demand that the Bulgarian army withdraw all of its troops from Thrace and Vardar Macedonia. With the army thus transformed and the administration of local order and administration in its hands, the BKP could await the end of the war with only the resurgent Agrarians to challenge their rapidly increasing membership. By January 1945 the Communist total had climbed to 250,000.

Yugoslavia, Albania, and Greece

To the west, the three Communist-led movements of rural resistance awaited the war's end as a reward for their Liberation Army's struggles against the Axis occupiers. In contrast to Romania and Bulgaria, they anticipated less accommodation with the major prewar parties, still less with the prewar monarchies, and none with the state institutions destroyed or taken over during the occupation. In Yugoslavia and Albania, these last months of the Second World War would not disappoint their Communist parties. In Greece, they would. In all three, Soviet, British, and American interventions, or the prospect thereof, would play their parts. Still, none would be as decisive as long assumed throughout the region.

For Tito's ascending Partisans, perhaps 400,000 strong by the summer of 1944, their leader's surreptitious trip from British-protected Vis in the Adriatic to Moscow in September strengthened their hand still further. Stalin not only promised Tito the arms to equip a dozen regular army divisions but also agreed that Partisan brigades could join the Red Army in liberating Belgrade. This last provision, and it was a concession given the Soviet reluctance to count on irregular units, paid the Partisans three dividends.[32] First, it brought them into Serbia where they could defeat or prompt the defection of what remained of the Chetniks' main force of 50,000 men. Red Army commanders had brushed aside Mihailović's deluded effort to link his own detachments up with the Red Army. Secondly, following the fall of Belgrade on October 20, Partisan commanders drafted all available young men in the city into their brigades, thus weakening subsequent opposition. Finally, the aforementioned press of the Red Army north into Hungary took its substantial numbers out of Yugoslavia almost as quickly as they had come.

A small Anglo-American air base established by early 1945 north of Belgrade served nicely to feed Communist suspicions of some significant Western intervention after all. The recent American military mission to Mihailović in Serbia, undertaken earlier in 1944 to evacuate the several hundred US airmen shot down while returning from raids on Ploeşti, was already suspected, albeit unjustifiably, of covering the delivery of arms to the Chetniks. Tito would not repudiate his tentative agreement in June 1944 to coordinate a postwar government with the new head of the London government, Ivan Šubašić, for the rest of the war. But Communist confidence and suspicion would quickly combine, as we shall see in Chapter 6, to sweep aside any sharing of significant power.

The one armed conflict contesting the Partisans' military sway helped Enver Hoxha's Liberation Movement to consolidate Communist power in Albania and ironically to resist Yugoslav domination. British military missions had already helped the Communist-led Partisans to advance during the German retreat that began in September. With that retreat went the credibility of the Ballist and Zogist forces that had accepted German aid. Even before the withdrawal finished in November 1944 with the capture of

Tirana, Hoxha had named himself Prime Minister. The British had helped even more by not planning the Anglo-American invasion that was Hoxha's worst fear. No Soviet mission, let alone the Red Army, ever had any prospect of reaching Albania.

A core of Yugoslav Partisan officers, plus some Albanian advocates, were pushing Hoxha to accept some confederal link between the two countries. But, beginning in December 1944, Kosovar Albanians, empowered by the Italian annexation, and then supported by a late infusion of German arms and the creation of their own SS Division, rose up in revolt. They engaged the heavily Serb Partisan brigades sent to replace the regime that had made the territory part of Albania. Fighting continued until the following June. Hoxha was obliged to send some of his own forces to join in suppressing the revolt, despite the fact that Tito's side was determined to return Kosovo permanently to Yugoslavia. This preview of a permanently subordinate position in any closer relationship with a Communist Yugoslavia helped Hoxha in putting off those in his own leadership, led by Koci Xoxe, who were encouraging it. Ignoring their advice, Hoxha went ahead with plans for a separate army, rather than more units simply attached to Yugoslav divisions.[33]

Several obstacles confronted the larger Greek movement, swollen to half a million for EAM and perhaps 50,000 for its ELAS fighting force by mid-1944. The barriers went beyond the British intervention that we can no longer accept as the sole reason for its failure to seize power. When it did come, British military intervention was indeed decisive in the bloody battle for Athens in December 1944. The subsequent Varkiza Agreement of February 1945 gave EAM a subordinate role in a new regime led by the exile government and obliged ELAS to disarm. Stalin stood by, observing the percentages agreement with Churchill for Greece after making sure that Bulgarian troops vacated Thrace and Aegean Macedonia. Before then, however, the story was more complicated.

EAM/ELAS already had weaknesses and rivals not faced by their Yugoslav or Albanian counterparts. Their own military strength had suffered during the summer of 1944. A month after their losses in a June attack on the EDES concentration in northwestern Greece, ELAS took at least 7000 casualties in Macedonia from Operation Steinadler, the last German offensive against any Communist-led force in the western Balkans. Then came the renewed specter of Slav Macedonian separatism.[34] Under Yugoslav Communist guidance, their Aegean and Vardar detachments created ASNOM (the Anti-Fascist Council for the Liberation of Macedonia) on August 2, the anniversary of the Illinden uprising in 1903. The ubiquitous tempo spoke of a single postwar Macedonia that would include Thessaloniki.

In addition to the smaller but still independent rival of EDES within Greece, EAM/ELAS also faced an exile government that, unlike Yugoslavia's, had maintained its own army throughout the war. The mutiny of its ELAS supporters earlier in 1944 had only allowed the British authorities in Cairo to replace its royalist leadership with the republican but strongly anti-Communist Gregorios Papandreou. The antiroyal basis for the mutiny removed, Papandreou was able to speak from renewed strength in reaching a September agreement in Italy with the Communist leadership. In return for six places in a new joint government, they signed an agreement to demobilize ELAS and join a new National Army. In early November the Papandreou regime transferred the royalist Mountain Brigade of nearly three thousand men from Cairo to Athens. After the city's rapturous public welcome, it was not disbanded as promised. EAM Ministers had objected in vain. There were few ELAS forces in the capital, but EAM's Labor Minister was able to organize a new Communist-dominated Provisional Committee for the General Confederation of Greek Workers (GSEE). It joined in organizing the KKE's massive demonstration to celebrate the anniversary of the party's founding on November 20. The domestic players were in place for the confrontation that became bloody December.[35]

The British military commander and Churchill himself played parts as well. By late November, General Ronald Scobie had built up a combat force of nearly twenty thousand men to keep Athens secure and press ahead with disarming ELAS. Surpassing this total on the government side were the hastily assembled National Guards and the larger part of the Security Battalions recruited by the Rallis occupation regime. Churchill continued to insist on the return of King George II. He rejected EAM's widely popular demand that a plebiscite on the monarchy be held first. After hesitating, the KKE, still under Siantos's leadership, decided on a new demonstration as a prelude to a general strike in Athens. When Papandreou refused to authorize the demonstration, it went ahead anyway on December 4. Fighting erupted between the crowd and police under still-disputed circumstances. ELAS moved in a couple of thousand men to help seize police stations and other government buildings, although under orders to avoid combat with British troops or the Mountain Brigade. Just such combat soon followed, despite the initial restraint of Scobie, if not Churchill, as well as the KKE leadership. The British army poured in reinforcements to double its contingent in Athens and Piraeus. It did not seek and could not afford at the time to challenge the predominance of EAM/ELAS in the majority of the countryside and most of the north. But to win the Battle of Athens, or the Second Round of the Greek Civil War as it is also called, Churchill had to come to Athens in late December. He finally agreed that the King should set aside the demand to return at once. Churchill then obliged George to accept representation by a regency under the Archbishop of Athens. Siantos and the other EAM leaders at the Athens meeting saw that Stalin's representative made no special pleas on their behalf. They had no choice but to sign the agreement at Varkiza near Athens on February 12, 1945. Its formal terms included the disarmament of ELAS but not the arrest of its combatants nor their exclusion from the new National Army.[36]

KKE militants in the north such as Aris disputed this decision to stand down from the start. But, unlike their colleagues in Yugoslavia and Albania, they would enter the postwar period not as revolutionary regimes in power but as the last of the region's rural resistance movements, tied as much to Balkan traditions as to Communist ideology. Nor would the Soviet support that proved crucial to the new Romanian and Bulgarian regimes be available.

As German forces were retreating from the region in late 1944, neither the Western allies nor the Soviet Union regarded Southeastern Europe as occupying the strategic position that it had early in the Second World War. The United States did not share the British interest in postwar Greece, nor did the British interest extend to the northern neighbors. Recall Winston Churchill's rejoinder in 1943 to concern about the Partisans' Communist leadership from Fitzroy Maclean, the head of the large British military mission in wartime Yugoslavia.[37] Did either of them intend to live there after the war? In October 1944, in the famous percentages agreement noted above, the British Prime Minister had ceded primary responsibility for Romania and Bulgaria to the Soviet Union. The Red Army had already swept through and was pressing the Germans through eastern Yugoslavia into Hungary by November.

From the first months of 1945, however, the region entered a postwar period that revived its strategic importance. By the war's end in May, the new Truman Administration in the US joined Churchill's government in regarding the local Communist advances and the presence of the Red Army as challenges to the postwar shape of Southeastern Europe. Stalin was prepared to cede only Greece to a postwar regime that would be hostile to the Soviet Union. Even there, battle lines appeared as the postwar transition began.

6 Communist and Cold War Transitions, 1945–1963

The century's second postwar transition would be less daunting for Southeastern Europe than its experience after the First World War in two respects. The period did not begin with a major redrawing of international boundaries. Nor was it followed a decade later by a collapse of the international economy. During the 1920s the new states of Albania and the Yugoslav Kingdom had struggled over their common border, while the borders of Bulgaria, Greece, and Romania remained in dispute throughout the interwar period. This time the region's prewar borders remained largely unchanged. Claims for their revision before 1989 were limited to the Yugoslav–Italian dispute over Trieste, resolved to mutual benefit as we shall see in 1954. Otherwise, the postwar map (Map 6.1) reveals only one addition in 1945, predominantly Slovene and Croatian Istria to Yugoslavia from Italy. Also ratified were Romania's 1940 losses of the southern Dobrudja to Bulgaria, and Bessarabia and the Bukovina to the Soviet Union.

Internally, the post-1918 political frameworks had barely ten years before the Great Depression began in 1929. Its impact combined with the rise of fascist or authoritarian governments across Europe to put an end to the liberal transition that most of them had pursued, however imperfectly. After 1945 nearly three decades of rising European prosperity and still more years of general peace lay ahead. This time, however, so did wrenching, often arbitrary systemic change.

As in the post-1918 period, the region had, like all of Eastern Europe, experienced more loss of civilian life, forced migration, and destruction of property during the world war than had Western Europe. This time Greece, along with Yugoslavia, had suffered the most civilian deaths – about 5 percent of their prewar populations. Only Romania matched Yugoslavia's further 5 percent of population forced to move. Overall, the toll from start to finish was about the same as for the First World War – over 2 million dead, military losses included, and nearly 2 million people uprooted. Upwards of half the prewar infrastructure had been destroyed. Once again,

Map 6.1 Southeastern Europe, 1945–1989

Source: Adapted from L. S. Stavrianos and Traian Stoianovich, *The Balkans Since 1453* (New York: New York University Press, 2000)

Greek acquisitions from Italy	— · — International boundaries
Bulgarian acquisitions from Romania	— · · — Republic boundary
Soviet acquisitions from Romania	– – – – – Autonomous province
Yugoslav acquisitions from Italy	boundaries

the region's large peasant majorities awaited some relief from rural isolation, limited opportunities, and official neglect. But the transition that awaited them, particularly the Communist choice between forced collectivization or forced migration into industrial jobs, would be far more daunting than their struggle with flawed land reforms had been in the 1920s.

Two further distinctions from the first postwar transition complete the wider context for the national cases. Before diverging increasingly, one from the other, by 1965, all five states began in 1945 with their prewar or wartime regimes discredited. Constitutional monarchies and multiparty elections had not even survived the 1930s. Ruling arbitrarily through nonparty regimes, and then accepting wartime collaboration or exile, now put the monarchies' political legitimacy into question. Broadly established peasant parties struggled to reemerge in Romania, Bulgaria, and Croatia but could not combine their scattered rural constituencies to match Communist mobilization, let alone confront the Red Army or Tito's Partisans. Narrower, nominally liberal parties in Greece and Serbia as well as in Romania were burdened with past compromises and ongoing divisions.

A new set of major powers now confronted these smaller states. The Soviet Union arrived to replace Germany's influence. The United States replaced Great Britain and France as the leading Western presence. Some combination of Soviet support and the domestic Communist advantages that followed from the Second World War (see Chapter 5) put Soviet-style regimes in power everywhere but Greece by 1947. Cold War confrontation brought American aid to help preserve an anti-Communist Greek government that did more, eventually if not at the start, to advance political pluralism than the one-party regimes surrounding it.

We typically date divergence within the region from Stalin's excommunication of Tito's Yugoslavia from the emerging Soviet bloc in 1948. There had, however, already appeared a damaging division within the Communist Party of Greece and a forceful Agrarian challenge in Bulgaria to what would later be assumed to be the easiest Communist assumption of power. By the early 1960s the Albanian regime had abandoned Soviet for Chinese support and Romania was pressing for greater economic independence within the bloc. Tito's Yugoslavia joined the Western framework for international trade and was trying to substantiate the social market economy promised by its workers' councils and enterprise self-management since the early 1950s. Multiparty elections in Greece allowed a Communist surrogate to win seats as early as 1951 and then the major opposition party to win power by 1963.

While the states of Southeastern Europe were going increasingly separate international ways and regional ties frayed as well, their national development proceeded along remarkably similar lines. Postwar recovery went rapidly ahead in every case but Romania's, only there without important Soviet or American assistance. From the 1950s forward, the ministries, state banks, or other agencies of centralization had taken the lead in a program of economic modernization. In Greece as well as the Communist regimes, their efforts transferred a significant share of the population to the urban labor force, improved rural health, and expanded primary education significantly. The Communist emphasis first on heavy industry and then on agricultural collectivization proved to be a less successful part of this process than advertised, as comparable economic advances for Greece at less social cost make clear. Yet their common neglect of internationally competitive manufacturing cost them all as the European trade boom pushed up aggregate economic growth after 1960.

A common, less constructive concentration on ethnically distinctive national identities emerged in all of the educational systems, although less successfully on a single shared identity in Yugoslavia. Religious identities survived but under official restriction outside of Greece and subject to official manipulation even there. Catholic clergy were harassed and arrested in Albania and Romania as well as Yugoslavia, where their real or presumed support for the wartime *Ustaša* regime made persecution easier. In Bosnia-Herzegovina, the Young Muslim movement, including the post-1991 President Alija Izetbegović, was suppressed on similar, more specious grounds. In Romania, the small Catholic Church and the much larger Uniate denomination of Transylvania, the so-called "Greek Catholics," were simply declared illegal. The still larger Orthodox Churches in Bulgaria, Romania, and Yugoslavia saw their lands confiscated, their hierarchies replaced by clerics subservient to the Communist regimes, and thousands of priests imprisoned. The Albanian Orthodox clergy received even harsher treatment as presumed Greek agents.

Before examining the broader transitions and impending contradictions of this longer period, we must first appreciate the initial struggle for political power, more intense and complex than previously assumed. It took place within the respective Communist parties as much as with their domestic opponents, and within the Communist camp as much as between the Soviet Union and the United States.

Recovering from the heavy material losses of the Second World War created a strong case for some new central authority to marshal all surviving resources for the task. The respective Communist parties all stepped forward with visions of duplicating the Soviet Five-Year Plans of the 1930s. In the USSR after all, these plans had just mobilized the war effort that defeated Nazi Germany. For Southeastern Europe, the cost of supporting the Red Army as the war was ending and the arrival of largely American recovery and relief aid through the United Nations (UNRRA) cut into those Communist credentials. Let us briefly review the balance of losses, costs, and assistance for each country.[1]

Postwar Albania, Greece, and Yugoslavia were all eligible for UNRRA assistance to recover from the damages of occupation. For Albania, damage was confined to the mines, livestock, and housing. But large fractions of all three had indeed been destroyed. UNRRA supplies arrived in time to prevent a famine in 1945, but the new Communist regime turned to assistance from Yugoslavia when upland flooding descended in 1946. UNRRA's Western staff aroused suspicion in any case. The Communist regime expelled them in early 1947 after only $26 million of aid had arrived. For Greece and Yugoslavia, far larger sums – $352 million and $415 million, respectively – helped their populations to deal with far greater losses. Both of their networks of rail and road transport had been heavily damaged, and bridges, rolling stock, and motor vehicles largely destroyed. Livestock and draft animals numbered half their reduced wartime levels. The cultivated area in Greece, already in food deficit through the century, shrank by one-quarter. Some 40 percent of Yugoslavia's industrial plant was in ruins. In Greece as well, systematic demolition during the German retreat caused far more damage than the Anglo-American bombing of 1944.

Unlike the western Balkans, the Romanian economy had actually benefited from German investment during the war. The major agricultural investments in soybean and sunflower cultivation had, however, taken place in Bessarabia. It was now part of the Soviet Union. Anglo-American bombing had destroyed improvements to the oil refineries of Ploești, although never stopping their capacity to produce for long. As we saw in Chapter 5, the first Romanian transitional government had been slow to provide the supplies to the Red Army that it had promised in addition to $300 million in reparations for the Romanian campaign in the Soviet Union. Its successor from March 1945 stood by while Soviet requisitions of grain, mineral oil, and cattle took the majority of domestic inventory. A drought in 1945 following the hasty land reform to redistribute large holdings cut the grain harvest to one-third of the previous year's level. For the hard winter of 1946–7, grain as well as oil and steel production struggled to reach half of wartime levels. The Red Army conscripted the rail network for the war's duration and beyond, depleting or badly damaging its rolling stock. Reparations claimed a third of reduced state revenues. And most resented in the later historiography of national Communism, almost one thousand enterprises including the large oil and metallurgical firms, were taken over, on the grounds of having supported the Nazi war effort. Russian administrators then arrived to run these supposedly joint entities, or Sovroms.

Bulgaria faced no Soviet demand for reparations and saw none of its less extensive industrial plant taken over as joint enterprises. There were other burdens. First, heavy contributions to supply the Red Army and then the aforementioned drought of 1945 created severe shortages of grain, meat, and draft animals. The arrival of 120,000 refugees from the occupied areas of Macedonia and Thrace, now ceded back to Yugoslavia and Greece, added to the strain. As for Romania, there would be no UNRRA assistance to a wartime German ally. But Bulgaria had committed no troops to the Russian Front, helping to encourage the shipments of Soviet grain and oil that relieved some of the shortage by the winter of 1945–6.

Romania, Bulgaria, and the Soviet Role, 1945–1949

These shipments, plus Stalin's initially cautious approach to Romania noted in Chapter 5, suggest that the larger Soviet role that we rightly anticipate in Bulgaria had appeared from the start. For the initial years of the postwar political transition, the reverse was true. First, the Anglo-American representatives on the Allied Control Commission for Bulgaria exerted more influence than their counterparts in Romania. More significant for Soviet leverage in Romania was the greater weakness not only of its Communist party but also of its opposition. By 1948, Soviet support had nonetheless come forward in Bulgaria as well, and both oppositions had been eliminated.

The tiny Romanian Communist Party still numbered barely 16,000 members when Soviet envoy Andrei Vyshinsky arrived in February 1945 to demand that a more favorable government be formed. Under what Vladimir Tismaneanu aptly calls "the fake pluralism" of the subsequent regime, party membership jumped past 250,000 by October and reached 700,000 by the following June.[2] Communist heads of the newly created Ministry of Propaganda as well as Justice and Transport plus a subsecretary in Agriculture encouraged this increase. Most importantly, the new Communist Minister of Internal Affairs used the established authority of that position to appoint members as prefects and key officials of the local *judeţ* councils. They extended the police powers that Red Army dismissals in the army, the gendarmerie, and the *Siguranţa* had already transferred to Communist supporters. By May 1946 those powers were used to arrest fully 4000 people on newly broadened charges of war crimes. The show trial and execution of Marshal Antonescu followed that same month.

By this time the governing coalition that Petru Groza still formally led on behalf of his Ploughman's Front, with the Communists, the Social Democrats, and a Liberal faction, had consolidated itself as the National Democratic Bloc. Already in the 1930s Groza had launched his party and begun collaboration with the PCR explicitly to undercut the National Peasant Party and its leader, Iuliu Maniu. Now his Front made it unnecessary for the Communists to split off a faction of Maniu's party to properly represent "the poorer peasantry." Groza's first act as Prime Minister in March 1945 had been to proclaim the confiscation of large private landholdings noted above. The Front's own village committees took the lead, even before the law was passed, in expelling owners of as little as 25 acres and parceling out a few acres each to landless or dwarfholding peasants.[3]

As for the other major historical party, the Liberals split themselves. The same Gheorghe Tătărescu who had broken with the continuing Brătianu family leadership of the Liberals to support King Carol's prewar regime now took his faction into the Groza government. The two historic parties struggled outside this government Bloc to find newsprint for their papers and Western support for their right to compete in the elections for a constituent assembly. They were successful in neither. Just as Vyshinsky was branding them "archaic parties," British Prime Minister Churchill omitted any mention of Romania in his request of March 1945 that Stalin respect the democratic process in Poland. Later in 1945, on the eve of September's London conference of Allied Foreign Ministers, Anglo-American encouragement did prompt King Michael to ask for Groza's resignation in favor of a more representative government. The Western powers took no further action, however, when Groza refused. Soviet Foreign Minister Molotov simply adjourned the conference. He refused to consider Western mediation in Romania or Bulgaria on the grounds that no Soviet role was permitted in Italy or Japan.

For the elections of November 1946, Communist activists disrupted National Peasant meetings, while the Propaganda Ministry censored what papers the opposition party managed to print. The Bloc claimed 70 percent of the votes in apparently winning the election of November 19, 1946. The delay in their announcement strengthened Western suspicions, confirmed since 1989, that the results had been falsified. As it was, the Bloc received 349 seats to 33 for the National Peasants and 32 for other opponents. Anglo-American officers on the Allied Control Commission and an active American Ambassador protested, but to little effect. Then Romania's signing of its peace treaty in February 1947 marked the end of the Control Commission. When the deputy Agrarian leader tried in vain to flee the country by plane in July, Maniu was promptly arrested on false charges of conspiring with Western intelligence. King Michael was forced to abdicate by the end of the year. From January 1948 the forced merger of the Social Democrats with the Communists to form the Romanian Workers' Party marked the end of the Groza government, poor semblance that it was of political pluralism in Romania.

Within the newly empowered Communist party, however, a fateful struggle for power was underway from 1945 to 1948. Recent research finds Soviet support ironically crucial in an earlier victory for the one Romanian Communist leader not schooled in Moscow than was previously believed. Surely Gheorghe Gheorghiu-Dej, it was assumed, had won out after 1948 because two of the three other leaders were not, like him, ethnically Romanian and had made themselves still more unpopular with a doubtful Romanian public by their hard-line support for rapid Sovietization. Instead, separate studies now suggest that Dej had won Soviet backing against all three of them precisely because of his greater loyalty.[4]

First to fall was the party's initial member of the coalition government that replaced the Antonescu regime, Lucretiu Pătrăşcanu. An urbane lawyer and longtime party member with some popular appeal, he clearly overshadowed Dej during these early months. His far shorter time in prison during the war helped to feed Dej's resentment. More important was the Soviet reaction to an allegedly nationalistic speech that the ethnically Romanian Pătrăşcanu made in Cluj in June 1945. He did stress the need for the remaining Hungarians to punish war criminals and accept the reunified Romanian state. From that time forward, Soviet representatives joined Dej in pushing him into lesser positions. His abortive effort to leave the country, albeit temporarily, in the wake of Maniu's arrest in 1947 increased his vulnerability. It took the Tito–Stalin split in 1948 to open him to charges of Yugoslav and other "imperialist" connections. Then tried and imprisoned, his eventual execution in 1954 belongs to the last Stalinist purges which we consider later in the chapter.

The reliability of Ana Pauker and Vasile Luca before the Tito–Stalin split, their respectively Jewish and Hungarian origins not yet a liability in the PCR, was also open to question from the Soviet side. Pauker and Luca did not return from Moscow to Bucharest until mid-September 1944. Until the fall of 1945, Pauker was indeed recognized as Party Secretary. But when Dej succeeded her, she held no position in the government until becoming Foreign Minister until early 1947. Dej's new position as Economics Minister trumped Luca's leverage as Finance Minister. He followed Pauker's lead in resisting the intentional hyperinflation of 1946, although he would later be blamed for the hardships it imposed. Pauker had the nerve to call on her own experience with a Soviet agricultural project in the early 1930s when she objected to the Soviet Embassy about its proposal for rushing ahead in 1946 with forced collectivization in Romania. She would repeat those objections to Stalin himself in 1948. These and other independent statements to accommodate the ever-larger mass membership of the party, plus a friendly relationship with Pătrășcanu, weakened her standing with Soviet representatives suspiciously watching a Romania they did not trust. Dej had no such handicaps.

Watching a Bulgaria that they undoubtedly trusted more, the Soviets were nonetheless obliged to accept the growth of a single, large opposition party and even to postpone the initial postwar election at Anglo-American urging. Given the much larger initial size and more active history of the Bulgarian Communist Party than its Romanian counterpart, this may seem surprising. Its growth to the same 250,000 members recorded in Romania by the end of 1945 started from a far larger base of 15,000 in September 1944 and included many more longtime sympathizers. Yet this higher standing and morale itself encouraged the Soviet representatives, fewer than in Romania from the start, to stand back. After all, BKP leader Georgi Dimitrov was in Moscow and in frequent contact with Stalin until returning in November 1945. Until then he had less contact with the acting Party Secretary in Bulgaria, Traicho Kostov. Not a Muscovite, he was nonetheless distinguished by an unbroken ideological commitment to the Soviet line as well as by a disabling back injury from a prison escape.

It was Kostov who sounded the first alarm about Nikola Petkov. The left Agrarian leader quickly became the most likely candidate to pull together the party's two factions and revive its post-1918 standing under Stamboliiski as the largest political movement in Bulgaria. But Dimitrov and the Soviets were more worried about "the other Dimitrov," G. M. Dimitrov. Gemeto, as he was dubbed, had returned from wartime exile in British-controlled Cairo to head the left faction. This British connection made him an easy target for the Communist Minister of Interior under the regime of the Fatherland Front. By January 1945, Gemeto had been forced to resign and was soon under house arrest, from which he shortly fled the country with American diplomatic assistance. As late as April 1945, Dimitrov and "our big friend" (as he called Stalin to the party leadership) agreed that Petkov needed to be "kept within the fold."[5] But Petkov was soon complaining about Soviet interference, even comparing it to the role of the Russian generals trying to control Bulgarian political life in the early 1880s. His demands for press freedom joined with similar pressures from Simon Georgiev, Zveno's Prime Minister within the Fatherland Front. Together they persuaded first the Anglo-American representatives and then the Soviet head of the Allied Control Commission to grant at least some access to paper and newsprint. By September, Dimitrov was calling Petkov "nothing less than a scoundrel" for asking the Control Commission to delay elections and to allow their international supervision. Stalin accepted only the first request for delay as a "last concession." The Truman Administration dispatched a senior journalist, Mark Ethridge, to report on the political process, but did no more. At a subsequent Moscow meeting, Molotov brushed aside the American's charge of Soviet interference and ignored the demand that a more representative government be appointed before the elections. The Fatherland Front handily won the November election with 75 percent of the vote versus 10 percent for the opposition, with 15 percent abstaining.

Yet the next year and the next election did not go as well for Communist accommodation with any kind of independent opposition.[6] Dimitrov had returned to head what would be called for 1945–8 the Bulgarian Workers Party (BRPk). He came with less confidence from Stalin and less consistent instruction from Moscow than was expected. Petkov's Agrarians (BZNS-NP) were attracting far more members, surpassing 50,000, than the rival Agrarian party set up under Communist auspices the year before. Petkov's party also reached out more successfully into the still predominant rural villages, organizing some 2000 local associations, or *druzhbi*. Its party paper and Zveno's both attracted a larger circulation than the Communists' *Rabotnichesko Delo*. Their articles raged at the electoral intimidations and other abuses of the People's Militia and the enterprise workers' councils. Outside of these institutions, the People's Courts and the state radio, moreover, the Communist presence in the rest of the judicial system, in the economic ministries and institutions, and in local government was small or shrinking. A party report of mid-1946 lamented that only 11 of 124 higher officials of the Interior Ministry were party members, only 5 of 38 in the Finance Ministry, and even fewer in the National Bank or the agricultural associations. The party's high initial share of town and village mayors was dropping toward one half. Only the army seemed more secure. Another 2000 officers were purged in July 1945. The dismissal of Zveno War Minister Damian Velchev and the assignment of party political officers to every unit offered further reassurance that this still-large force of 100,000 men could not turn on the Front.

In March 1946, the Communists had offered the BZNS-NP a last chance to join their Fatherland Front. Petkov's party quickly refused but did not oppose the September referendum to abolish the unpopular monarchy. The proposal's overwhelming approval by 94 percent of the votes cast offered the Communist leadership some encouragement. Yet the Agrarian base of village smallholders continued to endorse Petkov's opposition to the Front government. As elections to a constituent assembly in October approached, Communist anxiety rose. Dimitrov himself promised an article preserving private property in the new constitution. Both sides mobilized large public demonstrations in Sofia just before the balloting. Despite the continued disruption of their other meetings and publications, BZNS-NP won 30 percent of the vote and 101 of 465 seats in the assembly. The BRPk share of 53 percent and 264 seats, with the other 18 percent going to its partners in the Fatherland Front, hardly represented the overwhelming victory that the party anticipated and trumpeted anyway. Meanwhile, Agrarian party membership climbed past 90,000. Petkov continued his outspoken refusal to join a government that Dimitrov headed.

Dimitrov now joined his aggressive colleagues from the party's core to abandon any tolerance for a coalition government. Their allies in the Fatherland Front were given even fewer assembly seats than their reduced election votes indicated. Communists now moved into the great majority of higher positions in all ministries and other state agencies. The People's Courts reached beyond wartime charges to begin sentencing open opponents to forced labor. By June, new camps, if not yet the notorious Belene island complex, held 20,000 such prisoners. Western leverage for protest fell when the peace treaty with Bulgaria was finally signed in February 1947. It vanished with the subsequent British and American recognition of the new government. Petkov was arrested in the National Assembly, any immunity waved aside, on the day after US recognition was reluctantly granted on June 5. Anglo-American protests at his death sentence only hardened Dimitrov's personal determination that it be carried out.

By Petkov's execution in September, Communist plans for the nationalization of industry and a Soviet-style plan for 1947–8 were at least on the drawing board. They also predated August's founding of the Cominform and the formal creation of the Soviet bloc in Poland. A Higher Economic Council with supposed authority over all relevant ministries had been created in 1945 but had done little more than take over the functions of the wartime Directorate for Civilian Mobilization. For agriculture, only 5 percent of arable land had been collectivized by 1948. Forced deliveries to the *Hranoiznos* organization for sales and distribution, already expanded during the war (see Chapter 5), had served well enough. The complete control of industry essential to Communist planning was off to a slower start.[7] Some 200 larger enterprises had been confiscated from Bulgarian owners implicated in the German war effort, and the few foreign enterprises such as the French-owned tobacco monopoly and the large Granitoid cement factory taken over. But all together they put only one-quarter of industrial production into the state sector by 1946. Pressure to do more was, however, mounting. By the end of the year, military demobilization left nearly 40,000 industrial workers unemployed. In addition, the mushrooming of new, small, private manufacturers and other enterprises now made simply the nationalization of the relatively few large enterprises seem insufficient. Planned like a military operation, the full takeover of all 6000 enterprises remaining in private industry was accomplished in just two days in December 1947. By January the Council had given way to a State Planning Committee, supported by a new Ministry for each branch of industry. The program for transition to "total unity" and Soviet-style modernization under the sole control of the Bulgarian Communist leadership was finally underway.

From Balkan Federation and Greek Civil War to the Tito–Stalin Split

For Albania, Greece, and Yugoslavia, the postwar transition grew out of wartime occupation and significant resistance. We must therefore resist the simplifying temptation to rush ahead to 1948. Starting from this later date, US assistance to Greece's National Army and the Tito–Stalin split appear decisive. The Communist failure in Greece may thereby be laid to American intervention. Yugoslavia's independence follows from confrontation with the Soviet Union, and Albania's isolation from choosing Stalin's more powerful side in order to resist Yugoslavia as well as the West.

Starting instead from 1945, there emerges a more domestic and less disparate background to the three political transitions. For the three Communist parties, their prolonged involvement in armed internal conflict during the world war provided military experience and a sense of legitimacy that was missing in Romania and much exaggerated in Bulgaria. For Tito's Partisan-based regime in particular, the attendant hubris encouraged a more immediate political transition and a wider regional role than any of its neighbors. Its initiatives toward a Balkan Federation or at least a larger Yugoslav one, initially with Soviet approval, succeeded only in advancing the postwar division of Southeastern Europe.

Yugoslavia's Early Advantages

No other Communist party in Eastern Europe could match the unity of command and confidence in its supporting base enjoyed by Tito's regime.[8] Behind a smaller party membership of 140,000 in late 1945, versus a quarter of a million in Romanian and Bulgaria, stood a huge majority of members drawn from the victorious Partisan forces of the long wartime resistance. What was now renamed the Yugoslav National Army (JNA) amounted to half a million. Also in place was the first Soviet style security service, OZNa or the Department for the Protection of the People, to be available under domestic control to any postwar East European regime. The two of them combined to put down the Albanian revolt in Kosovo noted in Chapter 5. They were also responsible for executing the bulk of the 30,000 Croat *Ustaša* and regular Croat and Slovene soldiers from the collaborationist regimes handed back by British forces in the spring of 1945. Tito's National Front included no non-Communist groups of significance. In November it won over 90 percent of the votes cast in elections that allowed no independent opposition. Only in Serbia were there significant abstentions (30 percent); only in Croatia was there a party comparable to Bulgaria's Agrarians (Maček's Croatian Peasant Party). Communist pressure obliged Macek to flee the country, and the party was denied a place on the ballot. Delegates elected to the new Constituent Assembly, virtually all Communists, swept aside the 1944 coalition with Ivan Šubašić and the monarchy as well. Tito had been Prime Minister since March; now he stood at the head of the Federal People's Republic of Yugoslavia.

This was the first People's Republic, a list that Romania and Bulgaria would join by 1948, but the only federal state. The new constitution unanimously approved in January 1946 followed the Soviet pattern for federal rights and in all other respects save the mention of socialist institutions. This suggests the sort of initial caution that the Soviets were urging on other associated regimes. American films and Western publications were allowed to compete with celebrations of "the common Yugoslav spirit" from the new Department for Agitation and Propaganda, or Agitprop, under the zealous ideologue Milovan Djilas.[9] Otherwise, the regime was not cautious about cultural policy, pressing opposition newspapers and the religious press in particular. The Croatian Catholic Church, and not just its controversial Archbishop who had initially welcomed the *Ustasa* regime, was immediately confronted. Communist authorities rejected its efforts to resume the scores of various publications that had grown up in the interwar period.

Tito offered Archbishop Stepinac the chance to avoid trial for his war record in return for breaking with the Vatican and reconstituting the Church under the Communist authorization being forced on the Serbian Orthodox Church. The Archbishop refused and was promptly tried and sentenced to life imprisonment. The Catholic clergy in Slovenia as well faced the persecution that would come after 1948 to the Churches in Romania and Bulgaria. Enforcing these and other denials of the smallest dissent was the aforementioned OZNa, transformed in 1946 into the UDBa, or Administration for State Security. Its wartime head and leading Serbian member of Tito's inner circle, the dogged Aleksandar Ranković, remained in charge. A vast network of informants, a judicial system ready to convict anyone accused, and extrajudicial arrests by the UDBa sent another 100,000 to concentration camps by 1947. Over 10,000 people had simply been executed.

The party's large base of rural youth and the larger numbers of the new National Army plus some forced labor worked effectively to restore much of the transport network and some of the industrial plant by early 1947. UNRRA deliveries of construction materials were crucial. This most successful rebuilding of prewar infrastructure in the region drew on the competitive spirit among the various small groups assembled to do the job. This lesson did not inform the leaderships's overconfident decision to rush ahead with a fully centralized Five-Year Plan for 1947–51. The regime could indeed step into an institutional vacuum unparalleled in the region. It was easy to eliminate the major Zagreb banks as wartime collaborators and to merge Belgrade's mortgage and private banks into new state banks for investment and export. But the new Planning Commission in Belgrade proposed to control all investment through a country-wide system of targets and weekly reports that proved unworkable from the start. The plan itself weighed over a ton. Its 47 targets included meager funding for agriculture, 7 percent of the total for land that was still only 3 percent collectivized. The Commission failed even to collect the prescribed reports, let alone meet the wildly ambitious industrial targets. Its shortcomings were apparent after the first year.

The federal structure of the new state also worked against such central planning. The separate numbers of representatives allotted in the new Chamber of Nationalities to the six republics, with fewer to the Vojvodina as an autonomous province of Serbia and fewer still to Kosovo as a somehow subordinate autonomous region, posed no problem. Like the other new legislative body, the Federal Council with a delegate for each district of 50,000, its entirely Communist membership initiated no laws and rubber-stamped those presented to it. The trouble lay with the ministries, as it had for so much of the region for so much of the twentieth century. Concentrated, arbitrary authority remained but was now dispersed to central disadvantage. There were only six common ministries in Belgrade, and none dealt with the economy. The others shared authority with new republic ministries and bureaucracies. This division also allowed objections from Education Ministries in Serbia, Croatia, and Slovenia to prevent the development of common school textbooks. All of this was storing up trouble for the later survival of a single Yugoslavia.

At the time, Tito and his inner circle saw this federal structure as a set of units whose borders meant no more than "lines on a column." Their confidence from the wartime Partisan ordeal made problems of the economic transition to socialism seem secondary when compared to their standing as the preeminent Communist party in Southeastern Europe. This confidence pushed them out into the region and into conflict, first with the United States and then with the Soviet Union.

Those two conflicts are more familiar than the fateful origins of federal problems. Communist suspicion of postwar American intentions had begun with the belated US mission to Mihailović's Chetniks noted in Chapter 5. It grew with the small Anglo-American airstrip set up north of Belgrade and the US-uniformed staff that moved about remote areas to distribute UNRRA aid. Then came the overflights of US cargo planes taking shortcuts between Vienna and Rome. In 1946, relations reached their low point when first one US plane was forced to land and then a second one crashed with the deaths of all on board. Yugoslav demands for Trieste, which Partisan forces had briefly reached ahead of Commonwealth troops in 1945, added to the sharpest American confrontation with any Communist regime in the earliest postwar years. By 1947, however, Western diplomatic reporting from Belgrade was forecasting trouble in the apparently unshakeable relationship with the Soviet Union. Conspicuous by its absence was Soviet support for the Yugoslav insistence on Trieste, not surprising given the damage it would do to the Italian Communist Party. The internal sources of conflict are also well known. Soviet efforts to recruit Yugoslav party members to its own security services were resented. Rankovic's UDBa actively resisted them. Soviet management of the several joint companies set up on the arbitrary pattern of the Romanian Sovroms set off a series of increasingly open disputes with the Yugoslav partners.

For Stalin, however, it was Tito's continuing effort to play the first among equals for the region's Communist parties that made a break unavoidable. The Yugoslav effort began with the idea of a wider formal federation. It continued with initiatives whose effect would have been to spread informal Yugoslav control through Albania and northern Greece. Tito made his first move toward Bulgaria with Soviet support. Bulgarian party leader Dimitrov's Moscow conversations with Tito in September 1944 and then with his lieutenant Edvard Kardelj in November spoke of a common federation that would address the Macedonian question by creating a single entity from territory as yet undefined. But by January 1945 Stalin was backing Dimitrov's understandable objections to Bulgaria's simply becoming the seventh Yugoslav republic rather than entering into a coequal, two-part federation. He went on to tell Dimitrov that "the Yugoslavs want to take Greek Macedonia . . . Albania too . . . This is unreasonable."[10]

Albania and Yugoslavia

Albania was of course the most tempting prospect. Its small Communist party and its limited resistance movement had benefited, as we saw in

Chapter 5, from the compromising arrangements into which the German occupation had drawn all of its opponents by the time of its forced withdrawal in November 1944. By December 1945 the new regime had organized elections that did not allow parties or press outside its National Front to participate. Anglo-American diplomatic recognition in April had stipulated that they should participate. Party leader Enver Hoxha dismissed Western demands for the more open process with the charge that it would simply "create an opposition." To emphasize this rejection of any Western pressure, the British mission was forced to leave in April 1946. Albanian shore batteries subsequently fired on a British destroyer in the Corfu channel. In October, mines obtained from Yugoslavia sank another destroyer with the loss of all hands. Britain responded by withholding the return of Albania's gold reserves. The aforementioned expulsion of UNRRA staff followed shortly thereafter.

Only the wider assistance received from Yugoslavia made this defiance possible.[11] Whatever the controversial role of Tito's representatives in the wartime founding and resistance movement of the Albanian Communist Party, their predominant position from 1945 to 1947 was clear. Economic aid amounting to $33 million surpassed the UNRRA total. Wartime disruption had deepened Albania's traditional food deficit. The Communist regime's initial land reform of 1945 had indeed broken up the sharecropping estates, but left so much grain in the hands of peasant beneficiaries that the food deficit only worsened. Floods followed in 1946. The regime now reduced private holdings to a maximum of 8 acres and took 90 percent of the reduced crop in forced deliveries. Yugoslav shipments of food and transport equipment joined with the last UNRRA deliveries of livestock to prevent famine. Yugoslav political, military, and security representatives swarmed in. So did a set of joint companies that sold goods high and bought raw materials cheap. While they were provoking lower-level Albanian resentment, Hoxha made Koci Xoxe, the leading advocate of the Yugoslav connection, second in command and allowed him to press ahead as Interior Minister with joint security measures.

Hoxha's own sense of the regime's insecurity seems the best explanation for his grudging agreement to expand the Yugoslav connection. In June 1946 he traveled to Belgrade to discuss potential arrangements for a formal federation with Tito. Given the hard Yugoslav suppression of Kosovar Albanian resistance a year before, it seems unlikely that any prospect of including Kosovo on the Albanian side of the federation even came up. By November, Hoxha had signed an agreement for formal economic cooperation that promised a further $40 million of Yugoslav assistance. In December, although reaffirming his decision noted in Chapter 5 that Albania would indeed establish its own separate army, he had to ask for Yugoslav aid in training and equipping it. As late as March 1948, Hoxha sent a letter, perhaps disingenuous, to Tito suggesting that they still proceed with the federation. By then, Soviet objections to Yugoslav preeminence in Albania were boiling over. Hoxha seized the chance to stand up to Tito. He had already balked at the Yugoslav proposal to send its own troops to guard the Albanian coast and the border with Greece from a potential Anglo-American invasion. There was no such danger Stalin countered, and Hoxda could now openly agree.[12]

Yugoslavia's other potential partner in a wider federation was the Communist Republic of Northern Greece. When Tito met with Dimitrov at Lake Bled in July 1947, he had ceded Yugoslavia's rights to reparations in return for sending its Vardar Macedonian teachers and textbooks to replace their Bulgarian counterparts in the Pirin region. The agreement seemed to presage a similar proposal for Aegean Macedonia if the Greek Communist uprising succeeded.[13] By early 1948, Slav Macedonians did indeed make up nearly half of the 25,000 in the KKE's Democratic Army. In addition to rousing anti-Yugoslav sentiment in Greece, Tito's aid to those forces was by this time less effective than American support for the National Army. It represented the one internationally recognized government of Greece. The reduced force of the Democratic army, now without any Yugoslav support, had retreated into Albania in October 1949. As it fell back, the Slav Macedonian fraction had risen to two-thirds. Behind these final features of the Communist failure in Greece – American intervention, the specter of Yugoslav domination in Aegean Macedonia, and finally Yugoslav desertion – lies the most complex set of divisions – all of them to eventual Communist disadvantage – in postwar Southeastern Europe. They extended from the Greek political spectrum, the Anglo-American alliance and the KKE to Yugoslav–Soviet relations. In the process, the Greek economy and society started down a path that precluded not only Communist political control but also the emphasis on heavy industry and large enterprises into which the rest of the region was drawn.

Greece's Civil War, the Third Round

The Second World War had ended for Greece in December 1944 with the failure of the civil war's Second Round to give the Communist-led resistance movement EAM/ELAS political control of the country. The Varkiza Agreement in February 1945 (see Chapter 5) between the Communist Party (KKE) and the new British-backed government of George Papandreou promised instead the disarmament of ELAS and democratically representative elections. Neither took place. The British Embassy looked in vain for a moderate government that would draw the resistance movement's left and the royalist right back toward the weak Liberal center before parliamentary elections. British hopes for convergence prompted its embassy to run through a series of five Prime Ministers by March 1946. Meanwhile, the anti-ELAS recruits that the British military and police missions had hastily assembled as a National Guard to put down the December uprising included some members of the German-sponsored Security Batallions. Most stayed on in the new gendarmerie. They and predominantly royalist army officers led a purge of ELAS sympathizers from the civil administration.

It took only a few months in mid-1945 for an initial domestic effort to improve the desperate economic position of the region's largest urban population to fail, and thereby advance the egalitarian alternative promised by a socialist regime. The Governor of the Bank of Greece, Kyriakos Varvaressos, had hoped to undercut a black market that was well stocked but charged exorbitant prices. The Varvaressos Plan released inventories and drew on some of the UNRRA shipments in June to cut bread and other food prices by one half while increasing public service and manufacturing wages by one half. But the predominantly small Greek enterprises soon resisted the Special Contributions asked from their rents. Comprehensive price and wage controls proved unworkable. By August, rapid inflation had returned, further fueled by gold sales that allowed the Bank of Greece to print new money. Only the accelerating arrival of UNRRA aid, providing 70 per cent of the state budget for 1945, prevented starvation. These conditions made an appealing alternative out of the KKE proposal for "Heavy Industry in Greece." It featured public ownership of large new metallurgical and machinery enterprises powered by hydroelectric projects and financed by high internal taxation and a forced loan.[14]

The continuing crisis over economic recovery and the royalist takeover of the police and security services doubtless encouraged the KKE to boycott the parliamentary elections of March 1946. Just weeks before in Prague, Tito also encouraged party leader, Nikos Zakhariadis, not only to boycott the elections but to prepare for an armed revolt. The subsequent victory of the royalists' People's Party was all the greater: 55 percent of the vote and 206 of 354 seats. The British missions had counted on the elections as a democratic end in themselves, just as NATO would count on them in Bosnia 40 years later. But under the People's Party leader, Konstantinos Tsaldaris, the new government began to rule by decree. It introduced new and unaccountable committees who were responsible for national defense and the currency. The KKE was still legal but surely had no place in this regime. By February 1947, massive UNRRA aid had run its course, reparations from

Germany, Italy, and Bulgaria were well below expectations (barely $20 million), and the British capacity to provide more aid had exhausted itself. The KKE leadership now decided to launch the Third Round's uprising just as the US administration decided to replace the British, militarily as well as economically. It was a fatal coincidence for the Communists. The $354 million of US military equipment and supplies would nearly match the UNRRA aid total. The attendant Military Assistance Group tightened the training of the government's National Army and by 1948 its command structure as well. Its 150,000 men became a formidable force, its officer corps the source of support for an authoritarian, anti-Communist regime for decades to come. Its forced evacuation of 700,000 northern villagers late in the campaign aided final victory but was otherwise another authoritarian precedent.

Recent Greek scholarship has detailed serious failings on the Communist side after a long emphasis on American intervention as decisive.[15] Party Leader Zakhariadis remained committed to the old Bolshevik idea of revolution succeeding only from an urban base. He therefore delayed the movement of urban cadres into the hills as military commander Markos Vafiadis, an *andartes* veteran, demanded from the start. The delay allowed the regime's security service to round up many activists and exile them to island camps. Zakhariadis had continued to insist on the need to turn the guerrilla bands that were enjoying early success into a regular army. This army should then seize Thessaloniki as the center of a stronghold in Macedonia and Thrace. Absent the main northern city and a military victory in the first set piece encounter with the National Army, the KKE leadership nonetheless proclaimed the Democratic Republic of Northern Greece in December 1947. No foreign government, not even Tito's or Stalin's, recognized it. Supplies and sanctuary from the Yugoslav side continued to play an essential role in preserving what increasingly became a northern insurgency. Its chances to succeed had, however, vanished before the withdrawal of Yugoslav support in July of 1949. It never fielded more than half of the 50,000 fighters that Zakhariadis had promised. Nor did it receive the Soviet supplies that the party's Politburo had imagined would appear. By November 1948 Vafiadis lost his long struggle with Zakhariadis against increasingly forced recruitment to a regular army that could never match the National Army. He was formally ousted in February 1949, just as the able and also legendary hero of the Italian campaign of 1940, General Alexandros Papagos, took full command of the National Army under a broader new government. He proceeded to secure the south before turning to the final offensive in the north. It quickly defeated a Democratic Army whose theater of operations the KKE plenum in January had newly stretched.

The cost of the country's second postwar conflict in two generations was high. The military and civilian death toll of 150,000 surpassed losses from the expulsion from Anatolia in 1922. There was no catastrophic influx of refugees from abroad this time, but the aforementioned rural expulsions displaced 700,000 northern villagers. They were allowed to return from internal locations after the Communist defeat. Many ended up in the major cities, swelling their populations even further. Upwards of 100,000, many of them Slav Macedonians, fled to the northern Communist neighbors. They included over 20,000 children, most taken from their parents by the Communist authorities themselves, on the pattern of the *pedomasima* (children taken out of Athens after the defeat of December 1944). Three decades would pass before the ethnic Greeks who had left as adults or children would be allowed to return. In Greece, the psychological scars of the conflict remained for at least that long. By the 1970s the trauma opened public and scholarly controversy over the immediate postwar period that would appear in Yugoslavia only in the late 1980s and since the Communist collapse of 1989 elsewhere. In contrast especially to Poland and Hungary, the debate across Southeastern Europe has focused more on domestic dynamics than on the Soviet role.

Consolidating the Postwar Transitions after 1950

Over the next decade and a half, the anti-Communist but parliamentary Greek regime and its four Communist counterparts consolidated the political framework that they had all struggled to establish during the first postwar years. They pressed hard on their populations during the initial part of this longer period and then, with the exception of Albania, relaxed their tight hold. All of them succeeded in significantly increasing the proportions of urban numbers, literacy, and industrial production. These low levels had set them significantly apart from the European average through the interwar period. Agricultural sectors and the still-large rural populations, whether collectivized or not, did not make comparable advances. Only Albania and Bulgaria received significant Soviet aid, only Greece and Yugoslavia significant American aid. Although the latter two eventually made broad connections with Western popular culture, US aid came mainly in the earlier years when a siege mentality constrained public education and intellectual life.

By the early 1960s the contradictions between growing openness to Western Europe and domestic restriction were posing an economic challenge for Tito's regime and a political one for the Greek party that claimed credit for winning the civil war. In the other Communist regimes, Stalin's death in 1953 and Khrushchev's Secret Speech in 1956 denouncing Stalin's abuses advanced relaxation. Brutal Soviet suppression of the Hungarian Revolution late in 1956 set it back. For the entire region, the increasing growth of an educated urban population familiar with modern technology promised to frustrate simple reliance on repression. By 1960, foreign trade was also jumping ahead of all economic indicators across the region. Yet the wider integration that trade was promoting in Western Europe did not occur in Eastern Europe. Nor did other connections within Southeastern Europe, among regimes or peoples, move ahead during this prolonged postwar consolidation.

High Stalinism in Albania, Romania, and Bulgaria, 1950–1955

Accompanying the transition to a Soviet set of political and economic priorities was the equally Stalinist consolidation of the leader's life tenure heading the respective Communist parties. This the respective party heads proceeded to do from 1949 in Albania and before Stalin's death in Romania, but only later in Bulgaria. Hence the order that follows. Common features of the institutional transition still stand – party purges justified on the grounds of Titoist ties that reduced mass party membership, concentration camps for political opponents, restrictions on organized religion, the rapid launch of Five-Year Plans and industrialization drives, and struggles with collectivizing peasant agriculture. All this took place within an institutional framework of expanded state ministries that tightened control of local and regional government. There would be no place for the budding municipal autonomy of the interwar period in a vertical state hierarchy more rigid and comprehensive than any these societies had previously experienced. Serving this further ministerial centralization but also preserving the clientelism of prewar regimes was the Soviet practice of making key positions at every level of state administration and economic management *nomenklatura* appointees, i.e., party members selected by the hierarchy and responsible to it. This dual system of executive power, its second leg never mentioned in the resulting set of Soviet-style constitutions, subordinated the judiciary and selected representatives in all elected bodies. Party nominees ran unopposed in meaningless elections and unanimously approved all legislation put before them with rare exceptions.

Albania's experience was the most straightforward. Zog's interwar regime had of course established no precedent for the separation of powers. The Tito–Stalin split freed Hoxha's leadership of the Party of Labor of Albania (PPS), as it was renamed in 1947 at Stalin's urging, from the one significant source of internal opposition and external control. Second-ranked Koci

Xoxe, the main advocate of a close Yugoslav connection, was expelled from the party, tried, and executed by January 1949. While the expelled Yugoslav advisors included a number of Kosovar Albanians, the Soviet advisors who replaced them included none of the longtime Muscovite natives who would play important if different roles in Romania and Bulgaria. One-quarter of the party's 50,000 members had been purged by 1952.

Helping to keep the pressure on any possible dissent was the one Anglo-American effort to overthrow a newly established Communist regime in Eastern Europe. Their intelligence services selected Albania as "the most suitable target." Albanian emigrés promised widespread local support for an invasion force, however small. The several expeditions of 1950–3 were all quickly captured. Betrayed by Soviet penetration of the emigrés' Rome organization as well as their renowned agent, the British intelligence officer Kim Philby, the invaders received no local assistance either.[16] Their trials stretched from 1951 to 1954. Their Italian connections also facilitated the regime's persecution of Catholic clergy and justified the break in relations with the Vatican in 1951. As elsewhere in the region, the Orthodox Christian Metropolitan was simply replaced with a compliant cleric.

The regime still faced the challenge of feeding its population and proceeding with industrialization from the smallest manufacturing base in the region. Without Soviet aid, neither task could have been addressed. The droughts of 1950 and 1952, which affected Yugoslavia as well, cut the grain harvest by 15–20 percent. Collectivized farms still covered less than half of the small amount of arable land. The regime's first Five-Year Plan for 1951–5 nonetheless gave agriculture less than 10 percent of projected total investment. At least the major targets were rational choices – electrification, non-ferrous mining, and light industry, primarily textiles and sugar cane. By 1953 Hoxha approved the shift of some funding from industry to agriculture. Otherwise, the response to failing to meet overambitious targets was greater centralization. The number of state enterprises was nearly halved, from 300 to 171, and the 17 separate directorates over them eliminated. The regime also trimmed its 47 district administrations to 10. Whatever its own contribution, the PPS's first plan relied on Soviet and also East European aid to provide half of its imports and cover the bulk of a huge import surplus.[17] With the $156 million from the Soviets and $133 million from the rest of the bloc came technical advisors and training for Albanian personnel as well as shipments of grain, coal, and industrial equipment. Only US aid to Greece exceeded the bloc's assistance per capita to Albania.

The Stalinist transition in Romania proceeded along different lines. Soviet economic ties were a burden rather than an advantage. And crucial to the consolidation of party control for Gheorghe Gheorghiu-Dej was the final dismissal of the two main Muscovite colleagues, Pauker and Luca. The Soviets at least halved the reparations due to them in 1948, but there was little economic aid subsequently beyond credits for a new steel mill. As for foreign trade, Romania did not need the Soviet oil that was a valuable import elsewhere in Eastern Europe. Instead, the operation of the Romanian oil industry and related branches remained hostage to exploitative Soviet management of the Sovroms. The first full Five-Year Plan (1951–5) was at least counting on imports of iron ore until Moscow abruptly abandoned the planned delivery in 1952. Pig iron production fell by over one half, and the metallurgical sector suffered accordingly.

The regime hesitated to push the peasant majority too hard. Collectivization lagged, rising only from 3.1 to 7.7 percent of arable land by 1952. Some rural resisters had formed armed bands and confronted the regime in Transylvania through the late 1940s. The new *Securitate*, a security force with its own paramilitary units, not only rounded up such "gunners" but went on to arrest all manner of potential opponents. The total imprisoned by 1952 was the region's largest, 100,000. They were held in Soviet-style labor camps or worse, consigned to the construction of the Danube–Black Sea canal launched in 1949. Soviet advisors helped with the so-called currency reform of 1952, aligning Romanian lei with Russian rubles in order to soak up any remaining private deposits and reduce the growing gap between prices and wages. Yet wage-earners' real purchasing power only fell further as a result. To tighten its administrative grip in the face of these difficulties, the Dej regime reduced the number of regions from 28 to 18 as well.[18]

To tighten his control of the party, Dej built on efforts that had begun before the Tito–Stalin split, as we have seen, to push Ana Pauker and her close Muscovite associate Vasile Luca out of the leadership. Now he forced them into the dock. Dej's advantage as an ethnic Romanian over the Jewish Pauker and the Hungarian Luca now came into play. Pauker had continued to support the emigration of Romanian Jews to Palestine in 1950–1. Stalin had long since turned away from such facilitation, and her efforts were indeed used against her. Pauker was more vulnerable for past association with the leadership's initial purge victim Pătrășcanu, her role in broadening recruitment for the mass party membership of one million, purged back to 700,000 by 1950, and her continuing cautions against rapid collectivization.[19] If Pauker could be blamed for "peasantist politics," Luca was the Finance Minister who had worked with the Soviets on the ill-fated currency reform of 1952. The pair's arrest and conviction as "imperialist agents" by the year's end secured Dej's position as unchallenged party leader before

Stalin died. He was therefore able to resist the call for collective leadership afterward and to delay the second party congress from 1954 to the end of the next year. By then, Romania's admission to the United Nations secured his position further.

For Bulgaria, a more rapid agricultural transition accompanied the first Five-Year Plan (1949–53). Its wider economic impact and the intimidating political repression which made it possible did not help the new party leader, Vulko Chervenkov, to consolidate his position. A youthful Communist emigré to the Soviet Union in the 1920s who was educated as well as trained there, he had returned to Bulgaria after the war. Chervenkov occupied a subordinate position to longtime party leaders Georgi Dimitrov and Vasil Kolarov as well as to the non-Muscovites' leader in their absence, Traicho Kostov. Then the Tito–Stalin split and senior Muscovites' declining health (Dimitrov died in the Soviet Union in July 1949, Kolarov in January 1950) opened the way for him.[20] By March 1949 he had forced Kostov from the leadership for alleged association with various Yugoslav initiatives, including the dispatch of Macedonian teachers to the Pirin region (now sent packing). Kostov had in fact opposed this concession, but the charges at his show trial, delayed until after the first parliamentary elections in December, were even more bogus. Convicted as an American agent, he was quickly executed.

In 1950 Chervenkov forced what became a ten-year break in diplomatic relations with the United States by accusing its Ambassador of espionage and executing an Embassy translator on similar charges. He also launched a party purge, targeting the security service (*Drzhavna sigurnost* or DS) and the army, as well as the broader membership. About 100,000 of 460,000 party members were removed from the rolls. Some of them and a larger number of peasants resisting collectivization were sent to labor camps. They included the notoriously punitive and unhealthy Belene complex on the Danube. The uncertain total exceeded 20,000. The social cost to family members and to the much larger total who fled the collectivization campaign by volunteering for factory jobs is beyond counting.

No religious institution was in a position to protest, as already noted. The Bulgarian Orthodox Church had been subordinated to state control from 1945 forward. The new Communist regime had immediately abolished the Exarchate, with its headquarters in Istanbul and still representing the faithful in Thrace, Vardar, and Aegean Macedonia, as well as Bulgaria. The rights to religious instruction and Church lands were soon taken away. The popular Exarch Stefan, who had stood up for Bulgarian Jews (see Chapter 5) and even joined the Fatherland Front during the war, was obliged to retire by 1948.[21] The small Protestant clergy had meanwhile been tried as "imperialist agents" and the Vatican's representative denied residence. Joining the Jews departing for Israel, a migration that Chervenkov allowed to continue, were three times their number of Turks. Over 160,000, typically on good grain land in the Dobrudja ripe for collectivization, were forced to emigrate to Turkey by 1952.

The very advance of the harsh collectivization drive that began in 1950 was, however, storing up trouble for what seemed Chervenkov's unshakeable position. The year before, the huge private peasant majority had dared to withhold some of their crops from markets offering minimal prices. The new campaign dropped the previous emphasis on voluntary membership and put the DS to work assuring village agreement to join the collective farms, called Producers Cooperatives (TKZS) to sound like the 1930s Agrarian predecessors, or a state farm. The collectivized share of arable land jumped from 11 percent in 1949 to 61 percent by 1952. The Five-Year Plan had indeed allocated a larger share of investment, 17 percent, to agriculture than elsewhere in Eastern Europe. But only 13 percent was actually dispensed, as the same Soviet-inspired concentration on meeting the targets for heavy industry held sway. In addition, the flood of peasants leaving collectivized land for industrial jobs created an untrained labor force whose rapid turnover frustrated mining and manufacturing enterprises. Separate industrial and agricultural bureaucracies, at district as well as ministerial level, added to the difficulty. By January 1953, two months before Stalin died, Chervenkov was obliged to accept a new Five-Year Plan that acknowledged significant failings in the first one. Only months before, it had been triumphantly proclaimed as completed a year early. The shift hardly abandoned heavy industry but put more investment into agriculture and consumer goods, as the rest of the Soviet bloc would do once Stalin had died.[22]

A new political emphasis on collective leadership followed Stalin's death. The young, 36-year-old Todor Zhivkov now stepped forward as a representative of the broader, non-Muscovite core of the Bulgarian Party. He cautiously challenged Chervenkov. By 1954 he had replaced him as First Secretary, if not as Minister President. Backed by direct Soviet influence, Chervenkov and his Interior Minister, Anton Yugov, still held the preponderance of power. Two precedents were all the same established – the Bulgarian Party's readiness for economic reform within the post-Stalin Soviet framework and its disposition to placate rather than purge within the leadership. Communist confidence in the regime's wider popular acceptance grew, whether justifiably or not, and over ten thousand political prisoners, the bulk of the survivors, were released in 1955.

Yugoslavia and Greece: From Siege Mentalities and American Aid Forward

From 1948 into 1950, Tito's Yugoslavia considered itself under siege from both sides in the now established Cold War. Western political leaders, if not their diplomats, were yet to be convinced that the split with the Soviet Union was genuine. And Tito's regime spent these first two years trying to establish its Communist credentials according to prevailing Soviet standards. The major effort was faster, forced collectivization, thus responding to a specific Soviet criticism. Within the Communist Party itself, however, all Soviet sympathizers were suspect. Swollen like others in the region by 1948, the party began purging its half million members on this basis. Over 40,000 had been expelled by 1950, and another 100,000 by 1952. Ranković's UDBa summarily dispatched some 16,000 of the so-called Cominformists, more Serbs and Montenegrins than their shares of the population, to hard labor camps or the still harder punishment regime on the aptly named "barren island," *Goli otok*.[23] They were joined by some of the peasants resisting the new drive for collectivization. By 1950, 29 percent of arable land, much more in Macedonia and less in Serbia, had been taken over.

Then peasant resistance, that year's drought, and American readiness to accept the split with the Soviets as real combined to start the regime in a different direction. Army units had to be summoned to put down the multi-ethnic revolt in rural Bosnia around Bihać. The drought threatened to spread unrest through the food-deficit areas, prompting the first Yugoslav request for assistance. The new American Ambassador and then Washington were persuaded to ship grain and dried foodstuffs over as emergency relief. The Soviet bloc had by this time ceased all trade with Yugoslavia. Exports elsewhere fell well short of Western imports, and an imbalance of payments became a chronic problem. Payments relief and a second drought in 1952 secured another timely shipment, this time within the framework of the Marshall Plan. The collectivization drive had by now been abandoned. From 1952 as well, a resident US Military Assistance Group was funneling funds ($296 million by early 1953) and a much smaller amount of surplus equipment ($14 million) to the Yugoslav People's Army (JNA). Repeated Soviet maneuvers on the Hungarian border threatened invasions probably never planned but intended to provoke a pro-Soviet uprising within the Yugoslav Party. In response, the JNA had increased its already large numbers by one-third to 600,000. And then in 1953 Stalin was dead. By 1955 the new Soviet leadership was trying somehow to reestablish relations with the Tito regime.

As Tito began to balance Yugoslavia artfully between East and West, the country's new set of political and economic institutions struggled to come to constructive terms with their freedom from the Soviet framework. Decentralization and the growth of trade relations with Western Europe, Italy in particular, both offered initial promise. In the event, they tended to work against each other. By 1951 the huge Planning Ministry in Belgrade had been virtually eliminated. Kardelj and Djilas had persuaded Tito that elected Workers' Councils should run Yugoslav enterprises. What might better distinguish their system from the Soviet model? Yet when faced with implementing their new law on self-management, the inner circle did not wish to entrust management to the Workers' Councils. They soon placed the director's position and investment decisions in the hands of the local party leadership. The number of county and city committees was halved from 7000 to facilitate overall control.

The six republics, if not yet the two autonomous territories, also received rights that would grow by the early 1960s, as we shall see. An American effort in 1953–4 to channel its economic aid more efficiently had the ironic result of encouraging republic overinvestment in the heavy industry it was meant to discourage. The regime had artfully responded to a US demand to cut the large number of industrial investment projects by allowing each republic to protect its own sectors for heavy industry whatever the consequences for duplication.

Meanwhile, settling the dispute with Italy over Trieste and its environs allowed Western trade as a whole to grow. Croatian and Slovenian exports received a particular boost. By 1957 Italy had passed West Germany as Yugoslavia's largest trade partner. The restoration of trade ties with the Soviet bloc provided cheaper supplies of coal, iron ore, and oil that supported light as well as heavy industry. Further American grants and soft loans for surplus food allowed the neglect of agricultural investment to continue. Still, the unchanged amount of funds for development projects was now more rationally targeted.[24] These projects gave the Yugoslav side valuable experience that it used with international organizations by the early 1960s. World Bank loans would eventually total $4 billion, versus the $1.7 billion in American economic grants and loans, one billion berween 1953 and 1961. Tito's reconciliation, albeit on his own terms, with Khrushchev in 1955–6 and then Yugoslav support for the Soviet suppression of the Hungarian Revolution threatened to derail this assistance in 1956. By 1958, however, the start of Soviet efforts to assert supremacy over the Chinese Communist Party seemed to demand the same subordination from Yugoslavia. Tito's regime, newly confident from industrial growth and several good harvests, would have none of it. By 1961 renewed American aid and the growing advantages of West European trade had persuaded the regime to accommodate to Western markets. Reduced tariffs and currency devalued to a single rate won Yugoslavia's associate membership in the GATT (General Agreement on Trade and Tariffs). This international ascent, further complemented by Tito's adroit use of the new Non-Aligned Movement to demonstrate political distance from the West, obscured for many the country's harsh if less centralized internal framework. Milovan Djilas was the one member of the party's inner circle, and initiator of the 1952 decision to change its name to the League of Yugoslav Communists (SKJ), to protest at the growing abuse of power. He was easily dismissed by 1954 and famously imprisoned by 1956 for allowing his critical work, *The New Class*, to be published in the West.[25] These continuing Communist limitations would weigh down the full transition to market socialism attempted in the 1960s.

Such a transition's most powerful opponent was Aleksandar Ranković, Interior Minister through the 1950s and subsequently a rival only to Kardelj as Tito's likely successor. His Serb-dominated security forces continued to work outside any legal restraints in suppressing any sign of Albanian dissent in Kosovo. Some 150,000 Kosovars were simply deported as Turks to Turkey in 1953. A roundup of all private weapons in 1956 produced a wave of new arrests and disappearances. Elsewhere, this Serb predominance combined with overrepresentation in local police and party positions to create ethnic resentment in Bosnia and especially Croatia. The break in relations with the Vatican in 1952 and the new religious law of 1953, allowing only internal associations approved by Communist authorities, added to Croatian resentment.

The new Constitution of 1953 simply reaffirmed Tito's and Kardelj's supranational faith in Yugoslav socialism as superior to all past ethnic or religious distinctions and also republic rights. It created a new Chamber of Producers and merged the Chamber of Nationalities into the Federal Chamber. At the executive level, Tito became President for life. He now headed a new Federal Executive Council (SIV) intended to pull together ministries whose republic agencies were often more powerful.

None of this prevented local party leaders, often closely allied with the security service, from using their managerial leverage over enterprises and their control of the communal banks, numbering over 300 by the end of the 1950s, to resist market-oriented reforms.[26] By then, the Workers' Councils had received the right to determine how much of their enterprises' net income went to wage bonuses and how much to new investment. Their predictable preference for bonuses encouraged local recourse to loans from the communal banks. This combination created the first inflation to appear in a Communist economy. From 1962 forward, prices began rising by 15–20 percent a year. The regime's initial response to a growing economic crisis was the new Constitution of 1963, followed by the market-oriented reforms of 1965. Chapter 7 treats subsequent failings. Like the region's other postwar transitions, Yugoslavia's would not finish the 1960s in the same apparently successful form in which it had started the decade.

Greece's economic transition proceeded more smoothly into the Western framework during these years than its political process. Both transitions depended heavily on state intervention and, in the first years after the civil war, on American intervention as well as assistance. By 1955, however, the old struggles between domestic left and right, between the monarchy and its opponents, and between the army and parliamentary government had resumed their leading roles. They could at least contend in a political framework that had significantly opened by the early 1960s, in contrast to its neighbors to the north. Economic and social indicators made the same sort of advances trumpeted by the Communist regimes. The place for private investment and initiative was also smaller than the American formula for consolidation expected.

A massive National Army of 250,000 and the Ministry of Public Order kept their authority under extraparliamentary decrees after the lifting of martial law in February 1950. The "danger from the north" was used to justify paralegal detentions, and the 17,000 political prisoners through 1951 approached the Yugoslav and Bulgarian totals noted above. The 1947 law that made advocating revolution a crime stayed on the books. State employment, which accounted for a third of the urban labor force, required a police clearance. Local government did not receive back the rights it had lost under the prewar Metaxas dictatorship, nor was the school curriculum much changed. The 1952 constitution left the King as commander of the armed forces with the right to select the minister of National Defense in particular. Radio broadcasting was confined to the state and army stations. American advisors monitored key appointments in the army and the economic ministries in particular. Greece's membership in NATO from 1952 and the US provision of training and equipment to Greek military, totaling $2 billion from 1948 forward, added to this leverage.

The supposedly all-powerful American Embassy stood further back from an electoral process whose results allowed a wider political spectrum to survive. Parliamentary elections in 1950 took place in this continuing state of siege but still, under proportional representation, gave the ruling People's Party less than 20 percent of the vote. A majority of ballots cast went to three separate Liberal factions led by Venezelist republicans. The resulting centrist coalition reflected popular sentiment for reconciliation, distressing army leaders and the monarchy. Its instability distressed the American Embassy. For the 1951 elections, the fading People's Party gave way to the new Rally party, led by war hero General Alexandros Papagos. It was also denied a ruling majority. A Communist surrogate, the New Democratic Left (EDA), was already able to enter the contest and win over 10 percent of the vote. Here the American Embassy did use the leverage of its regime-sustaining economic aid to demand new elections based on majority rather than proportional representation. In November 1952 the Rally received 247 of 300 seats in return for winning 49 percent of the vote. General Papagos headed this new government until his death in 1955. By then, the number of political prisoners had fallen below 5000. King Paul used the monarch's privilege of naming the General's successor, Konstantinos Karamanlis. The uncharismatic northerner was also the Americans' choice, given his record for efficiency in heading a series of economic ministries, most recently public works.

The Rally's new leader sought to concentrate on economic policy. Yet Karamanlis was immediately confronted with a crisis over Cyprus that raised the specter of continuing American domination. As Britain's decolonization proceeded apace, the island just off the Turkish coast was an obvious candidate. If Turkey were allowed to reassert the sovereignty that the Ottoman Empire had ceded to Britain in 1878, the island's Greek population, a huge majority of 80 percent, would obviously object. Papagos had allowed a Greek army general born there to launch agitation and violence in favor of union (*enosis*) with Greece in April 1955. With the Turkish Cypriot minority potentially threatened, riots in Istanbul destroyed the remaining Greek minority's shops, churches, and houses. The British plan of 1958 proposed limited independence with disproportionate representation for the Turkish population rather than *enosis*. Once the island's powerful Orthodox Archbishop Makarios had reluctantly accepted the cumbersome arrangement, Karamanlis joined Turkey's Prime Minister Menderes in signing the agreement. NATO's interest in preventing war between its two well-armed members was clear.[27] So was the high political price that Karamanlis paid for appearing to give in to this American-led alliance.

The price did not seem too high at the time, given his party's predominant position. He had quickly changed its name to the National Radical Union (ERE) and pushed through a new electoral law that combined majority and proportional representation with interwar complexity. The full spectrum of opposing parties responded by forming a single Democratic Union slate that won slightly more votes but left the ERE with a majority, albeit reduced, of seats. Women now voted for the first time. It took three more of these elections, all based on "reinforced" proportional representation, for an opposition now led by the Center Union (EK) of George Papandreou to defeat the party in power by 1963. Already in 1958 the ruling ERE, the monarchy, and the army were shocked to see the Radical vote fall to 41 percent and the United Democratic Left (EDA) rise to second place with 24 percent. Discontent over Cyprus doubtless boosted the EDA vote. Army and police authorities sought to reverse this ominous result in the 1961 elections. Rural voters were indeed intimidated, urban numbers falsely added, and the Radical Union's majority restored, if barely.

Contrary to the army leaders' expectations, the emerging process of free elections worked to the advantage of the centrist Papandreou rather than the leftist EDA. It was still burdened with ties to the exiled KKE leadership and its Soviet-style disdain for practical electoral politics. The long-divided moderate opposition came together under the charismatic Papandreou. His Center Union ran a strong second in 1961, despite the abuses. His campaign questioned the election results and demanded an end to such abuses, familiar from prewar Balkan elections. Under its slogan of "unrelenting struggle," the Center Union won a narrow victory in 1963.[28] The victory signaled a rebuke to the monarchy as much as the army. Elections would not have been necessary in 1963 had Karamanlis himself not resigned in indignation at King Paul's refusal to defer a controversial trip to London. Queen Frederica's longer record of high-handed interference surely influenced his decision as well. Now the old republican Papandreou confronted the royal couple. After Paul died in 1964, Frederica and the young successor, their son Constantine, faced a final reckoning for the region's last surviving monarchy, as we shall see in Chapter 7.

Along with this halting political transition from proclaimed to elected legitimacy, Greece experienced a steadier if no less complex economic and social transition. Once again, American aid played an important early role but gave way to a mixture of state bank and foreign investment on large-scale projects. Domestic, generally small-scale private entrepreneurs predominated in trade, tourism, and construction. The state banks and the Karamanlis regime were crucial to the emergence of this uniquely mixed economy. Already in 1952 Bank of Greece Director Varvaressos put forward a report calling for a mix of public and private investment that would favor agricultural modernization and light over heavy industry.

American economic aid had gotten Greek agriculture off to a faster start than struggles over collectivization permitted in the Communist regimes. The larger part of the $976 million provided for 1948–52 went to electrification, rural road construction, irrigation, drainage, tractors, and a variety of health programs. The infant death rate in villages had already fallen by one half from 1938. American agronomists introduced crop rotation and improved seeds to boost grain production in particular. Another $800 million over the next decade supported further agricultural modernization. The Karamanlis regime added price supports for wheat, and encouraged membership in village cooperative associations. One-third of the predominantly small and still scattered family-plot owners resisted association membership as well as consolidation. Working under this presumably enduring peasant handicap, they nonetheless doubled agricultural production from the early 1950s to the mid-1960s. Productivity may be judged to have risen even more rapidly as agricultural employment dropped by 20 percent to less than half of the labor force. Agricultural exports now exceeded agricultural imports, helping to halve a still sizeable trade deficit.

For the rest of the economy, a sufficient foundation had been laid since 1953 for Karamanlis to apply for associate membership in the European Economic Community by 1961. A combination of US-encouraged measures devalued the drachma by 50 percent, ended import quotas and cut import tariffs by 20 percent. By 1955 inflation had been pushed below 3 percent a year, and the government was collecting enough income taxes to cover 27 percent of its budget. The tourism and remittances on which Yugoslavia would also rely to balance its current account by the 1960s were already closing the gap for Greece. The shipping services of the Greek emigré owners covered the rest. Aristotle Onassis and others had taken first advantage of loans from the three state banks that became the major source of investment capital under Karamanlis. Some 40 percent of direct state investment and also private domestic investment went into construction projects. For the state, it tended to be essential infrastructure, but for successful Greek merchants or small-scale manufacturers, it was private housing. They also resisted incorporation in favor of family ownership, further helping to keep the average size of a Greek industrial enterprise the smallest in Europe, barely 40 employees. This broadened the opening for direct Western investment by the early 1960s that the Greek left would find so objectionable. By the end of the decade, the foreign inflow to chemical and metallurgical enterprises as well as shipyards constituted over 30 percent of industrial assets. Yet the other 70 percent was directly or indirectly in the hands of the state banks. They had held off allowing any foreign competitors for most of this period.

The unevenness of social progress during this economic transition is open to more justifiable criticism.[29] Real urban wages began to move up only from 1956. The sizeable rural migration to towns, 560,000 during the 1950s and more in subsequent decades, struggled to stay above a poverty line that included 30 percent of the population. Emigration also moved past half a million by the early 1960s, rising further as the West European economy boomed. The state and the shipyards were the largest single employers, and also home to the largest number of union members. Urban unemployment insurance began in 1951, a rural counterpart in 1961. Higher education was slow to expand, but the expanding primary network cut the rate of illiteracy from 32 to 18 percent during the 1950s. Women found their way into jobs and higher education, but at a slower pace than their Communist neighbors. The state radio and now television kept their monopolies, but the press was free as long as supported by a political party. Basic political conflicts between the military, the monarchy, and civil society remained to be resolved in a country whose recovery from the civil war and economic advance was nonetheless remarkable.

The Stalinist Regimes after Hungary 1956

During the decade following Stalin's death in March 1953, the Stalinist regimes of Albania, Romania, and Bulgaria moved further apart from each other. By 1963 Albania had deserted the Soviet bloc for Chinese sponsorship, and Romania was beginning to assert its autonomy. Bulgaria remained the bloc's most loyal member and the only one to continue receiving Soviet assistance. Unlike Albania and Romania, its Communist regime had also followed the initial Soviet experiment with collective leadership in the years immediately after Stalin's death. Yet all three were still Stalinist regimes, dedicated to heavy industry, forced collectivization, and close cultural control. In 1956 the Soviet suppression of the Hungarian Revolution challenging that Communist regime ended whatever relaxations had appeared in each of these other three. The discomfort that their leaders had all felt at Soviet leader Khrushchev's famed Secret Speech earlier in the year, criticizing Stalin's arbitrary abuses, could now be set aside. They could continue the centralization of all authority under the party's *nomenklatura* and the state's bureaucracy. By the early 1960s, however, the transition to a modern industrial economy that was to justify this centralization began to show cracks under the impressive growth of aggregate industrial production that all the regimes could still advertize.

By then, the lack of Soviet support for creating a broader industrial base and the neglect of agricultural investment had created enough difficulties for the Albanian economy to justify the switch to Chinese assistance. The greater impetus came of course from the Soviet rapprochement with Yugoslavia in 1955–6 and again in 1959–60. Soviet diplomacy had arranged for Hoxha to meet with Tito's old regional representative Vukmanović-Tempo in 1955. Yet they failed to reconcile their differences, more over relations with the West than over Kosovo. Hoxha then seized on the Hungarian uprising of October 1956 to further distance Albania from Yugoslavia. Tito's initial support for the breakaway, still-Communist government, although quickly withdrawn, served nicely to make him the "counterrevolution's" mastermind for strident Albanian propaganda.

The Hungarian Revolution also served to consolidate Hoxha's leadership of the Party of Labor and to reset its economic course at the same time. Already in 1955, when the first Five-Year Plan was finishing short of meeting its industrial targets, he succeeded in forcing out of the Politburo the two main advocates of relaxing those targets in favor of agriculture in 1953. By April 1956, however, several speakers at a Tirana party plenum followed the lead offered by Khrushchev's Secret Speech. They criticized Hoxha and his closest associate, Mehmet Shehu, for their Stalinist rights to dismiss others out of hand and their refusal to reconcile with Yugoslavia. That October's image of a supposedly comparable dissenting party member, Imre Nagy, accepting the leadership of the Hungarian "counterrevolution" allowed Hoxha to expel the several who had spoken out.[30]

The coast was now clear for the second Five-Year Plan (1956–60) to proceed on Stalinist lines, although with increasing Soviet disapproval. The shift in investment from light to heavy industry (from consumers' to producers' goods) started with a population that was still over 70 percent rural and arable land only 40 percent collectivized. The plan's drive to bring the arable total up to 70 percent by 1960 did not include the increased investment in agriculture that Soviet advisors and Khrushchev himself were urging on the Hoxha regime. Too much of the now increased Soviet aid simply covered necessary imports of grain and other foodstuffs. Soviet industrial technicians and training for some 5000 Albanians in the USSR still constituted an important part of the assistance provided under the several generous grants of 1957. They converted all past credits to grants and added new credits worth half as much, totaling $156 million according to one careful Western calculation.[31] That sum nearly matched the Albanian trade deficit with the Soviet Union across the entire period 1947–61. But the continued drive for collectivization into larger units by 1958 proved so disruptive to the amount of grain actually harvested that Soviet wheat imports accounted for nearly half the country's consumption for 1959. Although the share of producers' goods did not advance, the regime could point to a tenfold increase in industrial production during the decade, even by Western calculations. Industry's share of Net Material Product (goods without services) rose from 16 to 44 percent. Health care had improved and primary education was made compulsory among a the huge rural majority. But basic consumer goods remained more scarce in the towns as well as the countryside than in any other member of the Soviet Bloc.[32]

The continuing emphasis on industrial over agricultural investment in the forthcoming Five-Year Plan for 1961–5 combined with the renewed Soviet reconciliation with Yugoslavia to prompt Albania's complete break with the bloc in 1961. The Hoxha regime's dissatisfaction had been brewing since the Soviet denial of promised support for an oil industry in 1957. It boiled over in 1959 when a visiting Khrushchev dismissed agricultural prospects as well. Better to stop growing grain entirely, he admonished, and simply import it all from the USSR. By April 1961, Soviet technicians, long resented for their comfortable living conditions, were obliged to leave and the Soviet ambassador was expelled. The deepening isolation did not help the new Chinese connection to make any lasting improvements, as we shall see in Chapter 7.

The Romanian road away from if hardly out of the Soviet bloc by the early 1960s followed from the same Stalinist commitment to the rapid growth of heavy industry and the same Soviet objections to its overemphasis. Agricultural investment also lagged, even after the belated effort to complete collectivization in the late 1950s. The Soviet Union had provided limited aid to the Galați steel mill and other metallurgical projects until 1958. Then the credits ended and Soviet pressure began for Romania to concentrate on light industry and agriculture as its proper specialization in the bloc's Council for Mutual Economic Assistance (CMEA). Founded by the Soviets in 1949 without consulting the other members and without any real impact for the next decade, the CMEA became the bloc's institution for matching the coordination that the European Economic Community provided for the booming foreign trade of its members. CMEA's "international coordination of socialist labor" would, however, continue to base all member trade on the bilateral clearing agreements introduced by the Germans in the 1930s, as we saw. They continued to provide an advantage to the larger partner or the seller of scarcer goods. Romania had neither advantage in its trade with the Soviet Union.

Only its past loyalty to the bloc during the 1950s, including the suppression of all internal dissent, allowed the Dej regime to begin its well-known economic confrontation with the Soviet Union.[33] It began almost immediately after Khrushchev had proclaimed the CMEA's new mandate in Moscow. This was in August 1961, the same month that he authorized the building of the Berlin Wall. Its further isolation of East from West Germany heightened the rationale for a better-coordinated Soviet bloc. Until then, Dej had been a faithful servant. His success, as we have seen, in eliminating party opposition to his leadership before Stalin's death meant that there would be little contention afterwards. Ana Pauker was released from prison but Vasile Luca was not. Lucretiu Pătrășcanu was finally executed in 1954. There was some cause for concern over the failure of the first Five-Year Plan to meet its targets and the still small share of industrial workers in the Romanian Workers' Party, despite the reduction in its overall membership from 1 million to under 600,000.

Once again, however, the abortive Hungarian Revolution swept away any challenge posed to a sitting Communist leader by Khrushchev's Secret Speech in February 1956. Dej did not even mention it in his address to the party leadership later that spring. The remarks of two other party leaders condemning Stalinist cults of personality wherever they might appear were simply not recorded. By May, however, the literary ferment starting in Budapest prompted several Romanian writers to speak out. Food lines and student chants of anti-Russian slogans appeared in the Romanian capital of Bucharest by the summer. The full-scale uprising in Budapest that October was the final danger signal for the Dej regime. The potential echo in Transylvania among its restricted Hungarian minority prompted a comprehensive crackdown on all opposition, real or imagined for the rest of the year. Within the party leadership, the two critics of the personality cult were soon dismissed. The young Dej-loyalist Nicolae Ceaușescu was promoted from the Politiburo to the Central Committee. Transylvania remained under what amounted to martial law for the next year. Its autonomous Magyar Region vanished for good.

The Soviet side tried to help the regime by ending the last of the Sovrom joint companies before the end of 1957 and then withdrawing its contingent of 35,000 troops in 1958. Insecure over their departure, the Dej regime introduced harsher new penalties for political dissent. It turned the Interior Ministry's feared secret police, the Securitate, loose to round up new numbers for more labor camps, this time in the daunting conditions of the Danube delta. Perhaps 40,000 people were arrested and sent there.

Some of them had opposed the new collectivization drive. In anticipation, agriculture's share of investment in the new 1956–60 plan had risen from 11 to 17 percent. Yet private smallholders still occupied 48 percent of arable land in 1956. The campaign launched in 1958 had increased that share to 84 percent two years later. By 1961 the regime could indeed point to an agricultural sector that had increased its output, by an annual average of 6 percent even according to Western calculations of Gross Domestic Product (GDP), more rapidly during the 1950s than any other economy in the region. The growth, however, rested on a larger share of the labor force remaining in agriculture, still 66 percent in 1960, and a smaller use of fertilizer per hectare and tractors than anywhere else save Albania. The agricultural share of Romania's exports also remained the smallest in the region, as did the share of exports in GDP, barely 10 percent.[34] The huge investments in metallurgy, chemicals, and petroleum were thus serving to expand heavy industry for domestic use. This was the classic Stalinist strategy that the Dej regime and its successor under Nicolae Ceauşescu would defend until 1989.

Bulgaria's Communist regime would until 1989 remain under the leadership of Todor Zhivkov. He did not consolidate his position as the sole leader until 1962. Along the way from appointment as the party's First Secretary in 1954, his own close if subordinate relation to Khrushchev's Soviet leadership and to its economic as well as foreign policies surely assisted Zhivkov. At the same time, the region's most rapid movement of population from countryside to town and the greatest turn to manufactured exports were creating challenges for central Communist control that would become unmanageable by the 1980s (see Chapter 7).

By the early 1960s, however, the party's internal discipline and the advantages of the Soviet connection seemed to have completed a successful postwar transition for Bulgaria's Communist regime. For Zhivkov, it was Khrushchev's Secret Speech denouncing the abuses of Stalinism rather than the Hungarian revolt later in 1956 that first advanced his own position. Vulko Chervenkov had remained Prime Minister and was there to take the blame not only for Stalinist abuses and a cult of personality before Stalin's death but also the economic setbacks and the continuing hostility to Yugoslavia afterwards. Khrushchev's rapprochement with Tito from 1955 forward left Chervenkov particularly exposed to criticism. Enough of it was voiced at the party's plenum in April 1956 for Zhivkov to force him out as Prime Minister. It was the powerful Interior Minister, Anton Yugov, rather than Zhivkov, who took his place. The Hungarian Revolution briefly strengthened Yugov's position and revived Chervenkov's influence. But Zhivkov's closer ties to Moscow and his ability to blame others for economic setbacks while claiming credit for the advances finally enabled him to dismiss Chervenkov before the 1962 party congress. Khrushchev's further and harsher denunciation of Stalin's abuses in 1961 then made Yugov vulnerable for having been Interior Minister in the early 1950s.

The longer and more important background to Zhivkov's becoming head of state as well as of the party came from the regime's contradictory economic record from 1954 to 1961. The rush into heavy industry was too closely tied to Soviet advisors and credits for its serious shortcomings to be criticized. Peasant flight from the countryside and overambitious targets for the region's most rapidly collectivized agricultural sector were blamed on

Chervenkov. Overall, food and tobacco processing plus textiles and other light manufactures had received enough investment since 1953 to make their export about two-thirds of a total that had grown fivefold across the full decade. In return came machinery imports from the bloc members, and oil and other raw materials from the Soviet Union. The Soviet share of foreign trade remained over half of the Bulgarian total, leaving the bloc share with 25–30 percent and Western Europe, primarily West Germany, with 15–20 percent. The Soviet decision to activate the CMEA helped the region's fastest advance in foreign trade, ahead of the less certain figures for national product, to continue past 1960.

Although "producers' goods" had risen to account for half of industrial production by 1960, the actual record of heavy industry did not augur well for the future. Metallurgy, machinery, and chemicals were primarily responsible for the large enterprises that boosted the average Bulgarian size past those of its neighbors. Their growth was too much tied to Soviet credits, technical advisors, or at a minimum the current state of Soviet technology. From 1953, Soviet geologists came to lead the search for uranium and iron ore. The first search was soon abandoned but the second concluded, contrary to a wartime German survey, that the low-grade iron ore in the country's one large field, near Sofia, could be sufficiently enriched to justify a major steel works. The Kremikovtsi *kombinat* there was to join the smaller one at Pernik, where at least low-grade coal was available. Both of them, as we shall see in Chapter 7, were soon forced to rely on imported Polish coal and Soviet iron ore. Both facilities were also tied to the Soviet steel technology of the 1930s. These future burdens were not foreseen when Zhivkov triumphantly launched Kremikovtsi in 1959 with the announcement of a large new Soviet credit for machinery and Soviet technicians for planning.[35] Zhivkov had long regarded such a "steel apex" as the best possible symbol of Bulgaria's becoming a modern economy. The project had indeed been on the drawing board since 1955. That Chervenkov had originally rejected it and Khrushchev favored it from the start added to Zhivkov's advantage.

Also to his advantage was Chervenkov's trip to China in 1958. He returned with Maoist enthusiasm to promote the experimental establishment of one huge collective farm of Chinese size. Its failure, at least absent the immense loss of life that accompanied Mao's Great Leap Forward, allowed Zhivkov to lay off on Chervenkov the shortfalls of his own proposal to complete the third Five-Year Plan in three years, 1958–60, and to consolidate an entirely collectivized agriculture into larger units, although on a smaller scale than in China, as introduced by Khrushchev in Central Asia. Their difficulties accelerated the peasant movement into towns that had already created urban unemployment by 1958. Over 10,000 workers had been sent to the Soviet Union to relieve the embarrassment.

By 1960 enough new jobs in light and especially heavy industry had relieved at least this problem. There remained the social adjustment to the most abrupt transition from agriculture to industry, and from rural to urban life, experienced anywhere in postwar Europe. Nearly 700,000 peasants, about one-fifth of the entire labor force had been pushed or pulled to industrial jobs, mainly in the larger towns, from 1948 to 1960. Unlike the other Communist states in Southeastern Europe, Bulgaria's agricultural production nonetheless grew at an annual rate ahead of the interwar advance when its labor force was increasing instead of falling.[36] Illiteracy had been virtually eliminated, and the number of scientists and engineers trained in an expanded Sofia university and other institutes passed 25,000. The Zhivkov regime celebrated these advances. The reorganization of regional government into 30 districts in 1959 promised to give the regional capitals some local autonomy.

What this transition now in place in Bulgaria and the rest of Southeastern Europe meant for the population at large, rather than the political leadership, concerns the next chapter. The further 25 years from 1964 to 1989 would more than double the period of postwar peace that the region had received after 1918. Now, after a difficult start, it would be Greece that made the better use of this further quarter century than the neighboring Communist regimes.

7 Continuity and Contradictions, 1964–1989

Southeastern Europe's second set of postwar transitions since 1918, uninterrupted this time by depression or world war, played themselves out over the next quarter century. On the one hand, the massive socioeconomic shifts under way by the early 1950s continued into the early 1980s. Populations were increasingly urban and employed in industry or services, amounting at least to majorities everywhere but Albania. The share of foreign trade in national income also advanced, as did public interest in the wider world, primarily in Western popular culture and consumer values. Higher education and access to modern media were making urban youth into a new social class of their own.

On the other hand, all of the region's postwar political regimes struggled, sooner or later, to maintain the legitimacy that they had appeared to consolidate by the early 1960s. A multi-party electoral process proved unable to prevent a group of anti-Communist army officers from seizing power in Greece and irrelevant to the aging Communist leaderships who controlled the single-party regimes elsewhere. The earlier access to financial support from the Soviet Union and its bloc or from the United States and Britain that all had enjoyed in varying measures, as we have seen, now gave way to Western commercial credit which had to be repaid. The initial rush of rural labor that had facilitated rapid industrialization also subsided. The postwar pace of economic modernization had, however, become one major source of political legitimacy across the region. Maintaining that pace would now depend on greater domestic productivity, or, in economists' terms, a further transition from extensive to intensive growth. By the 1980s the attraction to an increasingly integrated Western Europe and the start of serious regional relations seemed the most promising economic avenues.

The political promise of Cold War allegiances or balancing acts, more real in this region than in the rest of Europe, meanwhile faded. Détente between east and west peaked in 1975 with the Conference on Security and Cooperation in Europe (CSCE). Both sides signed its Helsinki Final Act, recognizing Eastern Europe's postwar borders as final in return for accept ing Western provisions for international standards on what were now called human rights. Although endorsing the "principle of self-determination" in its text, the Final Act itself advanced the subsuming of the controversial principle under equal rights for all citizens and their democratic representation, free from foreign control but within established borders. With all signatories as members, the CSCE became an ongoing organization responsible for monitoring observance of these standards. Virtually all European states and the US were members.[1] Communist regimes, Yugoslavia excepted until the late 1980s, received the greater scrutiny.

But for Greece as well as the Communist regimes, their other source of political legitimacy now became a distinctive national identity. Here the ideological attraction of populist nationalism itself rather than liberalism, socialism, or Communism proved strongest. Its imperatives hardly favored wider international connections. Wrapping the existing political regimes in ethnic celebration hardly inspired the new class of urban youth that the postwar transition had created. Here was a domestic contradiction that helped to create political crisis across all of Southeastern Europe by the end of the 1980s. The five states also faced the international contradiction of declining diplomatic importance or, for Albania, continuing isolation juxtaposed against the demands of growing interdependence.

Let us begin with societies rather than states, societies whose continuing evolution across a now lengthy postwar period came to strain the confines of their political regimes. These common strains created common problems for the politically distinctive regimes that persisted through the 1980s. Before then, Greece had weathered the Colonels' military regime of 1967–74, and the Communist regimes of Bulgaria, and Yugoslavia had proceeded respectively with centralizing and decentralizing reforms. The Stalinist regimes of Albania and Romania had survived the 1970s, respectively tightening and loosening their grips. By reversing these tendencies, the two would strive to continue on isolationist terms into the 1980s. Greece, Bulgaria, and Yugoslavia struggled to find new terms. The Greek experiment with socialist populism facilitated civil-war reconciliation but had run its costly economic course by 1989. Belated efforts to decentralize in Bulgaria and to recentralize in Yugoslavia failed to rebuild economic legitimacy. Only the nationalist card remained to be played, unsuccessfully in Bulgaria and disastrously in Yugoslavia.

Socioeconomic Transitions Continued

By 1980 the rural distinctions that had set Southeastern Europe apart from the developed European economies through the interwar period had

Table 7.1   Size of population and capital cities, 1939–80

Country (in millions)	1939	1947	1950	1960	1970	1980
Albania	1.1	1.1	1.2	1.6	2.1	2.6
Bulgaria	6.6	6.7	7.2	7.8	8.5	8.9
Greece	7.2	7.3	7.6*	8.4*	8.8*	9.6
Romania	16.0	15.9	17.2	18.5	20.1	22.2
Yugoslavia	16.4	15.8	17.4	18.3	19.4	22.4

Note: *For 1951, 1961, 1971.

Capitals (in thousands)	1939	1950–54	1970	1980
Tirana	30	–	115	175
Sofia	401	435	877	1057
Athens*	481	565	867	886
Bucharest	648	886	1475	1929
Belgrade	267	368	746	1088

Note: *Greater Athens had a population of 1.38 million in 1950 and 2.45 million in 1970.

Sources: John R. Lampe and Marvin R. Jackson, *Balkan Economic History, 1550–1950: From Imperial Borderlands to Developing Nations* (Bloomington, IN: Indiana University Press, 1982), Table 13.1, pp. 522–3; Godfrey Baldwin, "Population Estimates and Projections for Eastern Europe," Joint Economic Committee of US Congress, *East European Economic Assessment*, Part 2 (Washington, DC: US Government Printing Office, 1981), pp. 208–25; and *OECD Economic Survey, Greece 1972* (Paris: OECD, 1972), p. 73, and 2nd edn, 1921–82 (Paris: OECD, 1983), p. 79; B. R. Mitchell, *European Historical Statistics, 1750–2000* (New York: Palgrave, 2003), pp. 74–7.

significantly diminished. A peasantry bound to traditional agricultural practice could no longer be taken as representative. Nor was illiteracy, especially for females, any more the rule, or military service still the one likely point of male contact with the wider world. Massive movement to cities or towns, through schools and into new jobs, sometimes outside the country, had fashioned this new profile, modern and European in form if not always in substance.

While the reasons for this new internal migration varied, the results were roughly the same, with the exception of Albania. As may be seen in Tables 7.1 and 7.2, the rise in urban shares proceeded more rapidly between 1960

Table 7.2   Structure of population and labor force, 1950–80 (%)

Indicators	1950	1960–61	1970–71	1980–81
Urban population				
Albania	20.5	30.9	31.5	33.6
Bulgaria	27.5	38.8	54.7	62.5
Greece	36.3	43.3	53.2	58.0
Romania	24.7	32.5	41.1	47.0
Yugoslavia	25.9	28.3	39.0	47.0
Labor in agriculture				
Albania	76.2	–	–	40.0
Bulgaria	73.6 (1952)	55.5	35.7	23.8
Greece	48.2	55.3	40.5 (1971)	29.7
Romania	74.3	65.6	49.3	38.5
Yugoslavia	68.3 (1953)	56.3	47.4	20.0
Labor in industry				
Albania	11.0	–	–	–
Bulgaria	14.0 (1952)	21.9	30.3	35.2
Greece	19.4	19.7	25.6	30.0
Romania	14.2	20.0	30.8	33.5
Yugoslavia	7.5 (1953)	13.5	19.0	23.6

Sources: John R. Lampe and Marvin R. Jackson, *Balkan Economic History, 1550–1950, From Imperial Borderlands to Developing Nations* (Bloomington, IN: Indiana University Press, 1982), Table 14.2, p. 597; Godfrey Baldwin, "Population Estimates and Projections for Eastern Europe," Joint Economic Committee of US Congress, *East European Economic Assessment*, Part 2 (Washington, DC: US Government Printing Office, 1981), pp. 208–25; and *OECD Economic Survey, Greece 1972* (Paris: OECD, 1972), p. 73, and 2nd edn, 1921–82 (Paris: OECD, 1983), p. 79; B. R. Mitchell, *European Historical Statistics, 1750–2000* (New York: Palgrave, 2003), pp. 74–7.

and 1980 as the overall increase in population began to slow. The pressures of Communist collectivization and in Greece of civil-war destruction had started the movement from rural villages. But now it accelerated with the attractions of urban employment and life. Industry moved ahead of agriculture as an employer of active labor everywhere but Albania and Romania. By 1980 the populations of Bulgaria and Greece were predominantly in towns or cities. Urban proportions for Romania and Yugoslavia still approached one half, despite the large agricultural population remaining in Romania and the sizeable nonagricultural village numbers in Yugoslavia. Only Albania remained nearly two-thirds rural. Taking the full period from 1950 to 1980, Greece and Yugoslavia led in totals for internal migration, each shifting over 7 million people, versus 150,000 for Albania.

Most attractive for migrants were of course the major cities. These included the capital cities but were not confined to them. Yet only Zagreb managed to match Belgrade's growth and remain half as large. Elsewhere, Thessaloniki and Plovdiv were only one-quarter the size of Athens and Sofia, and the fractions were even smaller for Albanian and Romanian cities versus the populations of Tirana or Bucharest. Greater Athens had soon displaced Bucharest as the region's largest city. By 1980 it climbed past three million people. Bucharest's nearly two million still topped the one million plus in Sofia and Belgrade.

These four cities had now grown to a size comparable to the capitals of Belgium and the Netherlands, if not Britain and France. Their numbers and dispersion had also increased well beyond the size within which central governments had established rigid political control during the immediate postwar period. By the 1970s urban popular cultures had begun to take on lives of their own. American films appeared most prominently in Athens and Belgrade, while access was more restricted in Sofia and Bucharest. West European films were more influential in stimulating domestic productions, again in Greece and Yugoslavia. Only Athens could claim 300 movie theaters, but the smaller total in the others were well attended. British and West European popular music also swamped any Soviet bloc imports. With the spread of television sets, several American series became almost obligatory to watch. Since they typically centered on crime (as in *Mannix*) or corruption (as in *Dallas*), their content could pass ideological censorship in Romania. Antennas were increasingly set up in Sofia to receive such programs and the West European offerings of Eurovision from nearby Yugoslav Macedonia. Townspeople owning most of the several hundred thousand sets in Albania could also redirect antennas to receive Italian television.

Set against these visions of a wider world were struggles for housing in each of these sharply expanded urban populations. The share of investment devoted to meeting this need diverted funds from industrial projects as in Greece, created chances for state enterprises to control access to scarce housing as in Yugoslavia, and rationed out new apartments by political criteria in Albania, Bulgaria, and Romania. New residents, fresh from the villages, could of course turn away from an increasingly urban, European popular culture. Few turned back to relying on the regimes' mass organiza-

Table 7.3   Indicators for living standards, 1980

Per 1000 Population	Bulgaria	Greece	Romania	Yugoslavia	Portugal
Passenger cars	34.0	80.0	4.0	85.0	118.0
Telephones	12.0	28.0	5.6	79.0	132.0
Television sets	87.0	127.0	20.0	199.0	76.0
Doctors	4.5	2.7	1.6	1.3	1.5
Infant mortality	20.2	18.7	29.3	33.4	26.0
Secondary school enrollment* (% of eligible)	88.0	82.0	77.0	79.0	–
Higher education enrollment* (% of eligible)	18.0	21.0	10.0	21.0	–

Note: *1977.

Sources: *OECD Economic Survey, Greece 1981–82* (Paris: OECD, 1982), pp. 64–5; John R. Lampe, *The Bulgarian Economy in the Twentieth Century* (London: Croom Helm 1986), pp. 194–5; Joint Economic Committee of US Congress, *East European Economies: Slow Growth in the 1980s* (Washington, DC: US Government Printing Office, 1985), p. 257; Nicholas V. Gianaris, *The Economies of the Balkan Countries* (New York: Praeger, 1982), p. 83.

tions and official media. Many favored instead associations with fellows from their original area and its folk music, famously transformed in the "rurbanized" suburbs of Belgrade to defiantly nationalist "turbo-folk" by the end of the 1980s. Even in such locales, the desire for modern consumer goods reached beyond radios, television sets, and washing machines. Table 7.3 indicates the lead that Greece and Yugoslavia had established in automobiles by 1980, approximating the figures for Portugal. And in Bulgaria and Romania as well, if not in Albania, the taste for "little luxuries" like cosmetics, cigarettes, and blue jeans fed an informal "grey economy" that operated outside Communist planning or Greece's tax system.

Much less disparity from West European standards could be found in access to secondary and higher education. The figures in Table 7.3 reflect the impressive percentages of primary-school graduates who at least entered a secondary school (over 90 percent of the eligible cohort, even for Albania). The fraction of 20–24-year-olds going on to higher education is respectable by European standards for Bulgaria, Greece, and Yugoslavia. More detailed data for Yugoslavia indicate that about half of those entering secondary schooling graduated and about half of those went on to a university or a technical school. The number of schools had also increased across the region. By 1957 the first Albanian university had opened in Tirana. Campuses such as Plovdiv in Bulgaria, Ioannina in Greece, and Iaşi in Romania offered access beyond the capital city. Universities in Yugoslavia spread to every republic's capital and also to other cities within them. They totaled 17 by 1980, but scholarly interaction across the six republic and two provincial borders remained minimal.

Yugoslavia's new universities shared other problems with their counterparts elsewhere in the region. Too many of their faculty members were based in the established universities and appeared infrequently outside the capital. Even there, state funding for education neglected classrooms, equipment, and libraries. In Greece, the resulting limitations on enrollment encouraged the growth of private institutions and, even more, study outside the country, in Yugoslavia as well as in Western Europe. All this contributed to a common regional problem, prolonged periods before graduation. Another limitation across the Greek and Communist divide was the emphasis on rote learning inherited from Central European gymnasia and universities of the nineteenth century.[2] Memorization discouraged critical analysis in the humanities and the social sciences, further discouraged in the Communist regimes by required and resented courses in Marxism–Leninism. Still, these graduates plus the larger number in science and technology formed a new middle class conscious of professional standing as much or more than their state employment or party membership.

Such political indifference typically survived the indoctrination presented to the large majority of young males drafted for obligatory tours, typically of two years, in the national armies. For the Communist regimes, there were of course the Pioneer organizations for girls as well as boys aged 6–14, all started on the Soviet model in the immediate postwar period. Neither Greece's right-wing governments of the 1950s nor the Colonels' regime of 1967–74 would try to establish a comparable organization, perhaps wary of the excesses under Metaxas's EON youth organization before the war (see Chapter 4). Elsewhere in the 1950s the Communist organizations had provided rural youth in particular with holidays, excursions, and celebratory ceremonies that did indeed contribute to their regimes' legitimacy. Even then, the Tito regime's management of its Pioneers had shifted the emphasis from indoctrination to enjoyment.[3] By the 1970s, however, the popular culture and mass media noted above had stepped in everywhere but Albania to offer more attractive forms of enjoyment.

Foreign trade and, to a lesser extent, tourism and travel were further links between the region's new social profile and a wider world increasingly judged by West European standards. Only Albania's trade turnover (exports plus imports) failed to advance as a fraction of national income during the period 1960–80, remaining at a regional low of about 15 percent and falling even lower in terms of foreign trade per capita. Nor were there shipping income, tourist revenues, or remittances from workers abroad to help to cover the large import surpluses of nearly two to one as they did for Greece and Yugoslavia. Both of those economies saw their current account imbalances more than halved by the flood of West European tourists coming for summer holidays from the 1960s and the chances for their own workers to find jobs in the booming economies of the European Economic Community. Until the oil shocks of 1973 and 1979 started a reverse flow, over one million Greeks and one million Yugoslavs, primarily Croats, were working in the West, primarily in the Federal Republic of Germany. They sent back earnings and returned periodically as well, often bringing appliances and other favored consumer goods with them.

The Bulgarian economy, although without such invisible earnings other than a modest traffic in tourists, increased exports enough to avoid the large import surpluses typical for the rest of the region. Trade turnover (exports plus imports) jumped from 31 percent of estimated Net Material Product (NMP) in 1960 to 82 percent by 1980, a higher fraction than anywhere in Europe save Belgium and the Netherlands. This advance was large enough to make the absolute value of Western trade larger than Romania's, despite the continuing predominance of the Soviet Union and Eastern Europe in the overall distribution of trade indicated in Table 7.4. The roughly comparable turnover ratio to Gross National Product (GNP) for Greece went from 24 to 38 percent, and for Yugoslavia from 32 to 43 percent over the same period. Romania's efforts to continue its advance of the 1960s past 30 percent into the 1970s and to reduce a rising import surplus foundered on the more rapid increase in import prices from outside the Soviet bloc. Albania's limited trade and continuing import surplus kept its proportion under 20 percent.[4] Albania aside, the rest of the region and indeed all European economies, East and West, had been pushing foreign trade ahead faster from the mid-1950s than even the exaggerated East European figures for the growth of Net Material Product (GNP minus depreciation and services). How trade as an engine of growth could be sustained through the energy shocks and price inflation of the 1970s without growing dependence on Western commercial credit became a dilemma for the Communist regimes by the 1980s.

Contradicting these common trends was a set of political constraints that varied with the distinctive regimes that had consolidated postwar power across Southeastern Europe. Their different trajectories would reconverge

Table 7.4 Directions of foreign trade, 1938–80 (% of total)

Country	1938		1950		1965		1980	
	Exp.	*Imp.*	*Exp.*	*Imp.*	*Exp.*	*Imp.*	*Exp.*	*Imp.*
Albania								
Soviet Union	0	0	63.0	37.0	0	0	0	0
China	0	0	–	–	40.0	63.0	28.0	53.0
Eastern Europe*	3.3	26.3	37.0	63.0	18.0	37.0	48.0	27.0
Bulgaria								
Soviet Union	0	0	54.5	50.2	52.1	50.0	58.5	57.3
Eastern Europe*	17.1	24.1	37.1	35.6	27.2	24.3	23.5	21.6
Romania								
Soviet Union	0	0.1	58.9	44.4	39.8	37.7	18.1	16.3
Eastern Europe*	18.4	17.4	30.3	33.7	23.6	19.5	22.3	21.0
Yugoslavia								
Soviet Union	0	0.1	15.3**	11.1**	17.2	8.4	27.7	17.9
Eastern Europe*	23.2	28.4	52.0	54.0	14.8	20.6	18.5	12.2
Greece								
Germany	34.5	28.8	19.9	8.0	37.4	17.2	17.9	13.9
UK	8.3	11.3	15.0	12.4	9.9	9.1	4.1	4.6
USA	17.1	7.2	16.6	32.5	22.7	9.0	11.2	5.3

Notes: *Includes Czechoslovakia; **1948 figures; 0 for 1950 exports and imports.

Source: John R. Lampe and Marvin R. Jackson, *Balkan Economic History, 1550–1950: From Imperial Borderlands to Developing Nations* (Bloomington, IN: Indiana University Press, 1982), Table 13.2, pp. 524–5; *OECD Economic Survey, Greece 1972* (Paris: OECD, 1972), pp. 70–1; and Michael Kaser, "Trade and Aid in the Albanian Economy," Joint Economic Committee of US Congress, *East European Economies Post-Helsinki* (Washington, DC: US Government Printing Office, 1977), pp. 1325–40.

from the 1980s forward. A separate accounting is, however, needed to understand how they and their societies got there.

Greece Survives the Colonels' Regime

For Greece, the long political struggle between royalists and republicans came to an ironic end with the military regime that seized power in 1967 and held it until 1974. Officers from the same army that had won the civil war against the Communists and then supported King Paul and the right-wing regimes of the 1950s now became the instruments of the monarchy's destruction. Their abuse of power also put paid to any independent role for the military in Greece's political affairs after a history of intervention that began in 1909 (see Chapter 1). Their abuses and their failure to overcome the Turkish challenge on Cyprus did not, however, end the challenge from the Greek left to be the better representative of the national interest. That challenge still included the credentials acquired by the Communist-led resistance during the Second World War. By seeking to expunge them once and for all, the Colonels' regime succeeded only in reviving these credentials.

The leading Colonel, George Papadapoulos, had initially joined IDEA, the Sacred Band of Greek Officers, when it formed as a secret organization in the early 1950s. Its purpose was quite simply to prepare for a military dictatorship. Its leaders were junior officers who did not trust any parliamentary government to cement the civil-war victory over the Communists. Some of them came from the Sacred Battalion of Greek troops in wartime Cairo. It had opposed the British-brokered compromise of 1944 that made the republican George Papandreou Prime Minister and delayed the King's return.

Now that same Papandreou was Prime Minister again, thanks to his Center Union's narrow victory in the 1963 elections (see Chapter 6) and a decisive triumph in February 1964. Standing up to the US for its failure to take Greece's side in the Cyprus dispute and the promise of increased access to higher education gave the Center Union 53 percent of the vote, versus 35 percent for the royally favored Radical Union. Papandreou first appointed a royally favored Minister of Defense but soon found that the Ministry was resisting the advancement of generals not loyal to the Radicals and investigating left-wing officers, plus his own son, Andreas, for membership in a secret anti-NATO organization, ASPIDA. When the King rebuffed Papandreou's request to become his own Defense Minister, he resigned in protest in July 1965. Not reappointed as he expected, he also faced demands that Andreas's immunity as a member of parliament be lifted so that he could be arrested. Papandreou thereupon mobilized growing popular resentment against the interim governments that the King appointed. Finally, Constantine agreed to calling a new election in 1967.[5]

Explicitly in order to prevent this election, Papadopoulos mobilized the other Colonels whom he had been gathering together since 1965. They staged their coup d'état on April 21, with the King out of Athens and the highest-ranking Generals uninformed. Chief among the other Colonels in the 12-man Revolutionary Council was Dimitrios Ioannidis, previously a head of army intelligence in Cyprus and an advocate of simply expelling all Turks from the island. Papadapoulos's own prior service in the KPY, the Greek Central Intelligence Service modeled on and formed with the assistance of the American CIA, was less important for political leverage than his posting to the General Staff in Athens in 1965 by the new right-wing Chief of Staff appointed by the King. In the event, American officials showed no sign of anticipating or initially approving the coup. Its pretext was, however, a NATO-approved plan for assuming full powers under martial law in the case of an international emergency, helping to attach the stigma of US responsibility to the coup. This in turn helped to discredit the new regime from the start.

Reluctant American acceptance in fact came later, after a countercoup by the King and several senior Generals, that would have been an acceptable alternative, failed in December 1967. Constantine was obliged to flee the country, never to return. By then, the curious "political impasse and social veto" that the Colonels' regime imposed on Greece was underway, as the next seven years are well characterized by Thanos Veremis.[6] The first priority was to check any potential for public resistance and then to veto the changes that had been taking place in the country's military and, more broadly, in its educational system. Some 10,000 largely temporary arrests of suspected opponents discouraged the large political demonstrations that might have been expected. The Revolutionary Council provided the Ministry of Public Order with a 40 percent increase in its budget and put an expanded force of military police under Ioannidis. Then began the purge of any suspected opponents in the officer corps. About one-sixth of the total 20,000 were dismissed during the next few years, ironically forcing out senior royalist officers along with the younger and better educated men suspected of left-wing sympathies. Defense spending increased to one half of the state budget; expenditures for higher education were cut from 15 to 13 percent.

More importantly, the regime fired teachers and changed school curricula in an effort to cut Greek youth off from Western popular culture as well as any Communist sympathies. New textbooks, again printed in *katharevousa* rather than the demotic modern language, celebrated a "unique Hellenic–Christian civilization." It was to be preserved against class differences and all foreign influences. Textbooks read as though they had been written for the prewar Metaxas regime. As in the late 1930s, those foreign influences included Slav Macedonians wishing to speak their language or to travel to what was now the Yugoslav Republic of Macedonia. There was, however, no realistic prospect of re-creating a youth organization like Metaxas's beloved EON among the student population of the 1960s. All that could be done, to general European ridicule, was to ban short skirts and long hair, even for visiting tourists, and to restrict the films that could be shown.

Beyond concentrating more central powers in their hands, however, the Colonels' regime could define no political or economic program for the country's further development. The Defense Ministry passed from civilian to military control. The number of districts for local government was reduced from eighteen to seven. But while lower-level military and civilian authorities continued to operate on the basis of clientelist connections, major centralization took place at the top of the regime. And it soon became part of its undoing. Papadapoulos increasingly concentrated power in his own hands. The new constitution that his hasty plebiscite had been rigged to ratify in 1968 served to disband the Revolutionary Council and to force rival Colonels out of the government. Papadapoulos now assumed a number of cabinet positions for himself. In 1972 he proclaimed himself Regent in Constantine's enforced absence. Economic advance had continued until then, thanks to the ongoing boom of urban construction, the forgiving of farm debts in 1968, and concessions to the Greek shipbuilders. American and European investment declined, but ample credit from the Bank of Greece and other state banks allowed the large state enterprises and small private ones to go ahead.

Then, in 1973, the Papadapoulos regime failed to face down a series of gathering crises. The first oil shock combined with a rising trade deficit and lax credit policies to push prices up sharply. Wages already lagged behind in the absence of any effective union representation under the Colonels' continuing state of emergency. A May mutiny on a Greek destroyer persuaded Papadapoulos that he could do without the monarchy, the other Colonels, and martial law as well. Blaming the mutiny on Constantine's supporters, he declared the King deposed in June and conducted a tightly controlled plebiscite in July to make himself President of the Republic. His new cabinet replaced all military officers with civilians. His promise of parliamentary elections by 1974 included overtures to representatives of the major parties. They quickly rebuffed him and threatened to boycott the elections. Meanwhile, his army associates resented their exclusion from the new government. University students seized on wider public discontent to press their case for the restoration of political liberties.

Emboldened by the new republic's suspension of martial law, a group of them gathered in the Athens Polytechnic Institute in November 1973 to press their case. Soon several thousand protesters, workers and sympathizers now included, had assembled. Papadapoulos could not escape responsibility for turning loose the army and police units that stormed the building on November 17. Over the next five days, nearly one hundred protesters were killed, several hundred wounded, and seven thousand arrested. As public sympathy for the student victims spread and endangered the regime, Dimitrios Ioannidis ousted Papadapoulos from the Presidency a few days later. His first act was to reimpose martial law.

Ioannidis soon led the military regime into a confrontation with Turkey over Cyprus in 1974 that spelled its final doom. Returning to the cause of *enosis*, or Greece's sovereignty over the entire island, he bridled at the demand from Archbishop Makarios, the Greek President of the partly formed Republic of Cyprus, that mainland Greek officers leave its National Guard. Ioannidis authorized a coup to oust and possibly assassinate Makarios. As the Archbishop fled the island, Turkey's government responded by sending a sizeable invasion force on July 20. Greece's own military could not, and in some units would not, respond to Ioannidis's call for general mobilization. The regime's failure to use its huge military budgets to obtain new armaments, and its corrupt sale of ammunition stocks, turned the mobilization into a scandalous debacle. Faced with the alternative of declaring war and suffering a humiliating defeat, Ioannidis and the rest of his military leadership agreed to step down just four days after the Turkish invasion.[7]

Back from 11 years of exile in Paris came Konstantinos Karamanlis, the former Prime Minister from 1956 to 1963. The political steps that followed successfully restored multiparty elections and established a strong Presidency under a new constitution. The Prime Minister was automatically the leader of the largest party in the parliament. Neither the King nor the Greek military received another chance in the political process. Karamanlis reconstituted his Radical Union as New Democracy and led it to a sweeping victory in the November parliamentary elections, winning 54 percent of the vote. The old Center Union, minus the leadership of the elder Papandreou who had died in 1968, slipped to 21 percent. PASOK, the new Panhellenic Socialist Movement founded by his son Andreas in exile, secured 14 percent. Allowed to return open political activity, the Communists reconciled the domestic and pro-Soviet factions that had split in 1968 and won 9 percent as the United Left Party. By the next election in 1977, New Democracy's vote declined to 42 percent and PASOK's climbed to 25 percent. The Center Union continued to fade away at 12 percent and the United Left held its minority ground at 10 percent. The two major parties that have alternated in power and dominated Greek politics ever since were now in place.[8] Also in place was the new Constitution of 1975, following a referendum that rejected the monarchy once and for all. Karamanlis remained as Prime

Minister and left his designee, Konstantinos Tsatsos, as President. As for the considerable powers of the Presidency, such as to veto legislation or dissolve parliament, Tsatsos largely declined to use them during his five-year term. The restoration of parliamentary democracy did not smooth regional relations or significantly change a state-dominated economic course. Despite quick work by Karamanlis to force out the Greek radicals who had seized power on Cyprus, the invading Turkish troops pushed ahead on August 14 to secure 35 percent of the island's territory. Some 180,000 Greeks fled in front of them, from areas of largely Greek as well as mixed settlement. A provisional agreement with Turkey in 1977 did little more than recognize the so-called Green Line along this new internal border and provide for its monitoring by United Nations peacekeepers. Then the discovery of oil on the continental shelf extending from the Turkish mainland to Greece's small Aegean islands raised overlapping claims within each country's normal six-mile limit of territorial waters, let alone the 12-mile limit that Greece also advanced. The accumulated tension in Greek–Turkish relations kept Greece's military expenditures close to half the state budget. The modern armaments neglected by the Colonels, primarily tanks and planes, now received top priority. Except for Albania with whom a state of war still existed, the Communist neighbors supported Greece's claims against Turkey. Otherwise, despite Karamanlis's special interest and a Balkan conference he convened in Athens in 1976, Greece's regional relations did not advance beyond their limited level under the Colonels' regime.

Relations with the US suffered as the eventual American support for the Colonels had encouraged the comforting public sentiment that the CIA put them in power. If we acknowledge official US suspicion of the Makarios regime and also consider the Western failure to reverse the Turkish invasion of Cyprus, we can understand the decision of Karamanlis to withdraw Greece from NATO's military framework until 1980. He nonetheless pursued his long-standing enthusiasm for European integration, winning full Greek membership in the Europan Economic Community (EEC) by 1981.

Membership, as we shall see, did not mean integration. The PASOK governments of 1981–9 only added to the set of state enterprises, state banks and state subsidies whose predominance continued from the 1950s (see Chapter 6). Together, they troubled Greece's membership in the EEC and made the economy somewhat comparable to that of Yugoslavia. Distinctions of course remained. For Yugoslavia, the absence of any private sector or foreign investment to balance the political weight of large state enterprises made it more comparable to Bulgaria. Yet common economic problems would await Greece, Yugoslavia, and also Bulgaria in the 1980s.

Decentralized Yugoslavia and Centralized Bulgaria

Neither of the Communist regimes in Yugoslavia or Bulgaria responded to the foreign trade boom of the 1960s by opening their economies to Western investment or to private industrial enterprise. Neither of them would lose the party leader who had consolidated the Communist regime in the 1950s until Tito died in 1980. The two regimes still shared the common goal of maintaining the monopoly of political power that had eluded Greece's Colonels. By the early 1960s, however, the two were pursuing this goal in opposite directions. Both Yugoslavia's decentralization and Bulgaria's centralization proceeded ahead with the aim of continuing economic advance and the political dividend it would pay. In the event, both regimes favored political over economic priorities and paid the price in the 1980s, as the chapter's final section will demonstrate.

Republic Regimes Trump Federal Integration in Yugoslavia

Devolving political power and enterprise management downward while trusting the central organization and discipline of the League of Communists of Yugoslavia (SKJ) to keep the republic leaderships together could proceed as long as Tito's towering figure was there to act as final arbitrator. When the initial devolution of the early 1960s favored market reforms and political liberalization, Tito did not use his unique position to brake this potential threat to the party's authority. But when the first signs of ethnically based protest appeared later in the decade, he and Edvard Kardelj, the party's chief ideologist, launched a set of constitutional and economic changes. They also purged the reformers. New, more reliable republic party leaders found themselves in a potentially stronger position, market-oriented enterprise managers in a weaker one.

The new Constitution of 1963 had changed the state's name to the Socialist Federal Republic of Yugoslavia and declared the period of "socialist construction" completed. Yet two preliminary studies by Yugoslav economists argued that significant change, political as well as economic, was still needed.[9] Gathering inflation, now 15–20 percent a year as noted in Chapter 6, rising imports, and declining investment pushed the drafters to replace the powerless Council of Producers with four new socioeconomic chambers. Local assemblies were to select their delegates, and the six republic assemblies were to send ten additional delegates (and the two provinces five each) to join the 120 that the still centrally controlled communal assemblies had already nominated for direct election to the Federal Chamber. The principle of *rotacija* was also introduced to bring in new blood by barring delegates from successive terms. The ban did not apply to the party organizations themselves. By December 1964 the SKJ's Eighth Congress had authorized republic and provincial delegations to meet and formulate their program before attending such a national meeting.

In retrospect, this political devolution seems more important than the economic reform of 1965. Its imperatives help us to understand why Tito and Kardelj did not allow the economic reform to proceed. For reform advocates, dubbed "liberals" by their opponents and eventually Tito himself, their proposals assumed that greater enterprise and bank autonomy would promote federal integration rather than greater republic or local autonomy. Quickly put in place, the initial measures allowed enterprises to keep 70 percent of their net income. Federation-wide and international competition was expected to hold down the inflationary wage increases that the Workers' Councils had been voting themselves. To stem credit inflation flowing from some 380 communal banks to local enterprises under local party auspices, they were summarily replaced by a new set of 30 regional banks. Their mandate was to lend on commercial terms, across as well as within republic borders, to private farmers as well as "social enterprises." For the less-developed regions, a new fund (FADURK) was launched to funnel tax contributions to them from the more developed republics. A law encouraging direct foreign investment was to follow.

The coast for comprehensive implementation seemed to be clear in 1966 after the reform's primary opponent, and Tito's most likely successor, Aleksandar Ranković, suddenly fell from power. That July he was discovered using his continuing authority over the state security service (UDBa, by now the SDB) that he had founded to wiretap the residences of the top party leadership. This included Tito himself, who convened a hasty plenum to read Rankovic out of his high office and the party as well. The reformist leaderships in Serbia, Croatia, Slovenia, and Macedonia could not however proceed ahead as they expected. The severe limitations placed on the foreign investment law of 1967 pointed to the political reversal that would by 1972 force all of them from their positions.

Separate conflicts from 1967 forward – over ethnically related rights in Kosovo, Slovenia, and Croatia – encouraged the reversal. So ironically did the Soviet invasion of Czechoslovakia in August 1968. Tito's immediate criticism of the invasion and his readiness to mobilize the JNA if the Soviets threatened Yugoslavia not only boosted the regime's standing, it also made ethnic disunity seem disloyal. Student demonstrations had already erupted in Belgrade, inspired by Czech Communist ideas of "socialism with a human face" as well as the New Left in Western Europe. They raised no ethnic issues but questioned the inequalities and market rationale of the economic reform itself.

Tito and Kardelj doubtless welcomed this encouragement to retreat from the "rotten liberalism" that could spill over from the economy to a political process that now seemed vulnerable to ethnic disruption.[10] First came the ethnic Albanian demonstrations from Priština south to Tetovo in Macedonia in November 1967. Violence erupted over the restrictive Serb Communist regime that remained in power even after the fall of the man most responsible for its most repressive features, Aleksandar Ranković. Serbs still occupied a majority of official and enterprise positions despite an Albanian majority that had risen to 70 percent. The Tito regime responded by brutally suppressing the demonstrations, leaving Serb control of the SDB in place. Albanian party members then received the near-monopoly rights in administration and education that the Serbs had previously held. School textbooks and even teachers began arriving from Albania under an agreement with Tirana intended to make up for the previous lack of instruction in the Albanian language. This concession did little damage to the liberal Serbian party leadership at the time but would hurt its successors by the 1980s, eventually playing into the hands of Slobodan Milošević. So would the new, largely Albanian university in Pristina and the FADURK funds funneled in largest part to Kosovo. None of this stilled popular discontent there, among Albanians as well as Serbs. The province's level of unemployment rose past 20 percent during the 1970s.

Slovenia, the republic with the highest per capita income and lowest unemployment, sought to consolidate its advantage with the promised share of a World Bank loan for road-building in 1969. When the other republics agreed to withhold the Slovenian half, designated for a new road to the Austrian border and hence to the West European trade that they all sought, the aforementioned liberal coalition of party leaderships suffered a damaging division.

The more damaging division for economic and also political reform arose between Zagreb and Belgrade. Croatian cultural demands for recognition of a language distinct from Serbian, thereby acknowledging a separate literature of considerably longer standing, began in 1967. They soon spread to requests for greater access to the sizeable revenues that the booming tourist traffic to the Dalmatian coast was now generating. An increasingly autonomous Croatian media endorsed these claims. Magazine articles spread rumors such as "Serb plans for a separate republic around Dubrovnik," the most lucrative tourist center. The inland resentment of Serb predominance in lesser administrative positions that would arise in the late 1980s was not yet an issue. Instead, it was the danger of "the appearance on the political stage of people who are not ours," as the senior Croat Communist, Vladimir Bakarić, told Tito. The younger liberals now leading the party in Croatia and headed by Savka Dabčević-Kučar, had endorsed not only the doubling of the republic-nominated delegates to the former Federal Chamber (eventually the Chamber of Republics and Provinces) to 140 but also supported multicandidate elections to the other 120 in 1969. One of a growing number of constitutional amendments allowed such uncontrolled access at lower levels. Now the way seemed open for uncontrolled advocacy of Croatian interest, and perhaps others. Indeed, by 1970–1, students, intellectuals, journalists, and some enterprise managers had banded together to form a *maspok*, or mass movement, that demanded radical amendment of the constitution. What amounted to a separate Croatian financial system and diplomatic representation could of course never be accepted. When the Croatian liberal leadership did not openly reject their proposal, Tito had his chance. As a student strike proceeded unchecked in Zagreb, Tito summoned the Croat liberal leaders to his Karadjordjevo hunting lodge in late November 1971. He summarily dismissed them.

During the course of 1972, while the lower ranks of the Croatian party were being purged of Croats in particular, Tito forced the liberal leaderships of the Serbian, Slovenian, and Macedonian parties to resign as well. Strengthening his hand in Belgrade were the 1968 demonstrations by university students and intellectuals against the differences in income and the lack of social control that the reform measures had already encouraged. Their links were to the West European student demonstrations of that summer. They drew on the same early Marxist critique of capitalism and were also inspired by the anti-American opposition to the Vietnam War. Hence the Soviet invasion of Czechoslovakia that August to suppress "socialism with a human face" did not invalidate their criticisms. They remained particularly useful against Serbia's new party leader, summoned from his post as Foreign Minister after his predecessor had failed to prevent the demonstrations. Marko Nikezić was too strong an advocate of cooperation among the republics as equals to be criticized as a "Serbian unitarist." Only his strong commitment to the economic reform, explicitly favoring market-oriented management over the Workers' Councils, left him vulnerable.

To reestablish the Communist monopoly of power under newly or still reliable republic leaderships, Tito asked Kardelj to craft yet another constitution and to revive Workers' Council influence over enterprise management. Both endeavors favored Communist control of still more political assemblies or economic entities below the federal or the republic level. In the event, only federal leverage suffered under what Steven Burg has called the new regulatory framework.[11] The 1974 Constitution drew on a series of amendments from 1971–2 but went further. It created what amounted to a confederation of republics and the two provinces held together by Tito's predominance and the Yugoslav National Army's representation. Yet the specific powers of the new presidency were limited unless all the republic and provincial members agreed. The two new legislative bodies replacing the previous five were insulated from multiple candidacies and indeed any sort of direct election. Kardelj's series of closed assemblies elected delegates to the next level of assemblies until the legislators were finally chosen. The republic parties quickly mastered control of this process. Facing their legislative leverage plus their veto powers in the presidency, the central government's Federal Executive Council (SIV) in Belgrade could prevail only sporadically.

Then, in 1976, Kardelj's new law for Basic Associations of Organized Labor (OOUR) subdivided the existing Workers' Councils and made enterprise managers more dependent on political bargaining than market signals. Each occupational or specialized group within industrial or service enterprises was now entitled to its own Workers' Council. Enterprise management faced negotiations with all of them, leading typically to stalemate or to the playing off of one against the other. More damagingly, both enterprise and bank managements were pushed to bargain with each other as well as the OOURs. Kardelj much preferred these "social compacts," endorsed by the party's local leadership, to allowing market signals like interest rates and profit margins to prevail.

Such bargaining revived the chance for Workers' Councils to devote much more of net income to wage increases than to new investment. The 1965 reform's new regional banks, now numbering over a hundred, had generally failed to lend beyond republic borders or to avoid local party influence. Enterprises began trading credit arrangements among themselves, outside any contractual obligation for repayment. These "grey emissions" of unpaid debts climbed past 40 percent of enterprise liabilities, masked their losses, and helped to boost the rate of annual inflation for 1970–9 to 18 percent. So did the ability of local government, banks, and even enterprises to contract for Western bank loans, repayable all too soon in the absence of any significant foreign investment.[12] Only a few joint ventures fit the restrictive terms of the 1967 law. The monopoly powers of existing enterprises restricted entry more broadly, helping to drive up unemployment to 14 percent by the end of the 1970s. Meanwhile, dependence on trade with Western Europe and on the world oil market could be only partly reduced by shifting somewhat toward the Soviet bloc. The second international oil crisis descended in 1979 and pushed inflation further ahead. The

Yugoslav economy thus entered the 1980s with a series of burdens that, following Tito's death, republic parties and publics could openly blame on each other.

Bloc Integration Trumps Economic Reform in Bulgaria

The Zhivkov regime also experimented with economic reform during the mid-1960s but stopped short following the Soviet invasion of Czechoslovakia in 1968. Also simplifying the Bulgarian story was a consistent commitment to developing its own heavy industry while following the Soviet lead to an increasingly integrated Council for Mutual Economic Assistance (CMEA). Zhivkov sought out greater integration with the Soviet economy not for its markets for Bulgarian foodstuffs but rather for still cheaper access to the iron ore and other raw materials needed to expand domestic metallurgy. According to recent Bulgarian scholarship, this was the major reason that Zhivkov raised the prospect of Bulgaria's becoming the 16th republic of the Soviet Union in a 1963 meeting with Nikita Khrushchev.[13] His continuing commitment to matching Czech heavy industry was all the same storing up difficulties for the 1980s that bear comparison to those facing Tito's successors.

The continuing centralization of Bulgarian political life and economic management did indeed make for a simpler and therefore shorter story. Todor Zhivkov must be credited with artfully moving all potential rivals to the side before any real challenges to share or reduce his power emerged. Several army generals found some supporters only in the northwest of Bulgaria to support their easily aborted coup of 1965. It was apparently intended to follow Romania in asserting greater independence from the Soviet Union. This was the only effort to remove Zhivkov by force or any other means. In the event, it served to expand the requirement for training general officers in Soviet academies and assure the continuing assignment of Soviet officers to all Bulgarian units. This doubtless contributed to Bulgaria's dispatch in sending a contingent to join the Soviet army's occupation of Czechoslovakia in August 1968. The Bulgarian media also surpassed others across the bloc in its enthusiasm for the Soviet decision to oust the reform-minded if Communist regime of Aleksandar Dubček.

Zhivkov paid prompt attention in 1968 to silencing any internal echoes from the ill-fated Prague Spring. The Bulgarian Communist Party (BKP) reviewed party cards and expelled several thousand of its one million members. The Fatherland Front, still surviving from the war, expanded to include the few civic organizations outside its party-controlled framework. Directives from the Central Committee now sought to regulate the environment in and around the apartment complexes which accounted for most urban housing. To complement this growing centralization at lower levels, the Constitution of 1971 made Zhivkov the Chairman of the new State Council. Established to replace a committee from the National Assembly, it assumed executive powers and could initiate legislation as well. Zhivkov thus became head of state as well head of the party, a position matched only in the Stalinist regimes of Ceauşescu's Romania and Hoxha's Albania. Zhivkov dismissed a supposedly reformist member of his politburo in 1977, and as a further precaution another 40,000 party members, but otherwise proceeded unimpeded through the decade. Overall party membership continued to grow, from 500,000 in 1960 to 800,000 by 1980. So however did the average age of the Central Committee. Half were over 50 by 1976, and 80 percent over 40.[14]

Economic centralization had proceeded on a less direct and, by the end of the 1970s, a less successful course. The discrediting of the Prague Spring in 1968 helped to cut short the limited loosening of the planning process begun in 1964 as the New System of Management (NSR). Along lines suggested for selected consumer goods by the Soviet economist Evgenii Liberman, some 50 Bulgarian enterprises were freed from most planning targets, allowed to retain 70 percent of their net income, and left to seek external funding from state bank loans rather than the budget. By 1967, initial growth rates half again the industrial average had encouraged the NSR's spread to two-thirds of all enterprises, heavy industry conspicuously excluded. Price controls were also being relaxed along Czech lines. But disquiet and a demand for recentralization appeared as early as Todor Zhivkov's speech to a party plenum in 1966. By early 1968, prices were restored to control from the planning process, and a set of new targets and income controls placed on all enterprises. Several cases of genuine corruption, most notoriously the textile importing enterprise that had landed the contract for bottling Coca-Cola, helped to make the public case against continuing the New System. Considerable debate within the wider party leadership about preserving the reform's incentives to enterprise management ended with Soviet suppression of the Czech reformers later in 1968.

Three other continuities survived instead – the centrally planned concentration of industry in large enterprises, the determination to make metallurgy and machine production the center of Bulgarian industry, and the growth of market-based production in, of all places, collectivized agriculture. None of the three did much to advance the competitive advantage of a small economy more involved in foreign trade than any other member of the Soviet bloc. Yet access to uncompetitive markets, particularly the huge Soviet one as may be seen in Table 7.4 allowed all three continuities to reach the late 1970s before the regime felt renewed reform necessary along the lines of the New System.[15]

Until then, the only production based on domestic demand came from the "personal plots" permitted within the newly established Agro-industrial Complexes (APKs). They had originated in the Central Committee's 1968 pilot project to combine collective farms in order to introduce modern methods and economies of scale so as to process more foodstuffs for export. When fully implemented in 1971, the new framework merged Bulgaria's 800 collective and state farms into 161 complexes. By 1972 Zhivkov was promising that the APKs would also address increasing shortages in the domestic food supply and bring consumption up to the "scientific norms" set by the United Nations. Their record as large organizations helped increase exports to the Soviet bloc, more after their subdivision into smaller, more integrated units began in 1977. But domestic consumption gained primarily from the network of leased private plots that APK households soon began to assemble. No limit was placed on their number. The freeing of most weekends from Saturday work hours in 1973 allowed typically younger family members in town to join in cultivation and distribution. By 1978 they accounted for 22 percent of vegetable and 39 percent of fruit production, most of it sold for the higher prices permitted at town cooperative markets versus the state food stores.

The regime's concessions to private agriculture followed from its continuing determination after 1960 to give industry in general and heavy industry in particular the leading role even in an export-oriented economy. The original Soviet emphasis on heavy industry in the 1930s had however relied on domestic natural resources for industrialization to the virtual exclusion of foreign trade. Its aim was autarky, and Soviet trade had shrunk accordingly by 1935. The Bulgarian regime now bet on a growing capacity for machine and electronic exports that would be the primary beneficiary of self-sufficient metallurgy, built around Zhivkov's "steel apex" (see Chapter 6). Consequently, the rise in industry's share of fixed capital investment for 1960–70 from 34 to 45 percent, while that for agriculture plummeted from 30 to 16 percent. Within the industrial share, moreover, metallurgy and machine-building took over one half. Little wonder that the processed food, tobacco, and beverages that had amounted to 40 percent of Bulgarian export value as late as 1965 moved steadily down through the 1970s to 15 percent. The fractions of imported Soviet iron ore and Polish coal to supply the Kremikovtsi complex in particular rose through these decades, compounding the cost of using obsolete Soviet technology.[16]

Rather than turning to market incentives or away from heavy industry, the Zhivkov regime relied instead on closer coordination of a shrinking number of increasingly large organizational units to restore the high rates of industrial growth, 9–10 percent a year, that even American estimates had acknowledged for 1958–68. Bulgaria's industrial enterprises were large in themselves. Nearly one half of the industrial labor force worked in plants of over one thousand workers, a level of concentration surpassing East Germany as well as the regional neighbors. Already in the 1960s the regime had grouped enterprises into 120 State Industrial Associations (DSOs). First cut to 60 but given powers to decide enterprise investments and subsidies, the DSOs gave way by 1975 to a new set of only 11 combines, distributed among a set of seven new ministries. By 1979, however, these "units of the future," as Todor Zhivkov described them, had failed to prevent a significant decline in the rate of industrial growth, from 6 to 3 percent by American estimates, or to avoid the turn to Western credit markets for the investment needed to support unchanging industrial priorities. Hence the New Economic Mechanism and its return to market incentives in the decade that followed. The Zhivkov regime would, like PASOK's Greece, seek to combine further economic transition with a new nationalist legitimacy. The debate over further transition would only fragment post-Tito Yugoslavia.

National Stalinism in Albania and Romania

No such change of direction distinguished the two Communist regimes in Albania and Romania, at least as long as their Stalinist leaders lived. Enver Hoxha died in 1985, and his wife's effort to hold to an unchanging hard line lasted for another year. Even then, no new Albanian nationalist initiatives accompanied the limited relaxation of central economic controls. Nicolae Ceauşescu's Romania continued to play the nationalist card that had served it well internationally since 1968, when he denied the Soviet Union support in Czechoslovakia. National Stalinism also justified a repressive internal regime that hardened in the 1980s. Like Hoxha, he encouraged a Stalinist cult of personality to celebrate his unique political leadership and high scholarly standing. Like Hoxha and quite unlike Stalin, his family advanced into the highest ranks of the party. And, like Hoxha, he pressed ahead with the development of heavy industry in order to secure a Stalinist sort of economic independence while isolating the population from foreign influence.

Albania after China and after Hoxha

By 1963 Albania's anti-Yugoslav switch from Soviet to Chinese support was complete. Over the next five years the largest part of Chinese assistance, whose total by 1975 ($838 million) nearly tripled the $300 million previously provided by the Soviet bloc, arrived to cover imports and support Albanian industrial projects. These were also the years of Chairman Mao's Cultural Revolution. The Albanian regime launched a comparable set of egalitarian measures and purges to "cleanse the nation's superstructure." The legal profession was simply abolished, private agriculture was eliminated, and religious observance banned. Slogans for increasing women's rights and reducing wage differentials had a Maoist ring to them, but Hoxha's ideological commitment here was of longer standing. The ensuing campaigns for both also served the regime's growing need to increase the industrial labor force among a population still two-thirds rural. Full collectivization and Chinese assistance raised grain yields and production. This success eliminated one major component, bread grains, in the longstanding import surplus. Yet by the early 1970s the Sino-Albanian relationship cooled as China accepted detente with the United States. At the same time, the Hoxha regime softened its attitude toward Yugoslavia as the cultural access to an increasingly autonomous Kosovo noted above took hold.

None of this prevented the regime from ending the accompanying relaxation of tight political control as quickly as it had begun. By 1973 the brief opening to Western tourism closed down. *Zeri i popullit*, the party newspaper, blamed recent access to Italian television for the rising number of dropouts from the secondary schools. By 1975 Hoxha and his apparent successor, Mehmet Shehu, purged the military and economics ministers and eventually half of the Central Committee to tighten their hold. The new Constitution of 1976 explicitly placed the Party of Albanian Labor (PPS) over the army as well as the rest of society. To the extent that insecurity explained this increased rigor, we should note the small size of the Albanian party and the fact that half of its leadership were related to each other. The PPS's membership fell short of 100,000, its 3–4 percent of the population thus ranking slightly below the two major Greek parties, let alone Bulgaria and Yugoslavia's 10 percent and Romania's 15 percent. The party's elite resented the several thousand Chinese specialists only slightly less than they had their Soviet predecessors. This helps to explain the break that became final in 1978, as does the Chinese demand from the early 1970s that any further credits be repaid, perhaps accounting for the explicit ban on foreign credit in the 1976 constitution. By the late 1970s the glorification of Hoxha was growing. Publication of his own writings expanded to 19 volumes. The relationship with his successor suffered accordingly. Shehu's interest in reopening some of the Western economic contacts explored earlier in the decade may also have contributed to their estrangement.

Speculation also surrounds the circumstances of Shehu's sudden death in December 1981 but not its consequences. Dismissed as Defense Minister in 1980, he had already started to fall from grace. All subsequent sources, including his son, discount the official announcement of Shehu's suicide. The most likely scenario – a gun battle or assassination during a Politburo meeting where Hoxha demanded his resignation as Prime Minister – remains unconfirmed to this day. The Hoxha regime's subsequent demonization of Shehu as a long-standing agent for Western intelligence, his family's persecution, and his erasure from the party's history reminds us of Stalin's Soviet Union in the 1930s. So does a determination to isolate the regime and the country from outside influence that would not survive the longtime leader's death.[17]

The final push to insure isolation began with the departure of the last Chinese specialists and the end of rice imports in 1978. The regime launched an immediate drive to advance industrial production by centralizing the control of literally all financial transactions. It pressured collective farms for the deliveries needed to avoid any food imports. Shortfalls in meat deliveries led to the 1981 decision to absorb all privately held livestock into the collectives. What followed that year were food shortages in the towns and the first of the recurring declines in agricultural production per capita. As also calculated from fragmented official data, industrial production barely grew from year to year after 1982.[18]

These difficulties and the mushrooming number of television sets capable of receiving Italian programs without connection to a communal antenna favored some change of at least economic course after Hoxha's death in April 1985. His widow and Politburo member Nexhmije fought a delaying action against Ramiz Alia, who had replaced Shehu as Hoxha's successor. Alia used the party congress of 1986 to win approval for decentralization and some individual incentives. The number of plan targets and other controls were trimmed for a pilot group of industrial enterprises and a proposal for planning based at the district level announced. The congress also approved greater wage differentials for agriculture as well as industry. For agriculture in particular, the previously shrunken private plots could now enlarge. Control of livestock transferred down from the whole collective to the often related membership of the small work brigades. Yet production from both industry and agriculture probably kept falling in 1987–8. The long isolation even from Soviet technology and the absence of incentives outside of advancement within the small PPS were handicaps not quickly overcome.

The Alia regime reached out nonetheless to establish what regional and wider ties that it could,[19] Economic motives surely played a major part.

Negotiations to end the formal state of war that had existed with Greece since 1940 had already started in late 1985. An agreement on reopening the common border helped to boost the value of their trade by one half in 1986. By 1987 both sides formally signed off on ending the state of war. Greek authorities promptly put a $7 million bank credit into a new plant for chrome processing, the first direct Western investment ever permitted. Diplomatic relations with West Germany and Canada the same year opened the way to more trade and investment. Favorable signals to Yugoslavia soon distanced Alia from Nexhmije's provocative gesture at Hoxha's funeral, laying the Albanian flag on his heart "on behalf of the people of Kosova." Post-Tito Yugoslavia, eager for an Albania uninterested in the fate of the Kosovar Albanians, completed its long-delayed portion of the Titograd–Shkoder rail line in 1986 and signed a new cultural agreement in 1988 minus the university ties of the 1970s. That fall, Alia himself attended the Balkan Conference of Foreign Ministers that convened in Belgrade, on Greek as well as Yugoslav initiative. Unlike the Athens conference of 1976, all five regional states sent representatives, albeit from regimes whose time was running out.

Ceauşescu's Romania Descending

Just reversing Albania's experience, the Romanian regime of Nicolae Ceauşescu began in 1965 with the promise of reform and relaxed Communist control but soon turned back to Stalinist independence. Its harshness only depened when the regime confronted its declining economic fortunes during the 1980s. So did its celebration of the party's leader and his family. By then, the good first impression that his regime had made on the Romanian public had long since vanished. Even international favor had fallen away. By 1989 the sense everywhere else in the region that some significant change, for good or ill, was already under way could not be found in Romania.

Constructive change surely seemed to be afoot in the first years under the young General Secretary, only 47 in 1965. Half of the regional party leadership were replaced, typically with younger men. Past repression was admitted but blamed on the ousted Interior Minister, Alexandru Draghici. Building on his predecessor Dej's refusal of a subordinate, primary producer's position in the Soviet bloc, Ceauşescu sought out expanded trade with France. In 1967 he established diplomatic relations with West Germany despite the latter's refusal to recognize East Germany. French President de Gaulle visited in spring 1968. Then came the August windfall, for Ceauşescu, of Czechoslovakia's invasion by the Soviet Union. His decision to refuse participation and to mobilize the army in case Romania was invaded next won more popular support for the Communist regime than at any time before or since. The promise of more investment in two predominantly Hungarian districts in Transylvania accompanied the appearance of appeals to ethnic Romanian pride flooding newspapers and other media. Such openly nationalist rhetoric soon found its way into Romanian schoolbooks. The Patriotic Guard, a new people's militia meant to include literally all adult males and females, was hastily organized to supplement the army. University students and faculty attended the initial drills with enthusiasm. As for the Romanian army, it pulled back from the practice common elsewhere in the bloc of sending all potential general officers to the Soviet Union for advanced training.

The Western powers welcomed this turn with open arms. The American President, Richard Nixon, came for a visit in 1969. A cultural exchange agreement with the United States followed shortly thereafter. So did Most-Favored-Nation treatment in trade, as approved by the otherwise anti-Communist US Congress in 1975. Surely, the assumption became, Romania was on the road to becoming another Yugoslavia, another defector from the Soviet bloc. It took a full decade for the Western powers to understand that distance from the bloc alone did not mean political reform.

Ceauşescu's trip to China and North Korea in 1971, accompanied not incidentally by his wife Elena, has long been credited with inspiring the domestic retreat from relaxation that continued through the 1980s. And indeed what Vladimir Tismaneanu has called "dynastic Communism" and Dennis Deletant "sultanism" surely drew on the regimented hero worship of Mao and Kim Il Sung that the Ceauşescus appreciated on their visit.[20] The puritanical codes of public dress and behavior in Beijing and Pyongyang, the two capital cities, also impressed the couple from a small Romanian town. They brought with them a natural suspicion of their own large and long-sophisticated capital of Bucharest. Only weeks after returning, Ceauşescu proclaimed a set of 17 theses that demanded renewed ideological activity, education, and vigilance in the spirit of the Chinese cultural revolution. Students, for instance, were now required to wear their school uniforms in public as well as in class.

It was, however, the threat of contagion from Communist Eastern Europe that had started Romania's ideological retrenchment and renewed centralization before the Asian tour. By 1969 Ceauşescu was already criticizing the liberties being taken by Romanian fiction writers. Regime censors had given them freer reign after the Soviet invasion of Czechoslovakia in order to celebrate Romanian independence. Now, he complained publicly, this "literary inflation" was allowing veiled criticism of the regime. Such permissiveness, Ceauşescu told the Central Committee, had characterized the policy of Czechoslovakia's Communist Party during the reformist euphoria of the Prague Spring in 1968 and resulted only in the Russian intervention. By 1970 the regime's vaguely conceived program for industrial decentralization had clearly failed. Spring floods strained the urban food supply and created some open discontent. Then, in December, Polish workers rioted over higher food prices, forcing party secretary Wladislaw Gomulka to resign. The fact that he had just signed a trade agreement with West Germany, as Ceauşescu had done in 1967, was not lost on the Romanian leader. His measures for tighter control over Romanian workers began from this point.[21]

We may date Ceauşescu's reliance on family members from 1972. During his absence on a visit to Iran, a Romanian general tried to organize others trained in the Soviet Union to reestablish close relations with Moscow, even if it meant a new party leadership. The general was executed and the army never trusted again. Wife Elena now became a member of the party's Central Committee, their son Nicu and his wife soon after. By 1977 Elena had joined the Political Executive Committee, as the Politiburo had become known to distinguish it from the Soviet model. Seven of its dozen members in 1980 were related by blood, marriage, or rumor to the Ceauşescus.

Complementing this close concentration of party authority was an effort to merge it formally into the state's administrative structure. Ceauşescu's assumption of the state presidency in 1974 was one of the last steps in this direction. Others were under way by the late 1960s. The party's campaign to absorb the growing number of industrial workers and educated professionals had begun in the early 1960s, but Ceauşescu pushed it ahead with wider recruitment. From 1964 to 1975, the party doubled in size to 2.6 million members. From early 1971, before the visit to China and North Korea, he had begun the rotation of party appointees to lower-level state positions as a way of involving more of these large numbers and preventing any consolidation of local power. Multiple candidacies for local and national elections were tried out and then broadly implemented in 1975 but to serve the same restrictive purpose. They allowed the party hierarchy to draw more members into the political process in order to dismiss any sitting representatives who showed signs of independence. No such multiple candidacies were permitted for seats held by important figures in the hierarchy.[22]

The regime's wider determination to pursue a Stalinist economic strategy also emerged two years before the seminal visit of 1971. Here we find some initial success thanks to the un-Stalinist international connections that the regime had cultivated. The 10th Congress of the Romanian Communist

Party in 1969 had already adopted a Five-Year Plan for 1971–5 that gave metallurgy, machine-building, and petrochemical processing the highest priorities. At least for those years, concentrating 85–90 percent of new investment on heavy industry and the continued reliance on trade outside the Soviet bloc seemed to be paying off. Even by American estimates, industrial growth led the way in annual increases of 5 percent in Gross Domestic Product per capita that were the highest in the region and Eastern Europe. Living standards also advanced, if only to reach the modest levels for hard consumer goods indicated in Table 7.3. A larger contribution came from the construction of new urban apartments and the private house-building now allowed in the countryside. As bloc trade declined (see Table 7.4), the share with the developed Western economies had risen from 17 to 38 percent between 1958 and 1975. Romanian membership in the General Agreement on Trade and Tariffs (GATT) in 1971 and the International Monetary Fund (IMF) in 1972, plus Most-Favored-Nation treatment from US tariffs by 1975, promised a further rise.

But this was not to be. Partly to avoid such further dependence on Western trade but also to obtain the oil imports that were needed to support the huge investment in petrochemicals, the regime turned to the Third World, Iran in particular. As oil purchases grew sevenfold during the decade, their share of domestic consumption jumped to 53 percent by 1979. Romanian exports, petrochemicals in particular, had meanwhile failed to find the expected world markets. As the last surge of new industrial labor from the countryside tailed off, the official rates of industrial growth for 1976–80 were half those for 1971–5. To substitute capital for labor, the regime turned to Western banks still ready, despite the first oil shock of 1973, to lend to a European member of GATT and the IMF. Rebuilding the parts of Bucharest damaged in the severe earthquake of 1977 added to the demand for funds. By 1980 some $10 billion in relatively short-term debt had piled up, along with a large deficit on current account. Only a transition from extensive to intensive growth could hope to repay the interest and resume the advance in living standards that much of the urban population had experienced during the early 1970s.[23]

The Ceaușescu regime retreated instead into a cycle of economic retrenchment and political repression. It offered little encouragement for the increase in labor productivity essential to intensive growth. Nationalist rhetoric rose to offer what encouragement there was. The media dwelled on the leading role of both Ceaușescus in this last stage of Romania's two-thousand-year history. In 1981, building on its pride in hosting the World History Conference in Bucharest the year before, the regime celebrated "the 2050th anniversary of the centralized, independent Romanian state." Recognition of Ceaușescu's own credentials as an eminent scholar became required prefaces even to serious works of history. Some serious scholars retreated into philosophy, where the old interwar division between modernizers and Romanian essentialists (see Chapter 3) reappeared. The regime encouraged a new school of "protochronists" to combine the two. Rather than glorying in ethnic peasant traditions like Nicolae Iorga, they searched out prophetic, premodern Romanian anticipations of European high culture.[24]

This diversion combined with the growing size and authority of the *Securitate*, the secret political police, at the expense of the army as well as Romania's sizeable scholarly community. Together they prevented the sort of intellectual opposition growing in Poland and Hungary by the 1980s. Only science fiction emerged as a vehicle for veiled criticism. And unlike Poland's restive industrial workers, the coal and iron-ore miners in the Jiu valley who had struck for better conditions in 1977 remained unconnected with the intellectuals in distant Bucharest. Given the imprisonment of strike leaders and the persecution of their families that followed, we may doubt the argument that this lack of wider connection reflected some special Romanian deficiency. For intellectuals, they faced a requirement to turn in at least the keys of all typewriters not for official use. Then there was the threat of arrest for idle conversation recorded in the pervasive wiretaps. They numbered in the millions according to rumors spread by the *Securitate*.

The power of Ceauşescu's police state was otherwise sufficient to enforce his draconian solution to the debt problem and the shortage of new industrial labor. He determined that simply servicing this Western debt would not guarantee sufficient independence and decreed that the principal be paid off as well. And so it was by 1987. The cost was horrific. In order to generate the necessary trade surplus, imports were cut back sharply and exports expanded, particularly grain and other foodstuffs in both cases. Bread rationing began in 1981 and then spread to other daily necessities. Supplies often ran short, and lines formed before dawn in front of shops in the major cities. In the winter of 1984–5, imports of gas and heating oil were restricted to the needs of industrial facilities only. Housing and hospitals received none during the unusually harsh cold of early 1985. Pensioners in unheated apartments and newborn babies in hospitals died acordingly. By this time, births had risen in response to the regime's new ban on legal abortion. Ceauşescu sought to increase the birthrate not only to add to the supply of labor but also to push the country's total population toward 30 million.

The family members and sycophants who were his only advisors by this time supported such grandiose ambitions. Most grandiose of all was his plan for *sistematezarea* in the countryside and the construction of an immense new Palace of the People in Bucharest. The program to eliminate peasant villages and move their population into apartment complexes in new rural centers, where many could be recruited into industry, did not get very far. But the prospect fed anxiety, especially among the Hungarian villagers of Transylvania who believed that the program was aimed especially at them. Their protests had little effect. It was instead the destruction of existing houses, churches, and streets in Bucharest, displacing nearly 40,000 people, that created the basis for open defiance in the capital city by 1989.

Struggling with Reform and Remembrance: Bulgaria, Greece, and Yugoslavia in the 1980s

Across the rest of the region, its three apparently disparate regimes could not rely on repression or a Stalinist cult of leadership by 1980. They still had to face the economic challenges that their postwar transitions and now the end of the postwar European boom, East and West, left for them. They shared some common features. With the 1981 victory of PASOK's populist socialism in Greece and, in the early 1980s, the Communist concentration on reforming socialism in Bulgaria and Yugoslavia, the three governments moved on closer economic tracks than at any time since the Second World War. And, in each of them, their search for a new or renewed nationalist legitimacy led only to the revival of ethnic or wartime grievances – against the Turkish minority in Bulgaria, against Anglo-American intervention in Greece, and against each other among Yugoslavia's republics. Belated efforts at regional interconnection provided some more hopeful precedents for the regimes that were to succeed them after the seminal changes of 1989.

The Last Contradictions of Reform in Zhivkov's Bulgaria

The economy in which foreign trade weighed most heavily was not surprisingly the scene of the region's most concerted effort at improving enterprise efficiency throughout the 1980s. Its contradictory course from decentralization back to recentralization proceeded under two political handicaps that barred the way to significant improvement. The first was the entrenched and aging Communist leadership under Todor Zhivkov, 70 in 1981 but still able to prevent any significant sharing of power or challenge to his position. The second, plainly related to the first, was the regime's close and subordinate relationship to the Soviet Union.

Zhivkov had personally returned to relying on Soviet ties after allowing his controversial daughter Liudmila to stake out some distance in cultural relations. Rising from the chair of arts and culture for the Central Committee in 1975 to control of the media and science as well for the Politburo by 1980, she used her privileged family position to promote wider intellectual exchange. Foreign initiatives included a cultural agreement with the United States and neglected the predominant Soviet framework. Her crowning achievement was to be the celebration in 1981 of the 1300-year anniversary of the first founding of a Bulgarian state, obviously a millennium before any possible Russian connection. But then, as her increasingly erratic behavior kept her from overseeing the major ceremonies, she died that same year of a cerebral hemorrhage at age 39.[25]

The celebration's major regional legacy was to strain relations with Yugoslavia, once again over the historical identity of Vardar Macedonia. A film documentary calling it a Bulgarian land revived the contention that had just begun to heal after the centennial of the establishment of modern Bulgaria in 1878. Internationally, the polemics with Yugoslavia were soon overshadowed by Western allegations of Bulgarian involvement in the attempted assassination of the new Polish Pope, John Paul II, also in 1981. Although eventually disproved, the charges appeared against a background of real efforts by Bulgarian state security to use trading enterprises to funnel arms or assistance to dissident groups in Italy and Turkey. Souring relations with Western Europe and the United States only reinforced Zhivkov's commitment to the Soviet connection, as did the higher cost of Western credit, up since the second oil shock of 1979.

This was the unpromising context in which the regime's final program for enterprise reform struggled to get started in 1982. Projected since 1979, this New Economic Mechanism (NEM) tied the salaries of managers to net enterprise earnings, in hard currency for exporters, and the planning process to the new flexibility promised by computer technology. Credit from the Bulgarian National Bank rather than allocations from the state budget was supposed to further interenterprise competition. It foundered on the bank's lack of political independence. Zhivkov's aforementioned dedication to metallurgy kept large credits flowing to the loss-making Kremikovtsi complex and gave new allocations to the huge project planned for Burgas. This renewed concentration on heavy industry left the family networks of personal plots, which by now provided half of the meat, eggs, and potatoes to domestic markets, with reduced access to credit of any kind.

The NEM's only success came instructively from some 200 new enterprises, limited to 200 employees and authorized since 1980 to begin producing much-demanded consumer goods from blue jeans to baby wear and camping equipment. Their typically young managers took full advantage of freedom from any planned targets except net profit. Otherwise, the productivity per worker in the predominantly large enterprises failed to respond. The real value of overall industrial production increased by less than 2 percent a year for 1981–4, according to Western estimates. When Soviet authorities began to complain about the quality of Bulgarian exports, Zhivkov himself launched a 1983 campaign for *kachestvo* (quality). Its slogans generated little beyond a round of dismissive jokes in Sofia. By 1984 the NEM had gone as far as it could go.[26]

The regime now fastened on increasing the supply of industrial labor in order to reverse the overall decline in economic growth. It also faced two new handicaps. In 1983–5 one of the country's periodic droughts lasting beyond a single growing season descended. It exposed the failure of reduced agricultural investment to provide the comprehensive irrigation that would cut down the impact. As a result, overall agricultural production declined enough from 1983 forward to make a decrease of 2 percent the average annual for 1981–5. In addition, the drought cut deeply into the existing supply and future potential of hydroelectric power. That placed increasing reliance on nuclear power, supplying already 30 percent of the country's electricity from the facility at Kozlodui. A second was supposed to open at Belene by 1987. But in 1986 the Chernobyl nuclear disaster called that second project into question. Wider uncertainty about Soviet technology now spread across Bulgaria's large class of urban professionals.[27] Their anxiety encouraged instead reliance on the Western media, especially the BBC and Radio Free Europe, for information on current events in Bulgaria.

The regime had meanwhile distanced itself further from any alternative to Soviet support. Its ill-considered campaign of 1985 tried to force the large Turkish minority to exchange their names for ethnically Bulgarian ones and to abandon public use of the Turkish language, in the media, in schools, and even on the street. The initiative's still controversial origins seemed to lie in the regime's conviction that these measures would push significant numbers of this one large minority, approaching 900,000, to abandon their agricultural villages in two concentrated areas and seek industrial jobs. These were the very jobs that a declining birthrate for ethnic Bulgarians had ceased to fill. To sustain the initiative in the face of sizeable and sometimes violent Turkish resistance, Zhivkov turned loose a nationalist campaign in the media. It vilified any resistance as a denial of the minority's allegedly Bulgarian ethnic origins. Television programs and newspaper articles called them Bulgarians whose ancestors the Ottoman conquest had forced to adopt a Turkish identity, beyond simply converting to Islam as the smaller Pomak minority had admittedly done. The campaign, in obvious violation of the 1975 Helsinki Final Act on human rights, succeeded only in blackening Bulgaria's name further in the West. Opposition now began to stir among Bulgarian intellectuals. That opposition would grow after 1986 with a variety of environmental concerns, not just over Chernobyl but also over nonnuclear pollution around Kremikovtsi and elsewhere that was measurably increasing death rates. And under the new Soviet regime of Mikhail Gorbachev, these and other sensitive issues were now discussed in television talk shows from the Soviet Union that became widely popular in Sofia and other major cities. The Friday night of Soviet television that had previously been the evening for Bulgarians go out now became the one to stay in to watch this Third Channel in particular. Nor did Todor Zhivkov's personal failure to win a warm initial reception in Moscow from Gorbachev escape notice within the upper ranks of the BKP.

The Zhivkov regime thrashed about for a response during these last years before 1989 that would pass for the *perestroika* that Gorbachev advocated. According to one post-1989 recalculation based on physical units, industrial production ceased to grow after 1983 and then started to fall.[28] In order to pay for the Western equipment needed to reverse the decline, the regime's only recourse was the Western market for commercial credit. Foreign debt skyrocketed accordingly, from $3.2 to $9.2 billion between 1985 and 1989. The regime's domestic recourse was to recentralize the economy and also state administration. The last Five-Year Plan reduced the number of districts from 28 to 9. It sought to use the promise of self-managed municipalities within this smaller number to dismantle the separate district bureaucracies that had grown up in their 28 "central cities." Regime economists spoke of a new streamlined system of coordination that would make Bulgarian industry into "one large corporation." None of this reversed industry's decline, the growing shortages of basic supplies, or the start of price inflation. The distant relationship between the new Soviet leader and Todor Zhivkov stayed that way. At the time, it seemed that only Zhivkov's days were numbered.

Papandreou's PASOK in Power

As Bulgaria's "eternal friendship" with the Soviet Union turned against its Communist regime, Greece's looser and fraying ties with the United States helped bring to power a new government dedicated to trimming those ties. PASOK, the Panhellenic Socialist Movement, also took office with the populist promise of limited socialist reforms. Networks of new associations would make labor the equal of private capital and help to restrict foreign investment, still within the framework of a market economy and multiparty elections. But its newly independent, openly anti-American foreign policy provided nationalist appeal. The Cold War postulate of a northern border imperiled by the Warsaw Pact now seemed irrelevant. Led by the charismatic Andreas Papandreou, PASOK had championed a campaign for change, or *allagi*, to win 48 percent of the vote in the parliamentary election of 1981. It received a working majority of 172 seats to 115 for New Democracy, now deprived of its own charismatic leader since Konstantinos Karamanlis had won the previous parliament's approval as President of Greece. PASOK and Papandreou retained enough of their popularity to win a second four-year term in 1985, still taking 46 percent of the popular vote. By 1989, however, Papandreou's personal standing had fallen with doubtful health and his unpopular remarriage to a much younger women following a hasty divorce from his American wife, a longtime party activist. Also contributing to that year's narrow electoral defeat were problems that PASOK's record had created for a Greek economy that had entered the European Economic Community the same year that it had come to power.

By the late 1980s Papandreou's personal resentment of the postwar American presence, his presumption that the US had put the Colonels' regime in power, and his threat to close American naval bases unless they included support against Turkey had not proved to be the basis for significant change. Its rhetoric had previously offered PASOK domestic political advantage from a series of assertive nationalist gestures. Their defiance of the American-led NATO alliance began with the refusal to condemn Solidarity's 1981 suppression and martial law in Poland. But leaving the NATO alliance as promised or actually closing the American bases proved too uncertain an enterprise even for Papandreou. New confrontations with Turkey over the Aegean islands made one argument for Western accommodation. Another came from EEC subsidies, first for agriculture and then for infrastructure. They soon accounted for the largest part of invisible earnings on current account.[29]

PASOK's surviving effort to assert some new independence was regional accommodation. Its initiatives set useful precedents for the post-1989 period, as we shall see in Chapter 8. They ranged from the abovementioned peace treaty with Albania and more open borders with Bulgaria to the 1988 meeting of all five Foreign Ministers in Belgrade in 1988.

Domestic accommodation, perhaps inadvertently, became the major political accomplishment of Papandreou's two terms. By the late 1980s there was enough reconciliation between adversaries in the civil wars of 1944 and 1946–9 for Greek political life to proceed beyond the domestic Cold War that had by itself justified the anti-Communist side ever since. The PASOK regime, joined by a brace of younger, revisionist historians, recognized the

Communist case for a legitimate role at least in the wartime resistance. Open exchanges on the postwar period and the American role established higher standards both for revisionists and the increasing number of scholars who challenged them. At the same time, PASOK opened the way for long-exiled Greek Communists to return. Yet none of this, nor the broader introduction of proportional representation into all levels of Greek elections, advanced the parliamentary share of the KKE past the 10 percent it had held since recalled to life in 1975. PASOK and its rival major party, each with some 600,000 members, were left instead to vie for power between themselves and to make present-day issues the focus of their political platforms.

One such current issue from the first PASOK term turned against the regime during its second term. This was the populist promise of local empowerment free from the constraints of an austere state budget or profit-oriented private enterprise. This transition foundered on the party's abuse of empowerment to install its own people in the new associations that were supposed to represent civil society. And like the several Latin American cases that are most comparable, PASOK appointees swelled the size of the central government.[30]

The PASOK regime authorized new agricultural cooperatives in 1981–2 as the first in a series of associations that would eventually replace the state ministries and their patronage networks in place since 1914. The cooperatives' low fees attracted an initial membership of 130,000, but they soon failed to coordinate cultivation to any commercial advantage. PASOK replaced them the following year with a looser agricultural association, followed by merchant and crafts associations. Finally, a compulsory business association was intended to swamp the influence of large private firms with the small enterprise predominant in Greece. Trade unions and newly authorized enterprise unions received the greater effective power and used it to strike repeatedly for higher wages. They won instead nonwage benefits that kept wages substandard and labor productivity low. More important for the political impact of these organizations was their staffing with PASOK members. In the enterprise unions, these appointees worked effectively to prevent Communist influence. And within PASOK itself, what George Marvorgordatos calls the regime's other major *Gleichshaltung*, or leveling, the party eliminated the local and regional autonomy of its representatives, and hence their local clientelist capacity to put constituent interests first.[31]

These constraints do not however explain the increasing difficulties and rising popular discontent that marked PASOK's second term from 1985 to 1989. They came instead from the swelling size of the state budget and number of state employees, too many of them noticeably political appointees. The initial replacement of some 300 tenured civil servants, the recruitment of a large number of younger army and navy officers, and the injection of new, younger academics into an educational system at last conducted entirely in *demotiki* had been generally accepted as correcting a conservative bias. But export subsidies and other state aid mounted to 24 percent of manufacturers' value-added income by 1986. The state budget's share of Gross Domestic Product (GDP) climbed from 29 percent in 1975 to 51 percent by 1989. Inflation rose accordingly and the drachma lost value.[32] The Bank of Greece dropped its restriction of budget deficits and authorized budget aid to keep the still predominant state-controlled banks afloat. The EEC provided a balance of payments loan in 1985 in return for the promise of new austerity, kept only until 1987.

Real GDP slowed its annual increase to 1.2 percent for 1986–90. Net profits for manufacturers were now negative. Cushioning the effect of this "stagflation" for much of the population were the new agricultural pensions plus the health benefits and rising wages for state employees that the regime had provided. By 1987, however, the increase in state employment from 500,000 to 700,000 could not be sustained without wage restraint. PASOK was forced to confront the unions that had been their strongest supporters in a series of stormy strikes. The promise of state employment for all university graduates could no longer be kept. The regime's desperate addition of 90,000 new state employees on the eve of the 1989 elections only confirmed growing public disillusion. Too much of the central government's growth under PASOK looked like the clientelism of personal or family connections with which Greece's public administration had been plagued throughout the twentieth century.

Post-Tito Yugoslavia's Disastrous Descent

If the airing of issues from the Second World War and a distancing from divisions of the Cold War worked to the advantage of the Papandreou regime, the same two tendencies helped to bring post-Tito Yugoslavia to the brink of dissolution by 1989. Then the Communist collapse in Eastern Europe and finally in the Soviet Union itself, as we shall see in Chapter 8, removed the external justification both for a one-party regime and for balancing between Eastern and Western Europe. Already in the late 1980s, however, the banner of Communist reform had passed from the ensemble of republic leaderships and, as we shall see, two joint-party commissions into Slobodan Milošević's hands. He proposed recentralization but under widely suspected Serbian auspices. The last Western aid for Yugoslavia continuing its course independent of the Soviet bloc, now in the form of debt repayments renegotiated and further credits extended, had come and gone by 1985. By early 1989 a new American ambassador arrived with instructions to press hard on the Communist regime in general, and Milošević's Serbia in particular, over abuses of minority rights that had been ignored until then because of Cold War considerations. The CSCE's Helsinki standards on human rights were applied to Yugoslavia for the first time.

The economic decline and growing financial crisis that Harold Lydall's prescient 1989 analysis called "the great reversal" had already begun by 1981.[33] Retail prices rose by 42 percent that year despite efforts to reduce imports and new investment that already slowed industrial growth. Interenterprise credit continued to be the main domestic recourse, rising to 40 percent of all lending. Federal authorities joined republics, regional banks, and individual enterprises in searching for new Western credits. When one American bank turned down their largest request, the Federal Executive Council (SIV) was forced to acknowledge that they did not know the total amount of Yugoslavia's disparate foreign debt. Once calculated at $19 billion by an American accounting firm, the daunting aggregate did call forth an American-led consortium, the Friends of Yugoslavia. It assembled over $8 billion of debt rescheduling and new credits in 1983–4. Promises were made in return to reign in interenterprise credits and to reverse the negative interest rates from bank loans provided at well under the rate of inflation. Meanwhile, the aggregate declines in gross investment and real personal income for 1979–85 both topped 25 percent.

Some political response to the declining standard of living had already started not long after Tito's 1980 funeral seemed to bring the country together for some further joint effort. The specter of the Soviet invasion of Afghanistan in 1979 also promoted solidarity. Soon, however, the separate republic medias and academic communities were using greater post-Tito leeway to highlight current economic abuses originating in other republics. Serbian criticism focused on the restrictive practice of Slovenian enterprises operating in Belgrade. Magazine articles and books also opened inquiries into previously closed questions about the Partisans and the Great Powers in the Second World War. Many from Zagreb concentrated on the wartime abuse of Croats, many from Belgrade on the abuse of Serbs. Even Tito's own heroic role now came into question.

Any Yugoslavia-wide leadership depended, in Tito's absence from the multiple presidency with its rotating heads, on the Federal Executive Council. Here was the one body whose membership was not dictated by strict republic balance and nomination. First to take a four-year term as its chair after Tito's death was Milka Planinc, a Croatian Partisan veteran who must be credited with forcing the Federal Chamber to accept the demands for economic reform from the Friends of Yugoslavia in 1983. That same year, the federal party's special Commission for Economic Stabilization, chaired by an old Slovene advocate of the 1965 reforms, released a series of reports that endorsed comparable market incentives. But it stopped short of provisions to bankrupt loss-making enterprises or to eliminate the Basic Organizations whose subdivisions had burdened efficient firms since 1976.

Her successor, buttressed by the report of a second party commission, backed away from the commitment to market-based reform and the Western monitoring that might have provided further assistance. Branko Mikulić was a Bosnian Croat selected for his leadership of the republic's still hard-line party, his management of the 1984 Winter Olympics in Sarajevo, and his experience as a member of the federal presidency. A majority in that presidency also favored him because he was not a Serb, despite the ethnic balancing that would have demanded one after Planinc. He had no sooner departed Sarajevo than a huge financial scandal tarred major party allies among the Bosnian Muslims, leaving the Bosnian Communist leadership in disarray that also threatened its own long-standing ethnic balance. An emboldened local media stepped forward to press the advantage, exposing further scandals.[34] Thus ended the hard-line stability that had insulated Bosnia-Herzegovina into the 1980s.

Mikulić's arrival in Belgrade in 1986 coincided with the report of the party's commission on political reform. It endorsed his rejection of the further financial monitoring needed for another Standby credit from the IMF. The report, chaired by a Croatian hard-liner, called even the limited economic reforms of the 1983 commission "incompatible with a truly socialist system of self-management." It avoided any discussion of opening up the selection process for the layers of delegates who elected representatives to the two federal legislative bodies established by the 1974 constitution. There would still be no multiple candidacies even from within the League of Yugoslav Communists.[35]

Mikulić had assembled a Federal Council half of whose members were younger people drawn from outside the hierarchies of the republic parties. But neither he nor they were able to resist the pressures from the republic parties to protect their enterprises. They rejected restrictions that might reign in inflation but would risk a further rise in the rate of unemployment. It now averaged 14 percent for the socialist sector, more in the less developed republics and Kosovo. This problem alone was rising to threaten the legitimacy of an avowedly socialist regime.[36] As bank interest rates were once again allowed to lag behind, the annual rate of inflation climbed to 150 percent between 1986 and 1987. A new bank law of 1987 promised to empower the National Bank of Yugoslavia to restrict new credit according to enterprise accountability, but the threat it allegedly posed to the survival of thousands of loss-making enterprises quickly stifled its implementation.

By 1988 the Mikulić regime proposed the harder measures, including bankruptcy for insolvent firms, that were needed to reopen access to Western financial assistance. But it was now too late. The inflation rate continued its ascent to 250 percent by the end of the year. Mikulić felt obliged to resign in December, an unprecedented step among Communist regimes. By this time, moreover, two younger new leaders had come forward from within the republic party frameworks. Their prescriptions for a continuing single federation were incompatible. Slovenia's Milan Kučan represented the republic whose successful enterprises, highest average income, and lowest unemployment made its accommodation to rigorous market-based reforms the easiest. And that accommodation could most easily take place if the confederal rights latent in the 1974 constitution were affirmed or strengthened. Serbia's Slobodan Milošević, on the other hand, had taken control of his party's leadership in 1987 on the strength of resisting the autonomy that the 1974 constitution had given the Albanian ethnic majority in Kosovo. His initial championship of credit controls from the central bank and other reform measures rested on the recentralization of economic authority in Belgrade. Such a program was impossible to justify within the framework of post-Tito Yugoslavia even if put forward by someone who did not, like Milošević, regard political recentralization as equally important.

Beyond the contradictory approaches of Kučan and Milošević, the mounting economic burdens on the entire population and a series of strains between the republics, increasingly portrayed in their respective medias as ethnic conflicts, also began to tear apart the Socialist Federal Republic of Yugoslavia. Our final chapter must address its road to dissolution and war, a road which has made the entire region's post-1989 transition away from one-party regimes and state-centered economies more difficult.

This chapter has emphasized the failure of Yugoslavia's "really existing" market socialism to adopt the market mechanisms needed to preserve the socially owned enterprises that the Communist leadership could never abandon. As the economic crisis mounted, membership in the League of Yugoslav Communists steadily declined through the 1980s. It fell from 2.2 million in 1982 to 1.5 million by 1989. The slippage in Croatia and Slovenia was the most striking. With party membership dropping and its leadership divided, only the Yugoslav National Army (JNA) continued as a single institution representing the entire country. By the 1980s, however, the ethnic balancing that had kept the JNA leadership representative had given way to the same domination by Serbs and Montenegrins that had long characterized its corps of officers and noncommissioned officers. That new leadership had preceded the rise of Slobodan Milošević to power in Serbia. Their fateful intersection now impended.

The regional connections that had begun between the disparate regimes of Southeastern Europe by the late 1980s would not resume until after the Communist collapse of 1989 and the wars of Yugoslavia's dissolution. By then, at least, a more comparable and more representative set of regimes would be in place to pursue those connections.

8 Wars and Transitions since 1989

The Communist collapse of 1989 put "transition" into common and contended usage. Since then, as noted in our Introduction, a flood of first-hand accounts and scholarly analysis has poured out of and over Eastern Europe. For our region, however, the larger part of that outpouring has neglected systemic transition and concentrated on the wars of Yugoslavia's dissolution. And here, Western policy from the hesitant European mediation in Croatia to the American-led NATO interventions in Bosnia and Kosovo has received the greatest attention. We pay more attention to the domestic and regional consequences of disintegrating Yugoslavia's several wars. To be sure, they revived conflicting ethnocentric memories from the earlier warfare of the twentieth century. Yet the televised spectacle of renewed carnage and displacement also served as an object lesson that sobered the region as a whole, Greece included, and helped to draw it together. These connections, as much as the settlements imposed to stop the fighting, helped in turn to restart the post-Communist transitions. They had begun badly in the first half of the 1990s. Spurring this second wind as well has been a more constructive connection to the European Union than to either of the Cold War superpowers, one victorious and one vanquished.

The entire post-1989 decade and beyond has thus become another prolonged postwar transition, Southeastern Europe's third reconstruction in less than a century. The presumed reliability of a comparable, continuous statistical record from before and after 1989, grounded in the calculations of national product and income against which other indicators should be weighed, has made the economic shock seem all the worse. Yet even the OECD figures for Yugoslavia and the American recalculations of official data for the other Communist states now appear to have been considerable overestimates. By how much is uncertain. This doubtful data is often used to demonstrate catastrophic drops of one-quarter or more in national income from the last years before 1989. We may be more certain about the pace and structure of economic change from the 1990s forward. The pace did indeed lag, as may be seen in Table 8.1, before moving ahead by the end of the decade. The attendant, equally hesitant structural transformation

Table 8.1   State populations and urban shares, 1991–2001 (in millions)

State	1991	2001	Urban % 1991
Albania	3.26	3.11	37
Bulgaria	8.99	7.90	68
Greece	10.16	10.96	72
Romania	23.20	22.45	55
Yugoslavia*	10.39	10.63	57
Bosnia-Herzegovina	4.38	3.98	34
Croatia	4.78	4.38	54
Macedonia	2.04	2.03	58
Slovenia	1.91	1.96	50

Notes: * Serbia, inc. Kosovo and Montenegro.

Sources: *The Europa World Yearbook 2004* (London: Europa Publications, 2004), *passim*; Robert Paul Magocsi, *Historical Atlas of Central Europe*, revised and expanded edn (Seattle, WA: University of Washington Press, 2002), p. 194.

nonetheless merits comparison to the experience of the 1920s as well as contrast to the long Communist period. Political transitions faced the challenge of reversing statist centralization, reintroducing multiparty elections, and establishing legislative and judicial oversight. As previous chapters have made clear, this concentration of authority was already under way across the region during the 1930s. It advanced during the Communist regimes, increasingly for Yugoslavia *within* its republics.

The post-1989 transitions began with the domino effect of Communist collapse. Down came their one-party regimes one after the other, first in Poland, Hungary, and East Germany, and then in Czechoslovakia, Bulgaria, and Romania.[1] By August 1989 Poland had installed a non-Communist Prime Minister. By October Hungary was no longer a People's Republic nor was its Communist Party able to prevent a majority of members from splitting off to form a new Social Democratic Party. The fall of the Berlin Wall on November 9 spelled the end of the East German regime and, when the Soviet Union made no objection, the end of the Cold War. The next day, Todor Zhivkov was unable to resist demands from Bulgaria's party leadership for his resignation. The Bulgarian Communist Party managed to stay in power but was soon forced to disband the security service (DS), to withdraw its *nomenklatura* from enterprises or unions, and to allow opposition parties free reign. The new parties at least contested the initial multiparty elections of June 1990 but lost to the Communists' reconstituted Bulgarian Socialist Party (BSP). By the second parliamentary elections in October 1991, the Union of Democratic Forces (CDC) won enough seats to form a government. Their leader, Zheliu Zhelev, was elected to the new presidency, to which the prior BSP regime had already been obliged to appoint him in 1990.

The Romanian Communist Party did not survive the overthrow and execution of Nicolae Ceauşescu in the last month of 1989, surely the most dramatic transfer of power in Southeastern Europe. On December 16, ethnic Romanians joined the public demonstrations by local Hungarians protesting the eviction of their dissident cleric from his church in Timişoara. After security forces had killed over sixty demonstrators in suppressing the gathering, mass protests spread into the factories of Bucharest and other cities. Ceauşescu hurried back from a trip to Iran to call his last, ill-fated mass meeting of December 21. Hostile cries from the crowd forced him to abandon his televised speech and then the podium. Finding himself the next day without support from the army and with street protests raging out of control, Ceauşescu and his wife Elena sought to flee the capital. When their helicopter landed for fear that hostile army units were tracking them on radar, they sought out local authorities for protection. They delivered the couple instead to an army post where they were detained.

Meanwhile, in Bucharest, as fighting and rumors of *Securitate* forces ready to restore Ceauşescu spread, the hastily convened National Salvation Front (FSN) led by his one-time rival Ion Iliescu decided on an equally hasty trial. On December 25, a military tribunal took less than an hour to convict and sentence them to death. A firing squad flown in from Bucharest executed them both immediately thereafter. The images of their dead bodies on state television proclaimed the authority of the new Front as the government of Romania. Over a thousand people would die by the time that a confused mixture of resistance from security units and general disorder ended in early January.[2] The new regime's composition left many party members and the Communist economic framework in place, but at least the party was gone.

Albania would not replace its pre-1989 Communist President until April 1992, but Ramiz Alia had been obliged to allow political organization and activity outside the Albanian Party of Labor (PPS) by November 1990. The following month, university students in Tirana organized a strike that forced the PPS to recognize the legitimacy of the newly formed Democratic Party. Without reconstitution, the PPS also won an initial parliamentary election in 1991. It lost the next one and the presidency in 1992 to the Democrats and their leader Sali Berisha.

The collapse of Yugoslavia's Communist regime and the state itself may be dated from the breakup of the last party congress in January 1990. Serbian leader Slobodan Milošević had convened the meeting in Belgrade to assert dominance now that he controlled the parties of four of the country's eight federal units (Serbia, Montenegro, and the two autonomous provinces of Kosovo and the Vojvodina). A majority of delegates rebuffed the several Slovenian proposals to defer the recentralization that Milošević was demanding. When its delegates walked out, Croatia's representatives refused to continue without them. Milošević was obliged to adjourn the congress. The League of Yugoslav Communists ceased to exist.

Lacking any agreement on a country-wide referendum or a single set of elections, new parties now hastened to organize themselves within the republics. Multiparty elections for parliaments began in April. Slovenia unsurprisingly went first, its anti-Communist DEMOS coalition winning a majority of 75 seats. In a June referendum, 95 percent voted for secession and independence. In Croatia, a split within the former Communist ranks allowed the new Croatian Democratic Union (HDZ), led by the nationalist dissident Franjo Tudjman and supported by Croatian emigré funding, to win 42 percent of the vote. In the absence of proportional representation, the HDZ won a near-60 percent majority of seats. The new *Sabor* promptly elected Tudjman President. In November, the winning parties in Macedonia and Montenegro campaigned for staying within Yugoslavia. So of course did Milošević's renamed but hardly reconstituted Socialist Party of Serbia (SPS). It won over 80 percent of the parliamentary seats, and the National Assembly in Belgrade made Milošević President. In Bosnia-Herzegovina, the December elections seemed to offer one last chance to the one party running in all the republics, the Alliance for Democracy formed by the last federal Prime Minister Ante Marković. Despite the initial success of his currency reform in ending the hyperinflation of 1989, the Alliance won only 13 of 240 seats in the republic where no ethnic group had a majority and loyalty to the Yugoslav idea seemed strongest. Instead, the ethnic parties representing Serbs, Croats, and Bosnian Muslims, the SDS, the HDZ, and the SDA, won 196 seats between them.

As former republics declared themselves independent states, the new borders left large Serb minorities in Croatia and Bosnia-Herzegovina. Their memories of minority persecution during the Second World War played into the hands of a Milošević regime ready for its own reasons to revoke that independence by force. Enough paramilitary provocation and open warfare followed to create the disruptive background against which the region's first post-Communist regimes struggled and which entangled Greece in regional conflict as well. As may be seen from Map 8.1, the

Map 8.1 State borders, ethnic majorities and minorities, 1992

Source: Adapted from Paul Robert Magocsi, *Historical Atlas of Central Europe* (Seattle, WA: University of Washington Press, 2002)

Ethnic minorities, 1992

▦	Serbs *(SB)*	▨	Magyars *(MG)*	
▦	Croats *(CR)*	■	Turks and Pomaks *(TP)*	
▦	Bosnian Muslims *(BM)*	▨	Albanians *(AL)*	

☐ For Bosnia, no majority present

— · — International boundaries

----- Autonomous province boundaries

··········· Dayton Agreement lines for Bosnia, 1995

division of the former Yugoslavia by 1992 and the subdivision of Bosnia-Herzegovina by 1995 hardly eliminated the region's largest minority populations. Overall totals for Southeastern Europe, according to Table 8.1, had either declined or barely increased by 2000. Nor had their urban shares advanced beyond their generally low levels of 1990. The shock effect of this latest, and hopefully last, round of war, emigration, and forced migration has at least encouraged the rest of the region to pursue reconciliation and a permanent connection to European institutions during the most recent years.

Yugoslavia's Wars of Dissolution and the Western Response

The first two of these four wars began following the initial declarations of independence from the Socialist Federal Republic of Yugoslavia. Slovenia's announcement came on June 25, 1991, and Croatia's the next day. Western representatives had made hurried efforts to keep the federation together even on the confederal terms that Milošević would not accept. The Serbian leader fastened on the support for Yugoslavia's unity expressed by US Secretary of State James Baker during his daylong stop in Belgrade the week before, just as the Slovenian, Croatian, and Bosnian representatives fastened on Baker's rating democracy over unity if there were a choice between the two.[3] The longstanding American commitment only to the "unity, territorial integrity and independence of Yugoslavia" had come from the Cold War and no longer seemed to apply. British and French diplomacy paid more attention than the US to somehow keeping the country together, but their main concern was also keeping the peace. During the last days of June, it was however the European Community (EC; the European Union or EU from 1993) that sought to step forward in place of the US. Its Commission provided a hasty plan to delay the declarations of independence and restrain the Yugoslav National Army (JNA). Although it quickly became a dead letter, the plan made no mention of military intervention.

Two days after Slovenia's declaration of independence, JNA units tried briefly to secure the republic's borders with Italy and Austria, thereby reasserting federal sovereignty. Its few thousand poorly trained and armed draftees in Slovenia were either surrounded in their barracks or cut off from any concentration by road blocks. These maneuvers were more the work of a secretly retrained and rearmed police "protection force" than the new National Guard. Within ten days, at a cost of some fifty dead, largely from the JNA, Slobodan Milošević announced that the army was simply withdrawing. There would be no further dispute about Slovenia's independence. This now appears to have been his intention, if not that of the JNA leadership, from the start. Unlike Croatia and Bosnia-Herzegovina, there were virtually no Serbs in Slovenia. Perhaps more important to Milošević at the time, his vision of a recentralized Communist Yugoslavia would be more feasible without its most market- and Western-oriented republic. The size and resources of its Serb minority in Croatia did not make its departure a painless alternative. Many of its 600,000 Serbs, about 12 percent of the population, were unsettled by the new Croatian constitution. Its provisions recognized their rights as a minority but not as a constituent people. They balked at the new Croatian flag, which incorporated the checkerboard *šahovnica* used by the Independent State of Croatia in the Second World War. Such symbols and the return of Croat emigrés long opposed to Tito's Yugoslavia made Tudjman's aggressive campaign speeches in the 1990 election campaign seem all the more threatening. JNA efforts to arm the several heavy Serb concentrations from the Krajina, the old Military Border with Bosnia-Herzegovina, to eastern Slavonia and to deny such weaponry from arsenals for territorial defense to the Croats went rapidly ahead. But the new Croatian regime proceeded to obtain their own arms from Germany or Hungary. By August 1991 it was distributing them to the freshly formed National Guard (ZNG).

Two weeks later the JNA, now effectively a Serbian and Montenegrin army, launched an offensive into eastern Slavonia and up the Dalmatian coast toward Dubrovnik. Army support allowed the now autonomous Serb concentrations to establish their "autonomous regions" and to expel any remaining Croats in the process. When battle lines moved in their favor, the Croats did the same. Overall, the JNA's existing forces failed to sweep forward as expected. Its draft call was widely avoided in Serbia, almost completely in Belgrade. Infantry units mixing regulars and reserves proved ineffective. Mortar fire did serve to besiege Dubrovnik, at considerable cost in international reputation. JNA artillery destroyed the larger part of Vukovar, finally forcing the Danube city's Croat defenders to surrender. When Serbian forces executed out of hand a wounded Croat contingent left in hospital, the JNA's international standing suffered even more. The military result of the conflict was nonetheless a stalemate, and both sides agreed to a ceasefire from January 1, 1992. By then, however, some 20,000 people had died, many of them civilians. 250,000 Serbs and Croats had been displaced from their homes. The damage to housing, industry, and infrastructure has been estimated at over $4 billion.[4]

The warfare in Croatia did prompt further European involvement, also bringing the UN into the effort at peacekeeping. Violations of human rights as defined by the Helsinki Final Act obliged the participation of the Conference on Security and Cooperation in Europe. It was the American emphasis on those norms that had finally extended them to Yugoslavia in the late 1980s (see Chapter 7). But the European Community was eager to take the lead. The new Dutch President of its European Commission dispatched a small monitoring mission to the battlefront, but with little effect. After convening peace talks at the Hague between Milošević and Tudjman in the fall of 1991, it had authorized an arbitration commission to consider claims for new state borders and diplomatic recognition across the former Yugoslavia. Under the leadership of France's Robert Badinter, the Commission favored accepting the existing republic borders with attendant minority rights over redrawing them in response to mainly Serbian claims for ethnic self-determination. It nonetheless found Croatia still unqualified because the new constitution failed to offer sufficient autonomy to the large Serb minority. But the controversial German decision to recognize Croatia in December pushed ahead Western recognition. The Serb enclaves in the Krajina responded by formally declaring themselves autonomous regions.

The EC, now divided on its course of action and with no troops of its own to enforce the pending cease-fire, left the UN envoy, the American Cyrus Vance, to broker the final arrangements. The prospect of growing Western recognition for the breakaway republics and the army's failure to overwhelm Croatian forces pushed the Serbian side to agree to a cease-fire in January 1992. The terms demilitarized the Serb enclaves and made them UN Protected Areas. The Yugoslav Army (now renamed the VJ rather than the JNA) departed, and a small force of 15,000 UN peacekeepers, called UNPROFOR, moved in to secure the enclaves' borders. Yet the well-armed local Serb militias within them remained in place to bar the return of any Croat refugees. There they would stay until the Croatian Army offensives of 1995 forced them, and some 160,000 Serbs, to flee into Bosnia or Serbia.[5]

By the time that UNPROFOR was arriving in the Krajina in the spring of 1992, the still more deadly and destructive Bosnian conflict was erupting. Bosnian Serbs, led by the flamboyant psychoanalyst Radovan Karadžić and the SDS, boycotted the February referendum for the republic's statehood. Bosnian Muslims and Croats had voted almost unanimously in favor. Alija Izetbegović, the SDA's Islamic philosopher and activist leader, proclaimed independence on March 3. Although rejecting a European Community proposal for cantonal confederation after initially accepting it, he won Western diplomatic recognition on April 6 and 7. (The US delayed for a day in an effort to deny the Serb side the propaganda advantage of selecting the anniversary of the German bombing of Belgrade in 1941.) Serbian and Bosnian Serb media were however already busy recalling the wartime atrocities that Serbs had suffered in Bosnia at the hands of the Croat Ustaša and the Bosnian Muslim SS Handžar Division (see Chapter 5), as well as Izetbegović's dubious 1983 conviction for "Iranian-style fundamentalism." Under Milošević's disguised direction, the JNA had assembled its considerable number of Bosnian Serbs into a separate new force, complete with most of the JNA equipment and munitions stockpiled there. Supplies and salaries still came from Belgrade. The notorious Arkan's paramilitaries from Serbia had already moved into the northeast of Bosnia the week before diplomatic recognition and begun killing or expelling Bosnian Muslims. After recognition, the Bosnian Serb army pressed ahead with wider expulsions. They also moved into the largely Serb suburbs above Sarajevo to surround the city. Then, in July, the Bosnian Croats declared a separate entity, "Herceg-Bosna." Justified by President Tudjman himself as the area of southwestern Herzegovina that the 1939 *Sporazum* had added to the Croatian *banovina*, the new parastate formed its own army (HVO) with arms and equipment from Zagreb.

The Bosnian Muslims enlarged their own fledgling military force and then removed the criminal elements that were of necessity its first commanders. There followed three years of warfare. The conflict scarred Bosnia, prevented any change in the nationalist leadership in Serbia and Croatia, and brought NATO led by the United States "out of region," i.e., beyond its member-states' borders, for the first time.[6] The dead and missing, far more civilian than military, have been reckoned at 200,000, the forced migration or displacement at over 2 million.

The Bosnian Serbs held the initial military advantage. They used it to take control of nearly 70 percent of the former republic. But they could go no further, inhibited more by their own limitations than the scattered UNPROFOR force of 20,000 peacekeepers who had no peace to keep. In addition, the Serbs' siege of Sarajevo only turned the international community, with its press corps there to share the city's ordeal of shellfire and random sniping, further against them and the Milošević regime as well. The Bosnian Croats also put the Tudjman regime into disfavor when in 1993 its HVO turned on the Bosnian Muslim area in the center. Triggering the conflict was a last proposal from the joint EU and UN International Conference on the Former Yugoslavia. This Vance–Owen Plan had admittedly started both Muslims and Croats trying to increase the majorities to which the plan would have given proportional representation in a set of nine cantons. After its rejection and the subsequent warfare, American and Russian representatives joined with diplomats from Britain, France, and Germany in 1994 to form the so-called Contact Group. Relying on the new US role, it forced the Bosnian Croat and Muslim sides to agree to a confederal union of their two entities, also linked with Croatia as a guarantor.

The war ended in 1995. That summer the Serb side had pressed at Srebrenica. Its forces also held some of the scattered UNPROFOR troops as hostage in response to isolated NATO air attacks. Rather than evacuate UNPROFOR, its largely NATO contingents consolidated their units into secure positions. To eliminate the need for any such embarrassing evacuation and the need to supply American troops to secure it, the Clinton administration opted for leading a sustained NATO air attack on the Bosnian Serb army in September. Still more important, the Bosnian Muslim and Croat ground forces joined with Croatia's army, fresh from its victories in the Krajina. By November, the Karadžić leadership reluctantly allowed Slobodan Milošević to represent them at peace talks in the US, very much on NATO's terms. The resulting Dayton Agreement provided for 60,000 NATO troops to secure disarmament from all sides. It freed Sarajevo from encirclement by the Bosnian Serb army but left a Serb entity surviving behind reduced lines along with enlarged Bosnian Muslim and Croat entities. A European High Commissioner became the highest civilian authority. The Organization for Security and Cooperation in Europe (the former Conference now renamed the OSCE) and the UN High Commission for Refugees arrived to begin the slow process of refugee return. Within the complex of Western, international and nongovernmental organizations (NGOs) that soon assembled primarily in Sarajevo, the World Bank and USAID worked best together and led the way in physical reconstruction. Drawing on the commitment of $7.4 billion from a succession of international donors' conferences, it was largely completed by 2000. Yet market and judicial reforms within the entities and cooperation between them in the Dayton complex of confederal representation made little noteworthy progress. Only the overriding authority of the High Commissioner had allowed the creation of a common currency and vehicle license plates in 1998.

Meanwhile, in Kosovo, further violence was brewing. Kosovar Albanians had expected the Dayton Agreement to provide them some relief from the rigors of semimartial law in Milošević's Serbia. The subject was not even mentioned, undercutting the argument of Ibrahim Rugova, the leader of the major Kosovar party (LDK), that his strategy of nonviolent resistance should continue. Serbian personnel had taken over administration, police, and the judicial and educational systems in 1989. Rugova's passive resistance and election boycotts had at least allowed a shadow economy and full set of social services to emerge. Now political neglect at Dayton fed the rise of a small militant organization of emigré students and previously imprisoned young Kosovars. They called themselves the Kosovo Liberation Army (UCK). By 1998 their terrorist tactics of targeted assassinations had provoked the desired overreaction from the Milošević regime. Reprisal raids and widespread campaigns to force Kosovars out of the capital of Priština and areas of suspected opposition had made some 300,000 homeless by the summer. Bearing in mind the regime's unsavory reputation from the Bosnian war, the international community soon renewed UN sanctions against Serbia. They failed to stop what appeared to be an escalating Serbian campaign to cleanse the majority of Kosovars from the province. In March 1999 the US took the lead in negotiations with both sides at Rambouillet to force Serbian compliance in the face of threatened NATO air attacks. Milošević's representatives refused, and the air campaign began one week later. It continued for nearly three months, doing heavy damage to Serbia's and Kosovo's infrastructure, but little to the regime's military forces and equipment. Milošević made a last, futile effort to gain Russian support and gave up.[7] As the campaign had proceeded, his Yugoslav Army, Interior Ministry and paramilitaries had marshaled 50,000 men to force the flight of nearly half of the 1.8 million Kosovars into neighboring Macedonia and Albania. At least 5000 Kosovars, mainly civilians, were killed in this counter-campaign that the UCK proved powerless to prevent.

58,000 largely NATO troops poured into Kosovo in June. Called KFOR, they replaced the departing Serbian forces and brought with them a UN civilian mission (UNMIK) based in Priština. After a brief appearance by a Russian unit, NATO divided five zones between US, British, French, German, and Italian troops. Their initial success was the return of virtually all the refugees by August. By the end of 2001 the same mix of international agencies and NGOs as in Bosnia had received $2 billion in donor obligations, 65 percent from the EU or its members, in order to fund first physical reconstruction and then domestic governance and reform. With too little coordination on the ground, progress on the first priority fell short of the Bosnian pace. Even less was accomplished on the second, particularly ethnic reconciliation between the 100,000 remaining Serbs and an Albanian majority in which UCK leaders had simply taken over key positions. Elections in 2001, boycotted by the Serbs, put a more moderate Kosovar coalition in power by 2002. Yet the remaining Serbs found themselves either isolated in villages protected by KFOR or north of the Ibar River in territory from which the few Albanians were soon expelled.

Problems of the First Post-Communist Transitions

It has proved a powerful temptation, as already noted, to look at all of Southeastern Europe, the former Yugoslavia in particular, through the lens of these dysfunctional conflicts and massive international interventions in Bosnia and Kosovo. Exaggerated notions of ethnic difference and religious division have grown accordingly. The warfare admittedly revived regional anxiety over such distinctions. Intervention has kept the notion of Great Power predominance alive. At the same time, the domestic struggles to deal with post-Communist and post-Cold-War transition have proceeded on a recognizably common basis. The region's foreign relations are less and less bound to the sort of special bilateral relationship with a single Great Power that was typical, as we have seen, after the two world wars. The Anglo-French financial rivalry of the 1920s (see Chapter 3) has been replaced by a series of international organizations, starting with the American-influenced but independently funded International Monetary Fund and the World Bank and headed increasingly by the European Union. Their "conditionality," if not always coordinated, has offered more in return than the separate European capital markets struggling after the First World War. By the turn of the twenty-first century, multiparty and market transitions were making more consistent progress, with a growing sense of regional inter-relation if not integration.

For much of the 1990s, however, all of the post-Communist regimes save that in Slovenia struggled with several common problems. The presence of surviving Communists under new socialist labels and the absence of proportional representation encouraged confrontation with the new anti-Communist parties. They wrestled with the socialist survivors for the full control of the government that a bare majority would bring. The prewar agrarian parties sought to revive themselves but attracted little support. New parties representing ethnic minorities did better, but their commitment to one majority coalition or another could change. Women's representation declined all around, paying a price for its exaggerated emphasis (with no real authority or attention to gender issues) under the Communist regimes. The early economic transition was an unfortunate combination of hasty decollectivization in agriculture with the slow or corrupt privatization of industry. Foreign direct investment was minuscule. Exports faced lost markets in the Soviet bloc and the Bosnian war as well as domestic difficulties.

By 1998 a growing fraction of the region's foreign trade was conducted with members of the European Union. Yet exports still covered only 62 percent of imports for the seven post-Communist economies in the region, minus Slovenia which by this time had a nearly positive trade balance. Only Bulgaria was starting to close the gap with exports reaching 75 percent of imports. Its trade turnover also climbed back up toward the level of Gross

Domestic Product (GDP) that it had exceeded in the 1980s. Across the region, tourism and other services suffered from the Bosnian war in particular.

Other economic indicators were equally unpromising. Unemployment climbed past 15 percent, over 30 percent in the war zones. Declines in real GDP, catastrophic when calculated from the exaggerated figures for 1989 as noted above, were still sufficient when taken from the more comparable benchmark of 1991 to keep the region from showing any overall advance through 1998. The annual averages for Romania and Bulgaria, despite the absence of warfare, showed losses of 2 and 3 percent respectively Only Slovenia had joined Greece in recording a level of per capita GDP adjusted for purchasing power parity that reached 65 percent of the EU average. The rest lagged behind even the levels of roughly 30 percent from the late 1930s. Only Bulgaria and Croatia came close, and the others fell short of 20 percent.[8]

Serbia and Croatia as Special Cases

The two states most directly affected by the warfare in Bosnia and Kosovo were Serbia/Montenegro, still known as the Federal Republic of Yugoslavia (SRJ, or the FRY in English) and Croatia. Both of them shared one legacy from the former Yugoslavia with Slovenia that has proved difficult for any of them to dismiss. This was the framework of "socially owned" rather than state industrial enterprises. Their status as somehow belonging to managers and employees has survived the rapid demise of the Workers' Councils subdivided since 1976 into the Basic Organizations of Associated Labor. It served throughout the 1990s as a barrier to privatization, joint-stock issues, and direct foreign investment.

Slovenian banking was, however, much quicker to adjust, in part to prevent being taken over by Austrian or Italian interests. Maintaining independence from these two large neighbors had of course been a major reason for Slovenian allegiance to the two Yugoslavias across the century. The Nova Ljubljanska Banka took the lead in rehabilitating itself by 1994 in order to meet Western standards of accountability. Although losing a billion dollars' worth of foreign exchange deposited in Belgrade with Yugoslavia's central bank (NBJ), it also cut itself loose from the nonperforming loans and the obligation to return customer deposits from the other republics. Already, in 1991, Slovenia's new central bank had established a separate currency, the tolar, and held its exchange rate steady through the near-doubling of prices in 1992. By 1994 Slovenia's inflation rate had been reduced to 12 percent. The Slovenian government negotiated a bilateral agreement with the Paris Club of official lenders to the former Yugoslavia to cover Slovenia's share of the debt in 1993. A deal with the London Club of commercial bankers followed in 1998.[9]

Slovenian political life and its economy were, in addition, free from the cost of reconstituted armies, paramilitary corruption, and unchecked intelligence services that burdened both Serbia and Croatia under the Milošević and Tudjman regimes. Those two regimes also took advantage of another unfortunate legacy from the former Yugoslavia, each republic's right to control its own media. In addition, their pre-1989 newspapers, magazines, and television stations had enjoyed a reputation for relative credibility, certainly well above the standard for the Soviet bloc. Now pressed into wartime service in Belgrade and Zagreb, they helped with a few honorable exceptions to spread stories of the other side's war crimes. These in turn were often linked to earlier misdeeds from the two world wars or to allegedly long-standing plans to dominate the other.

In Serbia, the Milošević regime overcame a major economic crisis in 1994 only to face two major political challenges in 1996–7, one from domestic opposition and another from Montenegro, its only remaining partner in the Federal Republic of Yugoslavia.[10] Hyperinflation from October 1994 raced ahead to reach 500 trillion percent, surpassing the record set by Weimar Germany in 1923. The regime had already used inflation to suck up private reserves of foreign currency. The domestic currency's decline accelerated with the subsequent pyramid schemes that several doubtful new banks had used to draw in dinars with promises of high monthly returns. Their collapse triggered hyperinflation. The regime first blamed the 1992 UN economic sanctions that had indeed obstructed legal business and encouraged smuggling and the grey economy. Then in January 1995, as the daily rate of inflation reach 338 percent, Milošević felt obliged to call in a former World Bank official, Dragoslav Avramović, to take over the central bank. He promptly used the dwindling hard currency reserves to establish a hard dinar equal to one German mark.

As economic hardship and unemployment nonetheless continued into 1996, the previously divided opposition parties combined their efforts in September's national and local elections. Their coalition, *Zajedno* (Together), lost nationally but won the local elections in most of the major cities. When the regime invalidated those results, the coalition mobilized huge street demonstrations in Belgrade and promoted a boycott of state television news. The momentum that would overthrow Milošević in 2000 already seemed to be on their side. But this time he escaped, conceding the local elections and pulling back his wife's unpopular new political party JUL from near-equal standing with his SPS. Divisions also reappeared within

Zajedno, divisions that have returned to haunt the belated, still uncertain Serbian transition since 2000.

A more successful turn away from the Milošević regime had begun in 1996 in Montenegro. His loyal backer Momir Bulatović, the republic's President and head of the revised Socialist Party, had appointed a young Prime Minister, Milo Djukanović. The latter soon bridled at the UN economic sanctions that Montenegro still bore along with Serbia, even after the Dayton Agreement. By 1997 Djukanović had mobilized enough support, mainly from the southern core of pre-1912 Montenegro, to oppose Milosevic's selection as President of the Federal Republic of Yugoslavia. He then defeated Bulatović in a special election for the republic's presidency. The road to Western, principally American support opened, if only through the Kosovo intervention. So did the road to full independence, largely traveled at this writing despite a corrupted process of privatization, the disintegration of the pro-Western Liberal Alliance, and continuing opposition from the Serbophile northern territory added after the Balkan Wars of 1912–13. The north's essentially Bosnian Muslim minority and the Kosovar Albanian minority in the south have not surprisingly favored independence. A politicized process of privatization and an increasingly arbitrary ruling coalition, now minus the collapsed pro-Western Liberal Alliance, may however prove to be the greater challenge to an independent Montenegro.

Like Montenegro, Croatia did not find that Western support and separation from Milošević's Serbian-dominated version of Yugoslavia by themselves guaranteed a successful transition to political pluralism and a market economy. Franjo Tudjman and the Union of Democratic Forces (HDZ) were more concerned with consolidating their own power as the authoritarian regime allegedly needed to defend the nation. Their victory in the presidential and parliamentary elections of August 1992 gave them the chance. Tudjman won by an absolute majority of 57 percent. The HDZ benefited from the mixed majority and proportional electoral formula of 1990 to win 62 percent of the *Sabor* seats with 44 percent of the vote. Thus ended the wartime coalition government of 1991–2, one in which the HDZ was already strong enough to take virtual control of state television. But the primary reasons for their electoral mandate in 1992, and by nearly the same percentages again in 1995, were the two successful military campaigns, first to preserve independence and then to retake the former republic's Serb-controlled Krajina. Reinforcing these mandates were now total control of state television and radio. The privatization of newspapers and magazines also allowed regime favorites to take them over. The same process worked more fairly for smaller industrial or commercial enterprises. But a number of the larger "socially owned" firms found themselves "nationalized" as state enterprises. In others, the regime's Development Fund and state-owned banks handed management over to HDZ favorites.

While economic recovery from an admittedly significant amount of wartime damage favored the regime, the Croatian political spectrum showed hopeful signs of resisting subjugation. There was admittedly no revival of representation for the Serb minority, now reduced from 12 to 4 percent of the population and limited to three parliamentary delegates. Already in the local elections of 1993, however, a number of municipalities, across Istria and in Zagreb most noticeably, had voted for opponents of the regime. When Zagreb elected an opposition mayor in 1995, Tudjman refused to recognize the results, much as Milošević would do in Serbia. The regime's support for "Herzeg-Bosna," from its 1993 warfare with the Bosnian Muslims forward, became increasingly unpopular. Minister of Defense Gojko Šušak, a returned emigré from Canada but proud of his Herzegovina family and its world-war allegiance to the *Ustaša*, used his influence to make emigrés and others from that area into a major wing of the HDZ. Then Tudjman followed his 1995 electoral triumph with an embarrassing string of personal interventions. They ranged from the attempted suppression of independent Radio 101, a counterpart to B-92 in Belgrade, to the disqualification of the winner of the Miss Croatia contest for 1997 because she was Muslim.

That year as well, the new International Criminal Tribunal for Yugoslavia (ICTY) had convened in the Hague. The regime resisted any Croatian indictments on the grounds that the "Homeland War" justified whatever was done. Its resistance kept Croatia from receiving European aid under the PHARE program for post-Communist Eastern Europe, just as the $1.5 billion provided since 1991 was running out. This, plus the virtual absence of Serb refugee return, helped to sour relations with the United States. By this time, Tudjman's health was also deteriorating, and the evidence of financial abuses by his family and party favorites was mounting. Several weekly magazines had by this time joined the wickedly satirical newspaper *Feral Tribune* in defying the regime's efforts to suppress any exposure of abuse and corruption.

But it was the collapse of the apparent post-Dayton boom in the economy that provided the blow needed to bring the opposition parties, the divided Liberals and a revived Social Democratic Party, to power in the elections of 1999.[11] The boom had in fact started after the successful stabilization of the new kuna at the end of 1993. From the start, high interest rates had discouraged investment and an overvalued exchange rate discouraged exports. Still, the revival of tourism, the abovementioned aid for reconstruction from the European Union and its members, and another half billion dollars in international lending kept real GDP growing at over 6 percent a year for 1995–7. Then the aid ran down. The current account deficit mounted to 17 percent of GDP and international debt to one-third in 1997. The deepening debts of several state banks and leading "tycoon capitalists" such as Miroslav Kulte now caught up with them. Open bankruptcies followed. The unpaid debts of the regime-favored Globus Group amounted to one quarter of the total for the entire economy. As GDP turned downward by 1999, unemployment rose past 15 percent. Following the death of Tudjman and the defeat of HDZ in December of 1999, however, Croatian political pluralism has encouraged a more open and constructive economic transition. Its beleaguered Serbian counterpart would not make the same progress after the fall of Milošević just a year later.

Hard Roads for Romania and Albania

The National Salvation Front (FSN) took two-thirds of the vote in Romania's first multi-party elections in May 1990. The victory of Albania's Democratic Party in March 1992 enabled its new parliament to replace the Communist holdover President, Ramiz Alia, with Sali Berisha. Yet neither of these electoral triumphs placed its country in a position to proceed with positive transitions. The last decade of the Romanian Communist regime and the prior period of the cultural revolution in Albania had damaged the two economies and dispirited the two societies more than the setbacks and stagnation elsewhere in the region. The road back from the international isolation that the Ceauşescu regime had brought on itself and that the Hoxha regime had sought out would have been a hard one for any successor.

Whether because of the common legacy of Stalinist regimes or the disorder following their demise, both Romania and Albania saw considerable powers granted to their presidencies. Across post-Communist Eastern Europe, only Serbia, Montenegro, and Croatia had followed this pattern. At the same time, both of these presidencies would, after initial temptations, resist reliance on assertions of ethnic nationalism. Here the warfare in the former Yugoslavia and the international criticism it was provoking acted as a cautionary tale. So did the violent clashes between ethnic Hungarians, celebrating the anniversary of the 1848 revolt, and Romanians in several Transylvanian towns in March 1990, just two months before that first post-Communist election. Other sorts of disorder posed greater problems. Rural areas contained larger shares of total population in both countries than elsewhere in the region. Peasant resentment of the harsh terms and backward conditions of collectivized agriculture prompted spontaneous privatization and mass looting. In Albania particularly, much valuable equipment was destroyed in the process. The new regimes could do little more than codify the seizures, in 1991 in Romania and in 1993 in Albania. The resultant holdings were typically small in Romania (under 25 acres) and smaller in Albania (under 4 acres). Still missing was the clear title to the land and therefore access to mortgage credit whose absence had plagued the land reforms of the 1920s (see Chapter 3).

In urban areas, the Romanian problem was industrial unrest and for Albania a mass effort simply to flee across the Adriatic to Italy. Over ten thousand Albanians had succeeded in making the often hazardous trip by January 1990, creating a refugee problem that led to Italian restrictions and also assistance. By 1993 rural privation pushed the urban population up from 34 to 44 percent of the total while the majority of industrial plant still lay idle. The most profitable economic activity had become the smuggling trade generated by the warfare and sanctions in the former Yugoslavia. For Romania, the threat of still worse conditions for workers in the hugely unprofitable heavy industry that Ceauşescu had favored to the end made them potentially volatile. The coal miners of Transylvania's Jiu valley had already confronted him in 1977 (see Chapter 7). In 1990 the FSN was able to mobilize their decent on Bucharest to beat down student demonstrators protesting against its composition. But by September 1991 the miners came in larger numbers to unleash violence against the regime's failure to improve their deteriorating conditions.

From that time forward, the National Front began to split apart and the present political spectrum to take shape. Drawing on one of his aforementioned powers under the new constitution of 1991, President Ion Iliescu made the hasty resignation of Prime Minister Petre Roman stick. The miners' protest had indeed occasioned the resignation as well as subsequent debate in the FSN about holding back market reforms to provide more social support. Although favoring such reforms more than Iliescu, Roman's differences with him were mainly a personal struggle for leadership of the FSN. When Roman won that battle, Iliescu took his followers and the popular appeal that had won him 85 percent of the 1990 vote for the presidency into a new party. Despite or because of its greater reliance on members of the Communist regime, like Iliescu himself, the PDSN, or Democratic Party of National Salvation, won 28 percent in the parliamentary elections of 1992 to only 10 percent for the rump FSN, still led by the former if younger Communist Roman. Iliescu retained the presidency with a majority of 61 percent.

Despite the lack of much access to state television, several other political parties stepped forward to win sizeable support in this election. The only one that had already received a comparably significant share of the vote in 1990 was the Hungarian Democratic Union of Romania (UDMR), 7.2 versus the present 7.5 percent. The largest share among these others, 20 percent, went to the resolutely anti-Communist Democratic Convention of Romania (CDR). Its presidential candidate, Bucharest University Rector Emil Constantinescu, also reached the runoff election against Iliescu. Yet another 15 percent was divided among three anti-reform and anti-Hungarian parties. The two largest, the Romanian National Unity Party (PUNR) led by the stridently nationalist mayor of Cluj, Gheorghe Funar, and the Greater Romania Party (PRM) led by former Ceauşescu associate Corneliu Vadim Tudor, looked back approvingly to the authoritarian and anti-Semitic regime of Marshal Antonescu during the Second World War. Only the smallest, the Socialist Labor Party (PSM) led by Ceauşescu's former Prime Minister Ilie Verdeţ, represented the Communist legacy. All three were nonetheless brought into the coalition government under which Iliescu and his party, renamed as the Party of Social Democracy in Romania (PDSR) in 1993, ruled until 1996.

The reversal of fortune that brought the CDR to power and elected Constantinescu as President in 1996 started with the curiously contradictory record of the Iliescu regime in economic reform and in relations with European institutions.[12] By 1994 it had succeeded in bringing the annual inflation rates of 200 percent since 1991 under control, appropriately devaluing the leu, freeing prices and promoting export-led growth. Trade with Western Europe rose enough for the EU to grant Romania associate status by 1993. Yet this duty-free access helped to push up an import surplus that only a flood of direct Western investment or the restructuring of domestic industry could hope to balance. Neither was forthcoming. Western loans filled some of the payments gap, but the debt that Ceauşescu had ruthlessly eliminated climbed back to $9 billion by 1995. The major banks remained in state hands, leaving a pyramid scheme that soon collapsed to represent the private sector. At least privatized agriculture did better than expected, but the initial privatization of industry extended only to the smaller enterprises. The larger ones, employing the still larger number of workers whom the regime feared to dismiss, remained unreformed in any respect.

Mass privatization by vouchers in early 1996 attracted little Western capital and typically left existing managements in control. They continued to compete primarily through corrupt advantages provided by political connections to the regime. Social support for pensions and unemployment, now surpassing 10 percent, was trimmed in an effort to reduce the state's own budget deficit. In addition to these domestic difficulties, the complaints of the Hungarian minority over proposals such as Funar's to outlaw their political party, the UDMR, prompted the Council of Europe to deny Romania membership until 1993. The regime's reputation with the Council, and therefore with the EU as well, did not improve until 1996. Then Iliescu felt obliged to compromise with the new and more amenable Socialist government of Gyula Horn in Hungary. They soon signed the long-obstructed Basic Treaty between the two countries. The Council of Europe deemed the document's code of conduct and its promises of rights for the Hungarian minority a sufficient substitute for explicit recommendation of special status.

The Iliescu regime's credentials to move further ahead to a full set of Western connections, from membership in NATO to the EU, could not match those of the Constantinescu's CDR in the 1996 elections. In addition to the magnetic attraction of such membership, the CDR benefited from access to the new independent televison and newspaper outlets. A new generation of urban youth, called Generation PRO and known for their transformations of American rap and hip-hop music, used growing Internet access to exchange open criticism of official failings.[13] The presence of some 200 active NGOs, most with Western support, helped to open the political process to a previously inactive civil society. Living standards also slipped in the face of corrupt riches accumulating in the hands of familiar faces from the Ceaușescu era. A plurality of voters now decided to take a chance on a genuine transition to the market mechanism and the framework of European institutions. Iliescu's campaign resorted to newly nationalist rhetoric to make up for the fracturing of Funar's PUNR and a break with Tudor's Greater Romania Party. It lost him the presidency to Constantinescu. His party's share of the vote fell to 21.5 percent versus 30 percent for the CDR. As the Hungarian UDMR entered the new government, Romania took a decisive turn that even the subsequent economic struggles of the Constantinescu government and the return of Iliescu and the PDSR to power in the elections of 2000 have not undone. Enough accommodation to multiethnic as well as multiparty politics and enough economic restructuring was achieved by 2002 to persuade the European Union to begin a process that should lead to Romania's membership by 2007. Already in 2004, a new coalition under younger leadership defeated Iliescu's chosen PDSR successor for the presidency.

The turning point for Albania's transition came in 1997, about the same time as that for Romania and, as we shall see, Bulgaria. Until then, the presidency of Sali Berisha and the regime of his Democratic Party had increasingly abused its victory in the 1992 elections. Fairly won with a 62 percent majority to the Socialists' 26 percent, Berisha began forcing out centrist allies, starting with Gramoz Pashko, the major advocate of market reform. He extended his purge to the small Social Democratic and Republican parties. In part to solidify support among his Geg fellows, Berisha used the largely Tosk leadership of the discredited Hoxha regime and the former Communists now heading the Socialist Party to keep them tied together in public statements. The trials of Hoxha's successor Ramiz Alia and his widow for financial corruption helped to make this case, laying the groundwork for the conviction of Socialist Party leader Fatos Nano in 1994. Berisha also played the nationalist card early on. He charged that the small Greek minority and, by religious association, the Orthodox Albanians of the far Tosk south were seeking autonomy as a prelude to secession. By 1994, however, his effort to write requirements for a 20-year residence for Orthodox clergy into the new constitution helped to defeat its ratification. Helping more was the proposed presidential control of the judicial system. As for Kosovo and its fellow Gegs, Berisha advocated independence but only under the nonviolent leadership of Rugova's LDK. Even this support continued only until 1994, when Western urgings of restraint persuaded him to hold back.

His forced resignation in 1997 came neither from lack of American or West European support nor from an economic record that was through 1996, as judged by the average annual increase in GDP of 5.4 percent since 1992, the best in the region. Only Bosnia would receive more development aid and credit per capita during the 1990s than Albania, whose total in aid alone for 1992–5 was $928 million. Emigré remittances, from perhaps 300,000 Albanians in Greece alone, rose to $350 million by 1995. They helped to cover what remained the region's largest import surplus. Internally, too little income came from the equipment-starved agricultural sector or industrial enterprises. Their privatization by mass vouchers from 1995 achieved no more change in management than in Romania. Too much income came from smuggling and other illegal activities, most of them fed by the demands of the sanctioned sides in the former Yugoslavia. Cigarettes, vehicles, and enough gasoline in 1995 to cover half of Serbia's annual needs were the principal goods. But this corruption hardly seemed the exclusive province of the regime.

Berisha's downfall came instead from his probably unnecessary abuse of the electoral process in 1996, followed by the financial collapse of several pyramid funds. The regime's associates had used them to soak up remittances and illegal gains alike.[14] Despite a likely victory, his Democratic Party used police powers to harass the Socialist opposition and to deny it media access. The Socialists boycotted the May balloting. Their leaders were then beaten up. They unsurprisingly refused to recognize what had become a one-party parliament, with the Democrats holding 122 of 140 seats. Despite American displeasure, Berisha's regime might have survived had it not been for the collapse of first one and then all of the pyramid funds in 1997. As anarchy spread through the Tosk south and rioters broke into state arsenals, Berisha opened those in the north to his supporters. This decision succeeded only in dumping over half a million weapons into private hands, many of them sold or given to rising Kosovar movements, primarily the UCK, across the border. For Albania, however, the consequences were more peaceful, at least in the longer run. After some 2,000 people had died in the resulting unrest, Berisha and his government resigned. They have remained to contest legally for power in the multiparty framework that has prevailed ever since. The Socialist Party has not used its renewed mandate as Berisha, or before him Hoxha or King Zog, to close off opposition.

Both major parties have adhered instead to the terms of the new constitution overwhelmingly approved in a 1998 referendum. In 1999 the several months spent in Albania by 450,000 Kosovar refugees fleeing that spring's Serbian offensive and NATO's bombing generated enough misunderstanding and misconduct between them and their largely Geg host areas to push the appeal of a Greater Albania further into the background. All this, plus a new infusion of EU and US aid to deal with the refugee influx, has allowed Albania to proceed more hopefully into the new century, if hardly yet into the European Union.

Bulgaria and Macedonia as Comparable Cases

Any pairing of Bulgaria and its newly independent neighbor might suggest that the century-old Macedonian question had resurfaced to bedevil the post-1989 transitions in both countries. It has not. Although withholding recognition of Macedonian as a separate language until 2002, the Bulgarian government was in fact the first to recognize the independence of the former Yugoslav republic in 1990. Nor did the subsequent formation of two new VMRO parties in Bulgaria, divided by the same split between unitarists and autonomists as seen in the first half of the century, generate significant electoral support for either group. In Macedonia, the name selected by the largest anti-Communist party formed after independence put VMRO in front of its designation as the Democratic Party of Macedonian National Unity. Its leaders initially spoke in terms of a Greater Macedonia. Yet their irredentist pretensions were directed at Aegean (Greek) rather than Pirin (Bulgarian) Macedonia. Potential claims were modified by 1994 and virtually eliminated by the end of the decade.

There were common features other than the question of Macedonian ethnic identity that justify pairing the two states. A common border is of course one. The presence of significant Muslim minorities is another. Turks still made up 9.5 percent of Bulgaria's population in 2000, Bulgarian Muslim or Pomaks adding another 2 percent. For Macedonia, a larger proportion has come to pose a larger problem, although hardly for religious reasons. Ethnic Albanian numbers, geographically compact and bordering Albania and Kosovo, amount to at least 23 percent of the population. Turks and other Muslims add 6 percent. Yet throughout the 1990s, and beyond for Bulgaria, none of these minorities faced ethnic violence at the hands of the respective Bulgarian and ethnic Macedonian majorities. Large reformed Communist parties renamed as Socialists also came directly forward from the start to win the support of a significant part of the electorate. Finally, both states found their initial relations difficult with Greece and limited with the rest of the region. Both have since become a model for pursuing constructive connections there and with the European Union. Even at the start, they had the advantage of leaders who enjoyed more Western respect than any of the others across Southeastern Europe, the anti-Communist Zheliu Zhelev in Bulgaria and the former Communist Kiro Gligorov in Macedonia.

Zhelev could not, however, prevent the travails of the Bulgarian transition through much of the 1990s. An academic philosopher, he had won dissident distinction by his early expulsion from the BKP and then his 1981 book *Fashizmut*. Its critical study of fascist institutions clearly applied to the Communist regime as well. John Bell called his subsequent emphasis on eliminating totalitarian institutions Zhelev's major contribution to the framework for a peaceful and democratic transition.[15] He championed new laws that replaced the Communist Party's monopoly with free access to political organization, the printed word, and the electoral process. When the first open elections of June 1990 failed give his Union of Democratic Forces (CDC) the majority he had expected, Zhelev again displayed his commitment to a negotiated transition. He left the CDC to be voted President by a two-thirds parliamentary majority that came from the BSP as well as the CDC.

Despite welcoming the CDC's razor-thin electoral victory over the BSP that October, Zhelev now paid the price for his support of the "negotiated constitution" of 1991. The document did indeed delete provisions that would have penalized former Communists or their reconstituted Bulgarian Socialist Party. For this reason in particular, the CDC used its influence to reduce Zhelev's own presidential powers. The lack of wholehearted CDC endorsement also restricted the genuinely popular Zhelev to a second-round majority of 53 percent in Bulgaria's first presidential election of January 1992. His high international reputation still served Bulgaria well in its dealings with the West and with Turkey. He aroused resentment in Greece, however, and not just for repairing relations with Ankara after the Bulgarian Turkish name changes and refugee influx of the 1980s. He also supported the wider diplomatic recognition of the new Republic of Macedonia.

During the domestic course of his four-year term, the Bulgarian transition struggled under the disruptive succession of three ministerial regimes that followed two already during 1990–1. Admittedly compounding their economic problems was a Western debt that reached $11 billion by 1991, unrelieved by several billions more owed to Bulgaria but unpaid from Iraq. There was also the lost connection with a Soviet economy that had previously accounted for half of its foreign trade. The first two regimes reflected the BSP's parliamentary majority (211 of 400 seats) in the elections of June 1990 and allowed the reorganized Communists to bar the way to any real economic transition. Andrei Lukanov, who had headed the first government, was known as an economic reformer in the BKP. The party majority forced his resignation by December 1990, in considerable measure because they had distrusted his proposal for radical price liberalization on the Polish model. In the end he did little but declare a moratorium on debt servicing that cut off further borrowing. His nonparty successor, Dimitrur Popov, cut the state budget and freed the majority of prices but left the structure of industrial and agricultural enterprises unchanged.

The challenge of launching that change fell to Bulgaria's first government led by the anti-Communist opposition. Leading the CDC regime as Prime Minister was Filip Dimitrov, a founder of the environmentalist organization *Ecoglasnost* before 1989, and a strong advocate of removing all traces of the Communist system. Yet the CDC's margin of victory over the BSP in the October elections of 1991 was too narrow, 34.4 versus 33.1 percent and 110 seats to 106, to allow it govern without a coalition partner. Under the constitution's requirement of 4 percent of the vote, the two Agrarian parties seeking to represent a revival of the BZNS and other smaller ones all fell short. The only survivor, with 7.6 percent and 24 seats, was the Movement for Rights and Freedom (DPS). This was the Turkish party whose agile founder, Ahmed Dogan, had downplayed ethnic advocacy enough to keep it exempt from the constitution's ban on ethnic parties.

Despite Zhelev's encouragement, the coalition with the CDC lasted less then one year. Discouraged by lack of CDC attention to lost tobacco exports on which its largely rural members depended, the DPS joined in a vote of no confidence against the Dimitrov government on October 28, 1992. That government had done little either to launch the necessary economic transition or to win wider social support. It had neglected the privatization of industrial enterprises, a process opposed by the new union organization *Podkrepa*, whose support against BSP influence the CDC felt it needed. The regime did concentrate on agriculture. But in breaking up the collective farms and APKs, its "liquidation councils" were charged with returning land to their pre-Communist owners. This difficult process often prevented the present occupants from receiving clear, creditworthy titles or discouraged the profitable division of labor within larger units that had emerged under the Communist APKs or Stamboliiski's cooperatives of the interwar period. The result was too often the same widespread uncertainty about legal ownership and cooperative arrangements that had plagued land reforms elsewhere in the region in the 1920s (see Chapter 3). The relative decline in rural income worked to the political advantage of the BSP, already stronger in the smaller towns farther from the major cities. In addition, agricultural production even for the domestic market declined enough to create urban shortages by fall 1992.

The next government was, like Popov's, headed by a nonparty Prime Minister but beholden to the BSP and its new allies, Dogan's DPS. Liuben Berov, long Bulgaria's most respected economic historian, accepted the onerous assignment. The divided parliament of 1991 remained in place. Berov could do little to prevent the flow of new credits from the Bulgarian National Bank that were making up for reduced budget subsidies to the long-unprofitable metallurgical enterprises and the newly troubled export industries dependent on the vanished Soviet market. As a result, unemployment fell off in 1994 from its peak of 16.4 percent the year before, but the rate of inflation doubled to 121 percent. By December real wages had dropped back to the 1992 level of $95 a month. By then the Berov regime had at least arrested the lev's sharp decline earlier in the year and serviced the rising international debt in full. It also won new standby funding from the IMF to help restore the reserve of foreign exchange. Meanwhile, the CDC was fracturing badly, as Dimitrov took the lead in expelling admittedly contentious factions. And the BSP was coming together under the new leadership of the young Zhan Videnov and his Moscow-educated "Komsomol" (Communist youth) associates.

An apparently resounding victory for the BSP over the CDC in the elections of December 1994 (with 43.4 to 23.2 percent of the vote) put Videnov's cabinet in power. His was the last of these three short-lived and unsuccessful governments. Yet with two new, essentially populist parties sharing 46 seats, the BSP's parliamentary majority was much narrower, only 125 of 240 seats. The Videnov regime tried to govern as though it had a wider mandate, but without a specific plan for domestic reform. It staked its economic fortunes on a revival of economic ties with the Russian Federation and on a regional initiative to draw closer to Greece at Turkey's expense. The first initiative succeeded only in strengthening the illegal links with Russian oil and other enterprises. The second unsettled its coalition with the Turkish DPS. The regime negotiations with the IMF and the World Bank for new credits then failed. In their absence, the mounting number of nonperforming bank loans, some covered since 1994 by new government bonds, sent the lev and foreign reserves into a new downward spiral by the end of 1995. The reimposition of domestic price controls did not stop inflation from jumping up to 310 percent in 1996, taking real wages down still further to $54 a month. Half of the 27 state banks, unprivatized and dependent on the Bulgarian National Bank, had been forced to declare bankruptcy by December. Finally, and fatally for the Videnov government, state export enterprises had bought huge amounts of wheat that summer at a low, refixed domestic price and sold it abroad for much higher prices. But the grain harvest was unusually small, and by December bread shortages in Sofia and other cities brought out angry crowds. Their massive numbers and rising fury forced Videnov to resign. The Socialist candidate for President to replace Zheliu Zhelev had already lost the scheduled November election to the CDC candidate, the young Plovdiv lawyer Petar Stoyanov. Hyperinflation continued and left Videnov's successors dumbfounded. They agreed in February 1997 to a non-party government of "national consensus."[16] So ended the last of these initial post-1989 regimes that failed to finish the four-year term provided in the 1991 constitution.

By April 1997 the first one to succeed had won the largest victory so far in the parliamentary elections that would otherwise have taken place the following year. The CDC, reunited with the Dogan's Rights and Freedom Party, won the first numerical majority with 52.2 percent of the vote. Its 137 of 240 seats dwarfed the BSP and its allies, with 57 seats from 22.1 percent of the vote. The Videnov government had demonstrated that a BSP looking back to the pre-1989 framework had thus made a hard transition harder. Its failings were only partly responsible for the defeat. The restructuring of the CDC into a coherent party organization, tying together the distinct groups whose alliance had first created it, surely helped as well. Much of the credit belonged to the uncompromising Economics Minister from the Dimitrov government, Ivan Kostov. He now became Prime Minister. But credit must also go to the political culture that had emerged in Sofia, Plovdiv, and other major cities since 1989.

Their "blue Bulgaria" was not simply a voting bloc reflexively opposed to the BSP's "red Bulgaria" of villagers and pensioners. It also held the CDC's past disorganization to higher standards. They were being set by reviving attention to municipal government, by domestic NGOs, and by an openly, if wildly competitive press. It was the Mayor of Sofia who was selected to head the interim government that replaced the BSP in February 1997 until new elections could be held. Bulgarian-run NGOs, such as the Center for Liberal Strategies or the Economic Policy Institute, drew younger scholars with no place in the impoverished and unreformed university structure in order to mobilize demands for higher standards. And it was a free press whose largest daily paper, *Trud*, focused on economic issues, as did openly liberal economic weeklies named *Capital* and *Banker*. They all juxtaposed the rule of law and European business standards to the corruption that fed off unprivatized industry and banks. Many of the 7000 state security officers dismissed in 1990 had helped these enterprises to establish illegal connections to wartime Serbia and Yeltsin's Russia. The growing independence of Bulgaria's Constitutional Court at least provided an example for proper judicial standards. Guidelines for internal corporate governance have since come from the demands of an increasingly attractive stock market and an emphasis on business ethics in new organizations such as the Bulgarian Business Leaders Forum.

The central institution in the liberal economic transition launched by the Kostov government in 1997 was the new Currency Board. Composed of economists and representatives of the Bulgarian National Bank, the Board became a new part of the bank. It took the value of the lev away from the open market and fixed it as equivalent to one German mark. Its attendant restrictions recalled those attached to the central bank by the League of Nations 1928 stabilization loan (see Chapter 3) but went further and were more effective. Cutting off the refinancing of unsecured loans from other banks allowed a program of industrial and bank privatization to proceed. Fines for state or management interference in the process were levied, and prices freed from past controls by July. The fledgling stock market now began to list an increasing number of incorporated enterprises, whose growth and independence from bank ownership replicated the promising regional pattern of the 1930s (see Chapter 4).

Progress would hardly be unbroken. Emigration to the West has continued, helping, along with low birthrates, to pull the population down from 8.9 to 8.2 million during the 1990s. More concentrated corruption has remained. The widening economic gap between the major cities and the rest of the country has reinforced the political division between blue and red. Yet the Kostov government was not defeated by the BSP in the elections of 2001 but by a new party headed by Simeon Saxe-Coburg, the former King who had been forced to leave as a boy in 1947. Rather than royal nostalgia, its wider appeal was instead the promise of importing with Simeon a cadre of Bulgarians experienced in Western business. And the turn of the BSP itself to support membership for Bulgaria both in NATO and the European Union signaled that the economic direction taken in 1997 and the attendant commitment to accountable, representative government would be maintained. At work again may well have been the disposition of the Bulgarian body politic and public to favor economic imperatives since the political disappointments of the Balkan and First World Wars.

The struggling new state of Macedonia next door has enjoyed less chance to concentrate on its economic transition than its neighbor or to draw on a work ethic whose reputation was as well-established by its emigrants across the twentieth century as was Bulgaria's domestically. Macedonia benefitted politically from the longer and less-contended tenure of its first President. And Kiro Gligorov, unlike Zhelev, was an economist who had supported Yugoslavia's failed economic reform of 1965, rose to the party's Central Committee in the 1970s, and then reemerged to support Marković's belated market reforms of the late 1980s. Chosen almost unanimously as President in January 1991 by the multiparty parliament elected months before, Gligorov was reelected in 1994. He served his full five-year term before retiring at age 82 in 1999. He also survived an assassination attempt in October 1995 and returned to his duties three months later. Whether criminal elements worried about his interference in their smuggling to Serbia and the Bosnian war zone or nationalists resentful of his accommodations with the ethnic Albanian minority were responsible remains unclear. But one or the other or some combination of the two was surely the culprit.

The key to political stability in the new state has just as surely been the ethnic Macedonians' relationship with the Albanian minority, at least 23 percent, as noted above. Albanian representatives dispute the Council of Europe's 1994 census and maintain it is larger. Roma may now outnumber the six percent who are Turks and other Muslim minorities, but only the Serbs' 2 percent has political leverage in Kumanovo and several other northern towns. The Social Democratic Union of Macedonia succeeded the League of Communists. It had no choice after the 1990 elections but to collaborate with the Albanian's Party for Democratic Prosperity. Only by combining their respective 26 and 18 percent shares could they have prevented the VMRO's Democratic Party of National Unity, with its 32 percent, from forming its own coalition government. Instead, Gligorov's choice to head the Social Democratic Union, the 30-year-old Branko Crvenkovski, was able to replace the interim nonparty government with his own four-party coalition by September 1992. Four Albanian ministers were duly appointed. UN recognition followed in 1993. The promulgation of a promising plan for privatization of industrial enterprises won further approval from the European Community. After inviting a small UN military force (UNPREDEP) in 1992 that included an intimidating US contingent, President Gligorov also managed to steer Macedonia clear of any involvement in the Bosnian warfare.

All of this combined to win Crvenkovski's Democratic Union, now allied only with the small Liberal and Socialist Parties, a sweeping victory in the 1994 parliamentary elections. They won a combined 79 percent of the vote. But the victory was less conclusive that it appeared. Not only was there no ethnic Albanian partner. The rival VMRO party claimed electoral fraud in the first round of balloting and abstained from the second.[17] And there remained the unresolved dispute with Greece. Its government and northern public balked at recognizing a state called simply the Republic of Macedonia with a flag whose symbol from ancient Greece, the Star of Vergina, seemed to stake a claim to Greece's Aegean Macedonia as well.

The rest of the decade did not afford Macedonia the turning point for its transition that we have identified for the other post-Communist states who managed to avoid or move past armed violence. Four years of international sanctions against Serbia from 1992 and then the 18 months of Greece's economic embargo in 1994–5 (until at least the flag was changed) had imposed too heavy a burden on the attempt to introduce a legal market economy. Following runaway inflation, the tight monetary and fiscal policy demanded by the IMF for standby funding combined with continuing external restrictions to push production down. Industrial output fell 40 percent from 1991 to 1995. Unemployment stayed near 20 percent officially, over 30 percent by other estimates. These travails created too large a framework and too many incentives for organized crime for it to vanish in 1996, particularly with the Milošević regime still in power in Belgrade and Priština. Profits from smuggling and money-laundering also found their way into the privatization process that finally began in 1994. It favored insiders and attracted less than $250 million in Western investment. The police force was limited by its small size of 8000 and by low salaries that invited its own corruption. Enough charges of official corruption had surfaced by 1998 to support a Western judgment that transborder criminal enterprise occupied "the commanding heights" of Macedonia's economy.[18]

In the republic itself, the specter of corruption was sufficient to defeat Crvenkovski's Social Democratic Union in the parliamentary elections of 1998. An unlikely alliance between the VMRO and the new Albanian Democratic Party in a coalition led by the small Democratic Party won a majority of seats. The initially intransigent Arben Xhaferi, a Tetovo native returned like many of his followers after some years in Kosovo, headed the Albanian party. The VMRO's leader Ljubčo Georgievski, an aspiring poet the same age as Crvenkovski with a reputation as a strident, pro-Bulgarian Macedonian nationalist, became Prime Minister. The two parties and their newly restrained leaders, encouraged by Vasil Tupurkovski, the last Macedonian in Yugoslavia's presidency who now headed the coalition, promised ethnic reconciliation as well as reform. Neither was forthcoming. The division of cabinet positions on a 2–1 basis soon spread to all state positions. Notorious "10 percent commissions" went to officials approving a comparable division of privatized enterprises between the two parties. Industrial firms remained unreconstructed, and unemployment stayed above 30 percent.

The Albanian proportion in the police and among army officers was still less than 5 percent. The number of Albanian faculty at Skopje University grew only slightly. Xhaferi demanded state status for the new Albanian university opened at Tetovo in 1995 but was rebuffed. Another demand, that the VMRO regime agree to withdraw police patrols from the border with Kosovo, was accepted. Despite this destabilizing decision, the specter of Bosnian warfare, as seen on state television, joined with the small UNPREDEP force to prevent violence. Then China's veto (after Georgievski's illjudged recognition of Taiwan) obliged the UN to withdraw the force in March 1999. Most of the billion dollars' worth of credit and investment expected in return from Taiwan did not materialize, leaving the economy's dependence on political corruption and organized crime in place.

Later that year, the Kosovo crisis and NATO's intervention threatened to upset Macedonia's modus vivendi with the Albanian minority. First came 30,000 NATO troops into Macedonia and then a flood of Kosovar Albanian refugees, expelled by the Milošević offensive that his forces undertook on the pretext of NATO's bombing campaign. Nearly three hundred thousand Kosovars were soon jammed into refugee camps hastily thrown up with some international assistance on the Macedonian border. Others fled to Albania. By August, as noted above, virtually all of them had returned following the Serbian withdrawal of its forces. Milošević's surrender negated what would have been the last of many shifts in population across the region's long century of forced migrations. Instead, an initially small segment of Macedonia's existing Albanian population, swollen by the decade's previous emigration from Kosovo, from Priština and its university in particular, was emboldened. At least inspired if not supported by members of Kosovo's victorious UCK, first a thousand and then two thousand joined a new paramilitary force calling itself the National Liberation Army.

By 2001 its units were defying the authority of the largely ethnic Macedonian police and asserting the autonomy of their northwestern quadrant. The first reaction of VMRO leader Georgievksi was to allow his Interior Minister, Ljube Boškovski, to organize two paramilitary forces of their own, dubbed Lions and Tigers. Skirmishes that summer took some 200 lives and displaced over 100,000 people. An offensive by the republic's small regular army, hastily supported by the donation of Bulgarian tanks and Ukrainian helicopters and pilots, created wider Albanian support for the militants whose legitimacy Western diplomacy had been refusing to recognize. By August the violent stalemate prompted international intervention. American and British representatives led the brokering of the agreement between the two sides at Ohrid with which we began this volume. A NATO detachment of 4000 arrived to disarm the National Liberation Army, and a smaller, solely European successor has stayed to keep the peace.[19]

Ethnic Macedonian resentment over the perceived American lead in allowing the Albanian militants to negotiate has persisted. It feeds off widespread opposition to the NATO intervention in Kosovo and Serbia. But helping the Ohrid Agreement proceed at least to the centennial of the ill-fated Muerszteg program of 1903 was new domestic accommodation. The uncompromising Georgievski left the VMRO leadership, and the party has subsequently split. Meanwhile, Crvenkovski's Democratic Union won the 2002 elections thanks to another unlikely Albanian partnership. This time it was another new party, whose leader Ali Ahmeti came from the Albanians' main paramilitary force, that joined with Crvenkovski's Social Democrats. They formed the "guns and roses" coalition that has at least kept the peace while still struggling with Ohrid's terms for multiethnic representation. Also encouraging implementation are the prospects for the membership in the European Union raised by the recently completed feasibility study.

Greece and the Challenge of Regional Reconciliation

The survival of the new Republic of Macedonia and the post-Communist transition across the region owed some of the second wind that they were both finding by the turn of the new century to Greece. Its government turned from confrontation with Skopje, still short of recognizing any name other than the Former Yugoslav Republic of Macedonia (FYROM) at this writing, to the wider pursuit of regional reconciliation there and in all the capitals of Southeastern Europe. This is well recognized. The less obvious contribution has come from an upsurge in Greece's regional trade and investment, possible only because of a series of fiscal and monetary reforms significant enough to be called a transition in their own right. Together the two turns have also facilitated accommodation with the European Union and independence from the United States.

Movement up from the Macedonian embargo of 1994–5, which David Close dubbed "the nadir of Greek diplomacy toward the Balkans," began in the final months of the ailing Andreas Papandreou's term in office.[20] By that time, both Papandreou and public opinion were ready to accept the obvious compromise: lift the embargo in return for a new Macedonian flag, a revised constitution, and an end to other official statements implying any claim to Greece's territory. By 1996 Papandreou's death had allowed a younger group, headed by Kostas Simitis, to succeed to the leadership of PASOK. They won a narrow victory over New Democracy in the parliamentary elections that September, and a narrower one in 2000. But they maintained working majorities both times thanks to the complex 1985 modifications in proportional representation. Equally important for Greek foreign policy, however, was the general disposition of New Democracy to move in the same direction. The leading dissenter, the Communist Party of Greece, saw its share of the vote drop from 10 to 5 percent.

As with FYROM, relations with Albania and Bulgaria eased, and Greece launched several broader regional initiatives. Both sides of the respective borders were made more open to legal movement and less open to illegal traffic. Conditions for the several hundred thousand Albanians working in Greece, often undocumented, and the small Greek minority remaining in Albania were also relaxed. Greece's military even provided assistance to restructuring the Albanian army after its abovementioned disruption in 1997. That same year, the Simitis regime took the initiative in convening a meeting of the Southeastern Europe's Foreign Ministers in Thessaloniki. In 1998 their heads of government met in Crete. And in 1999 Greece pledged $100 million to the regional Stability Pact put forward by the European Commission and the World Bank in the wake of NATO's Kosovo intervention. Final status for a divided Cyprus still troubled relations with Turkey. Then, in 1999, the aid that each side rushed to the other when stricken by respective earthquakes helped to lighten their bilateral relations and encourage a common interest in regional cooperation.

Growing Greek trade with and investment in all of Southeastern Europe and not just its nearest neighbors offered substantial support to these official initiatives. After a century of limited interregional trade and virtually no capital movement, Greece and, to a lesser extent, Turkey took the lead in making significant increases. Between 1992 and 1999 Greece's exports to the region had tripled as a share of the total, from 4.3 to 12.6 percent. Imports more than doubled to reach 10.9 percent. Macedonia and Bulgaria saw the largest advances, so that 10 percent of their own exports went to Greece by 2000. Still more striking has been the increase in direct foreign investment from Greece, again to Macedonia and Bulgaria in particular. The overall total climbed from $2.5 billion in 1996 to $8 billion by 2004.[21] Projects ranged from telecommunications and oil refineries to soft drink and food processing firms. More recently, the entry of Greek banks into the newly privatized financial sectors has placed their affiliates in virtually every capital in the region, most noticeably in Sofia.

The banks would hardly have been able to play this regional role had the financial structure in which they functioned not changed significantly during the 1990s. Monetary and fiscal reform as well began under the New Democracy government of Mitsotakis in 1990 and continued on the same track when PASOK returned for its second decade in power from 1993 forward. This was what many have called a different PASOK from its first populist decade, increasingly concerned with the market reforms that facilitate Greece's commercial relations within the European Union and encourage further EU assistance. Consequently, support for the "hard drachma" launched by New Democracy's regime of 1990–3 continued even under the second Papandreou regime and even more under his successor Simitis. This policy not only maintained the currency's stable exchange rate but also allowed higher interest rates, nearly to EU levels. They were needed to cut down the inflationary flow of credit from what had been a state banking sector. From 1990 to 1995 the sum of domestic credit was trimmed from 65 percent of GDP to 35 percent, public credit alone from 15 to 7 percent. The state's budget deficit declined accordingly. A variety of opponents, from the Ministries of Industry and Agriculture to small businesses and the Agricultural Bank of Greece, had protested in vain against this contraction. Exporters were unhappy over losing their access to reductions in already low rates of interest. But the rate of inflation also declined, from 21 to 11 percent a year by 1994. By 1998 Greece's monetary and fiscal situation was strong enough to permit the limited devaluation of the drachma needed to join the EU's Exchange Rate Mechanism.[22] The way to membership in the European Monetary Union the following year was thereby opened, albeit a membership now stained by disputed budget deficits.

Crucial to this process of financial liberalization through the 1990s was the privatization of a banking sector previously dominated by state-controlled banks. In 1980 the National Bank of Greece held 42 percent of all bank assets and the five other leading "public banks" another 47 percent. The entire sector included only 18 banks, with the dominant public group drawing more of its profit from services and the state budget than interest-bearing loans. Foreign banks were largely excluded. The new Mitsotakis government of 1990–3 went ahead, with the strong encouragement of the European Economic Community (the European Union from 1993), to facilitate both the privatization of public banks and the entry of foreign commercial banks. By 1993 eight Western banks had opened for business. By 2000 the total was 23. Encouraging them and Greek commercial banking as well was enough deregulation of administrative controls to allow a profitable spread of 3–7 percent to open up between interest charged for loans and paid for deposits. By 1998 nine public banks had been privatized, including the large Ionian Bank. Its merger with Alpha, already the largest private bank in 1980 with 4.6 percent of total bank assets, helped to push the latter's share up to 12.5 percent by 1998. Meanwhile, the shares of the two remaining large public banks, the National Bank of Greece and the Commercial Bank, had seen their shares fall to 36 and 10 percent respectively. The public banks' share of lending fell more dramatically, from half in 1988 to 2 percent by 1999. As for the central bank, the Bank of Greece, it now turned to open market operations with short-term credit only for other banks. In this newly competitive framework, the interest rate for interbank lending dropped from 30 percent in 1994 to the general European level of 20 percent by 2000.[23] For Greece's domestic economy, this access to increasingly available and affordable credit helped the GDP to increase by an annual average of 3.2 percent for 1995–9, versus just 1.2 percent for the 1980s.

For its neighbors in Southeastern Europe, this access was the major reason that the new political disposition to regional interconnection could go forward with significant economic incentives. That those incentives were forthcoming from a financial sector now operating under competitive conditions also suggests that the neighbors' economies and at least some specific enterprises showed commercial promise, enough to justify the considerable credit extended and investments made across the region.

The Last Transition: From Regional Stability to European Integration

The greater promise of the new century for Southeastern Europe is integration not within the region itself but within Europe as a whole. For the 1990s, the greater concern of European political leadership, eventually joined and then dominated by the United States through the NATO alliance, was regional stability. And almost from the start stability was taken to include recognizing the series of states that emerged from the dissolution of Yugoslavia. Their ethnic claims to "self-determination" had never been seriously considered under the logic of liberal nationalism informing even the phrase's famed proponent, Woodrow Wilson, in 1918 (see Chapter 1).

Now the republics' claims won acknowledgment but only within their established borders and with guarantees of minority rights familiar from the League of Nations treaties forward. With political pluralism at the core of the post-Communist transition and the demagogic Milošević regime trying to hold Yugoslavia together by force, the claims of the other republics were hard to resist. Simply stopping the warfare within and across the newly recognized borders, from Croatia and Bosnia to Kosovo and Macedonia, was a principal concern of Western policy. So was a European framework for what were now called human rights for minorities within all state borders. Starting with the Council of Europe's High Commissioner for Minority Rights in 1993, this concern culminated in 2001 with the creation of a European Court for Human Rights. At the same time, economic assistance to the wider region undoubtedly grew in order to prevent further unrest.

The last and most comprehensive effort was the Stability Pact for Southeastern Europe, proclaimed in July 1999 in the wake of NATO's intervention in Kosovo and Serbia. Led by the EU's European Commission and the World Bank, some 40 countries and international institutions committed themselves to promoting democratization and economic development as well as regional security. Its model was the 1975 Helsinki Conference on Security and Cooperation in Europe, now the OSCE. Its funding was far more ambitious, projecting some 6 billion euros to the region within five years. Greece was a donor rather than a recipient. The United States would not only contribute up to 10 percent of the funds but would link its existing association of 11 regional and neighboring states, the Southeast European Cooperative Initiative (SECI), to the enterprise. By 2001, however, that link was slow in coming, and the initial Donors' Conference raised only 2.4 billion euros. A Quick-Start Program had to be introduced to move along at least some of the myriad of projects proposed.[24]

In addition to seeming more like intervention than its professed partnership to at least some of the recipients, the Stability Pact also fell far short of the funding extended during the wartime years. From 1991 through 1999, as noted in Table 8.2, the European Union, its members, and the European Bank for Reconstruction and Development had extended 22 billion euros in grants and loans to the states of Southeastern Europe, minus Greece and Slovenia. The United States provided $4 billion in nonmilitary assistance alone, plus $12 billion of military costs incurred in Bosnian and Kosovo. Adjusted for roughly tenfold inflation since 1945, the total matches only the American assistance given to Greece or Yugoslavia in the 15 years following the Second World War (see Chapter 6). The recent sum does however dwarf the $400 million largely lent in repayable credits for food and refugee relief after the First World War (see Chapter 3). Like the post-1945 total, the largest

Country	Annual average real GDP* growth 1992–96 (%)	Annual average real GDP* growth 1999–2004 (%)	Private share of GDP* 2001 (%)	Trade with EU 2004 (%)	EU aid** 1991–99/ 2001–04 (million euros)	FDI*** 1991–99/ 2001–4 (million euros)
Albania	5.4	6.4	75	89	1,840/1,143	456/773
Bosnia and Herzegovina	n.a.	6.0	40	53	2,957/1,457	203/1,272
Bulgaria	–3.2	4.4	70	56	3,675/2,775	2,292/4,703
Croatia	–1.0	3.6	60	52	2,133/2,328	4,031/4,742
Greece	1.1	4.1	95	49	-------	-------
Macedonia	–4.9	1.4	60	52	1,438/1,216	268/770
Romania	1.6	4.0	65	68	8,176/6,497	5,549/8,173
Serbia and Montenegro	–9.0	4.8	40	43	1,326/4,182	935/2,713
Slovenia	2.7	3.6	70	65	-------	-------
Regional cooperation****	–	–	–	–	517/390	-------
Totals					22,062/20,115	13,545/23,146

Notes: * Gross Domestic Product; ** EU, EU member states, European Investment Bank, European Bank for Recovery and Development; *** Foreign Direct Investment. ****Transferred from EU aid to accession framework by 1998.

Sources: George Petrakos and Stoyan Totev, eds, The Development of the Balkan Region (Aldershot: Ashgate, 2001), pp. 6–7; Milica Uvalić, "Economic Transition in Southeast Europe," Journal of Southeast European and Black Sea Studies, vol. 3, no. 1 (Jan., 2003), pp. 64–75; Laza Kekić, "Aid to the Balkans: Addicts and Pushers," Journal of Southeast European and Black Sea Studies, vol. 1, no. 1 (Jan., 2001), pp. 26–9 and Kekić, "Foreign Direct Investment in the Balkans: Recent Trends and Prospects," vol. 5, no. 2 (May, 2005), pp. 171–90; The Europa World Yearbook, 2004 (London: Europa Publications, 2004), passim; Plan Econ Review and Outlook for Eastern Europe, December, 2001 (Washington, DC: Plan Econ, 2001), passim; Office for South East Europe, European Commission/World Bank, Financial Flows to South East Europe 2001–2005, www.seerecon.org, May 27, 2005, passim.

part went to repairing war damage, providing emergency food supplies or refugee relief, repairing the current account balance, and military assistance. In both earlier cases, the sum of direct Western investment fell far short of the grants and credit provided. This time, according to Table 8.2, the 13.5 billion euros in direct investment was over half of the EU assistance provided for 1991–9. Over 90 percent of that overwhelmingly EU-member investment appeared in the last years of 1997–9. For 2003 alone, direct investment climbed to 8 billion euros and rose past 8 billion in 2004. Just the 16 billion euros for these last two years exceeded the 1991–9 investment total and approached the sum of EU aid for 2001–4, past EU member Greece and new member Slovenia aside. Note the recipients' higher rates of GDP growth for 1999–2004. And by 2004, EU members had also become the majority partners in foreign trade, with over 50 percent of exports and imports, for all the economies of the region save Serbia-Montenegro.

Like the still surviving Stability Pact, however, the overwhelming majority of the funding given to post-Communist Southeastern Europe since 1999 has gone directly to political and economic reform. A smaller share for security has moved through the American-initiated Partnership for Peace, culminating in the admission by 2002 of all states of the former Yugoslavia save Serbia-Montenegro and Bosnia-Herzegovina. By that time, Bulgaria, Romania, and Slovenia had moved from the Partnership into the NATO alliance as full members.[25] Most of the new financial support has come instead from the European Union. It has been aimed directly at the accession to its membership that was also promised as an aim of the Stability Pact. After holding back that prospect from the region's post-Communist states for the 1990s, the EU's leading members now turned to the systematic pursuit of bringing them all in.

By 2000 the EU was extending "potential membership" not only to Bulgaria, Romania, and Slovenia but also to what it called the Western Balkans, Yugoslavia's other successors plus Albania. A joint meeting in Denmark in June 2002 added regional cooperation to the standards for political pluralism and a "functioning market economy" already set down there in 1993 as "the Copenhagen criteria" for future membership. Bilateral agreements for free trade between virtually all of the region's states have indeed been negotiated, with the ironic exception of Serbia and Montenegro, otherwise identified as a political union. In return for efforts to meet the political and economic standards, an new EU program of Community Assistance for Reconstruction, Development, and Stabilization (CARDS) had since 2000 been providing these states with new annual assistance, to total 4.65 billion euros by 2006. Duty-free access to EU markets for over 80 percent of exports from this Western Balkans had already begun in 2000. Meanwhile, Slovenia was advancing to EU membership by 2004. From 2002 Bulgaria and Romania began receiving a variety of EU funding, totaling about 700 million euros a year, in order to prepare them for membership by 2007. Croatia was preparing to start on a similar track in 2005 until delayed by EU insistence that a general indicted by the ICTY for war crimes in Bosnia be handed over to the Hague tribunal.

These Stabilization and Association Agreements represented much more than stabilization. Their emphasis on regional cooperation made it a complement to potential EU membership, not the substitute for membership that it had appeared to be through the 1990s. They offered the chance, by fulfilling all 31 chapters of the EU's famously exacting *acquis communitaire*, to join a single European organization that has tied together the continent's trade, movement of labor and capital, and political standards. We may therefore speak of a broader "European consensus" replacing the narrower "Washington consensus" for financial stability from the 1990s.

Here is a more promising prospect than the one that had confronted Southeastern Europe in the aftermath of the two world wars or indeed immediately after the end of the Cold War in 1989. Then the centralization of individual states' executive powers, identified as "the structural narrative of twentieth-century European history" in our Introduction's citation from Charles Maier, still held sway. Its combination with the largest ethnic group to represent the nation-state proved to be unhelpful if hardly un-European during the 1920s and the 1990s. These two decades also marked the high points of Western political interest and intervention in the region, led by Britain and France immediately after the First World War and belatedly by the United States after the Cold War. During the long period from the Second World War to 1989, the Soviet Union and the US had divided that predominance. The American economic interest in the early 1990s relied on international financial organizations, especially the IMF whose anti-inflationary guidelines lay at the heart of the Washington consensus. Then US military intervention in Bosnia and Kosovo stimulated greater political interest, although narrowly focused on postwar reconstruction there and on stability elsewhere in the region.

The new century begins with Russia reduced to a lesser trading partner and the United States preoccupied with international terrorism and its interventions in Afghanistan and Iraq. For the newly expanded European Union, however, Southeastern Europe now holds center stage. Failure to include the entire region at least within the next decade has become a serious risk to the EU's broader blueprint for European integration, whether Turkey is successfully included or not.

Clouds remain on the region's horizon, although less dark than the ones that gathered during the Depression of the 1930s or under the repressive political regimes of the 1950s. The growth of the major European economies has slowed considerably over the past decade, but no crash is in prospect. The EU's struggle for its own Stability Pact to advance a single monetary union has proved difficult, and agreement on a political constitution harder still. Such an agreement must now include a constructive division of powers between a large number of member states, a common, increasingly assertive parliament, and an executive arm, the European Commission, long criticized for creating a "democratic deficit." The challenge of deepening democratically remains ahead, but we may hope that recent travails over an EU constitution will not derail the broadening of membership beyond Bulgaria and Romania.

In Southeastern Europe, clientism and corruption continue to trouble the executive and judicial branches of government. Paramilitary license has assassinated a Prime Minister in Serbia and threatened the peace in Kosovo and Macedonia. Elsewhere, opposition parties with attendant promises of higher standards are enjoying enough organizational freedom and media access to win parliamentary and presidential elections on a regular basis. Joining demographic decline is a growing gap in income and mobility between the largest cities, the capitals in particular, and the countryside of villages and small towns. With the failure of the interwar agrarian parties to revive, the shrinking but still sizeable hinterland is drawn to old Communist or new nationalist appeals. The devolution of power from the central government's ministries has however reached the larger cities. Witness the importance of their mayors in Greek, Serbian, Croatian, and Romanian as well as Bulgarian national politics. EU guidelines call for a still broader devolution to local government. With the sad exception of the international protectorates continuing in Bosnia-Herzegovina and Kosovo, the rest of the region seems ready if not uniformly able to accept this new structural narrative.

Its successful telling will require that all Southeastern European voices be heard in the democratic forum that the EU aspires to be. This economic and fledgling political framework offers the further promise of a common European institution to challenge the misdeeds of member governments and to preclude bilateral dependence on any foreign power. Here, after all, would be the "great result" that Woodrow Wilson had hoped would come to the "Balkan Peninsula" from the twentieth century's first postwar settlement in 1919. For with that liberation would also come the prospect of full European partnership, a prospect which the broadly representative International Commission on the Balkans foresees within the next decade.[26]

Their recent report calls Sarajevo the right place to celebrate the inclusion of all of Southeastern Europe in the European Union and 2014 the right date. That anniversary marks one hundred years since the assassination of Franz Ferdinand in the Bosnian capital started the war which disintegrated nineteenth-century Europe. In appraising the full twentieth century, however, let us remember the region's considerable European steps, false as well as true, along the hard, war-torn way that this volume has tried to trace.

Notes

Introduction – Transitions at the Turn of Two Centuries

1. The three Ottoman provinces of Monastir, Salonika, and Kosovo also included most of Aegean and Pirin Macedonia (respectively parts of Greece and Bulgaria since 1912 and with Greek and ethnic Bulgarian majorities since the First World War) and all of Kosovo (with an Albanian majority and a Serb minority throughout). It was from the present republic's Vardar region that the Slav majority (its designation as ethnically Macedonian at that time is still disputed) launched the ill-fated Illinden uprising to demand local autonomy and to force some European intervention. Ottoman authorities relied on paramilitary brutality to put down the armed revolt within a few weeks. Over 200 villages were burned and looted, often by Albanian irregulars. These reprisals left 50,000 people homeless in a pattern that Serbian forces would emulate as recently as the 1990s on a larger scale, and Kosovar Albanians, returning after their expulsion in 1999, now emulate on a smaller scale. On the several uprisings of 1902–3, see Duncan M. Perry, *The Politics of Terror, The Macedonian Revolutionary Movements, 1893–1903* (Durham, NC: Duke University Press, 1988), pp. 107–42, and on the fate of the Muerszteg Agreement, Steven W. Sowards, *Austria's Policy of Macedonian Reform* (New York: Columbia University Press, 1989), pp. 16–95.
2. See, for instance, Andre Gerolymatos, *The Balkan Wars* (New York: Basic Books, 2002).
3. The seminal work is Maria Todorova, *Imagining the Balkans* (London: Oxford University Press, 1997), now followed by Dusan I. Bjelić and Obrad Savić, eds, *Balkans as Metaphor, Between Globalization and Fragmentation* (Cambridge, MA: MIT Press, 2002).
4. Frank Boenker, Klaus Mueller and Andreas Pickel, eds, *Postcommunist Transformation and the Social Sciences* (Lanham, MD: Rowan and Littlefield, 2002); Michel Dobry, *Democratic and Capitalist Transitions in Eastern Europe, Lessons for Social Sciences* (Dordrecht: Kluwer Academic Publishers, 2000).
5. See Pridham's Introduction to Geoffrey Pridham and Tom Gallagher, eds, *Experimenting with Democracy, Regime Change in the Balkans* (London: Routledge, 2000), pp. 3–12, and also Valerie Bunce, "Comparative Democratization, Big and Bounded Generalizations," *Comparative Political Studies*, vol. 33, no. 6/7 (2000), pp. 703–35.

6. Claus Offe, *Varieties of Transition* (Cambridge: Cambridge University Press, 1996), pp. 138–44.

7. Eugen Weber, *Peasants into Frenchmen, The Modernization of Rural France, 1970–1914* (Stanford, CA: Stanford University Press, 1976).

8. Charles S. Maier, "Consigning the Twentieth Century to History: Alternative Narratives for the Modern Era," *American Historical Review,* 195 (Summer, 2000), pp. 807–31.

9. Eric Hobsbawm, *Nations and Nationalism since 1870, Programme, Myth and Reality,* 2nd edn (Cambridge: Cambridge University Press, 1992), pp. 30–42.

10. John Lampe and Mark Mazower, eds, *Ideologies and National Identities: The Case of Twentieth Century Southeastern Europe* (Budapest: CEU Press, 2004).

11. David Good, "Rethinking Economic Performance in Central and Eastern Europe, 1870–1039: Old Narratives and New Evidence," in Werner Baer and Joseph Love, eds, *Liberalization and its Consequences, A Comparative Perspective on Latin America and Eastern Europe* (Northampton, MA: Edward Elgar, 2000), pp. 42–65, and Valerie Bunce, *Subversive Institutions, The Design and Destruction of Socialism and the State* (Cambridge: Cambridge University Press, 1999).

1 Balkan States and Borderlands before the Balkan Wars

1. For a comprehensive review of the available record, see Michael Palairet, *The Balkan economies c.1800–1914, Evolution without development* (Cambridge: Cambridge University Press, 1997), pp. 3–33.

2. See Suiyana Faroqhi, Bruce McGowan, Donald Quataert and Sevket Pamuk, *An Economic and Social History of the Ottoman Empire, 1600–1914,* vol. II (Cambridge: Cambridge University Press, 1994). On the military border, see Karl Kaser, *Freier Bauer und Soldat, Die Militaerisierung der agrarischen Gesellschaft an der kroatischen-slavonischen Militaergrenze, 1535–1881* (Vienna: Bohlau Verlag, 1997).

3. John R. Lampe, *Yugoslavia as History, Twice There Was a Country,* 2nd edn (Cambridge: Cambridge University Press, 2000), pp. 20–38. For a broader view, see Karen Barkey, "Thinking About the Consequences of Empire," in Karen Barkey and Mark Van Hagen, *After Empire, Multiethnic Societies and Nation-Building, The Soviet Union, the Russian, Ottoman and Habsburg Empires* (Boulder, CO: Westview Press, 1997), pp. 9–114.

4. Francis W. Carter, ed., *An Historical Geography of the Balkans* (London: Seminar Press, 1972), pp. 6–10.

5. A good brief account of the Balkan diplomacy of the 1870s remains Charles and Barbara Jelavich, *The Establishment of the Independent Balkan National States, 1804–1920* (Seattle, WA: University of Washington Press, 1977), pp. 141–57; For the flavor of the Berlin meeting, see Misha Glenny, *The Balkans, Nationalism, War and the Great Powers, 1804–1999* (New York: Viking Penguin, 2000), pp. 135–51, and for the wider nineteenth century, Stevan K. Pavlowitch, *A History of the Balkans 1804 1945* (London: Longman, 1999), pp. 23–161.

6. For a brief account and wider references, see Lampe, *Yugoslavia as History*, pp. 71–91.
7. On Serbia, see Wayne S. Vucinich, *Serbia Between East and West, The Events of 1903–1908* (Stanford, CA: Stanford University Press, 1954), and, on Montenegro, John D. Treadway, *The Falcon and the Eagle: Montenegro and Austria–Hungary, 1908–1914* (West Lafayette, IN: Purdue University Press, 1983).
8. Richard C. Hall, *Bulgaria's Road to the First World War* (New York: Columbia University Press, East European Monographs, 1996), pp. 9–54; Richard J. Crampton, *A History of Bulgaria, 1878–1918* (New York: Columbia University Press, East European Monographs, 1983), pp. 287–346; Keith Hitchins, *Rumania, 1866–1947* (Oxford: Clarendon Press, 1994), pp. 90–154.
9. Mark Mazower, "The Messiah and the Bourgeoisie: Venizelos and Politics in Greece, 1909–1912," *The Historical Journal*, vol. 35, no. 4 (Dec., 1992), pp. 885–904.
10. Thanos Veremis, *The Greek Military in Politics, From Independence to Democracy* (Montreal: Black Rose Books, 1997), pp. 45–9, and, more broadly, John Koliopolis, *Brigands with a Cause, Brigandage and Irridentism in Modern Greece, 1821–1912* (Oxford: Clarendon Press, 1987), pp. 227–325.
11. Philip G. Eidelberg, *The Great Romanian Peasant Revolt of 1907, The First Modern Jacquerie* (Leiden: E. J. Brill, 1974).
12. John R. Lampe and Marvin R. Jackson, *Balkan Economic History, 1550–1950, From Imperial Borderlands to Developing Nations* (Bloomington, IN: Indiana University Press, 1982), pp. 159–201. On the poor agricultural performance of the pre-1914 Ottoman Balkans, Habsburg Bosnia and the independent states minus Romania, descending in that order, see Palairet, *The Balkan economies*, pp. 173–242, 298–346.
13. Lampe and Jackson, *Balkan Economic History*, pp. 282–302.
14. *Ibid.*, pp. 203–77.
15. John R. Lampe, "Modernization and Social Structure: The Case of the Pre-1914 Balkan Capitals," *Southeastern Europe*, vol. 5, pt. 2 (1979), pp. 11–32.
16. Palairet, *The Balkan economies*, p. 231.
17. Marin Pundev, *Bulgaria in American Perspective* (New York: Columbia University Press, East European Monographs, 1994).
18. David A. Norris, *In the Wake of the Balkan Myth, Questions of Identity and Modernity*, (New York: St. Martin's, 1999), pp. 93–4.
19. Charles Jelavich, *South Slav Nationalisms, Textbooks and Yugoslavism before 1914* (Columbus, OH: Ohio State University Press, 1991), pp. 37–40, 161, 240–1. On Skerlić generally, see Jelena Milojković-Djurić, *Tradition and Avant-Garde Literature and Arts in Serbian Culture, 1900–1918* (New York: Columbia University Press, East European Monographs, 1981), pp. 120–68.
20. Gerasimos Augostinos, *Consciousness and History: National Critics of Greek Society, 1897–1914* (New York: Columbia University Press, East European Monographs, 1977), pp. 84–116.
21. Irina Livezeanu, *Cultural Politics in Greater Romania, Regionalism, Nation Building and Ethnic Struggle, 1918–1930* (Ithaca, NY: Cornell University Press, 1995),

pp. 31–2; more broadly, see Nicholas M. Nagy-Talevera, *Nicolae Iorga, A Biography* (Oxford: The Center for Romanian Studies, 1998), pp. 69–183.

22. Mark Biondich, *Stjepan Radić, the Croat Peasant Party and the Politics of Mass Mobilization, 1904–1928* (Toronto: University of Toronto Press, 2000), pp. 62–119; Nicholas Miller, *Between Nation and State, Serbian Politics in Croatia Before the First World War* (Pittsburgh, PA: University of Pittsburgh Press, 1997).

23. Hitchins, *Rumania 1866–1947*, 1994, pp. 202–30.

24. Miranda Vickers, *The Albanians*, New York: I. B. Tauris, 1997), pp. 33–52; Anastasia N. Karakasidou, *Fields of Wheat, Hills of Blood, Passages to Nationhood in Greek Macedonia, 1870–1990* (Chicago: University of Chicago Press, 1997), p. 117; Mark Mazower, *Salonica, City of Ghosts, Christians, Muslims and Jews, 1430–1950* (New York: Alfred A. Knopf, 2005), pp. 255–77.

25. Lampe and Jackson, *Balkan Economic History*, 234; Richard C. Hall, *The Balkan Wars, 1912–13, Prelude to the First World War* (London: Routledge, 2002), pp. 16–19: Koliopoloulos, *Brigands with a Cause*, pp. 49–51.

2 Balkan Wars, First World War, Postwar Settlements, 1912–1922

1. Richard C. Hall, *The Balkan Wars, 1912–1913, Prelude to the First World War* (London: Routledge, 2000), p. 13. Also see Karin Boeckh, *Von den Balkankriegen zum Ersten Weltkrieg* (Munich: R. Oldenbourg Verlag, 1996).

2. Anxious for the Pope's acceptance of his conversion for Bulgarian legitimacy from Catholic to Orthodox, Ferdinand saw a joint ceremony for the two Christian faiths in the great church whose construction had preceded the split of 1054 as an added reason to pursue his "Byzantine dream." See Stephen Constant, *Foxy Ferdinand, Tsar of Bulgaria* (New York: Franklin Watts, 1980), pp. 153–74.

3. Richard C. Hall, *Bulgaria's Road to the First World War* (New York: Columbia University Press, East European Monographs, 1996), pp. 208–70.

4. On the role of all of the powers before and during the First World War, see Marian Kent, ed., *The Great Powers and the End of the Ottoman Empire* (London: Frank Cass, 1994).

5. Hall, *The Balkan Wars*, pp. 132–5.

6. Their report was republished by the Carnegie Endowment in 1993 as *The Other Balkan Wars*. The original is *Report of the International Commission to Inquire into the Causes and Conduct of the Balkan Wars* (Washington, DC: Carnegie Endowment for International Peace, 1914). On the respective abuses by Bulgarian, Greek, and Serbian troops against each other's perceived nationals, see pp. 78–107, 135–47, 160–200.

7. Stephen P. Ladas, *The Exchange of Minorities Bulgaria, Greece and Turkey* (New York: Macmillan, 1932), pp. 15–23.

8. On Greek pressures, see Anastasia Karakasidou, "Transforming Identity, Constructing Consciousness: Coercion and Hegemony in Northern Greece," in Victor Roudometof, ed., *The Macedonian Question, Culture, Historiography*

Politics (New York: Columbia University Press, East European Monographs, 2000), pp. 55–78. On Serbian pressures in Kosovo, see Noel Malcolm, *Kosovo, A Short History* (New York: New York University Press, 2000), pp. 249–58.

9. A similar Italo-Austrian ultimatum to Greece two weeks later, with no German objection in either case, signaled the predominance of alliance-bound Balkan policies for the powers' last prewar year. On the importance of the Albanian issue in breaking down the European Concert, see R. J. Crampton, *The Hollow Detente, Anglo-German Relations in the Balkans, 1911–1914* (London: George Prior, 1981), pp. 112–66.

10. The revival of those exclusively Serbian memories in late- and post-Tito Yugoslavia may be seen in the wide popularity of the four novels–historical narratives tracing the victories of 1914 and the final retreat of 1915 written by Dobrica Ćosić, then Communist dissident and later President of rump Yugoslavia, 1991–94. The three published in English translation are *A Time of Death, Reach to Eternity,* and *South to Destiny* (New York: Harcourt, Brace Jovanovich, 1978, 1980, 1981).

11. A detached treatment of these campaigns as military history may be found in Holger H. Hartwig, *The First World War, Germany and Austria-Hungary, 1914–1918* (London: Arnold, 1998), pp. 82–111, and on the Serbian retreat of 1915, pp. 157–9.

12. See John R. Lampe, *Yugoslavia as History, Twice There Was a Country*, 2nd edn (Cambridge: Cambridge University Press, 2000), pp. 102–3, and, more broadly, Andrej Mitrović, *Serbia's Great War, 1914–1918* (London: Hurst, 2007).

13. David L. Stevenson, *The First World War and International Politics* (Oxford: Clarendon Press, 1991), pp. 59–61.

14. The classic study is Alan Palmer's so titled *The Gardeners of Salonika* (New York: Simon and Schuster, 1965).

15. Keith Hitchins, *Rumania, 1866–1947* (London: Oxford University Press, 1994), p. 257, and, more broadly on Romania in the First World War, pp. 252–78.

16. This is well argued by V. N. Vinogradov, "Romania in the First World War: The Years of Neutrality," *International History Review*, XIV, 3 (1992), pp. 441–60.

17. Catherine Durandin, "Rumania, the War and the Army, 1914–1930," *War and Society*, vol. 3, no. 2 (1985), pp. 50–3; Glenn E. Torrey, "Romania in the First World War: The Years of Engagement, 1916–1918," *International History Review*, XIV, 3 (1992), pp. 462–79, and, more broadly, his *Romania and World War I, A Collection of Studies* (Oxford: Center for Romanian Studies, 1998).

18. Thanos Veremis, *The Greek Military in Politics from Independence to Democracy* (Montreal: Black Rose Books, 1997), pp. 64–9. On Greece from the Balkan Wars to the Anatolian disaster, a balanced overview is Richard Clogg, *A Concise History of Greece*, 2nd edn (Cambridge: Cambridge University Press, 2002), pp. 77–97.

19. John R. Lampe, *The Bulgarian Economy in the Twentieth Century* (London: Croom Helm, 1986), pp. 42–5.

20. R. J. Crampton, *Bulgaria, 1878–1918* (New York: Columbia University Press, 1983), pp. 452–4, 491–500. The most detailed account is Vera Katsaıkova,

"Ograbvaneto na Bulgariia ot germanskite imperializum," *Trudove na V.I.I. Karl Marx*, vol. II (1969), pp. 164–223.

21. Lampe, *Yugoslavia as History*, pp. 106–10.

22. Bernd Juergen Fischer, *King Zog and the Struggle for Stability in Albania* (New York: Columbia University Press, East European Monographs, 1984), pp. 5–40.

23. Ramadan Marmullaku, *Albania and the Albanians* (New York: Archon Books, 1975), pp. 32–5; Miranda Vickers, *The Albanians* (London: I. B. Tauris, 1997), pp. 91–8.

24. The classic study of the Romanian settlement remains Sherman D. Spector, *Rumania at the Paris Peace Conference* (New York: Bookman Associates, 1962). On the American role across the region, see Arthur Walworth, *Wilson and His Peacemakers, American Diplomacy at the Paris Peace Conference, 1919* (New York: W. W. Norton, 1986), pp. 443–67.

25. Mark Cornwall, *The Undermining of Austria–Hungary, The Battle for Hearts and Minds* (New York: St. Martin's, 2000), pp. 179–207. On the role of Seton-Watson and Steed throughout, see Hugh and Christopher Seton-Watson, *The Making of a New Europe, R. W. Seton Watson and the last years of Austria–Hungary* (Seattle, WA: University of Washington Press, 1976).

26. Lampe, *Yugoslavia as History*, pp. 105–6.

27. Janko Pleterski, "The Southern Slav Question," in Mark Cornwall, ed., *The Last Years of Austria–Hungary* (Exeter: University of Exeter Press, 2000), pp. 135–45; Andrew Wachtel, "Culture in the South Slav Lands, 1914–1918," in Aviel Roshwald and Richard Stites, *European Culture in the Great War, The Arts, Entertainment and Propaganda, 1914–1918* (Cambridge: Cambridge University Press, 2002), pp. 193–214.

28. On the Italian claims and pressures, see Dennison Rusinow, *Italy's Austrian Heritage, 1919–1946* (London: Oxford University Press, 1969), pp. 15–50, and Dragoljub Živojinović, *America, Italy and the Birth of Yugoslavia, 1917–1919* (Boulder, CO: East European Monographs, 1972).

29. On the Agrarians, see John D. Bell, *Peasants in Power, Alexander Stamboliiski and the Bulgarian Agrarian National Union, 1899–1923* (Princeton, NJ: Princeton University Press, 1977), pp. 85–153. On the Communists, see Lucien Karchmar, "Communism in Bulgaria, 1918–1921," in Ivo Banac, ed., *The Effects of World War I: The Rise of the Communist Parties in East Central Europe, 1918–1921* (New York: Atlantic Research, East European Monographs, 1983), pp. 231–77.

30. National Archives of the United States (NAUS), M 1207/1, 874.00, reports of February 22, August 26, October 12, and November 19, 1919, and March 6, May 21, and September 2, 1920.

31. For a concise description of the Anatolian expedition and expulsion, with emphasis on the British role, see David Fromkin, *A Peace to End All Peace, The Fall of the Ottoman Empire and the Creation of the Modern Middle East* (New York: Henry Holt, 1989), pp. 540–57.

32. On the Lausanne Convention in particular, see Kalliopi K. Koufa and Constantinos Svolopoulos, "The Compulsory Exchange of Populations Between Greece and Turkey. The Settlement of Minority Questions at the Conference of

Lausanne, 1923," in Paul Smith et al., eds, *Ethnic Groups in International Relations*, vol. V (New York: New York University Press, 1991), pp. 275–308, and Ladas, *The Exchange of Minorities*, pp. 338–52.

33. John S. Koliopoulos and Thanos M. Veremis, *Greece The Modern Sequel, From 1831 to the Present* (New York: New York University Press, 2002), p. 126.

3 Struggling with Liberal and National Transitions in the 1920s

1. Arthur S. Link, *The Deliberations of the Council of Four*, vol. I (Princeton, NJ: Princeton University Press, 1992), p. 283.

2. Legislation to reduce tariffs, deter monopoly, and establish an autonomous central bank had distinguished Wilson's first term as President. His New Freedom was a reform program that was explicitly called "liberal" rather than "progressive." It favored "regulated competition" over the "regulated monopoly" that he charged the rival Progressive and Socialist Parties with supporting in the election of 1912 that won him the Presidency. For a brief appraisal well informed by the continuing flow of scholarship on Wilson, see John A. Thompson, *Woodrow Wilson, Profiles in Power* (London: Pearson Education, 2002), pp. 65–78.

3. On Wilson's primary concern with the League and the problems encountered by him and his academic advisors over border questions and minority demands, see Arthur Walworth, *Wilson and His Peacemakers, American Diplomacy at the Paris Peace Conference, 1919* (New York: W. W. Norton, 1986), pp. 181–98, 435–84.

4. On the privatization and decentralization of American foreign policy in the 1920s, see Mark R. Brawley, *Liberal Leadership, Great Powers and Their Challengers in Peace and War* (Ithaca, NY: Cornell University Press, 1993), pp. 150–6.

5. James Barros, *The Corfu Incident, 1923* (Princeton, NJ: Princeton University Press, 1965) and Stefan Troebst, *Mussolini, Makedonien und die Maechte, 1922–1930* (Cologne: Bohlau Verlag, 1987).

6. On Norman's initiative, see Robert W. D. Boyce, *British Capitalism at the Crossroads, 1919–1932* (Cambridge: Cambridge University Press, 1987), pp. 39–47, and on the role of Emile Moreau, Governor of the Bank of France in the Romanian case, Kenneth Moure, "French Money Doctors in the 1920s," in Marc Flandreau, ed., *Money Doctors, The Experience of International Financial Advising, 1850–2000* (London: Routledge, 2003), pp. 138–65. On the failings of the restored gold exchange standard, see Barry Eichengreen, *Golden Fetters, The Gold Standard and the Great Depression, 1919–1939* (London: Oxford University Press, 1992), pp. 155–209.

7. On rail networks, see David Turnock, *Eastern Europe, An Historical Geography, 1815–1945* (London: Routledge, 1989), pp. 284–8.

8. John R. Lampe, "Unifying the Yugoslav Economy, 1918–1921," in Dimitrije Djordjevic, *The Creation of Yugoslavia, 1914–1918* (Santa Barbara, CA: ABC Clio Press, 1980), pp. 139–56.

9. Charles H. Feinstein, Peter Temin, Gianni Toniolo, *The European Economy Between the Wars* (London: Oxford University Press, 1997), p. 57, Fig. 4.1.

10. The most useful summary of the reforms and their impact for these three countries and Albania as well is Wojciech Roszkowsi, *Land Reforms in East Central Europe after World War One* (Warsaw: PAN, 1995), pp. 106–73.

11. This analysis derives from John R. Lampe and Marvin R. Jackson, *Balkan Economic History 1550–1950, From Imperial Borderlands to Developing Nations* (Bloomington, IN: Indiana University Press, 1982), p. 343, Table 10.6, and pp. 351–75.

12. See Table 10.13 on trade direction and Table 11.10 on tariff levels in Lampe and Jackson, *Balkan Economic History*, pp. 366 and 412–13.

13. Ibid., pp. 402–33.

14. On the British financial initiative, see Philip L. Cotrell, "Norman, Strakosch and the Development of Central Banking: From Conception to Practice, 1919–1924," in Philip L. Cottrell, ed., *Rebuilding the Financial System in Central and Eastern Europe, 1918–1994* (Brookfield, VT: Ashgate, 1994), pp. 29–74; on Bulgaria, Roumen Avramov, "Advising, Conditionality and Culture: Money Doctors in Bulgaria, 1900–2000," in Flandreau, ed., *Money Doctors*, pp. 190–216; on Greece, Mark Mazower, *Greece and the Interwar Economic Crisis* (Oxford, Clarendon Press, 1991), pp. 90–141.

15. Lampe and Jackson, *Balkan Economic History*, pp. 394–401.

16. George Th. Mavrogordatos, *Stillborn Republic, Social Coalitions and Party Strategies in Greece, 1922–1936* (Berkeley, CA: University of California Press, 1983), pp. 1–110.

17. Bernd J. Fischer, "Fan Noli and the Albanian Revolution of 1924," *East European Quarterly*, XXII, 2 (June, 1988), pp. 147–58.

18. Bernd J. Fischer, *King Zog and the Struggle for Stability in Albania* (New York: Columbia University Press, East European Monographs, 1984), pp. 76–81, 102–54.

19. Ibid., pp. 82–100. For an analysis of the limited class structure in Zogu's Albania and a review of Western scholarship, see Michael Schmidt-Neke, *Entstehung and Ausbau der Koenigsdiktatur in Albanien (1912–1939)* (Munich: R. Oldenbourg Verlag, 1987), pp. 280–304.

20. This is the recent and revised judgment of Bernd Fischer, in his "Perceptions and Reality in 20th Century Albanian Military Prowess," in Stephanie Schwander-Sievers and Bernd J. Fischer, eds, *Albanian Identities, Myth and History* (Bloomington, IN: Indiana University Press, 2002), pp. 134–42.

21. The best summary of the Agrarian initiatives remains John D. Bell, *Peasants in Power, Alexander Stamboliski and the Bulgarian Agrarian National Union, 1899–1923* (Princeton, NJ: Princeton University Press, 1977), pp. 154–83.

22. See Joseph Rothschild, *The Communist Party of Bulgaria, Origins and Development, 1883–1936* (New York: Columbia University Press, 1959), pp. 85–151.

23. George C. Logio, *Bulgaria Past and Present* (New York: ANS Press, 1971 reprint from 1936), pp. 43–7. On the increasingly constitutive rule of Tsar Boris, see

Stefane Groueff, *Crown of Thorns, The Reign of King Boris of Bulgaria, 1918–1943*
(Lanham, MD: Madison Books, 1978), pp. 67–162. A more critical and compre-
hensive but still positive study of Boris is the well-documented volume of Nedyu
Nedev, *Tsar Boris: Biografiia* (Sofia: Petar Beron, 2004).

24. See James Barros, *The League of Nations and the Great Powers, The Greek-
Bulgarian Incident, 1925* (Oxford: Clarendon Press, 1970).

25. Mavrogordatos, *Stillborn Republic*, pp. 28–43, 351–2 on the 1920s elections,
pp. 75–93 on the respective parties, and pp. 182–225 on the role of refugees.

26. The most comprehensive survey remains Dimitri Pentzopoulos, *The Balkan
Exchange of Minorities and its Impact on Greece* (The Hague: Mouton, 1962; repr.
London: Hurst, 2003), pp. 75–219. A useful review of the Commission's organi-
zation and activities from its American Chairman, 1926–30, is Charles B. Eddy,
Greece and the Greek Refugees (London: George, Allen & Unwin, 1931).

27. Ronald A. Helin, "The Volatile Administrative Map of Rumania," *Annals of the
Association of American Geographers*, vol. 57, no. 3 (Sept., 1967), pp. 486–91.

28. Keith Hitchins, *Rumania, 1866–1947* (Oxford: Clarendon Press, 1994), pp.
382–416, provides a judicious summary.

29. Maurice Pearton, *Oil and the Romanian State, 1895–1948* (London: Oxford
University Press, 1970), pp. 73–95.

30. Irina Livezeanu, *Cultural Politics in Greater Romania, Regionalism, Nation Building and Ethnic Struggle, 1918–1930* (Ithaca, NY: Cornell University Press, 1995),
pp. 34–48, 140–68, 221–3.

31. Hitchins, *Rumania, 1866–1947*, p. 414.

32. The following account is largely drawn from John R. Lampe, *Yugoslavia as
History, Twice There Was a Country*, 2nd edn (Cambridge: Cambridge Univer-
sity Press, 2000), pp. 129–62. Also see Charles A. Beard and George Radin, *The
Balkan Pivot: Yugoslavia* (New York: Macmillan, 1929).

33. Mark Biondich, *Stjepan Radić, the Croat Peasant Party, and the Politics of Mass
Mobilization, 1904–1928* (Toronto: University of Toronto Press, 2000), pp.
159–244.

34. See Vladan Jovanović, *Jugoslovenska država i južna Srbija, 1918–1929* (The
Yugoslav State and South Serbia, 1918–1929), Belgrade: INIS, 2002), pp. 177–226
on the gendarmerie, armed conflict and Serbian settlers, and pp. 309–39 on
educational limits.

35. Charles Jelavich, "Education, Textbooks and South Slav Nationalisms in the
Interwar Era," in Norbert Reiter and Holm Sundhaussen, eds, *Allgemeinbildung
als Modernizierungsfaktor* (Berlin: Harrasowitz Verlag, 1994), pp. 127–42.

36. See John S. Koliopoulis and Thanos M Veremis, *Greece, The Modern Sequel, From
1831 to the Present* (New York: New York University Press, 2002), pp. 197–9, 350–2,
and Helen Fessas-Emanouil, *Ideological and Cultural Issues in the Architecture of
Modern Greece* (Athens, 1987).

37. Lampe, *Yugoslavia as History*, pp. 145–9.

38. Andrew Baruch Wachtel, *Making a Nation, Breaking a Nation, Literature and
Cultural Politics in Yugoslavia* (Stanford, CA: Stanford University Press, 1998),
p. 82, and more generally, pp. 69–127.

39. Melissa Bokovoj, "Scattered Graves, Ordered Cemeteries, Commemorating Serbia's Wars of National Liberation," in Maria Bucur and Nancy M. Wingfield, eds, *Staging the Past, The Politics of Commemoration in Habsburg Central Europe, 1848 to the Present* (West Lafayette, IN: Purdue University Press, 2001), pp. 236–54.

40. Evelina Kelbetcheva, "Between Apology and Denial: Bulgarian Culture during World War I," in Aviel Roshwald and Richard Stites, eds, *European Culture in the Great War, The Arts, Entertainment and Propaganda, 1914–1918* (Cambridge: Cambridge University Press, 2002), pp. 215–42.

41. John R. Lampe, "Interwar Bucharest and the Promises of Urbanism," *Journal of Urban History*, vol. 9, no. 3 (May, 1983), pp. 267–90. On the city's industry and the wider Romanian setting, see David Turnock, *The Romanian Economy in the 20th Century* (London: Croom Helm, 1986), pp. 85–103, and on the universities, see Livezeanu, *Cultural Politics in Greater Romania*, pp. 211–43.

42. Hitchins, *Rumania, 1866–1947*, 292–334. On the interaction of ideology and national consciousness, see Katherine Verdery, "National Ideology and National Character in Interwar Romania," in Katherine Verdery and Ivo Banac, eds, *National Character and National Ideology in Interwar Eastern Europe* (New Haven, CT: Yale Center for International and Area Studies, 1995), pp. 103–33.

43. On Iorga's political as well as intellectual activity during the 1920s, see Nicholas M. Nagy-Talavera, *Nicolae Iorga, A Biography* (Portland, OR: Center for Romanian Studies, 1998), pp. 211–306.

44. Maria Bucur, "Edifices of the Past, War Memorials and Heroes in Twentieth Century Romania," in Maria Todorova, ed., *Balkan Identities* (London: Hurst, 2004), pp. 158–71. On the interwar and postwar autotochtonists, see Katherine Verdery, *National Identity under Socialism, Identity and Cultural Politics in Ceauşescu's Romania* (Berkeley, CA: University of California Press, 1991), pp. 41–71.

4 Illiberal Directions during the Depression Decade

1. For evidence of the full turn in Bulgarian historiography away from this pre-1989 interpretation of the 1930s, see Elena Statelova and Stoicho Gruncharov, *Istoriia na nova Bulgariia, 1878–1944*, vol. III (Sofia: Anubis, 1999), pp. 475–579.

2. Bernd. J. Fischer, *King Zog and the Struggle for Stability in Albania* (New York: Columbia University Press, East European Monographs, 1984), pp. 69–74, 212–44.

3. The one detailed and critical study of the administrative controls established during 1929–31 is Christian Axboe Nielsen, "One State, One Nation, One King: The Dictatorship of King Aleksandar and His Yugoslav Project. 1929–1935" (PhD dissertation, Columbia University, 2002).

4. The limitations and problems of the royal regime from 1931 forward are addressed in John R. Lampe, *Yugoslavia as History: Twice there Was a Country*, 2nd edn (Cambridge: Cambridge University Press, 2000), pp. 182–200. Also see

the classic chapter on Yugoslavia by Joseph Rothschild in his *East Central Europe between the Wars* (Seattle, WA: University of Washington Press, 1974), pp. 237–80.

5. On *Ustaša* origins, the one detailed, well-supported work remains Bogdan Krizman, *Ante Pavelić i Ustaše* (Zagreb: Globus, 1986). On the Croatian right in broader perspective, see Mark Biondich, "'We Were Defending the State': Nationalism, Myth and Memory in Twentieth Century Croatia," in John R. Lampe and Mark Mazower, eds, *Ideologies and National Identities: The Case of Twentieth Century Southeastern Europe* (Budapest: CEU Press, 2004), pp. 54–81.

6. On the party's interwar history from its founding in 1921, see Vladimir Tismaneanu, *Stalinism for All Seasons, A Political History of the Romania Communist Party* (Berkeley, CA: University of California Press, 2004), pp. 37–84.

7. The most recent study is Constantin Iordachi, "Charisma, Religion and Ideology: Romania's Interwar Legion of the Archangel Michael," in Lampe and Mazower, *Ideologies and National Identities*, pp. 19–53.

8. A useful guide through the mixture of politics and personalities that moved through the royal regime is Paul D. Quinlan, *The Playboy King, Carol II of Romania* (Westport, CT: Greenwood Press, 1995), pp. 107–224. Also see Keith Hitchins, *Rumania, 1866–1947* (Oxford: Clarendon Press, 1994), pp. 375–425.

9. Nissan Oren, *Revolution Administered: Agrarianism and Communism in Bulgaria* (Baltimore, MD: Johns Hopkins University Press, 1974), pp. 13–37; Tatiana Kostadinova, *Bulgaria, 1879–1946, The Challenge of Choice* (New York: Columbia University Press, East European Monographs, 1995), pp. 65–72.

10. R. J. Crampton, *A Short History of Bulgaria* (Cambridge: Cambridge University Press, 1987), pp. 14–19. A sympathetic yet well-supported biography of the Tsar is Stefane Groueff, *Crown of Thorns, The Reign of King Boris of Bulgaria, 1918–1943* (Lanham, MD: Madison Books, 1987). On the 1934 coup and its aftermath, see pp. 199–252.

11. Thanos Veremis, *The Greek Military in Politics from Independence to Democracy* (Montreal: Black Rose Books, 1997), pp. 101–33. On the political struggles of 1932–6, see George Mavrogordatos, *Stillborn Republic, Social Coalitions and Party Strategies in Greece, 1922–1936* (Berkeley, CA: University of California Press, 1983), pp. 38–51 and 296–345.

12. For two contrasting views of the regime, see P. J. Vatikiotis, *Popular Autocracy in Greece, 1936–1941, A Political Biography of General Ionnis Metaxas* (London: Frank Cass, 1998) and John V. Kofas, *Authoritarianism in Greece, The Metaxas Regime* (New York: Columbia University Press, 1983).

13. On changes in demography as well as education and employment, see Milan Hauner, "Human Resources," in M. C. Kaser and E. A. Radice, eds, *The Economic History of Eastern Europe, 1919–1975*, vol. I (Oxford: Clarendon Press, 1985), pp. 66–147.

14. The following account draws on John R. Lampe, "Interwar Bucharest and the Promises of Urbanism" and "Interwar Sofia Versus the Nazi-Style Garden City," *Journal of Urban History*, vol. 9, no. 3 (May, 1983), pp. 267–90, and vol. 11, no. 1 (Nov., 1984), pp. 39–62.

15. Lampe, *Yugoslavia as History*, pp. 191–4, which relies in turn on the unique survey of "the creative intelligentsia of interwar Yugoslavia" by Miroslav Janićijević, *Stvaralačka inteligencija medjuratne Jugoslavije* (Belgrade: Institut društvenih nauka, 1984).

16. Peter C. Kent, "The 'Proffered Gift,' The Vatican and the Abortive Yugoslav Concordat of 1935–37," in Dick Richardson and Glyn Stone, eds, *Decisions and Diplomacy in Twentieth Century International History* (London: Routledge, 1995), pp. 108–28.

17. Aleksandar Jakir, *Dalmatien zwischen den Weltkriegen, agrarischen und urbane Lebenswelt und das Scheitern der jugoslawischen Integration* (Munich: R. Oldenbourg Verlag, 1999), pp. 231–5. On the peasant problems of the food-deficit areas, see the translation of Rudolf Bićanić, *How the People Live: Life in the Passive Regions* (Amherst, MA: Research Report 21, Department of Anthropology, University of Massachusetts, 1981).

18. The path-breaking study is Sandra Prlenda, "Young, Religious and Radical: The Croat Catholic Youth Organizations, 1922–1945," in Lampe and Mazower, *Ideologies and National Identities*, pp. 82–109.

19. For overview and detail respectively, see Katherine Verdery "Ideology and National Character in Interwar Romania" and Keith Hitchins, "Orthodoxism: Polemics Over Ethnicity and Religion in Interwar Romania," in Ivo Banac and Katherine Verdery, eds, *National Character and National Ideology in Interwar Eastern Europe* (New Haven, CT: Yale Center for International and Area Studies, 1995), pp. 103–56. On links to the Iron Guard, see Z. Ornea, *The Romanian Extreme Right, The Nineteen Thirties* (New York: Columbia University Press, East European Monographs, 1999).

20. The pioneering study of Romanian eugenics is Maria Bucur, *Eugenics and Modernization in Interwar Romania* (Pittsburgh, PA: University of Pittsburgh Press, 2002).

21. The best summary remains Henry L. Roberts, *Rumania, Political Problems of an Agrarian State* (New Haven, CT: Yale University Press, 1951), pp. 142–205.

22. The following section is largely based on but also revises downward the emphasis on state initiative in John R. Lampe and Marvin R. Jackson, *Balkan Economic History, 1550–1950: From Imperial Borderlands to Developing Nations* (Bloomington, IN: Indiana University Press, 1982), pp. 434–519.

23. For detailed analysis on Bulgaria, Romania, and Yugoslavia, see E. Lethridge, "National Income and Product," in Kaser and Radice, eds, *Economic History of Eastern Europe*, vol. I, pp. 532–97.

24. Mark Mazower, *Greece and the Interwar Economic Crisis* (Oxford: Clarendon Press, 1991), pp. 117–22, 237–55.

25. Ivo Bićanić and Želko Ivanović, "Croatian Banking during the 1926–1936 Depression," in Edwin Green, John Lampe, and Franjo Štiblar, eds, *Crisis and Renewal in Twentieth Century Banking* (Aldershot: Ashgate, 2004), pp. 64–86.

26. Mazower, *Greece and the Interwar Economic Crisis*, pp. 197 ff.

27. For country data on interregional trade, see the editor's introduction to George Petrakos and Stoyan Totev, eds, *The Development of the Balkan Region* (Aldershot: Ashgate, 2001), pp. 41–6.
28. Theodore I. Geshkoff, *Balkan Union, A Road to Peace in Southeastern Europe* (New York: Columbia University Press, 1940), pp. 144–62, 203–31.
29. Lampe and Jackson, *Balkan Economic History, 1550–1950*, pp. 461–9.
30. Ibid., Table 12.7, pp. 462–3.
31. Grueff, *Crown of Thorns*, pp. 241–59.
32. The most comprehensive study for Romania as well as Yugoslavia is William S. Grenzbach, Jr, *Germany's Informal Empire in East-Central Europe, German Economic Policy Toward Yugoslavia and Romania, 1933–1939* (Stuttgart: Franz Steiner Verlag, 1988).
33. Lampe, *Yugoslavia as History*, pp. 181–6.
34. A useful summary of Schacht's *Neuer Plan* and the proposed application of *Grossraumwirtschaft* to Southeastern Europe is Gyorgi Ranki, *Economy and the Struggle of the Great Powers for Hegemony in the Danube Valley, 1919–1939* (New York: Columbia University Press, East European Monographs, 1983), pp. 145–60.
35. Grenzbach, *Germany's Informal Empire*, pp. 69–113. On foreign relations, see Dov B. Lungu, *Romania and the Great Powers, 1933–1940* (Durham, NC: Duke University Press, 1989), pp. 108–48, and Rebecca Haynes, *Romanian Policy toward Germany, 1936–1940* (New York: St Martin's, 2000).

5 World War, Civil War, and the Communist Advantage

1. An informed summary of German strategy is Norman Rich, *Hitler's War Aims, Ideology, the Nazi State and the Course of Expansion* (New York: W. W. Norton, 1973), pp. 180–203. On British policy, see Mark C. Wheeler, *Britain and the War for Yugoslavia, 1940–1943* (New York: Columbia University Press, 1980), pp. 34–61.
2. The classic study of Operation Maritsa remains Martin Van Creveld, *Hitler's Strategy, 1940–1941: The Balkan Clue* (Cambridge: Cambridge University Press, 1973). His conclusion that the campaign did not delay Barbarossa can however be challenged for considering only the availability of equipment and troop numbers rather than their state of readiness for this greater campaign.
3. Rebecca Haynes, *Romanian Policy toward Germany, 1936–1940* (New York: St Martin's, 2000), pp. 119–66.
4. Stefane Grueff, *Crown of Thorns, The Reign of King Boris III of Bulgaria, 1918–1943* (Lanham, MD: Madison Books, 1987), 259–95.
5. The most detailed account is Frank Littlefield, *Germany and Yugoslavia, 1933–1941, The German Conquest of Yugoslavia* (New York: Columbia University Press, East European Monographs, 1988), pp. 57–130.
6. Richard Clogg, *A Concise History of Greece* (Cambridge: Cambridge University Press, 1992), p. 212.
7. Tatiana Kostadinovoa, *Bulgaria, 1879–1946: The Challenge of Choice* (New York, Columbia University Press, 1995), pp. 78–82.

8. For evidence of comparably limited but nonetheless aggressive anti-Jewish sentiment and proposals in Serbia and Croatia, see Laszlo Sekelj, "Anti-Semitism in Yugoslavia, 1918–1941," *East European Quarterly*, vol. XXII, no. 2 (June, 1988), pp. 159–72.

9. The best summary of Antonescu's rise and the Guard's brief months in power is Keith Hitchins, *Rumania, 1866–1947* (Oxford: Clarendon Press, 1994), pp. 451–71. On Carol's last year, see Paul D. Quinlan, *The Playboy King, Carol II of Romania* (Westport, CT: Greenwood Press, 1995), pp. 204–18. On the benign attitude of interwar Romanian nationalists toward the Roma minority and the Iron Guard's belated borrowing from Nazi biopolitics to persecute them, see Viorel Achim, *The Roma in Romanian History* (Budapest: CEU Press, 2004), pp. 145–66.

10. Hitchins, *Rumania*, p. 469.

11. See Randolph L. Braham, ed., *The Tragedy of Romanian Jewry* (Boulder, CO: Social Science Monographs, 1994), and on the war in general, Kurt W. Treptow, ed., *Romania and World War II* (Iaşi: Center for Romanian Studies, 1996). On the Roma deportation and its abrupt halt, see Achim, *Roma in Romanian History*, pp. 170–85.

12. Henry L. Roberts, *Rumania, Political Problems of an Agrarian State* (New Haven, CT: Yale University Press, 1951), pp. 236–41.

13. John R. Lampe, *The Bulgarian Economy in the Twentieth Century* (London: Croom Helm, 1986), pp. 105–20.

14. A comprehensive if somewhat journalistic rendering of these events is Michael Bar-Zohar, *Beyond Hitler's Grasp, The Heroic Rescue of Bulgaria's Jews* (Holbrook, MA: Adams Media Corp., 1988). The first-hand recollection of the key Bulgarian official may now be found in Dimitur Peshev, *Spomeni* (Memoirs) (Sofia: Gutenberg, 2004), pp. 205–54.

15. This account appears even in the scholarly study most sympathetic to Kosovar Albanian grievances against Serbs, Noel Malcolm, *Kosovo, A Short History* (New York: New York University Press, 1998), pp. 294–9.

16. Bernd J. Fischer, *Albania at War, 1939–1945* (London: Hurst, 1999), pp. 89–97, and on the invasion and initial Italian advantages, see pp. 21–57.

17. Mark Mazower, *Inside Hitler's Greece, The Experience of Occupation, 1941–1944* (New Haven, CT: Yale University Press, 1993), pp. 15–84, provides detailed social as well as political–military history.

18. Michael Palairet, *The Four Ends of the Greek Hyperinflation* of 1941–1946 (Copenhagen: Museum Tusculanum Press, 2000), pp. 25–30.

19. Mazower, *Inside Hitler's Greece*, pp. 235–61, details Italian resistance as well as German persecution of Greek Jewry. Perhaps 10,000 of the 70,000 Jews in prewar Greece survived.

20. By far the most comprehensive, detailed, and balanced study of this much-contended subject is Jozo Tomasevich, *War and Revolution in Yugoslavia, 1941–1945, Occupation and Collaboration* (Stanford, CA: Stanford University Press, 2001).

21. The classic account of mutual German and Croatian disappointment is Holm Sundhausen, *Wirtschaftsgeschichte Kroatiens im nationalsozialistischen Grossraum, 1941–1945* (Stuttgart: Deutsche Verlags-Anstalt, 1983).

22. The pioneering work here is Phyllis Auty and Richard Clogg, eds, *British Policy toward Wartime Yugoslavia and Greece* (London: Macmillan, 1975).

23. For evidence of the further advance of Greek scholarship, away from heavy emphasis on British intervention, see John O. Iatrides and Linda Wrigley, eds, *Greece at the Crossroads, The Civil War and Its Legacy* (University Park, PA: Pennsylvania State University Press, 1995).

24. Especially valuable for its coverage of the disconnected and self-defeating Chetnik activity in Bosnia is Lucien Karchmar, *Draža Mihailović and the Rise of the Chetnik Movement, 1941–1942*, 2 vols (New York: Garland Publishers, 1987).

25. On British policy throughout, see Wheeler, *Britain and the War for Yugoslavia*. Analysis of German documents informs Walter R. Roberts, *Tito, Mihailović and the Allies, 1941–1945* (Durham, NC: Duke University Press, 1987 reprint from 1973).

26. A balanced, later view from a leading SOE officer from the British Military Missions is Christopher M. Woodhouse, *The Struggle for Greece, 1941–1949* (Chicago, IL: Ivan R. Dee, 2003, from the 1976 edition), pp. 21–81, and from British scholarship, Richard Clogg's 2002 Introduction, pp. ix–xxv. For a critical view of SOE, in particular from Greek scholarship, see Andre Gerolymatos, *Guerilla Warfare and Espionage in Greece, 1940–1944* (New York: Pella, 1992).

27. On the Communist Party of Albania and its subsequent wartime relations with the British missions, see the carefully considered account of another SOE insider, Reginald Hibbert, *Albania's National Liberation Struggle: The Bitter Victory* (London: Pinter Publishers, 1991), pp. 11–65.

28. Fischer, *Albania at War, 1939–1945*, pp. 177–9, 258–67.

29. Albert Resis, "The Churchill–Stalin Percentages Agreement on the Balkans, Moscow October 1944," *American Historical Review*, vol. 83, no. 2 (April, 1978), pp. 368–87.

30. Alfred J. Rieber, "The Crack in the Plaster: Crisis in Romania and the Origins of the Cold War," *Journal of Modern History*, vol. 76, no. 1 (March 2004), pp. 62–106.

31. A newly detailed account of the Communist ascension after September 9, 1944, and its serious limitations before then, drawing on previously unconsulted archival materials from Bulgaria and the Soviet Union, is Vesselin Dimitrov, "Stalin's Cold War: Soviet Foreign Policy, Democracy and Revolution in Bulgaria, 1944–1948" (PhD dissertation, London School of Economics and Political Science, 2001).

32. John R. Lampe, *Yugoslavia as History, Twice There Was a Country*, 2nd edn (Cambridge: Cambridge University Press, 2000), pp. 218–26.

33. Fischer, *Albania at War, 1939–1945*, 237–52; Hibbert, *Albania's National Liberation Struggle*, pp. 211–21.

34. John S. Koliopoulos, *Plundered Loyalties, World War II and Civil War in Greek West Macedonia* (New York: New York University Press, 1999), pp. 133–90, marshals the evidence for Greek concern while continuing to question the deeper roots of any separate Macedonian identity.
35. Woodhouse, *The Struggle for Greece*, pp. 86–138, provides an account of events on the ground from May through December 1944 which also pursues perceptions from the several sides and includes critical judgments of British policy.
36. For the full terms of the Varkiza Agreement, see Richard Clogg, ed. and trans., *Greece, 1940–1949, Occupation, Resistance and Civil War* (Basingstoke: Palgrave, 2002), pp. 188–90.
37. Fitzroy Maclean, *Eastern Approaches* (Harmondsworth: Penguin Books, 1991), pp. 402–3.

6 Communist and Cold War Transitions, 1945–1963

1. Military deaths for Romania and Yugoslavia amounted to about 300,000 apiece. Romania's civilian deaths, at least two-thirds of them Jews from outside the pre-1914 borders, totaled nearly 350,000. This matched Greece's civilian total, if not Yugoslavia's, of more than 700,000. The forced departure from Yugoslavia of half a million Germans, Hungarians, and Italians accounted for the largest part of the forced transfers from the end of the war through 1947. Marvin R. Jackson, "Changes in Ethnic Populations and Southeastern Europe: Holocaust, Migration and Assimilation – 1940 to 1970," in Roland Shoenfeld, ed., *Nationalitaetprobleme in Suedosteuropa* (Munich: R. Oldenbourg Verlag, 1987), pp. 73–104; Robert Paul Magocsi, *Historical Atlas of Central Europe*, revised and expanded edn (Seattle, WA: University of Washington Press, 2002), pp. 189–93.
2. The most recent and revealing analysis of the rapid Communist rise is Vladimir Tismaneanu, *Stalinism for All Seasons, A Political History of Romanian Communism* (Berkeley, CA: University of California Press, 2003), pp. 85–106.
3. A close account of agricultural policy and problems under the Groza regime may be found in Henry L. Roberts, *Rumania, Political Problems of an Agrarian State* (New Haven, CT: Yale University Press, 1951), pp. 290–9.
4. Dennis Deletant, "New Light on Gheorghiu-Dej's Struggle for Dominance in the Romanian Communist Party, 1944–1949," *Slavonic and East European Review*, vol. 73, no. 4 (Oct. 1995), pp. 659–90. Also see Robert Levy, *Ana Pauker, The Rise and Fall of a Jewish Communist* (Berkeley, CA: University of California Press, 2002), pp. 69–99.
5. For the text of and subsequent judgments on Petkov by Dimitrov and Stalin, down to the Bulgarian leader's insistence on his execution in September 1947, see Ivo Banac, ed., *The Diaries of Georgi Dimitrov, 1933–1949* (New Haven, CT: Yale University Press, 2003), pp. 369, 375, 377, 381, 384, 427.

6. Details of these setbacks may be found in Vesselin Dimitrov, "Stalin's Cold War: Soviet Foreign Policy, Democracy and Revolution in Bulgaria, 1944–1948" (PhD dissertation, London School of Economics and Political Science, 2001), pp. 168–89.

7. See John R. Lampe, *The Bulgarian Economy in the Twentieth Century* (London: Croom Helm, 1986), pp. 124–42.

8. For detail and further references on the period 1945–7, see John R. Lampe, *Yugoslavia as History, Twice There Was a Country*, 2nd edn (Cambridge: Cambridge University Press, 2000), pp. 226–49.

9. Carol S. Lilly, "Agitprop in Postwar Yugoslavia," *Slavic Review*, vol. 53, no. 24 (1995), pp. 395–413.

10. Banac, ed., *Diaries of Georgi Dimitrov*, pp. 337, 343, 352.

11. Paulin Kola, *The Search for Greater Albania* (London: Hurst, 2002), pp. 72–92.

12. On the importance of Albanian issues in provoking the Tito–Stalin split, see Ivo Banac, *With Stalin, Against Tito, Cominformist Splits in Yugoslav Communism* (Ithaca, NY: Cornell University Press, 1988), pp. 38–41, and on the further origins of the dispute, pp. 3–44.

13. The wider Greek anxiety about Tito's Macedonian initiatives is documented in Evangelos Kofos, "The Impact of the Macedonian Question of the Civil Conflict in Greece, 1943–1949," in John O. Iatrides and Linda Wrigley, eds, *Greece at the Crossroads, The Civil War and its Legacy* (University Park, PA: Pennsylvania State University Press, 1995), pp. 274–318.

14. Stavros B. Thomadakis, "Stabilization, Development and Government Activity in the 1940s," in Iatrides and Wrigley, eds, *Greece at the Crossroads*, pp. 183–211. On the predominant role of inflation, bank policy and the joint Anglo-American and Greek Currency Committee, see Athanasios Lykogiannis, *Britain and the Greek Economic Crisis, 1944–1947, From Liberation to the Truman Doctrine* (Columbia, MO: University of Missouri Press, 2002), pp. 119–39.

15. Haris Vlavianos, *Greece, 1941–1949, The Strategy of the Greek Communist Party* (London: Macmillan, 1992), pp. 225–45.

16. The most detailed if journalistic account is Nicholas Bethell, *Betrayed* (New York: Times Books, 1984).

17. Adi Schnytser, *Stalinist Economic Strategy in Practice, The Case of Albania* (London: Oxford University Press, 1982), pp. 67–9.

18. Ghita Ionescu, *Communism in Rumania, 1944–1962* (London: Oxford University Press, 1962), pp. 183–4, 203–36, 296–7. Also see Stelian Tanase, *Elite şi Societate, Guvernartea Gheorgiu-Dej, 1948–1965* (Bucharest: Humanitas, 1998).

19. Levy, *Ana Pauker*, pp. 115, 163–73, 201.

20. On Chervenkov's rise to power, see R. J. Crampton, *A Short History of Bulgaria* (Cambridge: Cambridge University Press, 1987), pp. 166–79.

21. A path-breaking account drawn from Church and State archives is provided by Daniela Kalkandzhieva, *Bulgaraskata provoslavna tsrkva i "narodnata demokratiia", 1944–1953* (The Bulgarian Orthodox Church and "Peoples Democracy") (Sofia: Demos, 2002).

22. Lampe, *Bulgarian Economy*, pp. 139–48.

23. On the controversy over numbers and the varying experiences of ethnic groups, see Banac, *With Stalin, Against Tito*, pp. 145–210.
24. John R. Lampe, Russell O. Prickett and Ljubisa Adamovic, *Yugoslav–American Economic Relations since World War II* (Durham, NC: Duke University Press, 1990), pp. 13–71, surveys the American assistance that continued through 1964.
25. Milovan Djilas, *The New Class* (London: Thames and Hudson, 1957).
26. Lampe, *Yugoslavia as History*, pp. 255–84.
27. See Stephen Xydis, *Cyprus: Conflict and Conciliation, 1954–1958* (Colombus, OH: Ohio State University Press, 1967).
28. For details of the elections from 1950 through 1963, see Richard Clogg, *Parties and Elections in Greece, The Search for Legitimacy* (London: Hurst, 1987), pp. 22–54.
29. A critical overview of the economic and social transition by the 1960s is David H. Close, *Greece since 1945* (London: Pearson Education, 2002), pp. 44–82.
30. On Soviet and Albanian relations and the role of Yugoslavia during the 1950s, see Kola, *Search for Greater Albania*, pp. 96–131.
31. Michael Kaser, "Trade and Aid in the Albanian Economy," Joint Economic Committee of the US Congress, *East European Economies Post-Helsinki* (Washington, DC: US Government Printing Office, 1977), pp. 1325–40.
32. On Albanian industry, see Schnytser, *Stalinist Economic Strategy*, pp. 68–77, and on agriculture, Orjan Sjoberg, *Rural Change in Albania* (Boulder, CO: Westview Press, 1991), pp. 81–104.
33. Expanded from the important Romanian edition is Dennis Deletant, *Romania under Communist Rule* (Portland, OR: Center for Romanian Studies, 1999), pp. 88–103. Also see Tismaneanu, *Stalinism for all Seasons*, pp. 136–67.
34. Lampe and Jackson, *Balkan Economic History*, pp. 584–5.
35. See Michael Palairet, " 'Lenin' and 'Brezhnev': Steel Making and the Bulgarian Economy, 1956–90," *Europe–Asia Studies*, vol. 47, no. 3 (1995), pp. 493–505.
36. Lampe, *Bulgarian Economy*, pp. 149–54.

7 Continuity and Contradictions, 1964–1989

1. For an overview of where the CSCE mandate fits into international treatment of territorial sovereignty versus self-determination, see Hurst Hannum, "Self-Determination in the Post-Colonial Era," in Donald Clark and Robert Williamson, eds, *Self-Determination, International Perspectives* (New York: St Martin's, 1996), pp. 12–44.
2. On Yugoslavia, see OECD, *Reviews of National Policies for Education, Yugoslavia* (Paris: Organization for Economic Cooperation and Development, 1981) and for Greece, David H. Close, *Greece since 1945, Politics, Economics, Society* (London: Pearson Education, 2002), pp. 74–6.
3. The Pioneers' initial role and later redirection as promoted by Milovan Djilas is detailed in Ildiko Erdei, " 'The Happy Child' as an Ikon of Socialist Transformation: Yugoslavia's Pioneer Organization," in John Lampe and Mark Mazower, eds, *Ideologies and National Identities, The Case of 20th Century Southeastern Europe* (Budapest: CEU Press, 2004), pp. 154–79.

4. A unique comparison of Romanian and Bulgarian trade patterns in real terms is Marvin R. Jackson, "Romania's Economy at the End of the 1970s: Turning the Corner on Intensive Development," Joint Economic Committee of the US Congress, *East European Economic Assessments*, Part I (Washington, DC: US Government Printing Office, 1981), pp. 267–70. On Greece and Yugoslavia, see the respective OECD Country Reports for 1981–2 and 1983.

5. The events and personalities of precoup years are summarized in Christopher M. Woodhouse, *The Rise and Fall of the Greek Colonels* (London: Granada, 1985), pp. 1–15.

6. Thanos Veremis, "Greece: Veto and Impasse, 1967–1974," in Christopher Clapham and George Philip, eds, *The Political Dilemmas of Military Regimes* (Totowa, NJ: Barnes & Noble, 1985), pp. 27–45.

7. On Cyprus, see Ioannis D. Stefanidis, *Isle of Discord: Nationalism, Imperialism and the Making of the Cyprus Problem* (New York: New York University Press, 1999).

8. Analysis of the Greek political spectrum and the detail of election procedures and results for 1946–84 are provided by Richard Clogg, *Parties and Elections in Greece, The Search for Legitimacy* (Durham, NC: Duke University Press, 1987).

9. On the background and content of the 1963 Constitution, see Dennison Rusinow, *The Yugoslav Experiment, 1948–1974* (Berkeley, CA: University of California Press, 1977), pp. 120–33.

10. On the crises of the late 1960s and how their "federalizing" of Yugoslav politics culminated in the 1974 Constitution, see Steven L. Burg, *Conflict and Cohesion in Socialist Yugoslavia, Political Decision Making Since 1966* (Princeton, NJ: Princeton University Press, 1983).

11. Burg, *Conflict and Cohesion*, pp. 242–300.

12. The features and subsequent failure of the 1965 economic reform are reviewed in John R. Lampe, *Yugoslavia as History, Twice There Was a Country*, 2nd edn (Cambridge: Cambridge University Press, 2000), pp. 284–320.

13. Iliana Marcheva, *Todor Zhivkov – Putiat kum vlastta* (The Road to Power) *Politika i ikonomika v Bulgariia 1953–1964* (Sofia: Institut po Istoriia-BAN, 2003), pp. 231–73.

14. The most useful summaries of these developments are John D. Bell, "Domestic Politics" and Wolfgang Hoepken, "Politisches System," in Klaus-Detlev Grothusen, ed., *Bulgarien, Suedosteurope-Handbuch*, vol. VI (Goettingen: Vandenhoeck & Ruprecht, 1990), pp. 54–83, 173–223.

15. On the New System of Management and the subsequent retreat until the early 1980s, see John R. Lampe, *The Bulgarian Economy in the 20th Century* (London: Croom Helm, 1986), pp. 199–222.

16. Michael Palairet, "'Lenin' and 'Brezhnev': Steel Making and the Bulgarian Economy, 1956–1990," *Europe–Asia Studies*, vol. 47, no. 3 (1995), pp. 493–505, provides the damning details.

17. On Hoxha's last years and the succession struggle that followed, see Nicolas Pano, "The Process of Democratization in Albania," in Karen Dawisha and Bruce Parrott, eds, *Politics, Power and the Struggle for Democracy in South-East Europe*

(Cambridge: Cambridge University Press, 1997), pp. 292–301. On Hoxha's replacement of Shehu after 1981 as the liberator of Tirana in 1944 in the party's widely distributed official history, see M. J. Alex Standish, "Enver Hoxha's Role in the Development of Socialist Albanian Myths," in Stephanie Schwandner-Sievers and Bernd J. Fischer, eds, *Albanian Identities, Myths and History* (Bloomington, IN: Indiana University Press, 2002), pp. 115–24.

18. Orjan Sjoberg, "The Albanian Economy in the 1980s," in Orjan Sjoberg and Michael L. Wyzan, eds, *Economic Change in the Balkan States: Albania, Bulgaria, Romania and Yugoslavia* (New York: St Martin's, 1991), pp. 115–21. On the limited and uneven progress for agricultural wage labor under full collectivization since 1967–8, see Sjoberg, *Rural Change and Development in Albania* (Boulder, CO: Westview Press, 1991), pp. 96–166.

19. On Albania's regional relations and the Kosovo question after Hoxha's death, see the Radio Free Europe/Radio Liberty Background Reports by Louis Zanga, No. 45 (May 21, 1985), No. 7 (Jan. 17, 1986), No. 152 (Sept. 3, 1987), No. 233 (Dec. 9, 1987), No. 31 (Feb. 26, 1988).

20. Vladimir Tismaneanu, *Stalinism for All Seasons, A Political History of Romanian Communism* (Berkeley, CA: California University Press, 2003), pp. 187–232; Dennis Deletant, *Romania under Communist Rule* (Portland, OR: Center for Romanian Studies, 1999), pp. 104–58.

21. For persuasive counterpoint to the customary emphasis on Ceauşescu's Maoist conversion, see the Radio Free Europe Research Reports for Romania by Henry Schaefer (May 5, 1969) and Robert R. King (November 11 and 18, 1971).

22. Robert R. King, *A History of the Romanian Communist Party* (Stanford, CA: Hoover Institution Press, 1980), pp. 85–119.

23. A well-supported statistical case for this judgement is Jackson, "Romania's Economy at the End of the 1970s," pp. 231–98. On the subsequent failures and hardships of the 1980s, see Per Ronnas, "The Economic Legacy of Ceauşescu," in Sjoberg and Wyzan, *Economic Change in the Balkan States*, pp. 51–61.

24. The course of the Romanian debate over "protochronism" in general and the enigmatic influence of the antiregime but also antiforeign philosopher Constantin Noica is explored at length in Katherine Verdery, *National Ideology under Socialism, Identity and Cultural Politics in Ceauşescu's Romania* (Berkeley, CA: University of California Press, 1991).

25. On the continuing controversy in Bulgaria over Zhivkova's life and death, see Ivanka Nedeva Atanassova, "Lyudmila Zhivkova and the Paradox of Ideology and Identity in Communist Bulgaria," *East European Politics and Society*, vol. 18, no. 2 (Spring, 2004), pp. 278–315.

26. John A. Bristow, *The Bulgarian Economy in Transition* (Cheltenham, UK: Edward Elgar, 1996), pp. 11–21; Lampe, *Bulgarian Economy*, pp. 216–19.

27. According to a 1986 population survey by social category, the "intelligentsia" comprised 7.5 percent, and nonagricultural "skilled salaried employees" 14.4 percent – over 400,000 people in all. Nikloai Genev and Anna Krasteva, eds, *Recent Social Trends in Bulgaria, 1960–1995* (Montreal: McGill-Queen's University Press, 2001), pp. 180–8.

28. Garabed Minassian, "Bulgarian Industrial Growth and Structure: 1970–89," *Soviet Studies*, vol. 44, no. 4 (1992), pp. 699–711.

29. The subsidies rose by 1983 to one quarter of invisible earnings, pushing their total up past 15 percent of GDP despite the drop in shipping and remittances. Nicholas G. Pirounakis, *The Greek Economy, Past, Present and Future* (London: Macmillan, 1997), pp. 25–7.

30. For historical perspective, see Nicos Mouzelis, "Continuities and Discontinuities in Greek Politics – from Eleftherios Venizelos to Andreas Papapandreou," in Kevin Featherstone and Dimitrios K. Katsoudas, eds, *Political Change in Greece before and after the Colonels* (London: Croom Helm, 1987), pp. 271–88.

31. George Th. Mavrogordatos, "Civil Society under Populism," in Richard Clogg, ed., *Greece, 1981–1989, The Populist Decade* (London: Macmillan, 1993), pp. 47–64.

32. On the financial problems of stagflation in the 1980s, see George Pagoulatos, *Greece's New Political Economy, State, Finance, and Growth from Postwar to EMU* (Basingstoke: Palgrave, 2003), pp. 87–127. For a persuasive indictment of the state's wider role, see Pirounakis, *The Greek Economy*, pp. 49–93.

33. Harold Lydall, *Yugoslavia in Crisis* (Oxford: Clarendon Press, 1989).

34. On the wider consequences of the Agrokomers scandal for the Bosnian party, media and civil society, see Neven Angelic, *Bosnia-Herzegovina, The End of a Legacy* (London: Frank Cass, 2003), pp. 51–78.

35. The League's incapacity for political change and the burdens of the delegate system are detailed in Laszlo Sekelj, *Yugoslavia: The Process of Disintegration* (New York: Columbia University Press, Atlantic Research and Publications, 1993).

36. Evidence focusing on the labor force is provided to support a socioeconomic argument that breakdown threatened by the 1980s in Susan L. Woodward, *Socialist Unemployment: The Political Economy of Yugoslavia, 1945–1990* (Princeton, NJ: Princeton University Press, 1995), pp. 191–370.

8 Wars and Transitions Since 1989

1. A succinct but informed summary is Gale Stokes, *The Walls Came Tumbling Down, The Collapse of Communism in Eastern Europe* (London: Oxford University Press, 1993), pp. 131–67.

2. A comprehensive analysis of these events and the controversies to which they gave rise is Peter Siani-Davies, *The Romanian Revolution of December 1989* (Ithaca, NY: Cornell University Press, 2005).

3. For a first-hand account from the American Ambassador to Yugoslavia himself of this often misrepresented meeting, see Warren Zimmerman, *Origins of a Catastrophe – Yugoslavia and its Destroyers* (New York: Times Books, 1996), pp. 133–40.

4. Ivo Bićanić, "Croatians Struggle to Make Ends Meet," *RFE/RL Research Report*, 2/26 (1993).

5. For informed surveys and contrasting analyses of the Croatian conflict and the

European role, see James Gow, *The Triumph of the Lack of Will, International Diplomacy and the Yugoslav War Dissolution* (New York: Columbia University Press, 1996), pp. 41–108, and Susan L. Woodward, *Balkan Tragedy, Chaos and Dissolution after the Cold War* (Washington, DC: The Brookings Institution, 1995), pp. 147–272.

6. The most balanced and comprehensive study is Steven L. Burg and Paul S. Shoup, *The War in Bosnia-Herzegovina, Ethnic Conflict and International Intervention* (Armonk, NY: M. E. Sharpe, 1999).

7. On the American-led military campaign, see Ivo H. Daalder and Michael E. O'Hanlon, *Winning Ugly, NATO's War to Save Kosovo* (Washington, DC: Brookings Institution, 2000). On the origins and course of the conflict in Kosovo itself, see Tim Judah, *Kosovo: War and Revenge* (New Haven, CT: Yale University Press, 2000) and Paulin Kola, *The Search for Greater Albania* (London: Hurst, 2003), pp. 222–376.

8. Recalculated from data in Milica Uvalić, "Economic Transition in Southeast Europe," *Journal of Southeast European and Black Sea Studies*, vol. 3, no. 1 (Jan., 2003), pp. 63–81.

9. For a detailed account of the economic transition in particular, see the essays of Slovenian scholars and participants assembled in Mojmir Mrak, Matija Rojec and Carlos Silva-Jauregui, *Slovenia From Yugoslavia to the European Union* (Washington, DC: The World Bank, 2004).

10. Nicholas J. Miller, "A Failed Transition: The Case of Serbia," in Karen Dawisha and Bruce Parrott, eds, *Politics, Power and the Struggle for Democracy in South-East Europe* (Cambridge: Cambridge University Press, 1997), pp. 146–88, and John R. Lampe, *Yugoslavia as History, Twice There Was a Country*, 2nd edn (Cambridge: Cambridge University Press, 2000), pp. 385–91. Of the several Milošević biographies, the most scholarly is Lenard Cohen, *Serpent in the Bosom: The Rise and Fall of Slobodan Milošević* (Boulder, CO: Westview Press, 2001).

11. The regime's later economic failings and the ongoing political struggle against its authoritarian features are described in William Bartlett, *Croatia between Europe and the Balkans* (London: Routledge, 2003), pp. 33–62, 87–120.

12. A concise review of these interrelations is Steven D. Roper, *Romania the Unfinished Revolution* (Amsterdam: Harwood Academic Publishers, 2000), pp. 69–129.

13. For the flavor of this new popular culture, see Denise Roman, *Fragmented Identities, Popular Culture, Sex, and Everyday Life in Postcommunist Romania* (Lanham, MD: Lexington Books, 2003), pp. 55–73.

14. See Kola, *Search for Greater Albania*, 321–8, and Anthony Clunies-Ross and Petar Sudar, eds, *Albania's Economy in Turmoil and Transition, 1990–1997* (Aldershot: Ashgate, 2000), pp. 7–21.

15. John D. Bell, "'Postcommunist' Bulgaria," in Dawisha and Parrott, eds, *Politics, Power*, pp. 362–74.

16. For an economist's account of Bulgaria's troubled transition through 1996 and the reversal of fortune that began in 1997, see Michael L. Wyzan, "Bulgarian Economic Policy and Performance," in John D. Bell, ed., *Bulgaria in Transition*

(Boulder, CO: Westview Press, 1998), pp. 93–122, and for a political scientist's overview of all aspects, Veselin Dimitrov, *Bulgaria, the Uneven Transition* (London: Routledge, 2001).

17. The most comprehensive survey of the period from 1991 to 1995 is Duncan M. Perry, "The Republic of Macedonia: Finding its Way," in Dawisha and Parrot, eds, *Politics, Power*, pp. 226–84.

18. Robert Hislope, "Crime and Honor in a Weak State, Paramilitary Forces and Violence on Macedonia," *Problems of Post-Communism*, vol. 51, no. 3 (May/June, 2004), pp. 18–26.

19. The international sequence is detailed in Alice Ackermann, "International Intervention in Macedonia, From Preventative Engagement to Peace Implementation," in Peter Siani-Davies, ed., *International Intervention in the Balkans since 1995* (London: Routledge, 2003), pp. 107–19. John Phillips, *Macedonia, Warlords & Rebels in the Balkans* (New Haven, CT: Yale University Press, 2004), pp. 85–200, traces the domestic conflict in 2001 and the play of forces since the Ohrid Agreement.

20. On Greece's reconciliation with what it still insisted be called the Former Yugoslav Republic of Macedonia (FYROM), movement toward detente with Turkey, and accommodation with the European Union, see David H. Close, *Greece since 1945, Politics, Economics and Society* (London: Pearson Education, 2002), pp. 231–82.

21. The course of Greece's foreign economic relations may be tracked through the annual *OECD Economic Surveys, Greece* (Paris: OECD). The series has included volumes for Bulgaria and Romania since 1996.

22. For an economist's overview of the progress of financial liberalization through the 1990s, see George Pagoulatos, *Greece's New Political Economy, State, Finance and Growth from Postwar to the EMU* (Basingstoke: Palgrave, 2003), pp. 125–67.

23. Details and analysis of bank profitability as well as restructuring may be found in Barry Eichengreen and Heather D. Gibson, "Greek Banking at the Dawn of the New Millennium," in Ralph C. Bryant, Nicholas C. Garganas, and George S. Tavias, eds, *Greece's Economic Performance and Prospects* (Athens: Bank of Greece and The Brookings Institution, 2001), pp. 545–97.

24. David Phinnemore and Peter Siani-Davies, "Beyond Intervention? The Balkans, the Stability Pact and the European Union," in Siani-Davies, ed., *International Intervention in the Balkans*, pp. 172–93.

25. Charles M. Perry and Dimitris Keridis, eds, *Defense Reform, Modernization, and Military Cooperation in Southeastern Europe* (Herndon, VA: Brassey's, 2004) provides chapters on all countries save Serbia-Montenegro.

26. International Commission on the Balkans, *The Balkans in Europe's Future* (www.balkan.commission.org, 2005), p. 38.

Select Bibliography

Balkans to 1918 and Beyond

Banac, Ivo. *The National Question in Yugoslavia: Origins, History, Politics*. Ithaca, NY: Cornell University Press, 1984.

Carter, Francis W., ed. *An Historical Geography of the Balkans*. London: Seminar Press, 1972.

Crampton, R. J. *A History of Bulgaria, 1878–1918*. New York: Columbia University Press, East European Monographs, 1983.

Dogo, Marco and Guido Franzinetti, eds. *Disrupting and Reshaping, Early Stages of Nation-Building in the Balkans*. Ravenna: Longo Editore, 2002.

Hall, Richard C. *The Balkan Wars, 1912–1913*. London: Routledge, 2000.

Hitchins, Keith. *Rumania, 1866–1947*. Oxford: Clarendon Press, 1994.

Jelavich, Charles. *South Slav Nationalisms, Textbooks and Yugoslavism before 1914*. Columbus, OH: Ohio State University Press, 1991.

Jelavich, Charles and Barbara Jelavich. *The Establishment of the Balkan National States, 1804–1920*. Seattle, WA: University of Washington Press, 1977.

Kent, Marian, ed. *The Great Powers and the End of the Ottoman Empire*. London: Frank Cass, 1994.

Koliopoulos, John. *Brigands with a Cause, Brigandage and Irridentism in Modern Greece, 1821–1912*. Oxford: Clarendon Press, 1987.

Miller, Nicholas J. *Between Nation and State, Serbian Politics in Croatia Before the First World War*. Pittsburgh, PA: Pittsburgh University Press, 1992.

Mitrović, Andrej. *Serbia's Great War, 1914–1918*. London: Hurst, 2007.

Pavlowitch, Stevan K. *A History of the Balkans, 1804–1945*. London: Longman, 1999.

Perry, Duncan M. *The Politics of Terror, The Macedonian Revolutionary Movements, 1893–1903*. Durham, NC: Duke University Press, 1988.

Torrey, Glenn E. *Romania and World War I, A Collection of Studies*. Oxford: Center for Romanian Studies, 1998.

Veremis, Thanos. *The Greek Military in Politics, From Independence to Democracy*. Montreal: Black Rose Books, 1997.

Interwar Parties and Politics

Banac, Ivo, ed. *The Effects of World War I: The Rise of the Communist Parties in East Central Europe, 1918–1921*. New York: Atlantic Research, East European Monographs, 1983.

Bell, John D. *Peasants in Power, Alexander Stamboliski and the Bulgarian Agrarian National Union, 1899–1923.* Princeton, NJ: Princeton University Press, 1977.

Biondich, Mark. *Stjepan Radić, the Croat Peasant Party, and the Politics of Mass Mobilization, 1904–1928.* Toronto: University of Toronto Press, 2000.

Fischer, Bernd J. *King Zog and the Struggle for Stability in Albania.* New York: Columbia University Press, East European Monographs, 1984.

Grueff, Stefane. *Crown of Thorns, The Reign of King Boris III of Bulgaria, 1918–1943.* Lanham, MD: Madison Books, 1987.

Kostadinova, Tatiana. *Bulgaria, 1879–1946: The Challenge of Choice.* New York, Columbia University Press, 1995.

Mavrogordatos, George Th. *Stillborn Republic, Social Coalitions and Party Strategies in Greece, 1922–1936.* Berkeley, CA: University of California Press, 1983.

Rothschild, Joseph. *The Communist Party of Bulgaria, Origins and Development, 1883–1936.* New York: Columbia University Press, 1959.

———. *East Central Europe between the Two Wars.* Seattle, WA: University of Washington Press, 1974.

Rusinow, Dennison *Italy's Austrian Heritage, 1919–1946.* London: Oxford University Press, 1969.

Second World War

Clogg, Richard, ed. and trans., *Greece, 1940–1949, Occupation, Resistance and Civil War.* Basingstoke: Palgrave, 2002.

Fischer, Bernd J. *Albania at War, 1939–1945.* London: Hurst, 1999.

Hibbert, Reginald. *Albania's National Liberation Struggle: The Bitter Victory.* London: Pinter, 1991.

Mazower, Mark. *Inside Hitler's Greece, The Experience of Occupation, 1941–1944.* New Haven, CT: Yale University Press, 1993.

Tomasevich, Jozo. *War and Revolution in Yugoslavia, 1941–1945, Occupation and Collaboration.* Stanford, CA: Stanford University Press, 2001.

Treptow, Kurt, ed. *Romania and World War II.* Iaşi: The Center for Romanian Studies, 1996.

Trew, Simon. *Britain, Mihailović and the Chetniks.* London: Macmillan, 1998.

Wheeler, Mark. *Britain and the War for Yugoslavia, 1940–43.* New York: Columbia University Press, East European Monographs, 1980.

Woodhouse, Christopher M. *The Struggle for Greece, 1941–1949.* Chicago, IL: Ivan R. Dee, 2003.

Economic Transitions before and after 1989

Bunce, Valerie. *Subversive Institutions, The Design and Destruction of Socialism and the State.* Cambridge: Cambridge University Press, 1999.

Dobry, Michel. *Democratic and Capitalist Transitions in Eastern Europe.* Dordrecht: Kluwer, 2000.

Eidelberg, Philip G. *The Great Romanian Peasant Revolt of 1907, The First Modern Jacquerie.* Leiden: E. J. Brill, 1974.

Grenzbach, Jr, William S. *Germany's Informal Empire in East-Central Europe, German Economic Policy Toward Yugoslavia and Romania, 1933–1939.* Stuttgart: Franz Steiner Verlag, 1988.

Lampe, John R. *The Bulgarian Economy in the Twentieth Century.* London: Croom Helm, 1986.

Lampe, John R. and Marvin R. Jackson. *Balkan Economic History 1550–1950, From Imperial Borderlands to Developing Nations.* Bloomington, IN: Indiana University Press, 1982.

Mazower, Mark. *Greece and the Interwar Economic Crisis.* Oxford, Clarendon Press, 1991.

Palairet, Michael. *The Balkan economies c. 1800–1914, Evolution without Development.* Cambridge: Cambridge University Press, 1997.

Pearton, Maurice. *Oil and the Romanian State, 1895–1948.* London: Oxford University Press, 1970.

Roberts, Henry L. *Rumania, Political Problems of an Agrarian State.* New Haven, CT: Yale University Press, 1951.

Tomasevich, Jozo. *Peasants, Politics, and Economic Change in Yugoslavia.* Stanford, CA: Stanford University Press, 1955.

National Identities, Societies, and Cultural Politics

Brown, Keith. *The Past in Question, Modern Macedonia and the Uncertainties of Nation.* Princeton: Princeton University Press, 2003.

Brunnbauer, Ulf, ed. *(Re)Writing History. Historiography in Southeastern Europe After Socialism.* Munster: LIT, 2004.

Bucur, Maria. *Eugenics and Modernization in Interwar Romania.* Pittsburgh, PA: University of Pittsburgh Press, 2002.

Bucur, Maria and Nancy M. Wingfield, eds. *Staging the Past, The Politics of Commemoration in Habsburg Central Europe, 1848 to the Present.* West Lafayette, IN: Purdue University Press, 2001.

Carter, F. W. and H. W. Norris, eds. *The Changing Shape of the Balkans.* Boulder, CO: Westview Press, 1996.

Karakasidou, Anastasia N. *Fields of Wheat, Hills of Blood, Passages to Nationhood in Greek Macedonia, 1870–1990.* Chicago: University of Chicago Press, 1997.

Koliopoulos, John S. and Thanos M. Veremis. *Greece, The Modern Sequel, from 1831 to the Present.* New York: New York University Press, 2002.

Lampe, John R. and Mark Mazower, eds. *Ideologies and National Identities: The Case of Twentieth-Century Southeastern Europe.* Budapest: CEU Press, 2004.

Livezeanu, Irina. *Cultural Politics in Greater Romania, Regionalism, Nation Building and Ethnic Struggle, 1918–1930.* Ithaca, NY: Cornell University Press, 1995.

Mazower, Mark. *Salonica, City of Ghosts, Christians, Muslims and Jews, 1430–1950.* New York: Alfred A. Knopf, 2005.

Perica, Vjekoslav. *Balkan Idols, Religion and Nationalism in Yugoslav States.* Oxford: Oxford University Press, 2001.

Roshwald, Aviel and Richard Stites, eds. *European Culture in the Great War, The Arts, Entertainment and Propaganda, 1914–1918.* Cambridge: Cambridge University Press, 2002.

Roudometof, Victor, ed. *The Macedonian Question: Culture, Historiography and Politics.* New York: Columbia University Press, East European Monographs, 2000.

Schwander-Sievers, Stephanie and Bernd J. Fischer, eds. *Albanian Identities, Myth and History.* Bloomington, IN: Indiana University Press, 2002.

Todorova, Maria. *Imagining the Balkans.* London: Oxford University Press, 1997.

Todorova, Maria, ed. *Balkan Identities.* London: Hurst, 2004.

Verdery, Katherine and Ivo Banac, eds. *National Character and National Ideology in Interwar Eastern Europe.* New Haven, CT: Yale Center for International and Area Studies, 1995.

Wachtel, Andrew Baruch. *Making a Nation, Breaking a Nation, Literature and Cultural Politics in Yugoslavia.* Stanford, CA: Stanford University Press, 1998.

Southeastern Europe 1945–1989

Banac, Ivo. *With Stalin, Against Tito, Cominformist Splits in Yugoslav Communism.* Ithaca, NY: Cornell University Press, 1988.

Burg, Steven L. *Conflict and Cohesion in Socialist Yugoslavia, Political Decision Making since 1966.* Princeton, NJ: Princeton University Press, 1983.

Clogg, Richard, ed. *Greece, 1981–1989, The Populist Decade.* London: Macmillan, 1993.

Close, David H. *Greece since 1945.* London: Pearson Education, 2002.

Crampton, R. J. *The Balkans since the Second World War.* London: Pearson Education, 2002.

Deletant, Dennis. *Romania under Communist Rule.* Portland, OR: Center for Romanian Studies, 1999.

Ionescu, Ghita. *Communism in Rumania, 1944–1962.* London: Oxford University Press, 1964.

Lampe, John R. *Yugoslavia as History: Twice There Was a Country,* 2nd edn. Cambridge: Cambridge University Press, 2000.

Mašević, Siniša. *Ideology, Legitimacy and the New State, Yugoslavia, Serbia and Croatia.* London: Frank Cass, 2003.

Rusinow, Dennison. *The Yugoslav Experiment, 1948–1974.* Berkeley, CA: University of California Press, 1977.

Stefanidis, Ioannis D. *Isle of Discord: Nationalism, Imperialism and the Making of the Cyprus Problem.* New York: New York University Press, 1999.

Tismaneanu, Vladimir. *Stalinism for All Seasons, A Political History of Romanian Communism.* Berkeley, CA: California University Press, 2003.

Verdery, Katherine. *National Ideology under Socialism, Identity and Cultural Politics in Ceauşescu's Romania.* Berkeley, CA: University of California Press, 1991.

Southeastern Europe since 1989

Bartlett, William. *Croatia Between Europe and the Balkans.* London: Routledge, 2003.

Bell, John D., ed. *Bulgaria in Transition.* Boulder, CO: Westview Press, 1998.

Burg, Steven L. and Paul S. Shoup. *The War in Bosnia-Herzegovina, Ethnic Conflict and International Intervention.* Armonk, NY: M. E. Sharpe, 1999.

Clunies-Ross, Anthony and Petar Sudar, eds. *Albania's Economy in Turmoil and Transition, 1990–1997.* Aldershot: Ashgate, 2000.

Dawisha, Karen and Bruce Parrott, eds. *Politics, Power and the Struggle for Democracy in South-East Europe.* Cambridge: Cambridge University Press, 1997.

Dimitrov, Veselin. *Bulgaria, the Uneven Transition.* London: Routledge, 2001.

Friedman, Francine. *Bosnia and Herzegovina, A Polity on the Brink.* London: Routledge, 2004.

Gallagher, Tom. *Modern Romania, The End of Communism, the Failure of Democratic Reform and the Theft of a Nation.* New York: New York University Press, 2005.

Kola, Paulin. *The Search for Greater Albania.* London: Hurst, 2003.

Light, Paulin and David Phinnemore, eds. *Post-Communist Romania: Coming to Terms with Transition.* Basingstoke: Palgrave, 2001.

Pagoulatos, George. *Greece's New Political Economy, State, Finance, and Growth from Postwar to EMU.* Basingstoke: Palgrave, 2003.

Petrakos, George and Stoyan Totev, eds. *The Development of the Balkan Region.* Aldershot: Ashgate, 2001.

Pridham, Geoffrey and Tom Gallagher, eds. *Experimenting with Democracy, Regime Change in the Balkans.* London: Routledge, 2000.

Roper, Steven D. *Romania the Unfinished Revolution.* Amsterdam: Harwood Academic Publishers, 2000.

Siani-Davies, Peter, ed. *International Intervention in the Balkans since 1995.* London: Routledge, 2003.

——. *The Romanian Revolution of December 1989.* Ithaca, NY: Cornell University Press, 2005.

Sjoberg, Orjan and Michael L. Wyzan, eds. *Economic Change in the Balkan States: Albania, Bulgaria, Romania and Yugoslavia.* New York: St Martin's, 1991.

Index

CPSIA information can be obtained at www.ICGtesting.com
Printed in the USA
LVOW061928220112

265019LV00002B/3/P